2005

WORLD DRUG REPORT

Volume 2: Statistics

The Office for Drug Control and Crime Prevention (UNODCCP) became the Office on Drugs and Crime (UNODC) on 1 October 2002. The Office on Drugs and Crime includes the United Nations International Drug Control Programme (UNDCP).

United Nations Publication
Sales No. E.05.XI.10
ISBN 92-1-148201-1
Volume 2

The boundaries, names and designations used in all maps in this book do not imply official endorsement or acceptance by the United Nations.

This publication has not been formally edited.

2005

WORLD DRUG REPORT

Volume 2: Statistics

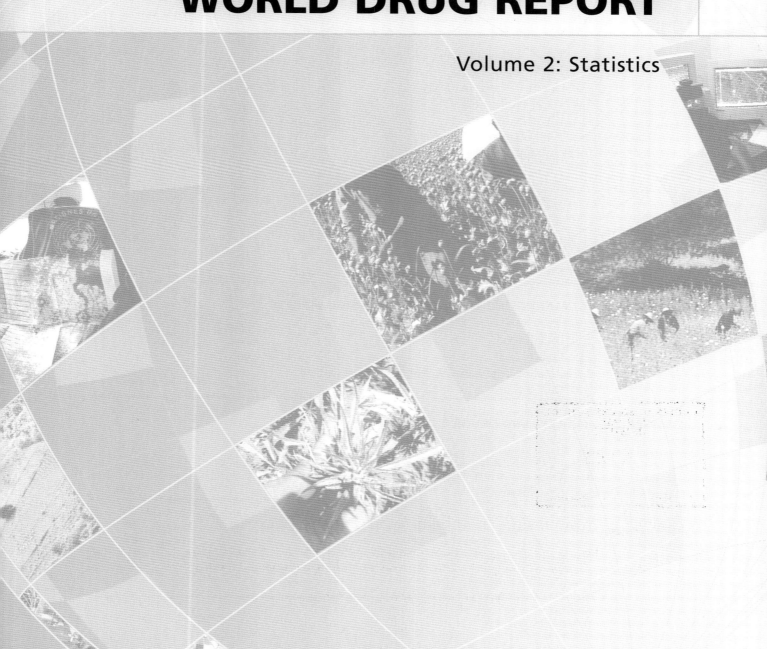

Contents

Volume I. Analysis

Volume II. Statistics

5. PRODUCTION

5.1. Opium/heroin

OPIUM

GLOBAL ILLICIT CULTIVATION OF OPIUM POPPY AND PRODUCTION OF OPIUM, 1990-2004

	1990	1991	1992	1993	1994	1995	1996	1997	1998	1999	2000	2001	2002	2003	2004
CULTIVATION[a] IN HECTARES															
SOUTH-WEST ASIA															
Afghanistan	41,300	50,800	49,300	58,300	71,470	53,759	56,824	58,416	63,674	90,583	82,171	7,606	74,100	80,000	131,000
Pakistan	7,488	7,962	9,493	7,329	5,759	5,091	873	874	950	284	260	213	622	2,500	1,500
Subtotal	48,788	58,762	58,793	65,629	77,229	58,850	57,697	59,290	64,624	90,867	82,431	7,819	74,722	82,500	132,500
SOUTH-EAST ASIA															
Lao PDR	30,580	29,625	19,190	26,040	18,520	19,650	21,601	24,082	26,837	22,543	19,052	17,255	14,000	12,000	6,600
Myanmar	150,100	160,000	153,700	165,800	146,600	154,070	163,000	155,150	130,300	89,500	108,700	105,000	81,400	62,200	44,200
Thailand [b]	1,782	3,727	3,016	998	478	168	368	352	716	702	890	820	750		
Viet Nam [b]	18,000	17,000	12,199	4,268	3,066	1,880	1,743	340	442	442					
Subtotal	200,462	210,352	188,105	197,106	168,664	175,768	186,712	179,924	158,295	113,187	128,642	123,075	96,150	74,200	50,800
LATIN AMERICA															
Colombia [c]		1,160	6,578	5,008	15,091	5,226	4,916	6,584	7,350	6,500	6,500	4,300	4,100	4,100	3,950
Mexico [d]	5,450	3,765	3,310	3,960	5,795	5,050	5,100	4,000	5,500	3,600	1,900	4,400	2,700	4,800	n.a.
Subtotal	5,450	4,925	9,888	8,968	20,886	10,276	10,016	10,584	12,850	10,100	8,400	8,700	6,800	8,900	8,750 [f]
OTHER															
Combined [e]	8,054	7,521	2,900	5,704	5,700	5,025	3,190	2,050	2,050	2,050	2,479	2,500	2,500	3,000	3,890
GRAND TOTAL	262,754	281,560	259,686	277,407	272,479	249,919	257,615	251,848	237,819	216,204	221,952	142,094	180,172	168,600	195,940

	1990	1991	1992	1993	1994	1995	1996	1997	1998	1999	2000	2001	2002	2003	2004
POTENTIAL PRODUCTION IN METRIC TONS — OPIUM															
SOUTH-WEST ASIA															
Afghanistan	1,570	1,980	1,970	2,330	3,416	2,335	2,248	2,804	2,693	4,565	3,276	185	3,400	3,600	4,200
Pakistan	150	160	181	161	128	112	24	24	26	9	8	5	5	52	40
Subtotal	1,720	2,140	2,151	2,491	3,544	2,447	2,272	2,828	2,719	4,574	3,284	190	3,405	3,652	4,240
SOUTH-EAST ASIA															
Lao PDR	202	196	127	169	120	128	140	147	124	124	167	134	112	120	43
Myanmar	1,621	1,728	1,660	1,791	1,583	1,664	1,760	1,676	1,303	895	1,087	1,097	828	810	370
Thailand [b]	20	23	14	17	3	2	5	4	8	8	6	6	9		
Viet Nam [b]	90	85	61	21	15	9	9	2	2	2					
Subtotal	1,933	2,032	1,862	1,998	1,721	1,803	1,914	1,829	1,437	1,029	1,260	1,237	949	930	413
LATIN AMERICA															
Colombia [c]		16	90	68	205	71	67	90	100	88	88	80	76	76	73
Mexico	62	41	40	49	60	53	54	46	60	43	21	71	47	84	n.a.
Subtotal	62	57	130	117	265	124	121	136	160	131	109	151	123	160	157 [f]
OTHER															
Combined [e]	45	45	-	4	90	78	48	30	30	30	38	18	14	24	40
GRAND TOTAL	3,760	4,274	4,143	4,610	5,620	4,452	4,355	4,823	4,346	5,764	4,691	1,596	4,491	4,765	4,850
HEROIN															
Potential HEROIN	376	427	414	461	562	445	436	482	435	576	469	160	449	477	565 [g]

a) Harvestable after eradication.
b) Due to small production, cultivation and production were included in the category " Other countries", for Viet Nam as of 2000 and for Thailand as of 2003.
c) According to the Government of Colombia, cultivation covered 7,350 ha and 6,500 ha and production amounted to 73 mt and 65 mt in 1998 and 1999 respectively.
d) Sources: As its survey system is under development, the Govt of Mexico indicates it can neither provide cultivation estimates nor endorse those published by UNODC which are derived from US Government surveys.
e) Includes countries such as Russia, Ukraine, Central Asia, Caucasus region, Egypt, Peru, Viet Nam (as of 2000) and Thailand (as of 2003).
f) For calculation of regional sub-total for 2004 previous year's estimates were used.
g) Based on the Afghanistan Opium Survey 2004, estimates of potential heroin production is 500 metric tons in Afghanistan. For other countries a 10 to 1 ratio is used for conversion from opium to heroin.

5.1.1. Afghanistan

During the 1990s, Afghanistan firmly established itself as the largest source of illicit opium and its derivative, heroin, in the world. In 2004, for the first time, opium cultivation was found in all 32 provinces, reaching an unprecedented total cultivation area of 131,000 hectares. The 64% increase, as compared to 2003, was in line with the assessment of farmers' intentions made by UNODC and the Afghan Government at the beginning of the planting season.

Results of the 2004 Afghanistan Annual Opium Survey

Opium poppy cultivation increased to a record level

The area under opium poppy cultivation in Afghanistan increased from about 80,000 hectares (ha) in 2003 to an unprecedented 131,000 hectares in 2004. The bulk of opium poppy cultivation is relatively concentrated with just three provinces accounting for 56% of the total area under cultivation: Hilmand, Nangarhar and Badakhshan.

Opium poppy cultivation is now found in all provinces

The 2004 opium survey confirmed the encroachment of opium poppy cultivation to previously unaffected areas and opium poppy cultivation is now found in all 32 provinces of the country, up from 18 provinces in 1999, 23 in 2000, 24 in 2002 and 28 provinces in 2003.

Expansion of opium cultivation at the expense of cereal cultivation

Ninety-two percent of opium poppy cultivation took place on fertile irrigated land. The expansion of opium poppy cultivation came at the expense of cereal cultivation, notably of wheat, which declined significantly in 2004.

Lower yields limit the increase of potential opium production

Potential opium production was estimated at around 4,200 metric tons (mt), representing an increase of about 17% compared to 2003. Unlike for the area under cultivation, this year did not set a record for production, which remained lower than the 1999 peak of 4,600 mt. This can be explained by relatively low opium yield per hectare in 2004 due to unfavourable weather conditions (insufficient rain and low temperatures) and disease.

Opium prices are declining

The average price for fresh opium at the time of harvest, weighted by regional opium production, amounted to US$ 92 per kilogram, a 67% decline compared to last year. Fresh opium prices at the farm-gate level were, however, still two to three times higher than in the second half of the 1990s.

Increased number of families involved in opium poppy cultivation

The number of families involved in opium poppy cultivation rose by 35% and was estimated at 356,000 families in 2004. This number represented about 2.3 million persons, 10% of the total population in Afghanistan or 12% - 14% of the rural population.

Estimated farmers' income from opium declined

The yearly gross income per opium growing family was estimated at around US$1,700 in 2004. The gross income from poppy cultivation per hectare amounted to US$4,600, a decline by 64% from a year earlier, but still almost 12 times higher than the gross income a farmer could expect from one hectare of wheat (US$390).

Total farm-gate value of opium decreased 41% to US$ 600 million

Based on opium production estimates and reported opium prices the farm-gate value of the opium harvest can be estimated at around US$ 600 million. This farm-gate value is equivalent to 13% of GDP (down from 22% in 2003) or three times the size of the Government's total domestic revenues (US$ 208 million in 2003/04). Due to the falling opium prices, the overall farm-gate value of opium production was some 41% lower than in 2003 and 50% lower than in 2002.

Fact Sheet : Afghanistan opium survey 2004

	2003	Variation on 2003	2004
Net opium poppy cultivation	80,000 ha	64%	131,000 ha
in percent of actual agricultural land	1.60%		2.90%
Number of provinces affected	28		32 (all)
Average opium yield	45 kg/ha		32 kg/ha
Production of opium	3,600 mt	17%	4,200 mt
in percent of world illicit opium production	76%		87%
Number of households involved in opium cultivation	264,000	35%	356,000
Number of persons involved in opium cultivation	1.7 million		2.3 million
in percent of total population (23 million)	7%		10%
Average farm-gate price of fresh opium at harvest time	US$ 283	-67%	US$ 92/kg
Average farm-gate price of dry opium at harvest time	US$ 425	-69%	US$ 142/kg
Total export value of opium to neighbouring countries	US$ 2.3 billion	22%	US$ 2.8 billion
in percent of 2003 GDP (US$ 4.6 billion)	50%		60%
Gross trafficking profits of Afghan traffickers	US$ 1.3 billion	69%	US$ 2.2 billion
Total farm-gate value of opium production	US$ 1.02 billion	-41%	US$ 0.6 billion
Household average yearly gross income from opium of opium growing families	US$ 3,900	-56%	US$ 1,700
Per capita gross income from opium of opium growing families	US$ 600	-56%	US$ 260
Afghanistan's GDP per capita	US$ 207	n.a.	n.a.
Indicative gross income from opium per ha	US$ 12,700	-64%	US$ 4,600
Gross income from wheat per ha	US$ 470	-17%	US$ 390

Graphs, tables, maps: Afghanistan

Afghanistan, Opium Poppy Cultivation, in thousands of ha, 1990 to 2004

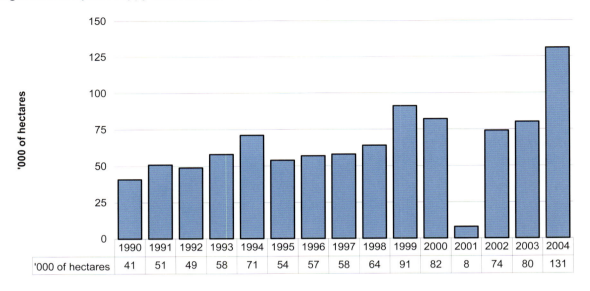

	1990	1991	1992	1993	1994	1995	1996	1997	1998	1999	2000	2001	2002	2003	2004
'000 of hectares	41	51	49	58	71	54	57	58	64	91	82	8	74	80	131

Afghanistan, largest opium poppy cultivating provinces in 2004 (ha)

Provinces	2003	2004	% one year change	% of total in 2004	Cumulative % in 2004
Hilmand	15,371	29,353	91	22%	44%
Nangarhar	18,904	28,213	49	22%	22%
Badakhshan	12,756	15,607	22	12%	56%
Uruzgan	7,143	11,080	55	8%	64%
Ghor	3,782	4,983	32	4%	68%
Kandahar	3,055	4,959	62	4%	72%
Rest of the country	19,471	36,441	87	28%	100%
Rounded Total	80,000	131,000	64		

Afghanistan, potential opium production by region and at national level in 2004

Survey Zone	Cultivation (hectares)	Average yield (kg/ha)	Confidence interval (± kg/ha)	Average production (metric tons)	Confidence interval (± metric tons)
Southern	48,431	27.8	2	1,346	97
Eastern	36,621	32.5	2	1,190	73
North-eastern	16,369	44.2	3.3	724	54
Northern	14,627	36.4	4	532	59
Western	9,917	34.9	2.5	346	25
Central	4,671	17.5	4.7	82	22
National average	130,636	32.3	2.5	4,220	327
(rounded)	131,000	32	2.5	4,200	± 330

Afghanistan, Opium production,1990 to 2004

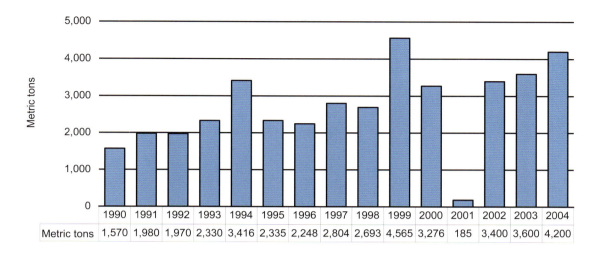

	1990	1991	1992	1993	1994	1995	1996	1997	1998	1999	2000	2001	2002	2003	2004
Metric tons	1,570	1,980	1,970	2,330	3,416	2,335	2,248	2,804	2,693	4,565	3,276	185	3,400	3,600	4,200

Afghanistan opium production by provinces in 2004

Provinces	Opium production in metric tons	% of total
Nangarhar	966	23%
Hilmand	840	20%
Badakhshan	756	18%
Uruzgan	336	8%
Ghor	168	4%
Kunar	168	4%
Others	966	23%
Rounded Total	**4,200**	100%

Afghanistan opium production by provinces in 2004

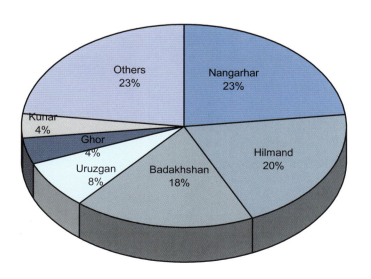

Afghanistan opium poppy cultivation 2000

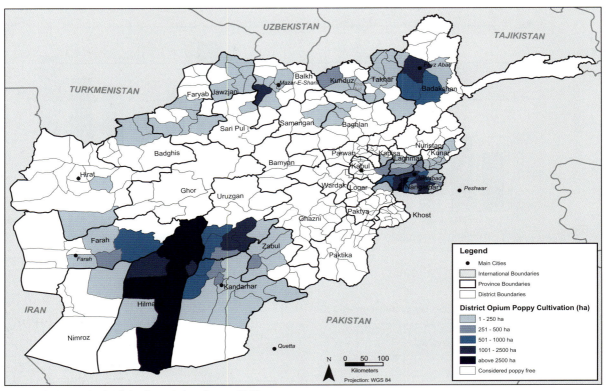

Source: CND - UNODC *Afghanistan Opium Survey 2000*

Afghanistan opium poppy cultivation 2001

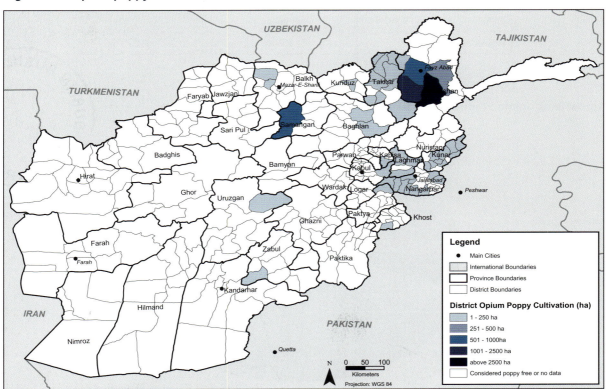

Source: CND - UNODC *Afghanistan Opium Survey 2001*

Afghanistan opium poppy cultivation 2002

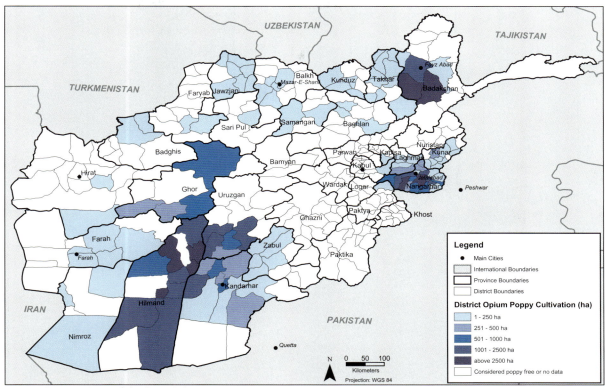

Source: CND - UNODC *Afghanistan Opium Survey 2002*

Afghanistan opium poppy cultivation 2003

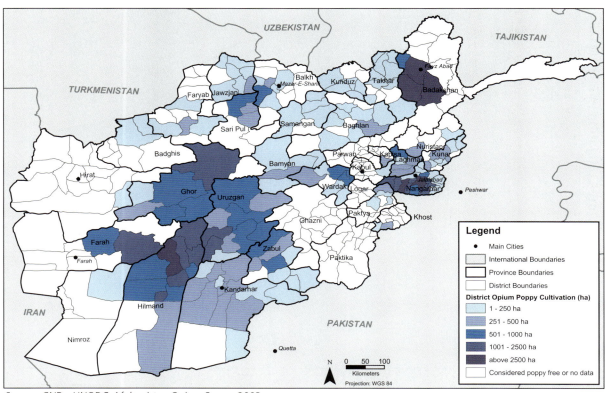

Source: CND - UNODC *Afghanistan Opium Survey 2003*

Afghanistan Opium Poppy Cultivation in 2004 (at district level)

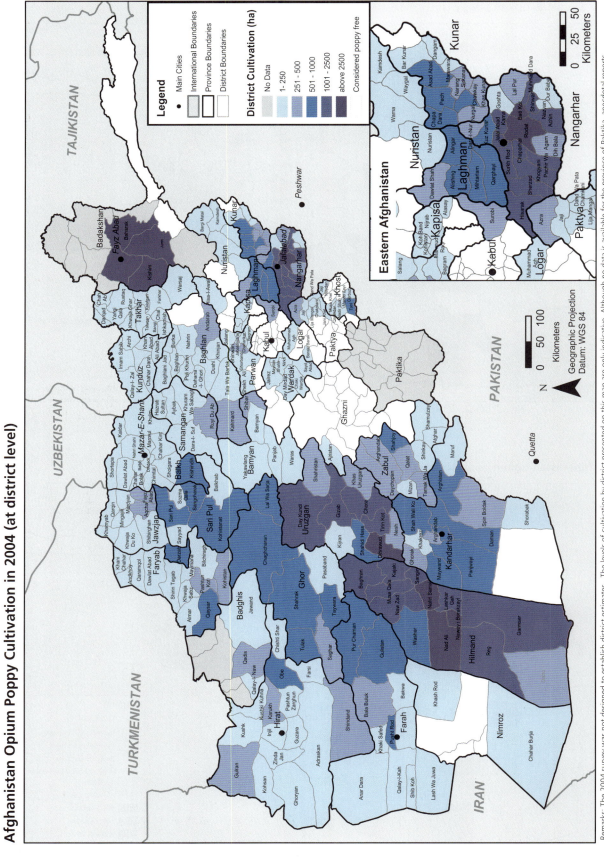

Remarks: The 2004 survey was not designed to establish district estimates. The levels of cultivation by district presented on this map are only indicative. Although no data is available for the province of Paktika, anecdotal reports confirm presence of opium poppy cultivation there.
Source: CND - UNODC Afghanistan Opium Survey 2004.

Afghanistan, farmgate prices for opium, US$/kg (all observations Nov. 2002 – Dec. 2004)

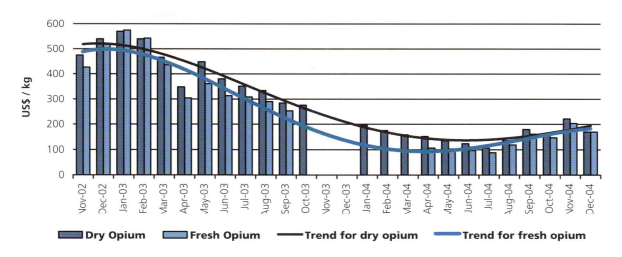

Source: UNODC (ICMP-AFG/F98 Monitoring of opium production in Afghanistan)

Afghanistan, opium farmgate prices in 2004 ($US/kg)

Period	Dry opium	n	Fresh opium	n
Jan-04	197	26		
Feb-04	176	20		
Mar-04	159	36		
Apr-04	153	60	107	40
May-04	135	47	103	47
Jun-04	124	84	97	93
Jul-04	107	93	88	93
Aug-04	136	92	119	76
Sep-04	180	64	162	62
Oct-04	154	63	147	47
Nov-04	222	90	204	27
Dec-04	170	73	170	27

n = number of observations

Empty cells = no data collection during the period considered

Source: *UNODC (ICMP-AFG/F98 Monitoring of opium production in Afghanistan)*

All transactions in the three provinces are reported by surveyors to be made in Pakistani Rupees. The prices were converted in US$, using the exchange rate prevailing on the day each observation was made.

Afghanistan: Prices of dry opium obtained from traders in Nangarhar and Kandahar in US$ per kg.

1997

Date	Nangarhar	Kandahar	Simple average
Jan-97			
Feb-97			
Mar-97	93		63
Apr-97	102		68
May-97	108		71
Jun-97	114		74
Jul-97	91		62
Aug-97	97	34	65
Sep-97	97	33	65
Oct-97	86	33	60
Nov-97	83	30	57
Dec-97	66	34	50

1998

Date	Nangarhar	Kandahar	Simple average
Jan-98	67	46	57
Feb-98	76	53	65
Mar-98	95	41	68
Apr-98	70	38	54
May-98	65	38	52
Jun-98	83	44	64
Jul-98	54	49	51
Aug-98	55	67	61
Sep-98	63	54	59
Oct-98	78	59	69
Nov-98	96	54	75
Dec-98	101	56	79

1999

Date	Nangarhar	Kandahar	Simple average
Jan-99	116	59	87
Feb-99	100	60	80
Mar-99	100	50	75
Apr-99	80	45	62
May-99	91	43	67
Jun-99	86	41	63
Jul-99	82	37	59
Aug-99	62	39	51
Sep-99	61	36	49
Oct-99	40	33	37
Nov-99	38	31	34
Dec-99	39	32	35

2000

Date	Nangarhar	Kandahar	Simple average
Jan-00	41	31	36
Feb-00	43	30	37
Mar-00	46	29	38
Apr-00	44	30	37
May-00	42	30	36
Jun-00	38	31	35
Jul-00	44	31	39
Aug-00	87	78	82
Sep-00	76	43	60
Oct-00	124	70	97
Nov-00	107	61	84
Dec-00	159	101	130

2001

Date	Nangarhar	Kandahar	Simple average
Jan-01	173	128	150
Feb-01	214	162	188
Mar-01	367	205	286
Apr-01	383	260	322
May-01	398	270	334
Jun-01	368	250	309
Jul-01	424	288	356
Aug-01	657	446	551
10 sept. 01	700	650	675
15 sept. 01	194	180	187
24 sept. 01	95	90	93
10 oct. 01	134	150	142
15 oct. 01	190	327	
28 oct. 01	210	270	
01 nov. 01	327	340	
05 nov. 01	330	350	
19 nov. 01	343	364	
15 dec. 01	316	275	

2002

Date	Nangarhar	Kandahar	Simple average
15 Jan 02	423	407	415
15 Feb 02	409	395	402
15 Mar 02	416	343	379
14 Apr 02	583	450	517
25 Apr 02	361	385	373
07 May 02	381	304	343
15 May 02	444	376	410
20 May 02	444	380	412
09 Jun 02	514	480	497
15 Jun 02	514	436	475
15 Jul 02	380	422	401
15 Aug 02	398	350	374
09 Sept. 02	418	370	394
23 Sept. 02	434	414	424
01 Oct 02	450	430	440
End Nov 02	481	538	510
Mid Dec 02	506	602	554
End Dec 02	524	556	540

2003

Date	Nangarhar	Kandahar	Simple average
Mid Jan 03	512	640	576
End Jan 03	499	609	554
Mid Feb 03	529	577	553
End Feb 03	447	577	512
Mid Mar 03	445	509	477
End Mar 03	381	444	412
Mid Apr 03	299	386	343
End Apr 03	355	426	390
Mid May 03	430	469	449
End May 03	416	452	434
Mid Jun 03	353	436	394
End Jun 03	339	415	377
Mid July 03	353	423	388
End July 03	327	379	353
Mid Aug 03	272	375	323
End Aug 03	286	432	359
Mid Sept 03	261	312	286
End Sept 03	247	321	284
Mid Oct 03	221	303	262
End Oct 03	197	249	223
Nov-03	219	225	222
Dec-03	229	203	216

2004

Date	Nangarhar	Kandahar	Simple average
Jan-04	211	184	197
Feb-04	184	177	180
Mar-04	193	159	176
Apr-04	176	154	165
May-04	138	145	141
Jun-04	143	143	143
Jul-04	140	98	119
Aug-04	126	142	134
Sep-04	129	223	176
Oct-04	158	197	178
Nov-04	273	234	254
Dec-04	206	203	204

2005

Date	Nangarhar	Kandahar	Simple average
Jan-05	190	222	206
Feb-05	165	173	169
Mar-05	166	149	158
Apr-05	156	148	152

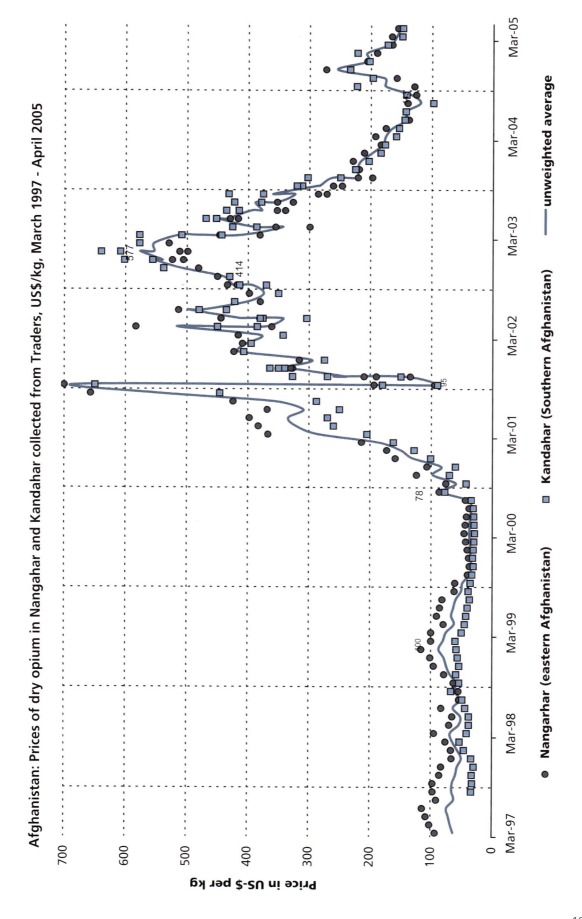

Afghanistan: Prices of dry opium in Nangahar and Kandahar collected from Traders, US$/kg, March 1997 - April 2005

● Nangarhar (eastern Afghanistan)   ■ Kandahar (Southern Afghanistan)   —— unweighted average

5.1.2. Myanmar

Myanmar is the main opium producer in Southeast Asia. However, despite its reputation as a leading producer, during the last decade, policies by both the central Government and local authorities continue to promote a rapid reduction in opium cultivation, in line with a national action plan to eradicate it by the year 2014.

Further decrease of opium poppy cultivation area

The total area under opium poppy cultivation in Myanmar, for the 2004 season was estimated to be 44,200 ha (ranging between 38,500 and 49,600 ha) representing a reduction of 29% from 2003. This value also represented a reduction of 73% compared to the opium cultivation estimate of 1996 (163,000 ha).

Yield and production affected by drought

In 2004 the North Shan experienced a severe drought. The maximum potential yield was estimated at 8 kg/ha, ranging between 7 kg/ha in the South Shan and 11 kg/ha in the East Shan. The average estimated opium production for the year 2004 thus amounted to 370 metric tons, a decline of 54% from 2003 and a decline of 72% from 1998.

Opium prices increase

The average farm gate sale price of opium in 2004 was estimated to be 200,310 Kyats (US$ 234) per kilogram. This corresponds to an increase of 80%, in US$ terms, compared with the farmgate price of US$130 reported in the 2003 survey.

Income of opium producing farmers still low

The average household income for opium producers was 207,000 Kyats per year (214 US$) and 266,680 Kyats (US $ 276) for non-opium producers. For opium producing farmers, the sale of opium represented 62% (or US$133) of their annual cash income.

Farm gate value of opium declines

With an estimated potential of 370 metric tons, the total farmgate value of opium production amounted to US$ 87 million in 2004, equivalent to 1-2% of the country's GDP.

Addiction

Opium addiction in the Shan State affected 0.6% of the adult population in 2004 (equivalent to about 17,000 addicts). In villages where opium cultivation took place in 2004, the average level of addiction was 2.2% and thus significantly higher than in non-producing villages where the average level of opium addiction amounted to just 0.2%.

Eradication

In 2004 a total of 2,820 ha cultivated with opium poppy were officially reported to have been eradicated. This represents an increase of more than 300% over the 638 ha eradicated in 2003.

Fact sheet: Myanmar Opium Survey 2004

	2004	Variation on 2003
Opium poppy planted area in the whole of the Union of Myanmar (including the Shan State)	44,200 ha	- 29 %
Opium poppy planted area in the Shan State	41,000 ha	- 28 %
Average opium yield	8 kg/ha	- 38%
Potential production of opium in the whole of the Union of Myanmar (including the Shan State)	370 mt	- 54%
Opium poppy eradication in the Union of Myanmar	2,820 ha	+ 342 %
Average farmgate price of opium	US$ 234/kg	+ 80%
Total potential value of opium production:	US$ 87 millions	- 17%
Addiction prevalence rate (Population aged 15 and above)	0.61%	- 3%
Estimated number of opium addicts in the Shan State	17,000	n.a.
Estimated number of households involved in opium poppy cultivation in Myanmar	260,000	n.a.
Estimated number of households involved in opium poppy cultivation in the Shan State	240,000	- 31%
Household average yearly income in opium poppy producing household (Shan State) of which from opium sale	US$ 214 US$ 133 (or 62%)	- 8%
Household average yearly income in non-opium poppy producing household (Shan State)	US$ 276	n.a.

Graphs, tables, maps: Myanmar

Myanmar, opium poppy cultivation 1990 – 2004 (in thousand of ha)

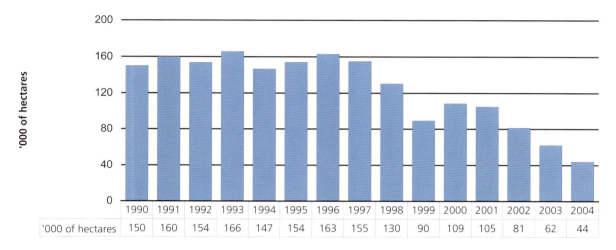

	1990	1991	1992	1993	1994	1995	1996	1997	1998	1999	2000	2001	2002	2003	2004
'000 of hectares	150	160	154	166	147	154	163	155	130	90	109	105	81	62	44

Myanmar, opium poppy cultivation in 2003 and 2004

Administrative Region	2003 Planted Surface Estimate (ha)	2004 Planted Surface Estimate (ha)	Variation (%)
North Shan	19,600	6,000	-69%
South Shan	10,500	10,500	0%
East Shan	6,700	7,750	16%
Special Region No. 2 (Wa)	20,400	16,750	-18%
Total (Shan States)	*57,200*	*41,000*	*-28%*
Outside Shan State	5,000	3,200	-36%
National Total	**62,200**	**44,200**	**-29%**

Myanmar, potential average regional yields 2004 (kg/ha)

Administrative Unit	Potential Yield (Kg/ha)	Production (metric tons)
North Shan	8	48
South Shan	7	74
East Shan	11	85
Special Region 2 (Wa)	8	134
Total Shan State	8	341
Kachin State	8	9
Sagaing Division	8	6
Kayah State	8	10
Rounded National Total	**8**	**370**

Myanmar opium production 1990 – 2004 (in metric tons)

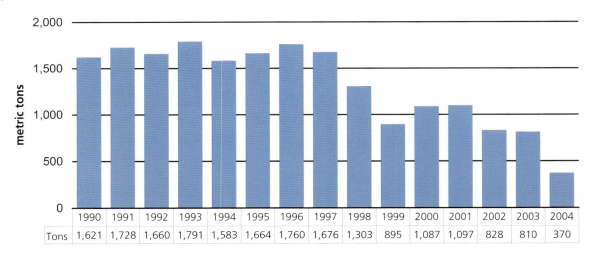

	1990	1991	1992	1993	1994	1995	1996	1997	1998	1999	2000	2001	2002	2003	2004
Tons	1,621	1,728	1,660	1,791	1,583	1,664	1,760	1,676	1,303	895	1,087	1,097	828	810	370

Myanmar, opium farmgate prices in Mong Pawk market, US$/kg (Wa Special Region 2)

Year	Jan	Feb	Mar	Apr	May	Jun	Jul	Aug	Sep	Oct	Nov	Dec
1999	172	97	110	125	136	123	133	152	119	173	144	163
2000	195	193	203	172	236	226	202	230	210	210	203	218
2001	234	216	194	205	187	182	195	195	186	162	150	151
2002	158	136	124	119	108	107	124	132	127	127	144	158
2003	165	127	117	128	132	138	139	139	138	146	152	155
2004	160	151	216	215	219	219	202	205	177	176	230	273

Myanmar, opium farmgate prices in Mong Pawk market, US$/kg (Wa Special Region 2)

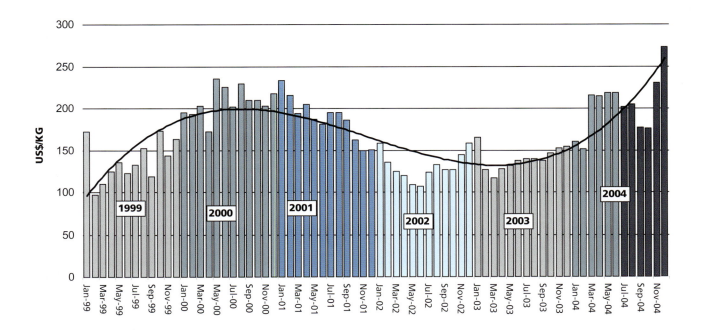

Myanmar, Opium prices per region in Shan States in 2004

	North Shan	South Shan	East Shan	S. R. No. 2 (Wa)	Average Shan State
Opium price in Kyats	196,556	243,684	179,741	200,012	200,310
Opium price in US-dollar	$230	$285	$210	$234	$234

Average cash income per opium producing household in Kyats

Source of income	North Shan	South Shan	East Shan	S. R. No. 2 (Wa)	Total Shan State	US-$	% of total
Opium	8,300	127,400	26,440	169,290	128,960	133	62.3%
Livestock	15,900	23,790	179,800	8,790	40,570	42	19.6%
Cereals	79,000	13,100	20,250		10,250	11	5.0%
Non-farm Employment	14,400	35,320	4,900	4,200	9,040	9	4.4%
Legume	25,500	5,900	2,300		2,800	3	1.4%
Forest Produce	5,900	560	8,400		1,900	2	0.9%
Vegetables	80	5,600	2,320	30	1,160	1	0.6%
Fruits	2,600	1770	530	880	1,040	1	0.5%
Other	6,100	47,160	5,140	6,100	11,280	12	5.4%
Total	157,780	255,000	250,080	189,290	207,000	214	100.0%
Opium in % of total income	5.30%	50.00%	10.60%	89.40%	62.30%		

Myanmar, Shan State opium addiction in the Shan State by regions in 2004

	North Shan	South Shan	East Shan	S. R. n. 2 (Wa)	Total
No. of villages surveyed	475	362	598	165	1,600
No. of headmen responding to question on addiction	204	253	216	137	810
Population of villages responding	73,726	85,763	29,945	32,163	221,597
Adult population[1] of villages responding	50,018	43,442	18,757	15,740	127,957
No. of headmen reporting addiction in their village	25	16	100	28	169
Adult population of villages reporting addiction	4,202	2,240	8,227	3,872	18,540
No. of opium addicts in sample	132	103	421	120	776
Addicts in % of adult population of villages responding to question of addiction	0.30%	0.20%	2.20%	0.80%	0.6%
Addicts in % of adult population of villages with opium addiction	3.30%	4.20%	4.90%	3.50%	4.2%

Myanmar, Shan State, demographic distribution of opium addicts by gender and age in 2004

Age	Men	Women	Total	% of total
0-10	3	3	6	0.81%
10-20	5		5	0.68%
20-30	28	7	35	4.73%
30-40	84	14	98	13.24%
40-50	137	16	153	20.68%
50-60	162	27	189	25.54%
60-70	140	16	156	21.08%
70-80	63	6	69	9.32%
80-90	23	5	28	3.78%
90-100	1		1	0.14%
	646	94	740	

Myanmar, Shan State, demographic distribution of opium addicts by age in 2004

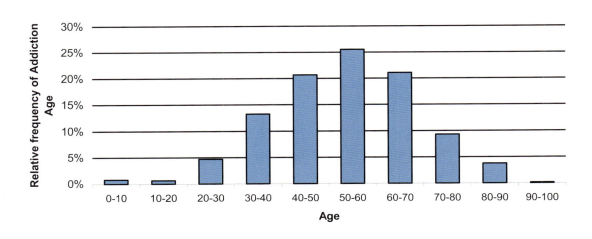

Myanmar, reported eradication by region and state in 2004

Administrative Unit	2003 (ha)	2004 (ha)	Variation (%)
North Shan State	235	172	-27%
South Shan State	182	2,170	1092%
East Shan State	91	195	114%
S. R. 2 (Wa)	55	0	-
Shan State	563	2,537	351%
Kachin State	56	126	125%
Chin State	2	0	-100%
Sagaing	0	74	-
Kayah State	9	83	824%
Mandalay Division	8	0	-
Total	638	2,820	342%

Myanmar Shan State* Opium Poppy Cultivation 2003-2004

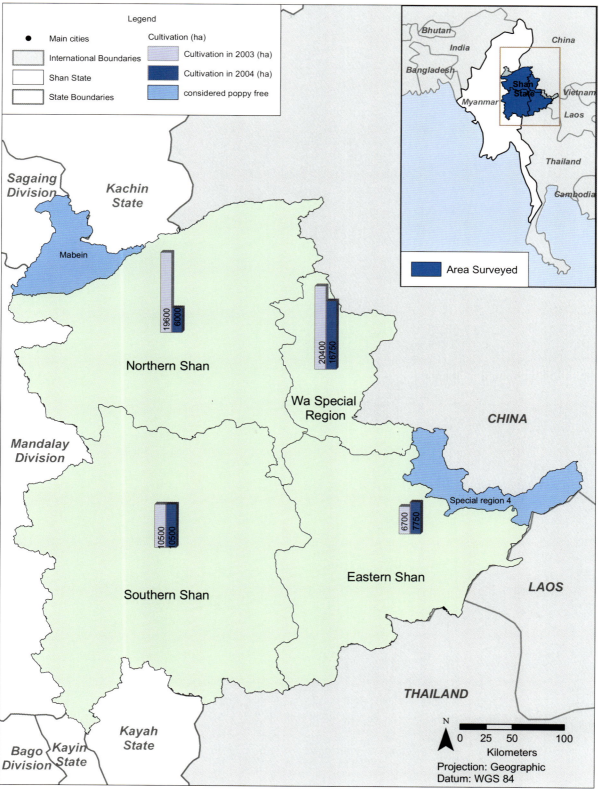

*Poppy cultivation in the Shan state counts for 90% of the national poppy area.
Source: Government of Myanmar - National monitoring system supported by UNODC.

5.1.3. Lao PDR

For many years Laos was an important producer and supplier of illicit opiates to the world. In 1998, the area under opium poppy cultivation was estimated at 26,800 hectares. However, since the Government decided to eliminate opium poppy cultivation in the Lao PDR by the year 2005, opium poppy cultivation has recorded a steady decline.

A further decline of opium poppy cultivation

The total area under opium poppy cultivation in the Lao PDR for the 2004 season was estimated at 6,600 ha, a decrease of 45% compared to the 2003 estimate of 12,000 ha. It was estimated that 22,800 households were engaged in opium cultivation, representing 5% of a total of 425,332 households in the Northern Provinces of Laos.

Low opium yield and production

The average national opium yield potential for 2004 was estimated at 6.5 kg/ha, ranging between 3.5 and 10.1 kg/ha, with a reduction of 34 % with respect to the 2003 estimate of 10 kg/ha. This outcome was due to unfavourable climatic conditions during the growing season and an ensuing drought. Based on the area planted, the average estimated production of opium for the year 2004 was 43 metric tons, with an overall reduction with respect to 2003, of over 64%.

Opium prices and trade

The average farm gate price of opium was 2,280,000 KIP per kilogram, corresponding to US$ 218. This represents an increase of 27% compared with the price attained during the previous season.

Household income from opium cultivation and trade

The average cash income of an opium-producing household was KIP 3,875,000 (US$ 371). This corresponds to 94 % of the average income of non-opium producing households (4,137,289 KIP, or 396 US$), who are less poor than their opium-producing neighbours.

Addiction

The 2004 opium survey showed that daily opium addiction took place in 60 % of the villages surveyed. In these villages, the average prevalence rate of addiction amounted to almost 3 % of the population age 15 and above. Opium smoking addiction is mainly a male phenomenon. For the country as a whole, the prevalence of opium use amounts to 0.9% of the population, age 15-64. Since 2000, opium use appears to have halved- a consequence of reduced availability in the country.

Fact sheet: Laos Opium Survey 2004

	2004	Variation on 2003
Opium poppy cultivation:	6,600 ha	- 45 %
Average opium yield:	6.5 kg/ha	- 34 %
Potential production of opium:	43 metric tons	- 64 %
Number of villages growing opium poppy:	846	- 45 %
Number of households cultivating opium poppy:	22,800	- 43 %
Average farm gate price of opium:	2,280,000 KIP/kg (US$ 218/kg)	+42 % (+27% in US$)
Total Potential value of opium production:	$9,400,000	-59 %
Household average total income in opium poppy cultivation villages:	KIP 3,875,000 (US$ 371)	-
Number of opium addicts	28,000	- 6%
Average male opium addiction prevalence rate (in the 11 Northern provinces)	2 %	-
Average female opium addiction prevalence rate (in the 11 Northern provinces)	0.6 %	-

Graphs, tables, maps: Lao PDR

Lao PDR, opium poppy cultivation 1990-2004 (in ha)

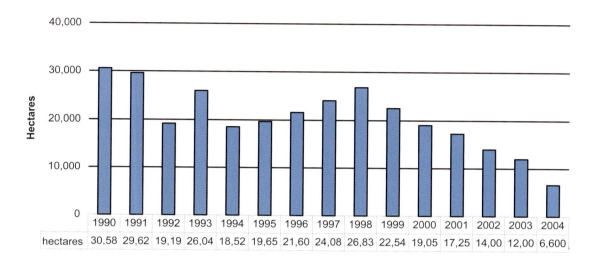

	1990	1991	1992	1993	1994	1995	1996	1997	1998	1999	2000	2001	2002	2003	2004
hectares	30,58	29,62	19,19	26,04	18,52	19,65	21,60	24,08	26,83	22,54	19,05	17,25	14,00	12,00	6,600

Lao PDR, evolution of the area under opium poppy cultivation by province, 1992-2004

	1992	1996	1998	2000	2001	2002	2003	2004***
Luang Prabang	3,510	3,550	2,786	3,036	2,950	3,400	2,576	
Huapanh	3,770	3,817	3,450	3,921	2,903	2,934	2,530	
Phongsaly	2,840	3,558	5,778	3,872	3,278	1,703	1,602	
UdomXay	1,860	2,416	5,597	4,061	3,112	1,901	1,579	
Luang Namtha	1,730	2,197	3,593	1,514	1,687	1,355	1197	
Xieng Khuang	2,880	2,916	2,902	1,376	1,426	1,078	979	
Bokeo	620	785	428	448	427	332	480	
Xayabouri	400	754	1,014	508	729	857	472	
Xaisombun	N/a	n/a	n/a	224	521**	240	354	
Vientiane	880*	900*	672*	19	117**	210	130	
Bolikhamsay	700	708	617	73	105	42	74	
Total	19,190	21,601	26,837	19,052	17,255	14,052	11,973	
Rounded Total	**19,200**	**21,600**	**26,800**	**19,100**	**17,300**	**14,100**	**12,000**	**6,600**

* Includes Xaisombun

** Previously within Xaisombun, the districts of Hom and Longxan are part of Vientiane Province since 2001.

*** Due to change of methodology in 2004 no provincial level estimates are available.

Lao PDR, potential opium production since 1990-2004 (in metric tons)

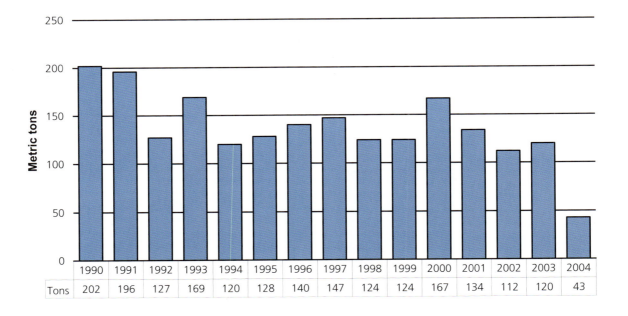

	1990	1991	1992	1993	1994	1995	1996	1997	1998	1999	2000	2001	2002	2003	2004
Tons	202	196	127	169	120	128	140	147	124	124	167	134	112	120	43

Lao PRD, Evolution of the value of opium production (2002-2004)

Year	2002	2003	2004
Price per kg of opium (KIP)	1,600,000	1,824,000	2,280,000
KIP/$ Exchange rate	10,166	10.59	10,441
Price per kg of opium ($)	$160	$172	$218
Value of Production ($)	$17,627,000	$20,669,000	$9,390,000
Variation	-	17%	-55%

Average sources of village household income

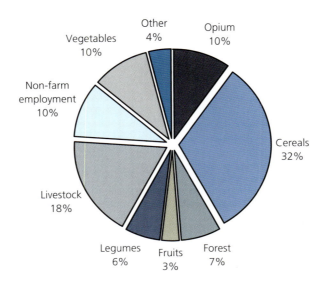

Lao PDR, Number of opium addicts 2000-2004

Year	Addicts
2000	63,000
2001	58,000
2002	53,000
2003	30,000
2004	28,000

Lao PDR, Demographic Distribution of Opium Addicts by Gender and Age in 2004

	2004	2003				2002	2001
Age	% of total	Male	Female	Total	% of Total	% of Total	% of Total
0-20	2%	1	0	1	0.10%	1.14%	1.20%
20-30	8%	22	6	28	4.10%	9.23%	10.85%
30-40	17%	56	12	68	10.00%	22.13%	21.90%
40-50	20%	93	23	116	17.10%	22.85%	23.27%
50-60	19%	146	41	187	27.60%	21.46%	22.53%
60-70	21%	149	38	187	27.60%	16.71%	14.52%
70-80	9%	44	15	59	8.70%	5.17%	4.57%
80-90	2%	13	13	26	3.90%	1.05%	0.90%
90-100	0%	4	2	6	0.90%	0.22%	0.27%
Total		528	150	678			
%	**98%**	**78%**	**22%**	**100%**	**100%**	**100%**	**100%**

Laos PDR, demographic distribution of opium addiction by age in 2004

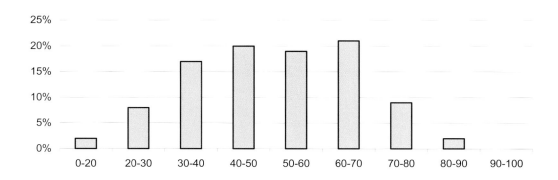

Lao PDR, reported eradication in 2004

Year	Hectares
2003	4,133
2004	3,556

5.1.4. Seizure of Illicit Laboratories

MANUFACTURE

SEIZURES OF ILLICIT LABORATORIES

REPORTED FOR 2002 - 2003

Remark: For convenience, an attempt was made to group the reported estimates by drug categories. however, due to inconsistencies and gaps in the reporting, no overall analysis of the data set was performed. Numbers are presented as reported to UNODC and should be interpreted with caution.

Source: Annual Report Questionnaire if not otherwise indicated

Country or Territory	Year	Name of drug seized	Number of laboratories (and quantity of drug)	Source
		OPIATE GROUP		
Americas				
North America				
Canada	2003	Heroin	1 Lab.	
Mexico	2002	Heroin	1 Lab.	
	2003	Heroin	3 Lab.	
Subtotal North America			5 Lab.	
South America				
Colombia	2002	Heroin	3 Lab.	
	2003	Heroin	3 Lab.	Govt
Subtotal South America			6 Lab.	
Total Americas			11 Lab.	
Asia				
East and South-East Asia				
Hong Kong Special Administrative Region of China	2002	Heroin	6 Lab.	
	2003	Heroin	3 Lab.	
Myanmar	2002	Heroin	9 Lab.	
	2003	Heroin	7 Lab.	
Subtotal East and South-East Asia			25 Lab.	
Near and Middle East /South-West Asia				
Afghanistan	2003	Heroin	(3780.000 kg)	
	2003	Morphine	12 Lab.(3800.000 kg)	
	2003	Opium	12 Lab.(38000.000 kg)	
Subtotal Near and Middle East /South-West Asia			24 Lab.(45580.000 kg)	
South Asia				
India	2002	Morphine	1 Lab.(5.000 kg)	
	2002	Heroin	7 Lab.(28.000 kg)	
	2003	Heroin	2 Lab.	
	2003	Morphine	2 Lab.	
Subtotal South Asia			12 Lab.(33.000 kg)	
Total Asia			61 Lab.(45613.000 kg)	
Europe				
East Europe				

Country or Territory	Year	Name of drug seized	Number of laboratories (and quantity of drug)	Source
Russian Federation	2002	Opium	91 Lab.	
	2003		304 Lab.	
Subtotal East Europe			395 Lab.	
Southeast Europe				
Romania	2003	Heroin	1 Lab.	
Turkey	2002	Heroin	10 Lab.	Govt
Subtotal Southeast Europe			11 Lab.	
West & Central Europe				
Poland	2002	Polish heroin	14 Lab.	
	2003	Polish heroin	13 Lab.	
Portugal	2003	Heroin	1 Lab.	
Subtotal West & Central Europe			28 Lab.	
Total Europe			434 Lab.	
Opiate group			506 Lab.(45613.000 kg)	

5.2. Coca/ Cocaine

GLOBAL ILLICIT CULTIVATION OF COCA BUSH AND PRODUCTION OF COCA LEAF AND COCAINE, 1990-2004															
	1990	1991	1992	1993	1994	1995	1996	1997	1998	1999	2000	2001	2002	2003	2004
CULTIVATION[a] OF COCA BUSH IN HECTARES															
Bolivia [b]	50,300	47,900	45,300	47,200	48,100	48,600	48,100	45,800	38,000	21,800	14,600	19,900	21,600	23,600	27,700
Colombia [c]	40,100	37,500	37,100	39,700	44,700	50,900	67,200	79,400	101,800	160,100	163,300	144,800	102,000	86,000	80,000
Peru [d]	121,300	120,800	129,100	108,800	108,600	115,300	94,400	68,800	51,000	38,700	43,400	46,200	46,700	44,200	50,300
Total	211,700	206,200	211,500	195,700	201,400	214,800	209,700	194,000	190,800	220,600	221,300	210,900	170,300	153,800	158,000

POTENTIAL PRODUCTION OF DRY COCA LEAF IN METRIC TONS															
Bolivia	77,000	78,000	80,300	84,400	89,800	85,000	75,100	70,100	52,900	22,800	13,400	20,200	19,800	18,500	25,000
Colombia	45,300	45,000	44,900	45,300	67,500	80,900	108,900	129,500	165,900	261,000	266,200	236,000	222,100	168,000	148,900
Peru	196,900	222,700	223,900	155,500	165,300	183,600	174,700	130,600	95,600	69,200	46,200	49,300	52,500	50,790	70,300
Total	319,200	345,700	349,100	285,200	322,600	349,500	358,700	330,200	314,400	353,000	325,800	305,500	294,400	237,290	244,200

POTENTIAL MANUFACTURE[e] OF COCAINE IN METRIC TONS															
Bolivia	189	220	225	240	255	240	215	200	150	70	43	60	60	79	107
Colombia	92	88	91	119	201	230	300	350	435	680	695	617	580	440	390
Peru	492	525	550	410	435	460	435	325	240	175	141	150	160	155	190
Total	774	833	866	769	891	930	950	875	825	925	879	827	800	674	687

a) Potentially harvestable, after eradication
b) Sources: 1990-2002: CICAD and US Department of State, International Narcotics Control Strategy Report; 2003-2004: National Illicit Crop Monitoring System supported by UNODC.
c) Sources: 1990-1998: CICAD and US Department of State, International Narcotics Control Strategy Report; 1999-2004: National Illicit Crop Monitoring System supported by UNODC.
d) Sources: 1990-1999: CICAD and US Department of State, International Narcotics Control Strategy Report; 2000-2004: National Illicit Crop Monitoring System supported by UNODC.
e) Amounts of cocaine that could be manufactured from locally produced coca leaf (due to imports and exports actual amounts of cocaine manufactured in a country can differ).

Coca cultivation density in the Andean Region, 2004

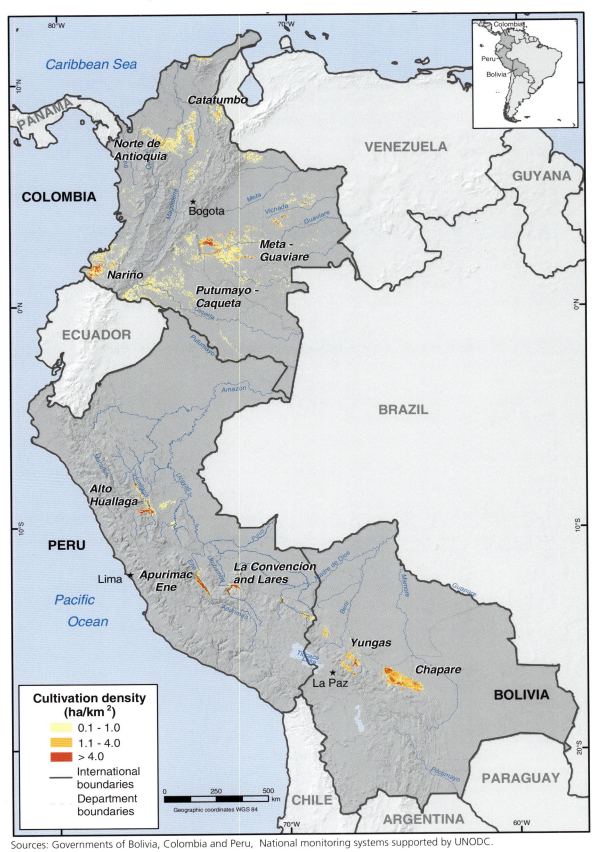

Sources: Governments of Bolivia, Colombia and Peru, National monitoring systems supported by UNODC.

5.2.1. Colombia

In 2004, the total area under coca cultivation in Colombia was estimated at about 80,000 ha, a 7% decrease compared to last year estimate of 86,000 ha. It was the fourth consecutive annual decrease of coca cultivation in Colombia, representing a reduction of 51% compared to the peak annual estimate of 163,000 ha in 2000 (-11% in 2001, -30% in 2002, -16% in 2003 and –7% in 2004).

Results of the 2004 UNODC Colombia Annual Survey

Coca Cultivation

The results of the Coca Survey showed that, at the end of December 2004, about 80,000 ha of coca were cultivated in Colombia. This represented a decrease of 6,000 ha since December 2003 when coca cultivation was estimated at about 86,000 ha. The decrease of coca cultivation corresponded to a sustained level of aerial spraying and manual eradication that peaked at 139,200 ha, an increase of 3% compared to 2003, as well as the implementation of alternative development projects. The budget for alternative development projects also increased between 2003 and 2004. The budget for alternative development projects implemented at the municipality and departmental levels increased from US$38 millions in 2003 to US$78 millions in 2004.

Geographical Distribution

In 2004 the department with the highest level of coca cultivation was Meta (18,700 ha), followed by Nariño (14,200 ha), Guaviare (9,800 ha), and Caqueta (6,500 ha). Putumayo department, which ranked first and accounted for 41% of the total coca cultivation in 2000, only accounted for 5% of the national total and ranked sixth in 2004. There are significant differences on the impact of aerial spraying and alternative development projects at the departmental level. Aerial spraying and alternative development efforts were intense in Putumayo and Caqueta between 2000 and 2004, producing a decrease of about 80,000 ha of coca cultivation. However, between 2000 and 2004, coca cultivation increased in Nariño by about 5,000 ha, despite of intense aerial spraying, and investment in alternative development amounting to US$ 11 millions. In Meta, coca cultivation increased by about 7,600 ha during the same period, which could be due to the absence of alternative development projects and the low level of aerial spraying of coca cultivation.

Coca Production

To establish an estimate of the cocaine production in 2004, UNODC relied on information available from other sources. The US government has done the most comprehensive work on this topic. The findings of this work indicated that the average cocaine yield per hectare of coca bushes amounts to 4.7 kg/ha in Colombia. In order to arrive at a realistic estimate for Colombia, UNODC calculated an average of the two cultivation figures recorded in December 2003 and in December 2004 by the UNODC supported national monitoring system. This average of 83,000 ha was then multiplied by the estimated yield per hectare. The result amounted to 390 metric tons of potential cocaine production in Colombia for 2004.

Coca prices

In 2004, the average price for one kg of coca paste amounted COP 2,121,000 (US$807). Compared to 2003, the prices decreased in Colombian pesos, but because of the depreciation of the US$, increased in US$ terms. Using the average price for coca paste of US$ 80/kg in 2004 and assuming a 1:1 conversion rate between coca paste and cocaine, the total farm-gate value of the 390 metric tons of coca paste produced in Colombia in 2004 would amount to about US$315 millions.

Opium cultivation and production

As of December 2004, the Colombian Anti-narcotics police's (DIRAN) estimates based on reconnaissance flights and spray operations, identified 3,950 hectares of opium poppy under cultivation, a stable situation compared to 4,026 hectares in 2003.

Opium prices in 2004 were rather similar to the opium prices reported in 2003. The price of opium latex in 2004 averaged US$ 164/kg. With an estimated opium latex production of 118 metric tons, the potential value of the 2004 farm-gate production of opium latex would amount to about US$ 19 millions. Trend in heroin and morphine prices per kg showed a similar pattern of a steady increase between 2003 and 2004. The average annual heroin price in 2004 was COP 20,067,000/kg or US$ 7,635/kg, representing an increase of 21% in COP and 33% in US$ compared to the annual average of 2003.

Eradication

The Colombian anti-drugs strategy includes a number of measures ranging from aerial spraying, to forced or voluntary manual eradication, including alternative development and crops substitution programmes. UNODC did not participate in or supervise any spraying activities. All data were received from DIRAN.

Reports from DIRAN showed that, for the fourth consecutive time, spraying activities reached record level in 2004. The DIRAN sprayed a total of 136,552 hectares (or +3% from 2003) and the Army manually eradicated 2,588 ha of coca. In addition, DIRAN sprayed 3,061 (or +71% from 2003) hectares and the Army manually eradicated 804 ha of opium poppy.

Fact Sheet: Colombia Coca Survey 2004

	2003	Variation on 2003	2004
Net coca cultivation (rounded total)	86,000 ha	- 7 %	80,000 ha
Of which			
Meta-Guaviare region	29,000 ha	-2%	28,500 ha
Pacific region	19,600 ha	-19%	15,800 ha
Central region	15,400 ha	-2%	15,100 ha
Putumayo-Caqueta region	10,900 ha	-	10,900 ha
Elsewhere	7,600 ha	+32%	10,100 ha
Reported accumulated aerial spraying and manual eradication of coca cultivation	136,800 ha	+3%	139,200 ha
Approximate annual budget for alternative development projects at department level (out of a total of US$ 230 millions for 1999-2007, not including US$ 350 millions for activities of national reach for 1999-2007)[1]	US$38 million	+ 105%	US$78 millions
Average farm-gate price of coca paste	780 US$ /kg	+ 4 %	810 US$/kg
Total farm-gate value of coca paste production	US$350 millions	-10 %	US$315 millions
GDP (in US$ billion)[2]	US$ 78.65 bn	n.a.	US$ 95.3 bn
Potential production of cocaine in percent of world cocaine production	440 mt 65 %	- 11 %	390 mt 57 %
Average cocaine price	US$ 1,565 /kg	+ 9%	US$1,713/kg
Reported opium poppy cultivation (rounded)	4,000 ha		4,000 ha
Average farm-gate price of opium latex	US$ 154 /kg	+ 6%	US$ 164 /kg
Total farm-gate value of opium production (rounded)	US$ 19 millions		US$19 millions
Potential heroin production	5 mt		5 mt
Average heroin price	US$ 5,700 /kg	+ 33%	US$7,600 /kg
Reported seizure of cocaine	113,142 kg		
Reported seizure of heroin	629 kg		
Reported destruction of illegal laboratories[3]	1,489	+ 15%	1,709

[1] Not including US$ 350 million for activities of national reach for 1997-2007.

[2] GDP for 2003 from the World Bank, not yet available for 2004. GDP for 2004 estimated from Economist Intelligence Unit. Sources were not comparable, but the Colombian Government reported a growth rate of 4.21% for 2003 and 4.12% for 2004.

[3] Includes laboratories processing coca paste/base (1,582), cocaine hydrochloride (243), heroin (8), morphine (1), Potassium permanganate (19), ammoniac (1) and non-specified (11).

Graphs, tables and maps: Colombia

Colombia, coca cultivation, in ha, 1990 – 2004

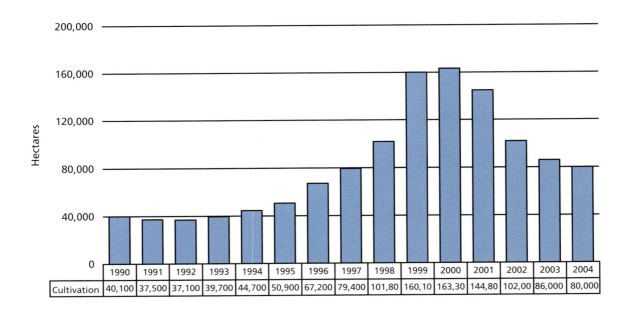

	1990	1991	1992	1993	1994	1995	1996	1997	1998	1999	2000	2001	2002	2003	2004
Cultivation	40,100	37,500	37,100	39,700	44,700	50,900	67,200	79,400	101,80	160,10	163,30	144,80	102,00	86,000	80,000

Colombia, main departments of coca cultivation, in ha, 2003 – 2004

Departments	2003	2004	% annual change	% of 2004 country total
Meta	12,814	18,740	46%	23%
Nariño	17,628	14,154	-20%	18%
Guaviare	16,163	9,769	-40%	12%
Caquetá	7,230	6,500	-10%	8%
Putumayo	7,559	4,386	-42%	5%
Norte de Santander	4,471	3,055	-32%	4%
Rest of the country	20,135	23,396	16%	29%
Rounded Total	86,000	80,000	-7%	100%

Colombia, coca cultivation trends by regions, in ha, 1999 – 2004

Region	1999	2000	2001	2002	2003	2004
Putumayo-Caqueta	82,015	92,625	61,636	22,137	14,789	10,886
Meta - Guaviare - Vaupes	40,833	30,235	38,896	38,088	30,134	29,593
Bolivar - Antioqua - Cordoba	11,461	8,624	8,647	6,150	9,581	10,106
Cauca - Nariño	10,250	13,919	10,633	17,251	19,071	15,420
Others	15,560	17,107	24,995	18,445	12,425	13,995
Grand Total	160,119	162,510	144,807	102,071	86,000	80,000

Colombia: Coca cultivation density change 2003 - 2004

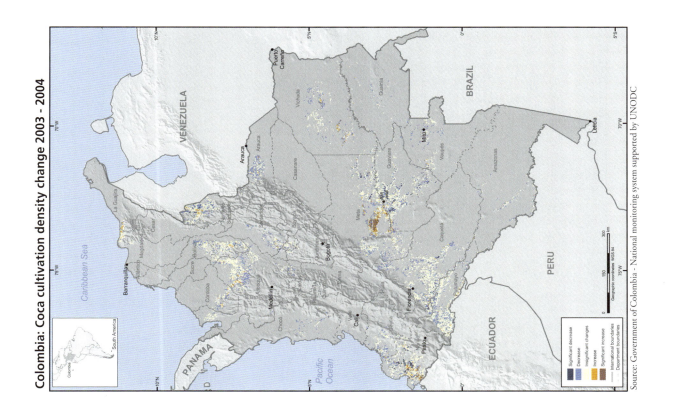

Source: Government of Colombia - National monitoring system supported by UNODC

Colombia: Coca cultivation density 2004

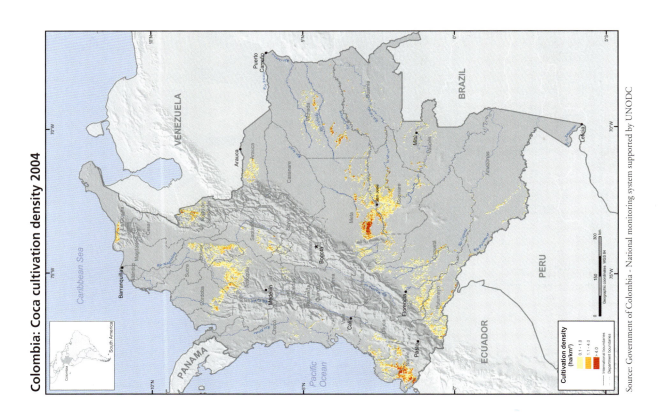

Source: Government of Colombia - National monitoring system supported by UNODC

Colombia: Coca cultivation by region 2001-2004

Source: Government of Colombia - National monitoring system supported by UNODC.

Colombia, potential cocaine production, 1990 - 2004

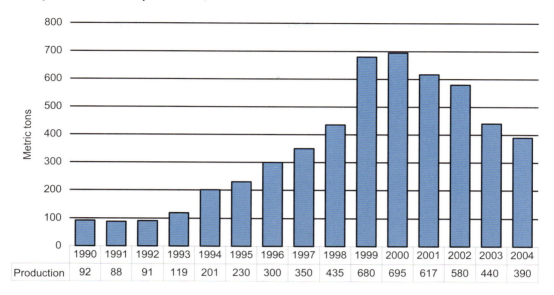

Production	1990	1991	1992	1993	1994	1995	1996	1997	1998	1999	2000	2001	2002	2003	2004
	92	88	91	119	201	230	300	350	435	680	695	617	580	440	390

Colombia, average coca base price, 2000 – 2004 (thousand of pesos /kg)

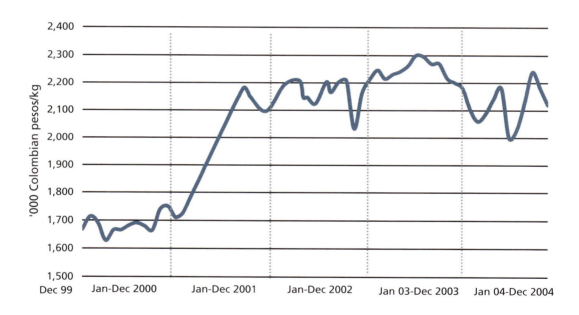

Colombia, average coca base price 2000 – 2004 (thousand of pesos /kg)

	Jan	Feb	Mar	Apr	May	Jun	Jul	Aug	Sept	Oct	Nov	Dec
2000	1,714	1,690	1,628	1,666	1,666	1,682	1,691	1,680	1,665	1,740	1,750	1,710
2001	1,730							2,179	2,150		2,096	
2002	2,192	2,208	2,146	2,146	2,124	2,204	2,165	2,203	2,208	2,034	2,162	
2003	2,213	2,247	2,215	2,231	2,242	2,263	2,300	2,295	2,269	2,270	2,217	2,200
2004	2,180	2,100	2,060	2,088	2,140	2,180	2,000	2,030	2,130	2,240	2,180	2,120

Colombia, cumulative aerial spraying of coca bushes by department (in ha), 1994- 2004

Sources	Environmental Audit of the National Narcotics Bureau						Antinarcotics Police Department				
Department	1994	1995	1996	1997	1998	1999	2000	2001	2002	2003	2004
Guaviare	3,142	21,394	14,425	30,192	37,081	17,376	8,241	7,477	7,207	37,493	30,892
Meta	729	2,471	2,524	6,725	5,920	2,296	1,345	3,251	1,496	6,973	3,888
Caqueta	-	-	537	4,370	18,433	15,656	9,172	17,252	18,567	1,059	16,276
Putumayo	-	-	-	574	3,949	4,980	13,508	32,506	71,891	8,342	17,524
Vichada	-	50	85	-	297	91	-	2,820	-	-	1,446
Antioquia	-	-	684	-	-	-	6,259	-	3,321	9,835	11,048
Cordoba	-	-	264	-	-	-	-	- -	734	550	-
Vaupes	-	-	-	-	349	-	-	-	-	-	756
Cauca	-	-	-	-	-	2,713	2,950	741	-	1,308	1,811
Norsantander	-	-	-	-	-	-	9,584	10,308	9,186	13,822	5,686
Nariño	-	-	-	-	-	-	6,442	8,216	17,962	36,910	31,307
Santander	-	-	-	-	-	-	470	-	-	5	1,855
Boyaca	-	-	-	-	-	-	102		-	-	-
Bolivar	-	-	-	-	-	-	-	11,581	-	4,783	6,456
Arauca	-	-	-	-	-	-	-	-	-	11,734	5,336
Magdalena											1,632
Guajira											449
Caldas											190
Sub-total	3,871	23,915	18,519	41,861	66,029	43,111	58,073	94,153	130,364	132,817	136,552
Manual eradication								1,745	2,752	4,011	2,609
Total eradication	3,871	23,915	18,519	41,861	66,029	43,111	58,073	95,898	133,116	136,828	139,161
Net cultivation	45,000	51,000	67,000	79,000	102,000	160,000	163,000	145,000	102,000	86,000	80,000

Colombia, comparison of net coca cultivation and reported cumulated sprayed area[4], in ha, 1990-2004

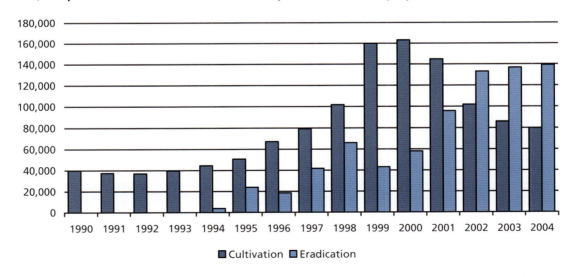

■ Cultivation ■ Eradication

---

[4] Reported cumulated spraying does not take into account the effectiveness of spraying nor the fact that some spraying paths can overlap, which explains that eradicated areas are larger then cultivated areas. Illicit crop cultivation estimates presented in this publication are net, i.e. post-eradication.

5.2.2. Peru

Peru is the second largest cultivator of coca after Colombia. It represented 33% of the 2004 global coca cultivation, compared to 29% in 2003. A percentage that remained much lower than 10 years ago, when coca cultivation in Peru accounted for 54% of the cultivation in the world. However, the increases in coca cultivation in Peru and Bolivia in 2004 neutralized reductions noted in Colombia so that global coca cultivation remained almost stable (+3%).

Results of the 2004 UNODC Peru Annual Survey

Coca Cultivation

In 2004, the total area under productive coca cultivation in Peru was estimated at about 50,300 ha. This represented an increase of 14% over the estimate for 2003 of 44,200 ha. Despite this increase, coca cultivation in 2004 remained below the levels registered in the mid-nineties, when cultivation was above 100,000 hectares.

Geographical Distribution

In Peru, most of the coca cultivation is concentrated in 14 large valleys and 8 small valleys. These valleys can be grouped in three main regions, making up to 88% of the total cultivation in 2004: Alto Huallaga, Apurimac-Ene and La Convencion y Lares. Each region has its own characteristics. While La Convencion y Lares is the main supplier of the domestic consumption of coca leaf, coca cultivation in Apurimac-Ene and Alto Huallaga are almost exclusively oriented for the production of cocaine for domestic and international markets.

Coca cultivation in other areas like San Gaban and Inambari-Tambopata at the border with Bolivia, Aguaytia and Pichis-Palcazu-Pitea in the central part of the country, and Putumayo of Loreto department close to Colombia, only accounted for 12% of the 2004. Coca cultivation in these areas has mainly been oriented towards the production of cocaine.

Coca Production

The total sun-dried leaf production in 2004 for Peru was estimated to range between 96,000 and 123,000 metric tons, with an average estimation of 110,000 metric tons, equivalent to a production of oven-dried coca leaf of about 76,500 metric tons (+/- 12%). Based on a conversion rate of 375 kg of oven-dried coca leaf for 1 kg of cocaine, the potential production of cocaine was estimated to range between 160 and 210 metric tons, with an average rounded estimate of 190 metric tons.

Coca prices

The annual average price of US$2.8/kg for coca leaves represented an increase of 33% compared to the annual average price of US$2.2/kg in 2003. On the long term, coca leaves prices have tended to increase since their lowest level of US$0.6/kg in 1996 when the interruption of the "air-bridge" between Peru and Colombia reduced demand for Peruvian coca leaf. The 2004 average annual price was the highest recorded since 1990. This sustained high price of coca leaf may have been the main motivation for the farmers to increase coca cultivation.

Opium cultivation and production

The UNODC-supported national illicit crop monitoring system has not yet established a reliable methodology for the detection of opium poppy in Peru. However, opium poppy cultivation was considered negligible in 2004. Opium poppy was mainly cultivated in the mountain range. The Anti-drugs Directorate Peruvian National Police (DIRANDRO) estimated at around 1,500 ha the total opium poppy cultivation in Peru in 2004. A stable situation compared to the latest available estimate of about 1,400 ha for 2001.

DIRANDRO reported annual opium latex yield of about 8 kg/ha, and a conversion rate of 10kg of opium latex for 1 kg of heroin. Based on this estimates, heroin production would be around 1 metric tons. A relatively small production compared to neighbouring Colombia where heroin production is estimated at 5 metric tons in 2004.

Eradication

In 2004, the Peruvian government reported the eradication of 10,257 ha of coca fields, 10% less than in 2003. It was however the third largest level of eradication since 1999. Of the total of 10,257 ha, about 75% were eradicated by the Control and Reduction of Coca Cultivation in Alto Huallaga (CORAH), the government entity in charge of forced eradication. CORAH operates throughout the country under the responsibility of the Ministry of interior.

Fact Sheet: Peru Coca Survey 2004

	2003	Variation on 2003	2004
Coca cultivation	44,200 ha	+14 %	50,300 ha
Of which			
Alto Huallaga	13,600 ha	+24%	28,500 ha
Apurimac-Ene	14,300 ha	+3%	15,800 ha
La Convencion y Lares	12,340 ha	+3%	15,100 ha
Elsewhere	3,940 ha	+52%	10,900 ha
Average sun-dried coca leaf yield from UNODC study in 2004			
In Alto Huallaga (except Monzon)			2,988 kg/ha
In Apurimac-Ene			3,627 kg/ha
In La Convencion y Lares	1,650 kg/ha	+ 32 %	1,457 kg/ha
Weighted average sun-dried coca leaf yield	1,650 kg/ha	+ 32 %	2,180 kg/ha
Potential production of sun-dried coca leaf	72,800 mt	+ 50 %	110,000 mt
Potential production of cocaine hydrochloride in percent of world illicit opium production	155 mt 23 %	+ 23 %	190 mt 28 %
Average farm-gate price of sun-dried coca leaf	US$ 2.2/kg	+ 27 %	US$ 2.8/kg
Potential farm-gate value of sun-dried coca leaf[5]			US$ 304 millions
GDP (Peru National Statistics Institute)			US$ 68.5 billions
Farm-gate value of coca leaf production			0.44%
Average farm-gate price of coca paste	US$ 530/kg	+21 %	US$ 640/kg
Reported eradication of coca cultivation	11,312 ha	- 9 %	10,257 ha
Reported seizure of cocaine paste	4,366 kg	+ 44 %	6,330 kg
Reported seizure of cocaine hydrochloride	3,574 kg	+ 104 %	7,303 kg
Reported opium poppy cultivation	n.a.		1,447 ha
Reported seizure of opium latex	433 kg	+ 4 %	451 kg

[5] Farm-gate value for 2004 was calculated based on coca leaf yield data obtained by UNODC in 2004. In 2003, farm-gate value for 2003 was estimated using coca leaf yield dating 2001. The total farm-gate value for 2003 and 2004 were therefore not directly comparable.

Graphs, tables and maps: Peru 2004

Peru, coca cultivation, in ha, 1990 – 2004

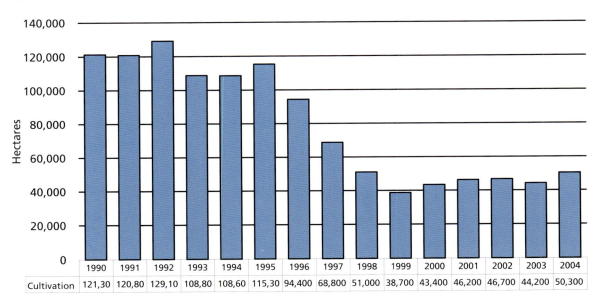

	1990	1991	1992	1993	1994	1995	1996	1997	1998	1999	2000	2001	2002	2003	2004
Cultivation	121,30	120,80	129,10	108,80	108,60	115,30	94,400	68,800	51,000	38,700	43,400	46,200	46,700	44,200	50,300

Peru, main areas of coca cultivation 2003 – 2004

Area	2003	2004	Change 2003 - 2004	Percentage of 2004 Total
Alto Huallaga	13,650	16,900	24%	34%
Aguaytia	510	500	-2%	1%
Apurimac	14,300	14,700	3%	29%
La Convencion - Lares	12,340	12,700	3%	25%
Inambari - Tambopata	2,260	2,000	-12%	4%
San Gaban	470	2700	474%	5%
Others	450	800	78%	2%
Total	44,200	50,300	14%	100%

Peru, potential cocaine production, 1990-2004

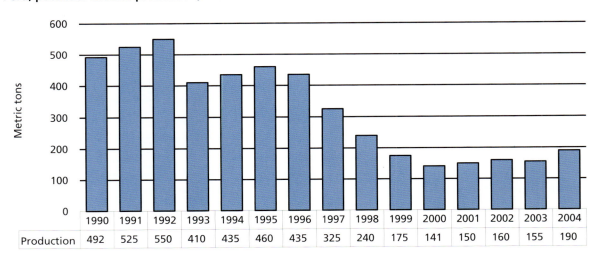

	1990	1991	1992	1993	1994	1995	1996	1997	1998	1999	2000	2001	2002	2003	2004
Production	492	525	550	410	435	460	435	325	240	175	141	150	160	155	190

Peru: Coca cultivation by region in 2001 - 2004

ECUADOR

COLOMBIA

BRAZIL

Putumayo

Loreto

Marañon

San Martín

La Libertad

16.950

Alto Huallaga

Huánuco

Ancash

Aguaytia

Palcazu - Pichis Pachitea

Pasco

12.737

La Convencion and Lares

Madre de Dios

Pacific Ocean

Junín

14.672

Lima

Huancavelica

Apurimac Ene

Ica

Ayacucho

Apurímac

Cusco

San Gaban

Inambari Tambopata

Arequipa

BOLIVIA

Moquegua

Tacna

CHILE

Tumbes
Piura
Lambayeque
Cajamarca
Amazonas

Coca cultivation (ha)

- 2001
- 2002
- 2003
- 2004

Coca growing areas 2004
International boundaries
Department boundaries

0   150   300
km
Geographic coordinates WGS 84

Source: Government of Peru - National of monitoring system supported by UNODC.

Peru, farm-gate prices of coca leaf 1990-2004 (US$/kg)

	1990	1991	1992	1993	1994	1995	1996	1997	1998	1999	2000	2001	2002	2003	2004
January	0.7	0.8	1.1	4.4	1.5	3.0	0.4	0.6	0.6	1.8	1.6	2.0	2.6	2.3	2.5
February	0.9	1.6	1.7	3.5	1.6	3.0	0.4	0.6	0.7	1.4	1.3	2.1	2.6	2.4	2.6
March	0.8	1.6	1.7	1.7	1.6	2.6	0.4	0.6	0.7	1.7	1.6	2.1	2.3	2.0	2.6
April	0.5	1.5	2.6	1.3	1.6	1.7	0.5	0.6	0.6	1.6	1.7	2.3	2.2	1.9	2.4
May	0.5	1.5	1.9	1.7	1.6	0.9	0.5	0.6	1.0	1.6	1.9	2.4	2.3	1.9	2.6
June	0.4	1.7	2.2	1.3	1.8	0.7	0.7	0.6	1.0	1.4	2.0	2.5	2.5	1.8	2.5
July	0.4	1.6	2.2	1.0	2.6	0.4	0.9	0.9	1.1	1.3	2.1	2.5	2.3	2.1	2.9
August	0.4	1.5	3.0	1.9	3.0	0.4	1.0	1.3	2.1	1.8	2.3	2.7	2.9	2.1	3.2
September	1.2	1.7	4.4	2.1	3.0	0.4	1.0	1.3	2.0	2.2	2.7	2.7	2.8	2.2	3.1
October	1.6	1.7	2.6	2.1	3.9	0.4	1.0	0.9	1.5	2.5	2.8	2.5	2.5	2.4	3.2
November	0.9	1.3	2.6	1.3	4.4	0.4	0.6	0.7	1.4	2.0	2.2	2.0	2.4	2.2	3.5
December	0.9	1.0	3.5	1.3	3.0	0.4	0.6	0.7	1.7	1.6	1.9	1.9	2.3	1.9	2.7
Annual Average US$/kg	0.8	1.5	2.5	2.0	2.5	1.2	0.7	0.8	1.2	1.7	2.0	2.3	2.5	2.1	2.8
In constant US$ of 2004	1.1	2.0	3.4	2.6	3.2	1.5	0.8	0.9	1.7	2.4	2.3	2.5	2.6	2.2	2.8

Peru, Upper Huallaga, farmgate prices of coca leaf 1991-2004 (US$/kg)

	1991	1992	1993	1994	1995	1996	1997	1998	1999	2000	2001	2002	2003	2004
January	1.1	1.3	3.8	1.5	3.0	0.4	0.6	0.7	1.9	2.6	2.2	3.9	2.2	2.3
February	1.3	1.5	3.2	1.6	2.9	0.4	0.6	0.7	2.1	2.5	2.2	3.5	2.4	2.6
March	1.6	2.0	2.2	1.6	2.4	0.4	0.6	0.7	2.0	2.4	2.3	2.7	1.9	2.8
April	1.5	2.1	1.6	1.6	1.7	0.5	0.6	0.9	2.1	1.9	2.6	3.0	2.1	2.4
May	1.6	2.2	1.5	1.7	1.1	0.6	0.6	1.1	1.8	2.2	2.5	3.2	2.0	2.6
June	1.6	2.1	1.4	2.0	0.7	0.7	0.7	1.3	1.6	2.3	2.7	3.8	2.2	2.4
July	1.6	2.5	1.4	2.5	0.5	0.8	0.9	1.9	1.7	2.3	2.6	3.0	2.4	2.6
August	1.6	3.2	1.7	2.9	0.4	1.0	1.2	2.2	2.1	2.6	2.9	3.3	2.4	2.9
September	1.6	3.3	2.0	3.3	0.4	1.0	1.2	2.4	2.8	3.0	3.1	3.1	2.5	3.0
October	1.6	3.2	1.8	3.8	0.4	0.9	1.0	2.0	3.1	3.0	2.8	2.2	2.6	3.2
November	1.4	2.9	1.6	3.8	0.4	0.8	0.8	1.8	3.0	2.4	1.8	2.4	2.5	3.5
December	1.2	3.5	1.4	3.5	0.4	0.6	0.7	1.9	2.8	1.9	1.9	2.4	1.9	2.7
Annual Average US$/kg	1.5	2.5	2.0	2.5	1.2	0.7	0.8	1.5	2.3	2.4	2.5	3.0	2.3	2.7
In constant US$ of 2004	2.0	3.4	2.6	3.2	1.5	0.8	0.9	1.7	2.6	2.7	2.6	3.2	2.3	2.7

Peru, average dry coca leaf prices for Peru and for Upper Huallaga, US$/kg, 1990-2004

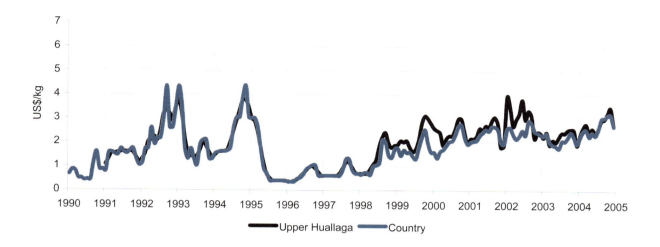

Peru, coca cultivation and reported eradication, in ha, 1983 – 2004 (source CORAH)

Years	Eradication (ha)	Cultivation (ha)
1983	700	45,000
1984	3,100	60,000
1985	4,800	70,000
1986	2,600	107,500
1987	400	110,146
1988	5,100	111,875
1989	1,300	123,007
1990	-	121,300
1991	-	120,800
1992	-	129,100
1993	-	108,800
1994	-	108,600
1995	-	115,300
1996	1,300	94,400
1997	3,500	68,800
1998	7,800	51,000
1999	14,700	38,700
2000	6,200	43,400
2001	6,400	46,200
2002	7,200	46,700
2003	11,312	44,200
2004	10,257	50,300

Peru, cultivation and reported eradication, in ha, 1983 - 2004

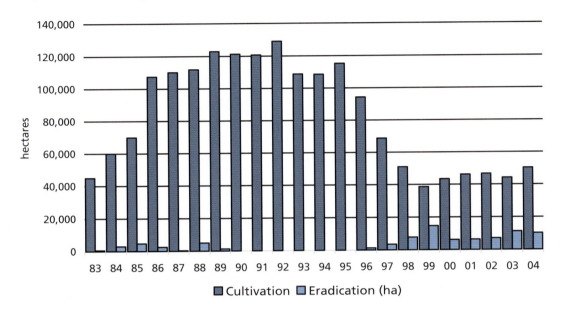

5.2.3. Bolivia

Under its Illicit Crop Monitoring Programme, UNODC has been assisting the Bolivian Government in the implementation of a national coca monitoring system. For the first time, in 2003, the Bolivian project was extended to the national level and consequently, able to provide estimates for coca cultivation at the national level. Bolivia is the third largest producer of coca in the world. It trails far behind Colombia, the world's largest producer.

Results of the 2004 UNODC Bolivia Annual Survey

Coca Cultivation

In 2004, the total area under coca cultivation in Bolivia was estimated to be 27,700 ha, an increase of 17% compared to last year's estimate of 23,600 ha. Although estimates for 2002 and before are not directly comparable with 2003 and 2004 estimates, it is widely recognized that there is an increasing trend in coca cultivation in Bolivia for the past few years.

Geographical Distribution

The increase in coca cultivation at the national level is mostly due to an increase in coca cultivation in the Chapare region from 7,300 ha to 10,100 ha, or 38%, between 2003 and 2004. The increase of 2,800 ha in Chapare represented 67% of the total increase of 4,150 ha. Coca cultivation in the Yungas increased by 7% between 2003 and 2004 to reach 17,300 ha, and it remained the most important region for coca cultivation in Bolivia, accounting for 62% of the total cultivation in 2004.

Coca Production

For the 2004 annual estimate of coca leaf and cocaine production, UNODC continues to rely on information available from other sources. The most comprehensive work on the subject was done by the US Government during the Operation Breakthrough that started in Bolivia in 1993.

No data are available on coca yield production in the hidden coca fields of Chapare but it is generally agreed that the coca yields from hidden fields are substantially lower than from open coca fields. As an approximation, the yield estimates from the traditional area were applied to the hidden coca cultivation in Chapare. Based on these data, the total coca leaf production amounted to 36,300 metric tons, of which 25,000 metric tons were estimated to be available for cocaine production, the rest correspond to the 12,000 ha of cultivation permitted under Bolivian law.

The potential cocaine production in Bolivia is estimated to have amounted to 107 metric tons in 2004. This corresponded an increase of 35% compared to the previous year's potential cocaine production of 79 metric tons.

Coca prices

Farm-gate prices of dry coca leaf have been collected in Chapare on a monthly basis by DIRECO since 1990, and by the UNODC monitoring project in the Yungas of La Paz since 2004. Average annual prices for coca leaf were higher in Chapare (US$ 5.2/kg) than in Yungas of La Paz (US$4.7/kg). Prices remained largely stable throughout 2004, although slightly increasing in the Yungas of La Paz to meet prices of Chapare for the last quarter of the year.

Eradication

In 2004, the Bolivian Government reported the eradication of 8,437 ha of coca fields. Only 4 ha were reported eradicated in the Yungas La Paz, and the remaining 8,433 ha in the Chapare region. This is a similar pattern as in the previous year. In 2004, the level of reported eradication was 16% less than in 2003. In Bolivia, the eradication of coca cultivation is exclusively manual, no chemicals are used.

Fact Sheet: Bolivia Coca Survey 2004

	2003	Variation on 2003	2004
Coca cultivation	23,600 ha	+17 %	27,700 ha
Of which			
in the Yungas of La Paz	16,200 ha	+7%	17,300 ha
in Chapare	7,300 ha	+38%	10,100 ha
in Apolo	50 ha	n.a.[6]	300 ha
Of which permitted by Bolivian law 1008	12,000 ha	0%	12,000 ha
non-permitted by Bolivian law 1008	11,600 ha	+35%	15,700 ha
Of which in national parks	2,400 ha	+71%	4100 ha
Average sun-dried coca leaf yield in traditional coca growing areas outside traditional growing areas	940 kg/ ha 1,800 kg/ha		940 kg/ha 1,800 kg/ha
Production of coca leaf	28,300 mt		36,200 mt
Maximum potential production of cocaine in percent of global cocaine production	79 mt 12%	+35%	107 mt 16%
National weighted average farm-gate price of coca leaf (outside state market)	n.a.		5.0 US$/kg
Chapare average farm-gate price of coca leaf	5.4 US$/kg	- 4%	5.2US$/kg
Total farm-gate value of coca leaf production	US$ 210 millions	+12 %	US$ 240 millions
GDP	US$ 7.8 billions	+ 3.8%	US$ 8.1[7] billions
Farm-gate value of coca leaf production in percent of GDP	1.9 %		2.1 %
Bolivia's agricultural GDP	US$ 1.4 billions	n.a.	n.a.
Farm-gate value of coca leaf production in percent of agricultural GDP	15%	+2%	17%
Reported seizure of cocaine paste	6,934 kg	+ 18%	8,189 kg
Reported seizure of cocaine hydrochloride	5,969 kg	- 91%	531 kg

---

[6] Survey areas not comparable.

[7] GDP of 2004 estimated from the 2003 GDP, and with a projected growth of 3.8% (source: INE)

Graphs, tables and maps: Bolivia

Bolivia, coca cultivation, in ha, 1990 – 2004

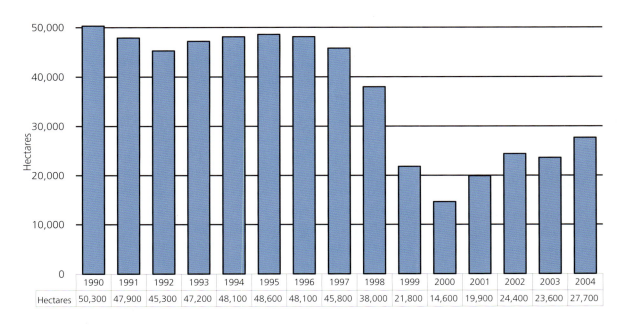

	1990	1991	1992	1993	1994	1995	1996	1997	1998	1999	2000	2001	2002	2003	2004
Hectares	50,300	47,900	45,300	47,200	48,100	48,600	48,100	45,800	38,000	21,800	14,600	19,900	24,400	23,600	27,700

Bolivia, Distribution of coca cultivation (2004 UNODC survey)

Area	2004 Coca Cultivation	% of 2004 total
Yungas of La Paz	17,300	63%
Chapare	10,100	36%
Apolo	300	1%
Rounded Total	27,700	100%

Bolivia, coca cultivation by municipalities (2004 UNODC survey)

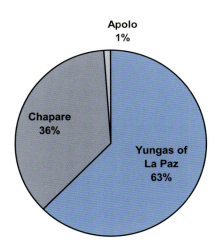

Bolivia: Coca cultivation 2002 - 2004 by region

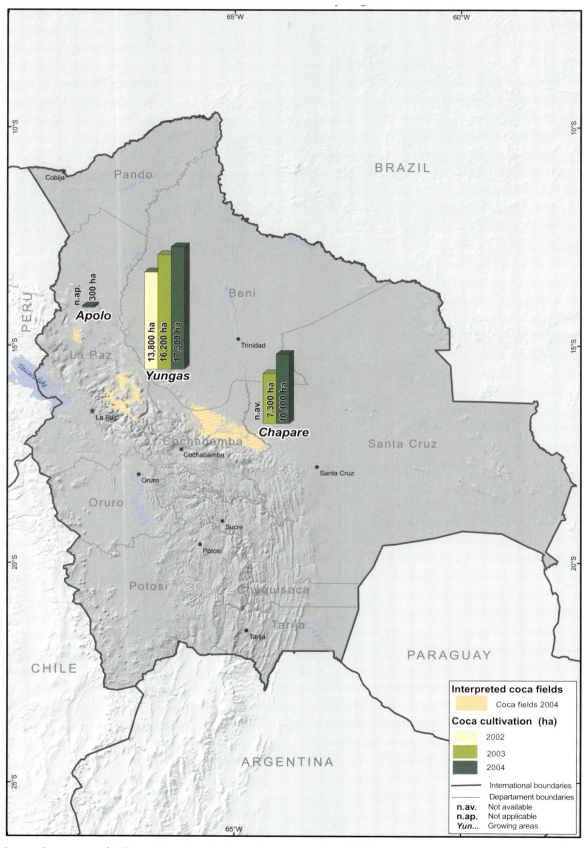

Source: Government of Bolivia - National monitoring system supported by UNODC.

Bolivia, potential cocaine production, 1990 - 2004

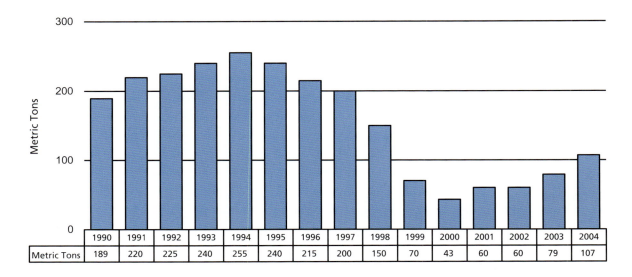

	1990	1991	1992	1993	1994	1995	1996	1997	1998	1999	2000	2001	2002	2003	2004
Metric Tons	189	220	225	240	255	240	215	200	150	70	43	60	60	79	107

Bolivia, farm-gate prices of coca leaf, 1991-2004 (US$/kg)

	1990	1991	1992	1993	1994	1995	1996	1997	1998	1999	2000	2001	2002	2003	2004
January	0.3	0.5		1.0	1.1	1.5	0.9	1.3	2.1	1.5	6.0	5.4	6.1	5.4	5.3
February	0.3	1.2	0.9	1.0	1.1	1.7	1.4	1.2	2.0	1.5	5.1	5.3	5.8	5.3	5.1
March	0.3	1.5	1.0	1.0	0.6	1.5	0.9	1.1	1.3	1.7	5.4	5.3	5.7	5.2	5.2
April	0.2	1.1	0.8	1.1	0.9	1.3	0.9	1.0	1.4	2.0	5.7	5.5	5.7	5.2	5.3
May	0.4	0.8	0.9	1.0	0.9	1.4	0.9	1.1	1.3	2.0	5.9	5.4	5.6	5.3	5.2
June	0.6	1.2	1.0	1.4	0.9	1.3	1.3	1.2	1.5	2.4	6.0	5.5	5.6	5.4	5.1
July	0.8	0.8	0.8	1.8	0.7	1.3	0.8	1.4	1.5	2.4	6.0	5.6	5.7	5.5	5.1
August	1.0	1.0	0.9	1.5	0.8	1.4	1.1	1.9	1.4	3.7	6.0	5.6	5.7	5.5	5.1
September	1.1	1.2	1.2	1.5	1.2	1.4	1.7	2.2	1.5	4.8	5.3	5.3	5.4	5.4	5.3
October	0.7	0.9	0.9	1.4	1.6	1.4	1.4	2.2	1.4	4.9	4.8	5.6	5.4	5.4	5.0
November	0.5	1.1	0.9	1.2	1.8	1.4	1.3	2.3	1.4	4.9	5.3	5.6	5.4	5.4	5.0
December	0.3	0.8	0.9	1.2	1.7	1.4	1.2	2.1	1.4	5.0	5.3	5.7	5.5	5.5	5.1
Annual Average US$/kg	0.5	1.0	0.9	1.3	1.1	1.4	1.1	1.6	1.5	3.1	5.6	5.5	5.6	5.4	5.2

Bolivia, coca leaf prices, US$/kg, 1990-2004

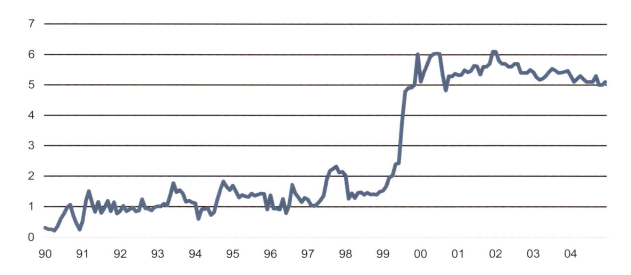

Bolivia, reported eradication and cultivation, in ha, 1997-2004

Year	Eradicated (ha)	Cultivated (ha)
1997	7,026	45,800
1998	11,621	38,000
1999	16,999	21,800
2000	7,953	19,600
2001	9,435	19,900
2002	11,853	24,400
2003	10,087	23,600
2004	8,437	27,700

Source: DIRECO

Bolivia, reported eradication and cultivation, in ha, 1997-2004

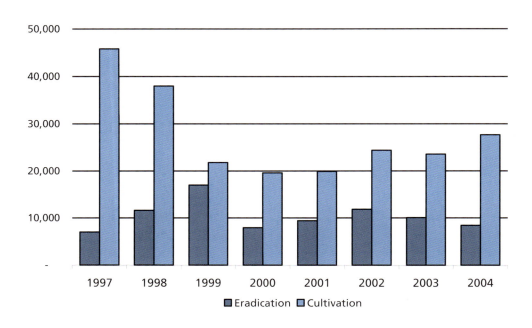

5.2.4. Seizure of Illicit laboratories

MANUFACTURE

SEIZURES OF ILLICIT LABORATORIES

REPORTED FOR 2002 - 2003

Remark: For convenience, an attempt was made to group the reported estimates by drug categories. however, due to inconsistencies and gaps in the reporting, no overall analysis of the data set was performed. Numbers are presented as reported to UNODC and should be interpreted with caution.

Source: Annual Report Questionnaire if not otherwise indicated

Country or Territory	Year	Name of drug seized	Number of laboratories (and quantity of drug)	Source
			COCA GROUP	
Africa				
Southern Africa				
South Africa	2003	Cocaine	1 Lab.	
Subtotal Southern Africa			1 Lab.	
Total Africa			1 Lab.	
Americas				
Central America				
Honduras	2003		3 Lab.	
Subtotal Central America			3 Lab.	
North America				
United States	2002	Cocaine	5 Lab.(1.000 kg)	
Subtotal North America			5 Lab.(1.000 kg)	
South America				
Argentina	2002	Cocaine	9 Lab.	
	2003	Cocaine	8 Lab.	
	2003	Coca paste	3 Lab.	
Bolivia	2002	Coca paste	1950 Lab.*	F.O
	2002		1 Lab.	F.O
	2002	Cocaine base	1426 Lab.	F.O
	2003	Coca paste	2544 Lab.*	F.O
	2003	Cocaine base	1769 Lab.	F.O
Chile	2002		1 Lab.	
	2003		3 Lab.	
Colombia	2002		138 Lab.	Govt
	2002	Cocaine base	1273 Lab.	Govt
	2002		23 Lab.	Govt
	2003		637 Lab.	Govt
	2003		12 Lab.	Govt
	2003	Cocaine base	822 Lab.	Govt
Peru	2003		964 Lab.(19280.000 kg)	
Subtotal South America			11583 Lab.(19280.000 kg)	
Total Americas			11591 Lab.(19281.000 kg)	
Asia				
East and South-East Asia				

* Maceration pits

Country or Territory	Year	Name of drug seized	Number of laboratories (and quantity of drug)	Source
Hong Kong Special Administrative Region of China	2002	Cocaine	2 Lab.	
Subtotal East and South-East Asia			2 Lab.	
Total Asia			2 Lab.	
Europe				
<u>West & Central Europe</u>				
France	2002	Cocaine	1 Lab.	
Germany, Federal Republic of	2002		1 Lab.	
Slovenia	2002	Cocaine base	1 Lab.	
Subtotal West & Central Europe			3 Lab.	
Total Europe			3 Lab.	
Coca group			11597 Lab.(19281.000 kg)	

233

5.3. Cannabis

5.3.1. Morocco

Morocco remains one of the main producers of cannabis resin (hashish) in the world. It supplies primarily the European market. The Northern Region of Morocco, where most of the cannabis cultivation is concentrated, is spread over 5 provinces and covers an area of roughly 20,000 square km. In 2003, the Government of Morocco and UNODC undertook the first survey of cannabis cultivation in Morocco and provided an initial estimate of the extent of cannabis cultivation in the country. The second survey conducted in 2004, provided some new information leading to the revision of selected 2003 estimates.

Results of the 2004 UNODC Morocco Cannabis Survey

Cannabis cultivation decreased slightly

The survey estimated cannabis cultivation at about 120,500 hectares, or a decrease of 10% compared to 2003. The most important decreases took place in the provinces of Al Hoceima (-54%) and Taounate (-43%) while a smaller decrease was noted in the province of Larache (- 1%). These decreases are attributed to outreach activities by the local administration. In contrast cannabis cultivation increased significantly in the provinces of Tetouan (+19%) and Chefchaouen (+13%).

Cannabis and cannabis resin production figures updated

Based on a raw cannabis yield of 1,270 kg/ha on irrigated land and 750 kg/ha yield on rain-fed land, the total potential production of raw cannabis was estimated at 98,000 metric tons. Its conversion into cannabis resin (hashish) was estimated at about 2,760 metric tons, or a decrease of about 10% compared to a revised 2003 potential production of cannabis resin of 3,070 mt, (instead of 3,080 mt published last year).

Cannabis producers' revenues declined by 26%

The calculation of raw cannabis is based on the estimates of production, the extraction rate of cannabis resin from raw cannabis and the distribution of the sales between raw cannabis and cannabis resin. Using these estimates as a basis, the total gross farmers income from cannabis cultivation is estimated at about 3 billion Dh (US$325 million). This represents 0.7% of GDP in 2003 (Dh242.6 billion or US$47 billion). Based on an estimate of 96,600 households (804,000 persons) benefiting from cannabis cultivation in the Rif region (2003 estimates), this represents a gross per capita income of 3,600 Dh (US$400), well below the country's overall 2003 GDP per capita of 14,106 Dh (US$ 1478).

A lower overall turnover of the market of cannabis resin of Moroccan origin

Assuming that, as in 2003, 853 metric tons of cannabis resin were seized in 2004 (of which 96 metric tons in Morocco), about 1,927 metric tons of cannabis resin have remained available for consumption in 2004. With an average street price for cannabis resin of 6.9$ per gram in Western Europe, the overall turnover of the market of cannabis resin of Moroccan origin would have been US$ 13 billion, or €10.8 billion in 2004 in Europe.

Fact Sheet : Morocco Cannabis Survey 2004

	2003	Change	2004
Cannabis cultivation: (88% rain fed and 12% irrigated)	134,000 ha	-10%	120,500 ha
No. of households cultivating cannabis	96,600 families		n/a
Cannabis yield on rain fed land on irrigated land	750* kg/ha 1,270* kg/ha		750 kg/ha 1,270 kg/ha
Gross cannabis production	109,000* mt.	-10%	98,000 mt.
Cannabis extraction rate	2.82*%		2.82%
Potential production of cannabis resin	3,070* mt.	-10%	2,760 mt.
Distribution of farm gate sales Sale of raw cannabis Sale of cannabis resin	66% 34%		66% 34%
Cannabis sale prices at farmgate Raw cannabis Cannabis resin	35 dh/kg 1,400* dh/kg		25 dh/kg 1,400 dh/kg
Total farmers income from cannabis	Dh4.0 bn* (US$ 417 mn €362 mn)	-26%	Dh2.9 bn (US$ 325 mn €263 mn)
Average cannabis income per capita	Dh4,900 (US$ 520, €450)		Dh3,600 (US$ 400, €330)
2003 GDP per capita	US$ 1,478		n/a
Seizure of cannabis resin in Morocco	96* mt.		n/a
in Western and Central Europe of which of Moroccan origin (80%)	946* mt. 757* mt.		n/a n/a
Annual turn-over of international trade in cannabis resin of Moroccan origin	US$ 15* bn €12.4* bn	- 14%	US$ 13 bn €10.8 bn (based on 2003 seizures estimates)

* 2003 results updated based on more recent or more precise informationand data obtained during the 2004 survey.

Graphs, tables, maps: Morocco 2004

Morocco, provincial cannabis cultivation

Province	Total area (ha)	Cannabis cultivation (ha)	Cannabis cultivation in % of total area
Al Hoceima	375,008	10,524	9%
Chefchaouen	529,503	75,195	62%
Larache	278,968	11,892	10%
Taounate	525,568	14,718	12%
Tétouan	245,771	8,225	7%
Total	1,956,818	120,554	100%

Morocco, provincial cannabis cultivation (ha) 2004

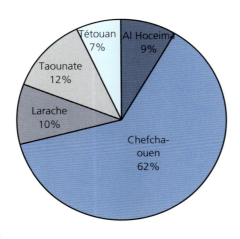

Morocco, provincial raw cannabis production (mt) 2004

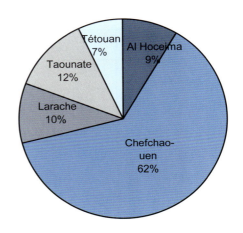

Morocco, provincial raw cannabis production 2004

Province	Ha rainfed	Ha irrigated	Yield rainfed (kg/ha)	Yield irrigated (kg/ha)	Production rainfed (tonnes)	Production irrigated (tonnes)	Production Total (tonnes)
Al Hoceima	9,261	1,263	750	1,270	7,001	1,604	8,605
Chefchaouen	66,172	9,023	750	1,270	50,026	11,459	61,485
Larache	10,465	1,427	750	1,270	7,912	1,812	9,724
Taounate	12,952	1,766	750	1,270	9,792	2,243	12,035
Tétouan	7,238	987	750	1,270	5,472	1,253	6,725
Total	106,088	14,466			80,203	18,371	98,574
Total (Rounded)					80,000	18,000	98,000

Morocco, potential farmers income from cannabis 2004

Production	Quantity (kg)	Price (Dh/kg)	Total (Dh)
Total raw cannabis production	97,900,000		
Sale as raw cannabis (66%)	64,610,000	25	1,615,250,000
Sale as cannabis resine (34%)	939,000	1,400	1,314,600,000
Total income from cannabis (rounded)			3,000,000,000

Morocco, cannabis area as percentage of agricultural land per province

Province	Total agicultural area (ha)*	Cannabis (ha)	Cannabis in % of agricultural area
Al Hoceima	169,400	10,524	6%
Chefchaouen	162,500	75,195	46%
Larache	175,900	11,892	7%
Taounate	370,800	14,718	4%
Tétouan	78,600	8,225	10%
Total	957,200	120,554	13%

* Source DPAE, Ministry of Agriculture

Morocco, Northern Provinces: Cannabis cultivation in 2004 (per commune)

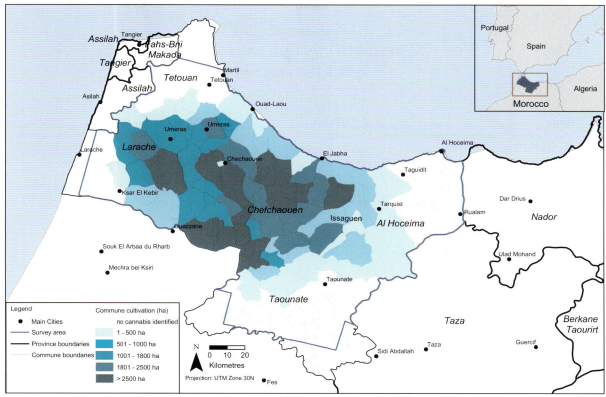

Source: APDN (Morocco) - UNODC/ICMP *Cannabis Survey 2004*

Morocco, Northern Provinces: Cannabis production in 2004 (per commune)

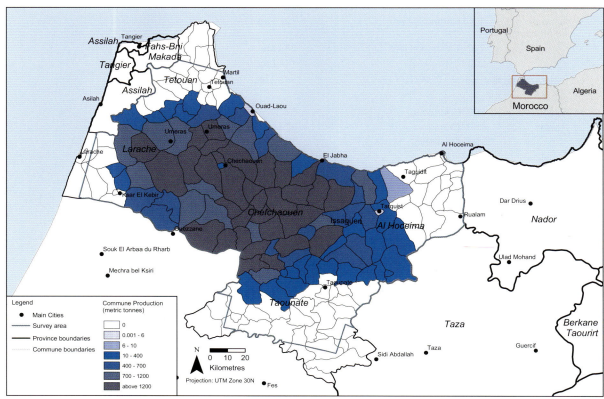

Source: APDN (Morocco) - UNODC/ICMP *Cannabis Survey 2004*

5.3.2. Seizure of Illicit laboratories

MANUFACTURE
SEIZURES OF ILLICIT LABORATORIES
REPORTED FOR 2002 - 2003

Remark: For convenience, an attempt was made to group the reported estimates by drug categories. however, due to inconsistencies and gaps in the reporting, no overall analysis of the data set was performed. Numbers are presented as reported to UNODC and should be interpreted with caution.

Source: Annual Report Questionnaire if not otherwise indicated

Country or Territory	Year	Name of drug seized	Number of laboratories (and quantity of drug)	Source
		CANNABIS GROUP		
Africa				
Southern Africa				
South Africa	2003	Cannabis	3 Lab.(100.000 kg)	
Subtotal Southern Africa			3 Lab.(100.000 kg)	
Total Africa			3 Lab.(100.000 kg)	
Americas				
North America				
Canada	2002		1 Lab.	
	2003		3 Lab.	
Subtotal North America			4 Lab.	
Total Americas			4 Lab.	
Europe				
East Europe				
Russian Federation	2002	Cannabis herb	121 Lab.	
	2003	Cannabis herb	83 Lab.	
	2003		114 Lab.	
Subtotal East Europe			318 Lab.	
West & Central Europe				
Czech Republic	2003	Cannabis	3 Lab.	
Poland	2002	Cannabis	32 Lab.	
	2003	Cannabis	32 Lab.	
Slovakia	2003		1 Lab.	
Subtotal West & Central Europe			68 Lab.	
Total Europe			386 Lab.	
Cannabis group			393 Lab.(100.000 kg)	

5.4. Amphetamine-type stimulants

5.4.1. Seizure of Illicit laboratories

MANUFACTURE
SEIZURES OF ILLICIT LABORATORIES
REPORTED FOR 2002 - 2003

Remark: For convenience, an attempt was made to group the reported estimates by drug categories. however, due to inconsistencies and gaps in the reporting, no overall analysis of the data set was performed. Numbers are presented as reported to UNODC and should be interpreted with caution.

Source: Annual Report Questionnaire if not otherwise indicated

Country or Territory	Year	Name of drug seized	Number of laboratories (and quantity of drug)	Source
COMBINED AMPHETAMINE, METHAMPHETAMINE GROUP				
Europe				
West & Central Europe				
Lithuania	2002	Amphetamine, methamphetamine	2 Lab.(1460.000 kg)	
Subtotal West & Central Europe			2 Lab.(1460.000 kg)	
Total Europe			2 Lab.(1460.000 kg)	
Oceania				
Oceania				
Australia	2002	Methamphetamine, amphetamine	240 Lab.	
	2003	Methamphetamine, amphetamine	314 Lab.	
Subtotal Oceania			554 Lab. *	
Total Oceania			554 Lab.	
Combined amphetamine, methamphetamine group			556 Lab.(1460.000 kg)	
AMPHETAMINE GROUP				
Americas				
North America				
Mexico	2003	Amphetamine	1 Lab.	
United States	2003	Amphetamine	10 Lab.	
Subtotal North America			11 Lab.	
South America				
Chile	2002	Amphetamine	1 Lab.	
Subtotal South America			1 Lab.	
Total Americas			12 Lab.	
Asia				
East and South-East Asia				
Indonesia	2003	Amphetamine	6 Lab.	
Subtotal East and South-East Asia			6 Lab.	
Total Asia			6 Lab.	
Europe				
East Europe				
Russian Federation	2002	Amphetamine	97 Lab.	
	2003		101 Lab.	

* for the period July 2001 – June 2003

Country or Territory	Year	Name of drug seized	Number of laboratories (and quantity of drug)	Source
Subtotal East Europe			198 Lab.	
Southeast Europe				
Bulgaria	2002	Amphetamine	2 Lab.(1500.000 kg)	
	2003	Amphetamine	5 Lab.	
Serbia and Montenegro	2003		1 Lab.(167000 u.)	
	2003		2 Lab.(150.000 kg)	
Subtotal Southeast Europe			10 Lab.(1650.000 kg)(167000 u.)	
West & Central Europe				
Belgium	2002	Amphetamine	1 Lab.	
	2002		1 Lab.	
	2003	Amphetamine	1 Lab.	
Estonia	2002	Amphetamine	1 Lab.	
	2003	Amphetamine	2 Lab.	
France	2002	Amphetamine	1 Lab.	
Germany, Federal Republic of	2002		2 Lab.	
	2003	Amphetamine	1 Lab.	
	2003		3 Lab.	
Lithuania	2003	Amphetamine	1 Lab.	
Luxembourg	2003	Amphetamine	1 Lab.	
Netherlands	2002	Amphetamine	10 Lab.	
	2003	Amphetamine	15 Lab.(36000.000 kg)	
Poland	2002	Amphetamine	15 Lab.	
	2003	Amphetamine	10 Lab.	
United Kingdom	2002	Amphetamine	1 Lab.	
	2003	Amphetamine	1 Lab.	
Subtotal West & Central Europe			67 Lab.(36000.000 kg)	
Total Europe			275 Lab.(37650.000 kg)(167000 u.)	
Amphetamine group			293 Lab.(37650.000 kg)(167000 u.)	

METHAMPHETAMINE GROUP

Africa

Southern Africa

Country or Territory	Year	Name of drug seized	Number of laboratories (and quantity of drug)	Source
South Africa	2002	Methamphetamine	1 Lab.	
Subtotal Southern Africa			1 Lab.	
Total Africa			1 Lab.	

Americas

North America

Country or Territory	Year	Name of drug seized	Number of laboratories (and quantity of drug)	Source
Canada	2002	Methamphetamine	14 Lab.	
	2003	Methamphetamine	39 Lab.	
Mexico	2002	Methamphetamine	10 Lab.	
	2003	Methamphetamine	17 Lab.	
United States	2002	Methamphetamine	9024 Lab.(3367.000 kg)	
	2003	Methamphetamine	10182 Lab.	Govt
Subtotal North America			19286 Lab.(3367.000 kg)	
Total Americas			19286 Lab.(3367.000 kg)	

Asia

East and South-East Asia

Country or Territory	Year	Name of drug seized	Number of laboratories (and quantity of drug)	Source
Cambodia	2003	Methamphetamine	7 Lab.	F.O
China	2002	Methamphetamine	13 Lab.	
Myanmar	2002	Methamphetamine	4 Lab.	
	2003		1 Lab.	
Philippines	2002	Methamphetamine	4 Lab.	
	2003		11 Lab.	
Taiwan, Province of China	2003	Methamphetamine	10 Lab.	INCSR
Subtotal East and South-East Asia			50 Lab.	
Total Asia			50 Lab.	

Europe

West & Central Europe

Czech Republic	2002	Methamphetamine	104 Lab.	
	2003	Methamphetamine	188 Lab.	
Germany, Federal Republic of	2002	Methamphetamine	2 Lab.	
Lithuania	2003	Methamphetamine	1 Lab.	
Slovakia	2003	Methamphetamine	3 Lab.	
Subtotal West & Central Europe			298 Lab.	
Total Europe			298 Lab.	

Oceania

Oceania

New Zealand	2002	Methamphetamine	147 Lab.	
	2003	Methamphetamine	201 Lab.	
Subtotal Oceania			348 Lab.	
Total Oceania			348 Lab.	
Methamphetamine group			19983 Lab.(3367.000 kg)	

ECSTASY GROUP

Africa

Southern Africa

South Africa	2003		1 Lab.(0.020 kg)	
Subtotal Southern Africa			1 Lab.(0.020 kg)	
Total Africa			1 Lab.(0.020 kg)	

Americas

North America

Canada	2002	MDMA	8 Lab.	
	2003	MDA	3 Lab.	
	2003	MDMA	12 Lab.	
Mexico	2002	MDMA	1 Lab.	
United States	2002	MDMA	9 Lab.(1.500 kg)	
	2003	MDMA	10 Lab.	
Subtotal North America			43 Lab.(1.500 kg)	

South America

Argentina	2003		1 Lab.	
Subtotal South America			1 Lab.	
Total Americas			44 Lab.(1.500 kg)	

Country or Territory	Year	Name of drug seized	Number of laboratories (and quantity of drug)	Source
Asia				
East and South-East Asia				
China	2002		11 Lab.	
Hong Kong Special Administrative Region of China	2003		1 Lab.	Govt
	2003		1 Lab.	
Indonesia	2002		2 Lab.	
Subtotal East and South-East Asia			15 Lab.	
Total Asia			15 Lab.	
Europe				
East Europe				
Russian Federation	2003		1 Lab.(120.000 kg)	
Subtotal East Europe			1 Lab.(120.000 kg)	
West & Central Europe				
Belgium	2002		4 Lab.	
	2003		1 Lab.	
	2003	MDMA	1 Lab.	
Estonia	2002	MDMA	1 Lab.	
	2003	MDMA	2 Lab.	
France	2002	MDMA	1 Lab.	
Lithuania	2003		2 Lab.	
Netherlands	2002	MDMA	18 Lab.	
	2003	MDMA	12 Lab.(14400.000 kg)	
United Kingdom	2002		1 Lab.	
	2002	MDMA	2 Lab.(4160000 u.)	
Subtotal West & Central Europe			45 Lab.(14400.000 kg)(4160000 u.)	
Total Europe			46 Lab.(14520.000 kg)(4160000 u.)	
Oceania				
Oceania				
New Zealand	2003	MDMA	1 Lab.	
Subtotal Oceania			1 Lab.	
Total Oceania			1 Lab.	
Ecstasy group			107 Lab.(14521.520 kg)(4160000 u.)	

5.5. Other Drugs

5.5.1. Seizures of Illicit Laboratories

MANUFACTURE

SEIZURES OF ILLICIT LABORATORIES

REPORTED FOR 2002 - 2003

Remark: For convenience, an attempt was made to group the reported estimates by drug categories. however, due to inconsistencies and gaps in the reporting, no overall analysis of the data set was performed. Numbers are presented as reported to UNODC and should be interpreted with caution.

Source: Annual Report Questionnaire if not otherwise indicated

Country or Territory	Year	Name of drug seized	Number of laboratories (and quantity of drug)	Source
OTHER SYNTHETIC STIMULANTS				
Africa				
Southern Africa				
South Africa	2002	Methcathinone	13 Lab.	
	2003	Methcathinone	36 Lab.(12.751 kg)	
Subtotal Southern Africa			49 Lab.(12.751 kg)	
Total Africa			49 Lab.(12.751 kg)	
Americas				
North America				
United States	2002	Methcathinone	9 Lab.(1.190 kg)	
	2003	Methcathinone	33 Lab.	
Subtotal North America			42 Lab.(1.190 kg)	
South America				
Colombia	2002		1 Lab.	
Subtotal South America			1 Lab.	
Total Americas			43 Lab.(1.190 kg)	
Europe				
West & Central Europe				
Netherlands	2002		1 Lab.	
Subtotal West & Central Europe			1 Lab.	
Total Europe			1 Lab.	
Other synthetic stimulants			93 Lab.(13.941 kg)	
DEPRESSANT GROUP				
Africa				
Southern Africa				
South Africa	2002	GHB	1 Lab.	
	2002	Methaqualone	4 Lab.	
	2003	Methaqualone	15 Lab.(1697000 u.)	
	2003	GHB	6 Lab.(4.000 lt.)	
Subtotal Southern Africa			26 Lab.(4.000 lt.)(1697000 u.)	
Total Africa			26 Lab.(4.000 lt.)(1697000 u.)	
Americas				
North America				
Canada	2002		2 Lab.	
United States	2002	GHB	7 Lab.(1.360 kg)	

Country or Territory	Year	Name of drug seized	Number of laboratories (and quantity of drug)	Source
United States	2003	GHB	6 Lab.	
Subtotal North America			15 Lab.(1.360 kg)	
Total Americas			15 Lab.(1.360 kg)	
Asia				
East and South-East Asia				
China	2002	Methaqualone	1 Lab.	
Subtotal East and South-East Asia			1 Lab.	
South Asia				
India	2002	Methaqualone	1 Lab.(442.000 kg)	
Subtotal South Asia			1 Lab.(442.000 kg)	
Total Asia			2 Lab.(442.000 kg)	
Europe				
West & Central Europe				
Estonia	2002	GHB	1 Lab.	
Germany, Federal Republic of	2003	GHB	9 Lab.	
Subtotal West & Central Europe			10 Lab.	
Total Europe			10 Lab.	
Depressant group			53 Lab.(443.360 kg)(4.000 lt.)(1697000 u.)	

HALLUCINOGEN GROUP

Country or Territory	Year	Name of drug seized	Number of laboratories (and quantity of drug)	Source
Americas				
North America				
Canada	2002		2 Lab.	
	2003		1 Lab.	
United States	2002		6 Lab.(8.000 kg)	
	2003		16 Lab.	
	2003	LSD	1 Lab.	
Subtotal North America			26 Lab.(8.000 kg)	
Total Americas			26 Lab.(8.000 kg)	
Europe				
West & Central Europe				
Germany, Federal Republic of	2002		1 Lab.	
Subtotal West & Central Europe			1 Lab.	
Total Europe			1 Lab.	
Hallucinogen group			27 Lab.(8.000 kg)	

OTHER

Country or Territory	Year	Name of drug seized	Number of laboratories (and quantity of drug)	Source
Europe				
East Europe				
Russian Federation	2003	Other drugs	103 Lab.	
Subtotal East Europe			103 Lab.	
West & Central Europe				
Estonia	2002		1 Lab.	
Germany, Federal Republic of	2003		1 Lab.	

Country or Territory	Year	Name of drug seized	Number of laboratories (and quantity of drug)	Source
Subtotal West & Central Europe			2 Lab.	
Total Europe			105 Lab.	
Other			105 Lab.	

PRECURSORS

Americas

North America

Canada	2003		1 Lab.	
Subtotal North America			1 Lab.	
Total Americas			1 Lab.	
Precursors			1 Lab.	

UNSPECIFIED

Americas

South America

Peru	2002	unknown	238 Lab.	
Subtotal South America			238 Lab.	
Total Americas			238 Lab.	

Europe

West & Central Europe

Netherlands	2002	Unspecified	15 Lab.	Govt
Spain	2002	Unspecified	8 Lab.	
Subtotal West & Central Europe			23 Lab.	
Total Europe			23 Lab.	
Unspecified			261 Lab.	

6. SEIZURES

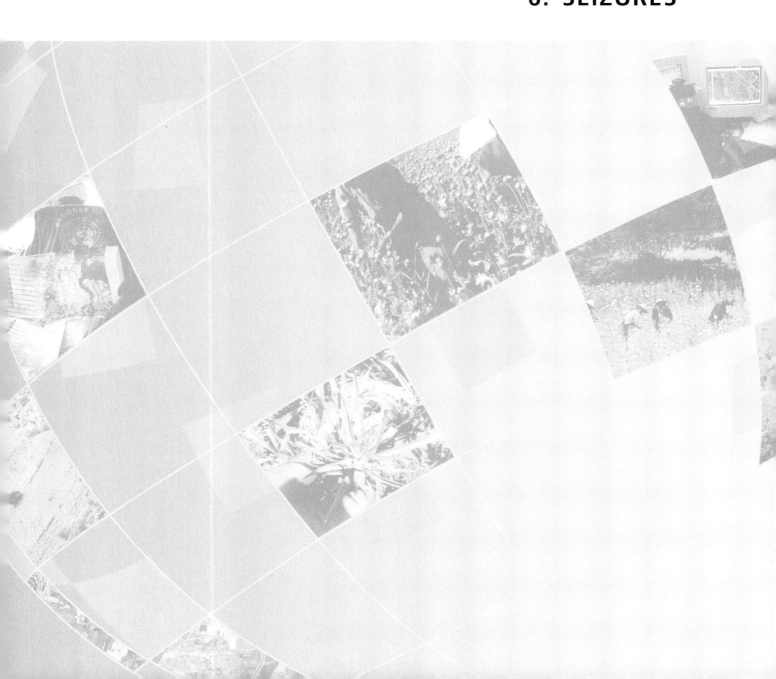

6.1. Opiates: Seizures 1998-2003

SEIZURES, 1998 - 2003
Opium (raw and prepared)

Region/country or territory	1998	1999	2000	2001	2002	2003
AFRICA						
East Africa						
Mauritius	No Report	No Report	No Report	0.001 kg	No Report	No Report
Sub-Total				0.001 kg		
North Africa						
Egypt	25.894 kg	24.702 kg	75.283 kg	40.000 kg	33.000 kg	44.500 kg
Tunisia	No Report	No Report	0.017 kg [ICPO]	No Report	No Report	No Report
Sub-Total	25.894 kg	24.702 kg	75.300 kg	40.000 kg	33.000 kg	44.500 kg
Southern Africa						
Zambia	6.770 kg [Govt]	8.622 kg	0.000 kg [Govt]	0.000 kg [Govt]	No Report	No Report
Sub-Total	6.770 kg	8.622 kg				
West and Central Africa						
Benin	No Report	No Report	No Report	0.414 kg [ICPO]	No Report	No Report
Gambia	No Report	No Report	No Report	0.024 kg [Govt]	No Report	No Report
Niger	No Report	0.013 kg [ICPO]	No Report	No Report	No Report	No Report
Sub-Total		0.013 kg		0.438 kg		
Total region	32.664 kg	33.337 kg	75.300 kg	40.439 kg	33.000 kg	44.500 kg
AMERICAS						
Caribbean						
Netherlands Antilles	No Report	No Report	No Report	No Report	0.440 kg [ICPO]	No Report
Sub-Total					0.440 kg	
North America						
Canada	61.310 kg	57.000 kg 10061 u.	18.788 kg 140 u.	27.307 kg	12.320 kg 1313 u.	30.080 kg
Mexico	149.640 kg	801.180 kg	469.445 kg	516.369 kg	309.902 kg [(1]	192.014 kg
United States	No Report	68.970 kg	No Report	24.500 kg	95.779 kg	201.722 kg
Sub-Total	210.950 kg	927.150 kg 10061 u.	488.233 kg 140 u.	568.176 kg	418.001 kg 1313 u.	423.816 kg
South America						
Colombia	99.950 kg [Govt]	32.680 kg [Govt]	16.630 kg [Govt]	3.740 kg [Govt]	110.270 kg [Govt]	27.180 kg [Govt]
Peru	11.528 kg	No Report	No Report	146.950 kg	244.753 kg	181.915 kg
Sub-Total	111.478 kg	32.680 kg	16.630 kg	150.690 kg	355.023 kg	209.095 kg
Total region	322.428 kg	959.830 kg 10061 u.	504.863 kg 140 u.	718.866 kg	773.464 kg 1313 u.	632.911 kg
ASIA						
Central Asia and Transcaucasian countries						
Armenia	No Report	2.032 kg [Govt.]	2.188 kg	0.090 kg	0.078 kg	0.039 kg
Azerbaijan	48.541 kg	52.218 kg	87.617 kg [ICPO]	10.500 kg	0.127 kg	No Report
Georgia	No Report	14.700 kg [ICPO]	33.500 kg [ICPO]	No Report	No Report	8.400 kg
Kazakhstan	296.574 kg	170.236 kg	136.000 kg [F.O]	36.000 kg [F.O]	13.571 kg [F.O]	192.000 kg [F.O]
Kyrgyzstan	171.872 kg	151.174 kg	1405.232 kg	469.225 kg	109.295 kg	45.684 kg

Source: Annual Report Questionnaire if not otherwise indicated

251

SEIZURES, 1998 - 2003
Opium (raw and prepared)

Region/country or territory	1998	1999	2000	2001	2002	2003
ASIA						
Central Asia and Transcaucasian countries						
Tajikistan	1190.400 kg	1269.278 kg [F.O]	4778.448 kg [F.O]	3664.277 kg	1624.101 kg	2371.005 kg
Turkmenistan	1412.000 kg [Govt.]	4600.000 kg [F.O]	2300.000 kg [F.O]	No Report	1200.000 kg [F.O]	138.000 kg [F.O]
Uzbekistan	1935.315 kg	3292.342 kg	2008.200 kg	241.680 kg [F.O]	76.000 kg [F.O]	151.200 kg
Sub-Total	5054.702 kg	9551.979 kg	10751.180 kg	4421.772 kg	3023.172 kg	2906.328 kg
East and South-East Asia						
China	1215.000 kg	1193.000 kg [ICPO]	2428.000 kg [Govt.]	2820.000 kg [Govt.]	1219.300 kg	905.400 kg
Hong Kong Special Administrative Region of China	No Report	0.100 kg	0.090 kg	2.500 kg	No Report	No Report
Indonesia	0.030 kg [HNLP]	3.097 kg [HNLP]	0.034 kg [ICPO]	0.009 kg	0.000 kg [Govt]	0.000 kg [Govt]
Japan	19.811 kg	7.688 kg	8.979 kg	No Report	5.700 kg [Govt]	6.600 kg
Lao People's Democratic Republic	442.000 kg [INCSR]	225.800 kg [HNLP]	78.000 kg [INCSR]	372.600 kg [Govt]	123.150 kg	209.200 kg
Malaysia	32.747 kg	21.066 kg	0.710 kg	69.270 kg [ICPO]	No Report	66.120 kg
Myanmar	5705.881 kg	1759.538 kg	1773.652 kg	1770.773 kg	1989.222 kg	1685.566 kg
Republic of Korea	1.035 kg	3.064 kg	14996 u. [ICPO]	0.218 kg	0.258 kg [ICPO]	25.284 kg
Singapore	22.781 kg	98.144 kg	4.504 kg	13.375 kg	No Report	No Report
Thailand	1631.124 kg	421.939 kg	1595.000 kg [HNLP]	2289.000 kg [HNLP]	3458.000 kg [ICPO]	10240.000 kg [Govt.]
Viet Nam	800.000 kg [F.O]	495.000 kg [F.O]	567.000 kg [F.O]	583.005 kg	613.000 kg [F.O]	280.000 kg
Sub-Total	9870.408 kg	4228.436 kg	6455.969 kg 14996 u.	7920.750 kg	7408.630 kg	13418.170 kg
Near and Middle East /South-West Asia						
Afghanistan	No Report	No Report	No Report	No Report	5581.615 kg	8412.000 kg
Bahrain	0.014 kg [ICPO]	0.323 kg [ICPO]	0.001 kg [ICPO]	No Report	0.007 kg	No Report
Iran (Islamic Republic of)	154453.569 kg	204485.000 kg	179053.000 kg [NAPOL]	81061.000 kg	72856.000 kg [Govt]	97575.000 kg
Iraq	No Report	No Report	10.511 kg	0.993 kg	No Report	No Report
Israel	0.556 kg	0.005 kg [ICPO]	0.194 kg	4.405 kg	0.006 kg	1.824 kg
Jordan	No Report	61.700 kg	No Report	0.327 kg	19.326 kg	No Report
Kuwait	4.720 kg	14.000 kg [INCB]	32.500 kg [ICPO]	No Report	6.367 kg [ICPO]	No Report
Lebanon	No Report	44.226 kg	0.052 kg	7.028 kg	0.762 kg	2.703 kg
Oman	No Report	No Report	1.647 kg [ICPO]	0.308 kg	0.591 kg	No Report
Pakistan	5021.712 kg	16319.918 kg	8867.407 kg	5175.000 kg [F.O]	2686.257 kg	5785.710 kg
Qatar	0.030 kg [ICPO]	0.100 kg [ICPO]	2.700 kg [ICPO]	No Report	0.225 kg	0.200 kg
Saudi Arabia	16.721 kg [(2]	No Report	13.472 kg	0.954 kg	4.561 kg [ICPO]	0.300 kg [ICPO]
Syrian Arab Republic	1.200 kg [Govt]	5.876 kg [Govt]	35.400 kg [Govt]	1.862 kg [Govt]	16.066 kg	7.136 kg
United Arab Emirates	9.717 kg	8.389 kg	27.236 kg	8.899 kg	22.669 kg	7.461 kg
Sub-Total	159508.300 kg	220939.500 kg	188044.100 kg	86260.770 kg	81194.470 kg	111792.300 kg
South Asia						
Bangladesh	1.012 kg [Govt]	0.014 kg [Govt]	2.500 kg [Govt]	2.810 kg [Govt]	0.190 kg [Govt]	0.000 kg [Govt]

Source: Annual Report Questionnaire if not otherwise indicated

SEIZURES, 1998 - 2003
Opium (raw and prepared)

Region/country or territory	1998	1999	2000	2001	2002	2003
ASIA						
South Asia						
India	2031.000 kg	1588.000 kg	2684.000 kg	2533.000 kg	1867.000 kg	1635.000 kg
Nepal	0.950 kg	1.440 kg	No Report	No Report	No Report	No Report
Sri Lanka	0.020 kg	0.008 kg	36.452 kg	1.658 kg	16.800 kg	3.960 kg
Sub-Total	2032.982 kg	1589.462 kg	2722.952 kg	2537.468 kg	1883.990 kg	1638.960 kg
Total region	176466.300 kg	236309.400 kg	207974.200 kg 14996 u.	101140.800 kg	93510.270 kg	129755.800 kg
EUROPE						
East Europe						
Belarus	0.001 kg	0.033 kg	0.090 kg	No Report	0.056 kg	0.053 kg [Govt]
Republic of Moldova	No Report	28.000 kg [ICPO]	1485.000 kg [ICPO] 98.550 lt.	1891.000 kg	1505.000 kg [Govt]	No Report
Russian Federation	1803.700 kg [F.O]	1506.966 kg	2186.000 kg [F.O]	862.645 kg	445.254 kg [F.O]	2232.280 kg
Ukraine	No Report	No Report	166.056 kg [ICPO]	151.009 kg	42.000 kg	3.367 kg
Sub-Total	1803.701 kg	1534.999 kg	3837.146 kg 98.550 lt.	2904.654 kg	1992.310 kg	2235.700 kg
Southeast Europe						
Albania	No Report	0.026 kg [ICPO]	No Report	No Report	No Report	No Report
Bosnia and Herzegovina	No Report	No Report	No Report	No Report	0.074 kg [ICPO]	No Report
Bulgaria	1.970 kg	4.466 kg	No Report	1.980 kg	1.440 kg	0.053 kg
Croatia	[(3]	0.103 kg	0.011 kg	No Report	No Report	No Report
Romania	0.728 kg	2.470 kg	0.060 kg	15.530 kg	0.794 kg	0.570 kg
Serbia and Montenegro	No Report	No Report	No Report	No Report	0.587 kg	No Report
The former Yugoslav Republic of Macedonia	19.985 kg	12.239 kg [NAPOL]	27.395 kg [NAPOL]	3.494 kg [Govt]	22.930 kg	17.947 kg
Turkey	141.655 kg [Govt]	358.012 kg [Govt]	470.950 kg [Govt]	262.759 kg [Govt]	161.054 kg [Govt]	305.736 kg [Govt]
Sub-Total	164.338 kg	377.316 kg	498.416 kg	283.763 kg	186.879 kg	324.306 kg
West & Central Europe						
Austria	10.447 kg	33.646 kg	69.873 kg	4.488 kg	25.160 kg	11.948 kg
Belgium	0.011 kg	0.200 kg	No Report	No Report		0.145 kg
Cyprus	0.021 kg	0.062 kg	0.575 kg	0.367 kg	No Report	0.094 kg
Denmark	5.428 kg	0.330 kg	1.405 kg	5.000 kg	5.274 kg	No Report
Estonia	No Report	No Report	19.426 kg 20 u.	No Report	169.509 kg [ICPO]	0.002 kg
Finland	0.007 kg	No Report	No Report	No Report	No Report	No Report
France	3.194 kg	0.503 kg	18.701 kg	2.720 kg	1.376 kg	1.596 kg
Germany, Federal Republic of	286.074 kg	79.500 kg	30.900 kg	4.115 kg	62.674 kg	322.405 kg
Greece	No Report	46.208 kg [ICPO]	1.742 kg	0.955 kg	No Report	0.582 kg
Hungary	No Report	2.149 kg	17.905 kg	0.003 kg	0.892 kg	0.002 kg

Source: Annual Report Questionnaire if not otherwise indicated

253

SEIZURES, 1998 - 2003
Opium (raw and prepared)

Region/country or territory	1998	1999	2000	2001	2002	2003
EUROPE						
West & Central Europe						
Italy	2.895 kg	0.401 kg [ICPO]	28.672 kg	0.189 kg 6 u.	0.539 kg 17 u.	0.942 kg
Latvia	0.755 kg	0.005 kg	0.005 kg	No Report	No Report	No Report
Lithuania	0.101 kg	0.190 kg	0.129 kg	436.505 kg	261.373 kg	269.454 kg 54 u.
Netherlands	No Report	No Report	No Report	No Report	No Report	0.100 kg
Norway	2.498 kg	1.661 kg	9.800 kg	3.214 kg	0.121 kg	0.042 kg
Poland	No Report	No Report	55.000 kg	No Report	16.000 kg	54.000 kg
Portugal	0.001 kg	No Report	2.850 kg [ICPO]	0.015 kg 77 u.	0.082 kg 1014 u.	0.250 kg 1112 u.
Spain	0.002 kg	1.080 kg	5.264 kg	84.900 kg	0.153 kg	0.147 kg
Sweden	15.641 kg	9.867 kg	24.030 kg	16.153 kg	10.100 kg	12.157 kg
Switzerland	0.015 kg	0.775 kg	0.009 kg [ICPO]	No Report	0.005 kg	0.016 kg
United Kingdom	54.263 kg	37.700 kg [NCIS]	18.481 kg	34.971 kg	32.000 kg	32.000 kg [4]
Sub-Total	381.353 kg	214.277 kg	304.767 kg 20 u.	593.595 kg 83 u.	585.258 kg 1031 u.	705.882 kg 1166 u.
Total region	2349.392 kg	2126.592 kg	4640.329 kg 98.550 lt. 20 u.	3782.012 kg 83 u.	2764.447 kg 1031 u.	3265.888 kg 1166 u.
OCEANIA						
Oceania						
Australia	No Report	3.000 kg [INCB]	2.279 kg	68.410 kg 397 u.	12.535 kg	6.899 kg [5]
New Zealand	0.006 kg	No Report	No Report	0.008 kg	0.004 kg	0.003 kg 220 u.
Sub-Total	0.006 kg	3.000 kg	2.279 kg	68.418 kg 397 u.	12.539 kg	6.902 kg 220 u.
Total region	0.006 kg	3.000 kg	2.279 kg	68.418 kg 397 u.	12.539 kg	6.902 kg 220 u.
TOTAL	179170.800 kg	239432.200 kg 10061 u.	213197.000 kg 98.550 lt. 15156 u.	105750.500 kg 480 u.	97093.710 kg 2344 u.	133706.000 kg 1386 u.

1) opium latex 2) Including other opiates. 3) Small quantity. 4) Due to unavailability of 2003 data, year 2002 data were used for analysis purposes. 5) Sum of seizures reported by national, State & Territory law enforcement agencies

Source: Annual Report Questionnaire if not otherwise indicated

SEIZURES, 1998 - 2003
Opium (liquid)

Region/country or territory	1998	1999	2000	2001	2002	2003
AFRICA						
North Africa						
Egypt	0.030 lt.	0.001 lt.	0.005 lt.	No Report	No Report	No Report
Sub-Total	0.030 lt.	0.001 lt.	0.005 lt.			
Total region	0.030 lt.	0.001 lt.	0.005 lt.			
AMERICAS						
Caribbean						
Cayman Islands	No Report	No Report	0.628 kg 1 u.	No Report	No Report	No Report
Sub-Total			0.628 kg 1 u.			
South America						
Peru	No Report	66.088 kg	508.358 kg	No Report	No Report	No Report
Sub-Total		66.088 kg	508.358 kg			
Total region		66.088 kg	508.986 kg 1 u.			
ASIA						
Central Asia and Transcaucasian countries						
Armenia	2.000 kg	No Report	0.002 kg	No Report	No Report	No Report
Kazakhstan	1.265 kg	No Report	No Report	No Report	No Report	No Report
Sub-Total	3.265 kg		0.002 kg			
East and South-East Asia						
Hong Kong Special Administrative Region of China	No Report	No Report	2 u.	No Report	No Report	No Report
Indonesia	0.030 kg	3.097 kg	0.034 kg	0.000 kg^{Govt}	0.000 kg^{Govt}	0.000 kg^{Govt}
Japan	0.130 lt.	No Report	No Report	No Report	No Report	No Report
Lao People's Democratic Republic	No Report	No Report	No Report	No Report	98.000 lt.	No Report
Myanmar	383.251 kg	332.495 kg	16.086 kg	18.684 kg	18.025 kg	51.737 kg
Sub-Total	383.281 kg 0.130 lt.	335.592 kg	16.120 kg 2 u.	18.684 kg	18.025 kg 98.000 lt.	51.737 kg
Near and Middle East /South-West Asia						
Jordan	No Report	No Report	41.150 kg	No Report	No Report	No Report
Lebanon	35.840 kg	No Report	0.000 kg[1]	No Report	No Report	No Report
Sub-Total	35.840 kg		41.150 kg			
Total region	422.386 kg 0.130 lt.	335.592 kg	57.272 kg 2 u.	18.684 kg	18.025 kg 98.000 lt.	51.737 kg
EUROPE						
East Europe						
Belarus	330.882 kg	244.034 kg[2]	220.520 kg	No Report	334.225 kg[3]	251.524 kg^{Govt}

Source: Annual Report Questionnaire if not otherwise indicated

255

SEIZURES, 1998 - 2003
Opium (liquid)

Region/country or territory	1998	1999	2000	2001	2002	2003
EUROPE						
East Europe						
Republic of Moldova	13.480 kg	No Report	No Report	No Report	No Report	No Report
Ukraine	127.000 kg	No Report	No Report	No Report	No Report	No Report
Sub-Total	471.362 kg	244.034 kg	220.520 kg		334.225 kg	251.524 kg
Southeast Europe						
Croatia	8.600 lt.	No Report	1.500 kg	No Report	No Report	No Report
Sub-Total	8.600 lt.		1.500 kg			
West & Central Europe						
Austria	No Report	No Report	0.075 kg	No Report	No Report	No Report
Denmark	0.004 kg	2.640 kg	No Report	No Report	No Report	No Report
Estonia	19.200 kg 293 u.	0.276 kg 61 u.	0.027 kg 19 u.	No Report	No Report	No Report
Italy	No Report	No Report	35 u.	No Report	No Report	No Report
Latvia	64.800 kg	17.300 kg	7.170 kg	No Report	No Report	No Report
Lithuania	49.490 lt.	190.000 lt.	77.000 lt.	No Report	No Report	No Report
Sweden	0.326 lt.	16.000 lt.	0.018 kg	No Report	No Report	No Report
Sub-Total	84.004 kg 49.816 lt. 293 u.	20.216 kg 206.000 lt. 61 u.	7.290 kg 77.000 lt. 54 u.			
Total region	555.366 kg 58.416 lt. 293 u.	264.250 kg 206.000 lt. 61 u.	229.310 kg 77.000 lt. 54 u.		334.225 kg	251.524 kg
TOTAL	977.752 kg 58.576 lt. 293 u.	665.930 kg 206.001 lt. 61 u.	795.568 kg 77.005 lt. 57 u.	18.684 kg	352.250 kg 98.000 lt.	303.261 kg

1) Small quantity. 2) Includes liquid heroin (1.160kg) 3) poppy brew

Source: Annual Report Questionnaire if not otherwise indicated

SEIZURES, 1998 - 2003
Opium (plant,capsule)

Region/country or territory	1998	1999	2000	2001	2002	2003
AFRICA						
North Africa						
Egypt	0.352 kg 30214000 u.	14.552 kg	No Report	No Report	No Report	419 u.
Sub-Total	0.352 kg 30214000 u.	14.552 kg				419 u.
West and Central Africa						
Niger	0.040 kg [ICPO]	No Report	No Report	No Report	No Report	No Report
Sao Tome and Principe	No Report	0.300 kg	No Report	No Report	No Report	No Report
Sub-Total	0.040 kg	0.300 kg				
Total region	0.392 kg 30214000 u.	14.852 kg				419 u.
AMERICAS						
Central America						
Guatemala	114238 u.	23100 u.	20619 u.	No Report	No Report	9300 u. [HONL]
Sub-Total	114238 u.	23100 u.	20619 u.			9300 u.
North America						
Canada	2.016 kg	15000 u.	No Report	No Report	No Report	No Report
Sub-Total	2.016 kg	15000 u.				
South America						
Argentina	408 u.	No Report	No Report	No Report	No Report	No Report
Ecuador	100873 u. [Govt]	No Report	30 u. [Govt]	No Report	No Report	200 u. [Govt]
Peru	964 u.	63703.614 kg	20837.016 kg	No Report	No Report	No Report
Sub-Total	102245 u.	63703.610 kg	20837.020 kg 30 u.			200 u.
Total region	2.016 kg 216483 u.	63703.610 kg 38100 u.	20837.020 kg 20649 u.			9500 u.
ASIA						
Central Asia and Transcaucasian countries						
Armenia	18.725 kg	No Report	No Report	No Report	No Report	No Report
Azerbaijan	6.200 kg	No Report	No Report	No Report	No Report	No Report
Georgia	7.500 kg [ICPO]	No Report	No Report	No Report	No Report	No Report
Kazakhstan	113.895 kg	No Report	No Report	No Report	No Report	No Report
Tajikistan	No Report	No Report	No Report	No Report	143.141 kg [(1]	No Report
Turkmenistan	No Report	No Report	No Report	No Report	No Report	83.500 kg [Govt]
Uzbekistan	54.496 kg	No Report	14.700 kg	No Report	No Report	No Report
Sub-Total	200.816 kg		14.700 kg		143.141 kg	83.500 kg
East and South-East Asia						
Hong Kong Special Administrative Region of China	No Report	32 u.	3.001 kg	No Report	No Report	No Report
Indonesia	0.030 kg	0.000 kg [Govt]	0.000 kg [Govt]	0.000 kg [Govt]	0.000 kg [Govt]	0.000 kg [Govt]

Source: Annual Report Questionnaire if not otherwise indicated

257

SEIZURES, 1998 - 2003
Opium (plant,capsule)

Region/country or territory	1998	1999	2000	2001	2002	2003
ASIA						
East and South-East Asia						
Japan	0.063 kg 6807 u.	No Report	0.022 kg 11571 u.	No Report	0.092 kg 1424 u.	0.001 kg [Govt] 11756 u.
Republic of Korea	21944 u.	No Report	No Report	No Report	No Report	No Report
Thailand	No Report	312.837 kg	No Report	No Report	No Report	No Report
Viet Nam	1.100 kg [ICPO]	No Report	No Report	No Report	No Report	No Report
Sub-Total	1.193 kg 28751 u.	312.837 kg 32 u.	3.023 kg 11571 u.		0.092 kg 1424 u.	0.001 kg 11756 u.
Near and Middle East /South-West Asia						
Pakistan	No Report	No Report	No Report	No Report	21757.000 kg	No Report
Yemen	No Report [ICPO]	No Report	No Report	No Report	No Report	No Report
Sub-Total					21757.000 kg	
Total region	202.009 kg 28751 u.	312.837 kg 32 u.	17.723 kg 11571 u.		21900.230 kg 1424 u.	83.501 kg 11756 u.
EUROPE						
East Europe						
Belarus	1621.000 kg	1056.000 kg	1084.000 kg	1106.000 kg [Govt]	1412.000 kg [Govt]	1176.000 kg [Govt]
Republic of Moldova	406.550 kg	No Report	No Report	No Report	3635.000 kg [Govt]	No Report
Russian Federation	16511.359 kg	18366.055 kg	No Report	No Report	No Report	No Report
Ukraine	26632.801 kg	No Report	No Report	No Report	23115.000 kg	No Report
Sub-Total	45171.710 kg	19422.050 kg	1084.000 kg	1106.000 kg	28162.000 kg	1176.000 kg
Southeast Europe						
Bulgaria	No Report	No Report	No Report	1415.000 kg	No Report	No Report
Croatia	3504 u.	6206 u.	1.607 kg 519 u.	No Report	No Report	No Report
Turkey	No Report	No Report	1820.000 kg 3550 u.	No Report	No Report	No Report
Sub-Total	3504 u.	6206 u.	1821.607 kg 4069 u.	1415.000 kg		
West & Central Europe						
Austria	9.367 kg	9.349 kg	No Report	No Report	No Report	No Report
Estonia	36.011 kg 111 u.	No Report	37.883 kg 69 u.	No Report	No Report	No Report
Finland	1.000 kg	No Report	No Report	No Report	No Report	No Report
Italy	5991 u.	No Report	4449 u. [(2]	No Report	No Report	No Report
Latvia	192.000 kg	30.200 kg	145.950 kg	No Report	No Report	No Report
Lithuania	1525.000 kg	744.000 kg	623.000 kg	No Report	No Report	No Report
Norway	0.070 kg	No Report	0.001 kg	No Report	No Report	No Report
Poland	4000.000 kg	3553.000 kg	No Report	No Report	No Report	No Report
Portugal	28848 u.	351 u.	2.850 kg 1348 u.	No Report	No Report	No Report
Spain	4.800 kg	1003.004 kg	22755.700 kg	No Report	49.737 kg	No Report

Source: Annual Report Questionnaire if not otherwise indicated

SEIZURES, 1998 - 2003
Opium (plant,capsule)

Region/country or territory	1998	1999	2000	2001	2002	2003
EUROPE						
West & Central Europe						
Sweden	No Report	3615 u.	No Report	No Report	No Report	No Report
Sub-Total	5768.248 kg 34950 u.	5339.553 kg 3966 u.	23565.380 kg 5866 u.		49.737 kg	
Total region	50939.960 kg 38454 u.	24761.610 kg 10172 u.	26470.990 kg 9935 u.	2521.000 kg	28211.740 kg	1176.000 kg
OCEANIA						
Oceania						
Australia	No Report	No Report	0.407 kg 2083 u.	No Report	79.533 kg	No Report
New Zealand	20249 u.	338 u.	No Report	No Report	No Report	No Report
Sub-Total	20249 u.	338 u.	0.407 kg 2083 u.		79.533 kg	
Total region	20249 u.	338 u.	0.407 kg 2083 u.		79.533 kg	
TOTAL	51144.380 kg 30517940 u.	88792.910 kg 48642 u.	47326.140 kg 44238 u.	2521.000 kg	50191.500 kg 1424 u.	1259.501 kg 21675 u.

1) Poppystraw, heads,stems & leaves 2) 221buds(1), 4,228 plants(6)

Source: Annual Report Questionnaire if not otherwise indicated

259

SEIZURES, 1998 - 2003
Heroin

Region/country or territory	1998	1999	2000	2001	2002	2003
AFRICA						
East Africa						
Burundi	No Report	0.006 kg [ICPO] 260 u.	No Report	No Report	No Report	No Report
Ethiopia	8.987 kg	12.582 kg	18.042 kg	5.650 kg	33.505 kg	11.812 kg
Kenya	9.954 kg	17.459 kg	28.657 kg	19.438 kg [Govt]	41.272 kg	30.650 kg
Madagascar	No Report	0.005 kg [ICPO]	No Report	No Report	No Report	No Report
Mauritius	6.060 kg	3.067 kg	4.062 kg	24.532 kg	6.973 kg	15.949 kg
Rwanda	No Report	No Report	No Report	No Report	0.500 kg	No Report
Uganda	1.302 kg	14.170 kg	3.400 kg	5.772 kg	11.190 kg	No Report
United Republic of Tanzania	2.745 kg	7.583 kg	5.322 kg [ICPO]	7.997 kg [Govt]	1.458 kg [ICPO]	4.071 kg
Sub-Total	29.048 kg	54.872 kg 260 u.	59.483 kg	63.389 kg	94.898 kg	62.483 kg
North Africa						
Algeria	0.256 kg [ICPO]	0.002 kg	No Report	0.006 kg [ICPO]	0.024 kg	1.454 kg
Egypt	24.416 kg 0.266 lt.	23.627 kg	37.114 kg	38.000 kg 385 u.	55.000 kg	27.000 kg
Libyan Arab Jamahiriya	4.809 kg	4.809 kg [F.O]	15.000 kg [F.O]	12.000 kg [F.O]	No Report	No Report
Morocco	1.282 kg	0.437 kg	0.152 kg	3.971 kg 110 u.	3.528 kg 18 u.	0.760 kg
Sudan	No Report	0.250 kg [Govt]	No Report	0.505 kg [Govt]	No Report	No Report
Tunisia	0.474 kg	1.391 kg	1.020 kg [ICPO]	No Report	0.254 kg	No Report
Sub-Total	31.237 kg 0.266 lt.	30.516 kg	53.286 kg	54.482 kg 495 u.	58.806 kg 18 u.	29.214 kg
Southern Africa						
Angola	No Report	[(1]	0.005 kg [ICPO]	21.500 kg [ICPO]	No Report	No Report
Lesotho	No Report	0.500 kg [ICPO]	No Report	No Report	No Report	No Report
Malawi	0.200 kg	0.500 kg	No Report	No Report	No Report	No Report
Mozambique	No Report	No Report	232 u. [ICPO]	0.005 kg [ICPO]	No Report	No Report
Namibia	No Report	0.003 kg [ICPO]	0.100 kg	0.003 kg	0.002 kg	No Report
South Africa	5.383 kg	7.435 kg [ICPO]	15.386 kg	8.465 kg	15.020 kg	33.953 kg
Swaziland	0.010 kg	0.097 kg	1.919 kg	0.093 kg	0.004 kg	0.002 kg
Zambia	0.001 kg [Govt]	0.369 kg	0.005 kg	0.002 kg [Govt]	0.360 kg	1.529 kg
Zimbabwe	0.740 kg	No Report	No Report	No Report	0.077 kg	No Report
Sub-Total	6.334 kg	8.904 kg	17.415 kg 232 u.	30.068 kg	15.463 kg	35.484 kg
West and Central Africa						
Benin	0.888 kg	18.670 kg [Govt]	7.572 kg [F.O]	0.079 kg [ICPO]	0.014 kg [ICPO]	No Report
Burkina Faso	No Report	No Report	No Report	0.038 kg	No Report	0.061 kg
Cameroon	2.150 kg	0.400 kg	No Report	No Report	No Report	No Report
Chad	No Report	1.800 kg [ICPO]	No Report	No Report	No Report	No Report
Congo	No Report	No Report	No Report	0.010 kg	0.016 kg	No Report

Source: Annual Report Questionnaire if not otherwise indicated

SEIZURES, 1998 - 2003
Heroin

Region/country or territory	1998	1999	2000	2001	2002	2003
AFRICA						
West and Central Africa						
Côte d'Ivoire	0.060 kg 16 u.	1.889 kg 19 u.	3.035 kg [ICPO]	10.394 kg	34.085 kg	No Report
Gabon	No Report	0.106 kg [ICPO]	No Report	No Report	No Report	No Report
Gambia	0.590 kg [ICPO]	0.039 kg	No Report	4.000 kg	No Report	0.003 kg [Govt]
Ghana	18.023 kg	21.020 kg	No Report	No Report	19.060 kg	8.180 kg
Guinea	No Report	No Report	2.215 kg [ICPO]	0.592 kg [ICPO]	0.057 kg [ICPO]	0.901 kg
Mauritania	0.005 kg [Govt]	No Report	No Report	No Report	No Report	No Report
Niger	0.412 kg [ICPO]	No Report	No Report	No Report	No Report	No Report
Nigeria	362.000 kg [Govt]	81.035 kg	55.100 kg	46.639 kg	55.626 kg	87.580 kg
Senegal	0.234 kg [ICPO]	0.071 kg [ICPO] 382 u.	198 u. [ICPO]	No Report	0.336 kg [ICPO]	No Report
Togo	No Report	12.764 kg [HNLF]	10.808 kg	15.253 kg	4.727 kg	1.850 kg
Sub-Total	384.362 kg 16 u.	137.794 kg 401 u.	78.730 kg 198 u.	77.005 kg	113.921 kg	98.574 kg
Total region	450.981 kg 0.266 lt. 16 u.	232.086 kg 661 u.	208.914 kg 430 u.	224.944 kg 495 u.	283.089 kg 18 u.	225.755 kg
AMERICAS						
Caribbean						
Aruba	No Report	6.000 kg [F.O]	78.000 kg [F.O]	65.000 kg [F.O]	25.677 kg [ICPO]	No Report
Bahamas	No Report	No Report	No Report	No Report	No Report	0.272 kg
Barbados	No Report	3.230 kg [HONLC]	No Report	No Report	No Report	No Report
Bermuda	No Report	0.836 kg	0.292 kg	2.000 kg [F.O]	2.630 kg	0.600 kg [PROJ.S]
British Virgin Islands	No Report	No Report	No Report	1.200 kg 1 u.	No Report	No Report
Cayman Islands	No Report	No Report	1.000 kg [F.O]	0.213 kg	No Report	No Report
Cuba	No Report	3.000 kg [F.O]	No Report	No Report	No Report	6.800 kg [HONL]
Dominican Republic	6.891 kg	11.909 kg	24.000 kg [F.O]	33.003 kg	67.000 kg [HONLC]	58.860 kg
Guadeloupe	No Report	No Report	No Report	4.000 kg [F.O]	No Report	No Report
Haiti	No Report	No Report	No Report	No Report	No Report	1.000 kg [CICAD]
Jamaica	No Report	No Report	No Report	0.450 kg	No Report	No Report
Netherlands Antilles	No Report	2.000 kg [INCB]	2.032 kg [ICPO]	72.000 kg [F.O]	62.622 kg [ICPO]	44.300 kg [PROJ.S]
Puerto Rico	No Report	No Report	24.000 kg [F.O]	42.000 kg [F.O]	12.070 kg [ICPO] 24619 u.	No Report
Saint Lucia	No Report	No Report	2.000 kg	No Report	No Report	No Report
Trinidad and Tobago	No Report	No Report	5.000 kg [INCSR]	No Report	10.380 kg [ICPO]	10.540 kg
Turks and Caicos Islands	No Report	No Report	No Report	No Report	No Report	1.100 kg
Sub-Total	6.891 kg	26.975 kg	136.324 kg	219.866 kg	180.379 kg 1 u.	123.472 kg 24619 u.

Source: Annual Report Questionnaire if not otherwise indicated

SEIZURES, 1998 - 2003
Heroin

Region/country or territory	1998	1999	2000	2001	2002	2003
AMERICAS						
Central America						
Belize	No Report	No Report	No Report	3.399 kg	No Report	No Report
Costa Rica	13.500 kg	2.400 kg	7.787 kg	20.290 kg [Govt]	61.770 kg [Govt]	121.300 kg
El Salvador	0.697 kg [ICPO]	0.099 kg	6.900 kg [ICPO]	9.368 kg	13.229 kg	22.100 kg
Guatemala	3.650 kg	53.000 kg	9.740 kg	21.170 kg	0.050 kg	0.050 kg
Honduras	No Report	No Report	No Report	No Report	No Report	13.250 kg
Nicaragua	No Report	2.000 kg [CICAD]	2.000 kg [CICAD]	8.422 kg [ICPO]	53.189 kg	90.300 kg [HONL]
Panama	22.825 kg	46.456 kg	39.045 kg	87.000 kg	101.100 kg [HONLC]	205.000 kg [INCSR]
Sub-Total	40.672 kg	103.955 kg	65.472 kg	149.649 kg	229.338 kg	452.000 kg
North America						
Canada	22.295 kg 0.176 lt. 994 u.	88.000 kg 91 u.	6.970 kg 0.117 lt. 2 u.	73.979 kg	3.295 kg	5.073 kg 148 u.
Mexico	120.896 kg	260.191 kg	299.102 kg	269.614 kg [Govt]	282.692 kg	288.576 kg
United States	1580.700 kg [Govt.]	1200.000 kg 437 u.	1705.188 kg 1.850 lt. 593 u.	1983.700 kg	2765.600 kg	2380.900 kg
Sub-Total	1723.891 kg 0.176 lt. 994 u.	1548.191 kg 528 u.	2011.260 kg 1.967 lt. 595 u.	2327.293 kg	3051.587 kg	2674.549 kg 148 u.
South America						
Argentina	31.040 kg	7.962 kg	47.664 kg	84.683 kg	32.296 kg	175.784 kg
Bolivia	0.760 kg	No Report	No Report	No Report	No Report	No Report
Brazil	0.950 kg	No Report	[ICPO]	12.500 kg [Govt]	56.600 kg [F.O]	66.265 kg
Chile	No Report	No Report	21.088 kg	33.234 kg	13.649 kg	4.641 kg
Colombia	239.154 kg	584.200 kg [Govt]	567.200 kg [Govt]	787.600 kg	776.870 kg [Govt]	628.820 kg [Govt]
Ecuador	58.300 kg [Govt]	80.600 kg [Govt]	108.100 kg [Govt]	253.600 kg [Govt]	352.200 kg [Govt]	296.280 kg [Govt]
Guyana	No Report	No Report	No Report	No Report	No Report	0.600 kg
Peru	No Report	No Report	2.186 kg	0.004 kg	15.793 kg	4.764 kg
Suriname	0.030 kg	No Report	No Report	No Report	No Report	No Report
Uruguay	No Report	No Report	No Report	5.872 kg [ICPO]	7.200 kg	12.133 kg
Venezuela	No Report	41.514 kg	195.580 kg	228.430 kg	562.950 kg	443.460 kg
Sub-Total	330.234 kg	714.276 kg	941.818 kg	1405.923 kg	1817.558 kg	1632.747 kg
Total region	2101.688 kg 0.176 lt. 994 u.	2393.396 kg 528 u.	3154.874 kg 1.967 lt. 595 u.	4102.731 kg 1 u.	5278.862 kg 24619 u.	4882.768 kg 148 u.
ASIA						
Central Asia and Transcaucasian countries						
Armenia	0.065 kg	0.191 kg	0.109 kg	0.016 kg	0.175 kg	0.309 kg
Azerbaijan	4.332 kg	4.018 kg	9.917 kg [ICPO]	4.000 kg	0.704 kg	No Report
Georgia	0.083 kg [ICPO]	2.300 kg [ICPO]	3.993 kg [ICPO]	5.518 kg [ICPO]	No Report	3.000 kg
Kazakhstan	24.196 kg	54.264 kg	262.400 kg [F.O]	136.700 kg [F.O]	167.690 kg [F.O]	707.000 kg [F.O]

Source: Annual Report Questionnaire if not otherwise indicated

SEIZURES, 1998 - 2003
Heroin

Region/country or territory	1998	1999	2000	2001	2002	2003
ASIA						
Central Asia and Transcaucasian countries						
Kyrgyzstan	24.732 kg	26.870 kg	216.780 kg	170.898 kg	271.250 kg	104.580 kg
Tajikistan	271.471 kg	708.820 kg	1882.929 kg [F.O]	4239.005 kg	3958.182 kg	5600.309 kg
Turkmenistan	495.000 kg [Govt.]	240.000 kg [F.O]	200.000 kg [F.O]	71.000 kg [NAPOL]	400.000 kg [F.O]	80.500 kg [F.O]
Uzbekistan	194.679 kg	324.843 kg	675.000 kg	466.601 kg [F.O]	256.320 kg	336.400 kg
Sub-Total	1014.558 kg	1361.306 kg	3251.128 kg	5093.738 kg	5054.322 kg	6832.098 kg
East and South-East Asia						
Brunei Darussalam	0.003 kg	No Report	0.001 kg	No Report	0.004 kg [ICPO]	No Report
China	7358.000 kg	5364.000 kg [ICPO]	6281.000 kg [Govt.]	13200.000 kg	9290.800 kg	9530.000 kg
Hong Kong Special Administrative Region of China	209.000 kg [Govt.]	284.001 kg / 0.003 lt.	339.003 kg	156.400 kg	105.590 kg	No Report
Indonesia	27.761 kg	14.049 kg	22.655 kg	16.641 kg	20.004 kg	21.872 kg [Govt]
Japan	3.947 kg	2.150 kg	7.006 kg	4.944 kg	20.900 kg / 0.000 lt.	5.100 kg
Lao People's Democratic Republic	80.000 kg [INCSR]	14.750 kg [HNLP]	20.000 kg [INCSR]	49.700 kg [Govt]	21.245 kg / 30 u.	39.350 kg
Macao Special Administrative Region of China	2.217 kg [ICPO]	1.000 kg [INCB]	0.147 kg	0.069 kg	0.052 kg	0.087 kg
Malaysia	289.664 kg	200.937 kg	109.170 kg	227.058 kg [ICPO]	294.471 kg [ICPO]	133.420 kg
Myanmar	403.805 kg	273.193 kg	158.921 kg	96.744 kg	333.888 kg	568.083 kg
Philippines	1.741 kg [ICPO]	0.022 kg	No Report	0.010 kg	No Report	No Report
Republic of Korea	2.126 kg	0.342 kg	No Report	0.567 kg	1.078 kg [ICPO]	0.007 kg
Singapore	141.852 kg	56.730 kg	52.083 kg	106.678 kg	63.420 kg	0.951 kg
Taiwan, Province of China	No Report	No Report	273.000 kg [PRESS]	153.000 kg [PRESS]	No Report	No Report
Thailand	507.769 kg	405.034 kg	384.000 kg [HNLP]	501.000 kg [F.O]	697.000 kg [F.O]	439.000 kg [Govt.]
Viet Nam	60.000 kg [F.O]	66.700 kg [F.O]	60.000 kg [F.O]	40.300 kg	57.390 kg [F.O]	160.000 kg
Sub-Total	9087.884 kg	6682.908 kg / 0.003 lt.	7706.985 kg	14553.110 kg	10905.840 kg / 30 u.	10897.870 kg
Near and Middle East /South-West Asia						
Afghanistan	No Report	No Report	No Report	No Report	1291.700 kg	815.000 kg
Bahrain	3.982 kg [ICPO]	2.856 kg [ICPO]	1.643 kg [ICPO]	0.001 kg [ICPO]	2.473 kg	No Report
Iran (Islamic Republic of)	2894.462 kg	6030.000 kg	6189.000 kg [NAPOL]	4001.000 kg	3977.000 kg [Govt]	3327.000 kg
Iraq	8.300 kg	No Report	1.020 kg	No Report	No Report	No Report
Israel	137.800 kg	111.830 kg [ICPO]	80.000 kg	67.625 kg	66.590 kg	62.006 kg
Jordan	52.397 kg	41.397 kg	127.712 kg	35.545 kg	14.666 kg	104.741 kg
Kuwait	21.601 kg	35.000 kg [INCB]	No Report	No Report	17.186 kg [ICPO]	0.500 kg [ICPO]
Lebanon	3.093 kg	8.149 kg	2.363 kg	13.002 kg	2.005 kg	9.117 kg
Oman	No Report	54.109 kg	14.008 kg [ICPO]	8.485 kg	28.734 kg	No Report

Source: Annual Report Questionnaire if not otherwise indicated

SEIZURES, 1998 - 2003
Heroin

Region/country or territory	1998	1999	2000	2001	2002	2003
ASIA						
Near and Middle East /South-West Asia						
Pakistan	3363.723 kg	4973.711 kg	9492.029 kg	6931.470 kg	5870.498 kg	6363.931 kg
Qatar	1.480 kg ICPO	0.108 kg ICPO	0.534 kg ICPO	0.404 kg	7.045 kg	0.284 kg
Saudi Arabia	63.107 kg	No Report	200.922 kg	178.825 kg	28.564 kg ICPO	2.800 kg ICPO
Syrian Arab Republic	36.204 kg Govt	57.659 kg Govt	50.441 kg Govt	30.342 kg Govt	28.663 kg Govt	7.943 kg
United Arab Emirates	34.450 kg	65.909 kg	82.176 kg	40.100 kg	115.031 kg	66.372 kg
Yemen	0.027 kg ICPO	No Report	No Report	No Report	No Report	No Report
Sub-Total	6620.626 kg	11380.730 kg	16241.850 kg	11306.800 kg	11450.160 kg	10759.690 kg
South Asia						
Bangladesh	14.555 kg Govt	41.510 kg Govt	53.103 kg Govt	49.290 kg Govt	54.913 kg Govt	38.239 kg Govt
India	655.000 kg	839.000 kg	1240.000 kg	889.000 kg	933.000 kg Govt	1008.000 kg
Maldives	1.142 kg	0.357 kg	No Report	0.167 kg	0.300 kg ICPO	No Report
Nepal	9.400 kg Govt	1.515 kg Govt	1.705 kg Govt	9.360 kg ICPO	10.493 kg	22.710 kg
Sri Lanka	56.942 kg	68.500 kg	94.150 kg	102.216 kg	62.545 kg	54.017 kg
Sub-Total	737.039 kg	950.882 kg	1388.958 kg	1050.033 kg	1061.251 kg	1122.966 kg
Total region	17460.110 kg	20375.820 kg 0.003 lt.	28588.920 kg	32003.680 kg	28471.570 kg 30 u.	29612.630 kg
EUROPE						
East Europe						
Belarus	0.907 kg	1.977 kg	3.442 kg	3.257 kg ICPO	6.171 kg	5.113 kg Govt
Republic of Moldova	No Report	No Report	1.313 kg ICPO	0.041 kg	No Report	No Report
Russian Federation	442.900 kg	695.085 kg	984.000 kg F.O	1287.226 kg	842.163 kg F.O	3248.814 kg
Ukraine	8.940 kg	21.530 kg ICPO	21.743 kg ICPO	8.669 kg	206.600 kg	2.406 kg
Sub-Total	452.747 kg	718.592 kg	1010.498 kg	1299.193 kg	1054.934 kg	3256.333 kg
Southeast Europe						
Albania	No Report	7.122 kg ICPO	47.000 kg Govt	4.500 kg Govt	71.714 kg	114.475 kg
Bosnia and Herzegovina	0.686 kg NAPOL	1.125 kg ICPO	0.375 kg NAPOL	1.900 kg ICPO 5 u.	3.265 kg ICPO	No Report
Bulgaria	219.632 kg	265.249 kg	2067.201 kg	1550.629 kg	535.090 kg	778.637 kg
Croatia	50.095 kg	13.232 kg	7.041 kg	19.569 kg	46.359 kg	85.727 kg
Romania	412.327 kg	63.630 kg	52.940 kg	41.770 kg	202.180 kg	320.700 kg
Serbia and Montenegro	No Report	No Report	No Report	62.518 kg	43.462 kg	278.760 kg
The former Yugoslav Republic of Macedonia	91.672 kg	14.375 kg NAPOL	90.789 kg NAPOL	110.882 kg Govt	28.572 kg	66.145 kg
Turkey	4651.486 kg	3862.472 kg Govt	6337.747 kg Govt	3998.880 kg Govt	2582.676 kg Govt	4704.736 kg
Sub-Total	5425.898 kg	4227.205 kg	8603.093 kg	5790.648 kg 5 u.	3513.318 kg	6349.180 kg

Source: Annual Report Questionnaire if not otherwise indicated

SEIZURES, 1998 - 2003
Heroin

Region/country or territory	1998	1999	2000	2001	2002
EUROPE					
West & Central Europe					
Andorra	0.003 kg [ICPO]	0.013 kg	0.009 kg [ICPO]	0.009 kg	[1] No Report
Austria	118.213 kg	78.914 kg	230.747 kg	288.312 kg	59.473 kg	42.876 kg
Belgium	75.790 kg	73.537 kg	187.739 kg	187.739 kg [UNODC (2]	262.000 kg	51.000 kg
Cyprus	0.035 kg	2.193 kg	4.949 kg	1.638 kg	0.283 kg	1.568 kg
Czech Republic	240.000 kg	108.380 kg	114.520 kg	88.590 kg / 478 u.	34.033 kg / 40 u.	9.135 kg / 142 u.
Denmark	55.136 kg	96.040 kg	32.080 kg	25.125 kg	62.495 kg	16.028 kg
Estonia	0.091 kg / 129 u.	0.518 kg / 1269 u.	0.438 kg / 2129 u.	1.163 kg	3.783 kg	0.143 kg
Finland	1.965 kg	2.884 kg	6.026 kg	7.500 kg		1.600 kg
France	343.783 kg	203.313 kg	443.935 kg	351.055 kg	476.149 kg	545.003 kg
Germany, Federal Republic of	685.920 kg	796.400 kg	796.000 kg	835.836 kg	519.598 kg	626.185 kg
Greece	232.110 kg / 6 u.	98.401 kg / 10 u.	1179.526 kg / 14 u.	329.725 kg	201.176 kg [3]	246.719 kg
Hungary	634.613 kg	172.703 kg	819.000 kg	154.410 kg	320.129 kg	256.334 kg
Iceland	No Report	0.001 kg	No Report	No Report	[1]	0.003 kg
Ireland	36.963 kg	15.921 kg	23.942 kg	29.527 kg	16.606 kg	26.981 kg
Italy	703.335 kg / 3069 u.	1313.708 kg [ICPO]	980.379 kg / 1678 u.	2004.588 kg / 1423 u.	2584.564 kg / 1697 u.	2582.568 kg / 4698 u.
Latvia	0.098 kg	0.768 kg	0.775 kg	0.465 kg	No Report	0.600 kg
Liechtenstein	No Report	14.388 kg	0.005 kg	0.003 kg	0.004 kg	2.983 kg
Lithuania	0.423 kg	0.923 kg	0.943 kg	2.740 kg	2.761 kg	0.807 kg
Luxembourg	3.592 kg	1.914 kg	11.358 kg [ICPO]	No Report	2.956 kg [ICPO]	3.611 kg
Malta	0.498 kg	1.724 kg	5.912 kg	2.600 kg	1.218 kg [ICPO]	5.500 kg
Monaco	[4]	No Report	No Report	No Report	No Report	0.011 kg
Netherlands	784.000 kg [Govt]	770.000 kg [Govt]	896.000 kg [Govt]	739.000 kg	1122.000 kg	417.000 kg
Norway	37.347 kg	45.810 kg	51.500 kg	67.905 kg	59.106 kg	52.126 kg
Poland	67.405 kg	44.947 kg	120.063 kg [5] / 388.000 lt.	208.106 kg	293.207 kg	6.913 kg
Portugal	96.666 kg	76.417 kg	567.577 kg [6]	316.039 kg / 5.000 lt.	96.315 kg	72.365 kg
Slovakia	13.671 kg	5.808 kg	98.507 kg	15.680 kg	15.400 kg	6.902 kg
Slovenia	46.106 kg	32.270 kg	392.065 kg	88.930 kg	68.670 kg	150.173 kg
Spain	444.243 kg	1159.297 kg	484.854 kg	630.600 kg	274.777 kg	242.434 kg
Sweden	70.927 kg / 0.011 lt.	63.009 kg / 0.509 lt.	27.649 kg	32.627 kg	58.600 kg	15.987 kg
Switzerland	403.680 kg	397.527 kg	372.061 kg	227.515 kg	208.510 kg	300.113 kg
United Kingdom	1345.804 kg	2341.700 kg [NCIS]	3382.392 kg	3928.976 kg	2730.000 kg	2730.000 kg [7]
Sub-Total	6442.417 kg / 0.011 lt. / 3204 u.	7919.428 kg / 0.509 lt. / 1279 u.	11230.950 kg / 388.000 lt. / 3821 u.	10566.400 kg / 5.000 lt. / 1901 u.	9473.813 kg / 1737 u.	8413.668 kg / 4840 u.

Source: Annual Report Questionnaire if not otherwise indicated

SEIZURES, 1998 - 2003
Morphine

Region/country or territory	1998	1999	2000	2001	2002	2003
AFRICA						
East Africa						
Ethiopia	0.001 kg 6 u.	No Report	No Report	No Report	No Report	No Report
United Republic of Tanzania	No Report	0.020 kg	No Report	3.338 kg [Govt]	0.850 kg [ICPO]	No Report
Sub-Total	0.001 kg 6 u.	0.020 kg		3.338 kg	0.850 kg	
North Africa						
Egypt	0.012 lt.	0.007 kg	No Report	4 u.	No Report	No Report
Morocco	0.997 kg	No Report	No Report	247 u.	No Report	No Report
Sudan	No Report	No Report	No Report	18408 u. [Govt]	No Report	No Report
Sub-Total	0.997 kg 0.012 lt.	0.007 kg		18659 u.		
Southern Africa						
Mozambique	No Report	0.085 kg [ICPO]	No Report	No Report	No Report	No Report
Zambia	3.200 kg [Govt]	0.028 kg	0.061 kg	0.860 kg [Govt]	No Report	0.137 kg
Sub-Total	3.200 kg	0.113 kg	0.061 kg	0.860 kg		0.137 kg
West and Central Africa						
Benin	3.190 kg	No Report	No Report	No Report	No Report	No Report
Chad	No Report	No Report	0.090 kg	No Report	No Report	No Report
Nigeria	No Report	No Report	21.120 kg	No Report	No Report	No Report
Sub-Total	3.190 kg		21.210 kg			
Total region	7.388 kg 0.012 lt. 6 u.	0.140 kg	21.271 kg	4.198 kg 18659 u.	0.850 kg	0.137 kg
AMERICAS						
Caribbean						
Aruba	No Report	No Report	No Report	No Report	0.509 kg [ICPO]	No Report
Cuba	No Report	No Report	No Report	No Report	63 u. [ICPO]	No Report
Dominican Republic	No Report	No Report	19.000 kg [CICAD]	No Report	No Report	No Report
Turks and Caicos Islands	No Report	No Report	No Report	No Report	No Report	0.001 kg
Sub-Total			19.000 kg		0.509 kg 63 u.	0.001 kg
North America						
Canada	1.662 kg 0.433 lt. 1166 u.	1.000 kg 1.016 lt. 1826 u.	0.751 kg 1.285 lt. 1842 u.	0.267 kg 3807 u.	0.239 kg 3591 u.	1.842 kg 4033 u.
Mexico	No Report	1.130 kg	4.480 kg	0.539 kg	0.002 kg	1409.645 kg
United States	No Report	3.134 kg 998 u.	180.108 kg 15.723 lt. 134 u.	812 u.	652 u.	16870 u.

Source: Annual Report Questionnaire if not otherwise indicated

SEIZURES, 1998 - 2003
Morphine

Region/country or territory	1998	1999	2000	2001	2002	2003
AMERICAS						
North America						
Sub-Total	1.662 kg	5.264 kg	185.339 kg	0.806 kg	0.241 kg	1411.487 kg
	0.433 lt.	1.016 lt.	17.008 lt.	4619 u.	4243 u.	20903 u.
	1166 u.	2824 u.	1976 u.			
South America						
Argentina	No Report	650.000 kg	No Report	No Report	No Report	No Report
Brazil	No Report	0.150 kg	No Report	No Report	No Report	0.046 kg
Chile	29 u.	1 u. [ICPO]	No Report	No Report	5 u.	24 u.
Colombia	79.111 kg	154.023 kg	107.890 kg [Govt]	47.390 kg [Govt]	20.260 kg [Govt]	78.240 kg [Govt]
Peru	No Report	No Report	11.979 kg	0.492 kg	6.230 kg	0.040 kg
Sub-Total	79.111 kg	804.173 kg	119.869 kg	47.882 kg	26.490 kg	78.326 kg
	29 u.	1 u.			5 u.	24 u.
Total region	80.773 kg	809.437 kg	324.208 kg	48.688 kg	27.240 kg	1489.814 kg
	0.433 lt.	1.016 lt.	17.008 lt.	4619 u.	4311 u.	20927 u.
	1195 u.	2825 u.	1976 u.			
ASIA						
Central Asia and Transcaucasian countries						
Armenia	[(1]	No Report	0.000 kg [(1]	0.351 kg	[(1]	[(1]
Azerbaijan	No Report	0.085 kg	No Report	No Report	No Report	No Report
Georgia	No Report	0.003 kg [ICPO]	0.262 kg [ICPO]	0.107 kg [ICPO]	No Report	0.014 kg
Kazakhstan	4.172 kg	1.493 kg	No Report	No Report	No Report	No Report
Uzbekistan	0.030 kg	3.400 kg [ICPO]	No Report	No Report	No Report	No Report
Sub-Total	4.202 kg	4.981 kg	0.262 kg	0.458 kg		0.014 kg
East and South-East Asia						
Brunei Darussalam	No Report	No Report	No Report	No Report	0.004 kg	No Report
China	146.000 kg	No Report	No Report	No Report	No Report	No Report
Hong Kong Special Administrative Region of China	No Report	[(1]	No Report	1462 u.	No Report	No Report
Indonesia	0.000 kg [Govt]	3.174 kg	0.223 kg	0.001 kg	0.000 kg [Govt]	0.000 kg [Govt]
		202 u.				
Japan	0.363 kg	0.002 kg	200 u.	1.275 kg	0.001 lt.	0.124 kg
	0.002 lt.			117 u.		1002 u.
	146 u.					
Lao People's Democratic Republic	No Report	No Report	No Report	No Report	18.100 kg	14.470 kg
Mongolia	No Report	No Report	0.270 kg [ICPO]	No Report	No Report	126 u.
Myanmar	95.087 kg	24.001 kg	22.696 kg	6.052 kg	314.004 kg	156.250 kg
				107 u.	177 u.	6 u.
Singapore	No Report	No Report	No Report	0.076 kg	No Report	No Report
				24 u.		
Thailand	No Report	0.200 kg [ICPO]	0.005 kg [ICPO]	No Report	No Report	No Report

Source: Annual Report Questionnaire if not otherwise indicated

SEIZURES, 1998 - 2003
Morphine

Region/country or territory	1998	1999	2000	2001	2002	2003
ASIA						
East and South-East Asia						
Sub-Total	241.450 kg	27.377 kg	23.194 kg	7.404 kg	332.108 kg	170.844 kg
	0.002 lt.	202 u.	200 u.	1710 u.	0.001 lt.	1134 u.
	146 u.				177 u.	
Near and Middle East /South-West Asia						
Afghanistan	No Report	No Report	No Report	No Report	No Report	85.066 kg
Iran (Islamic Republic of)	22291.102 kg	22764.000 kg	20764.000 kg NAPOL	8668.000 kg	9521.000 kg Govt	13063.000 kg
Israel	No Report	0.028 kg ICPO	18 u.	0.041 kg	50 u.	137 u.
Kuwait	No Report	34.813 kg ICPO	10.611 kg ICPO	No Report	No Report	No Report
Oman	No Report	1.006 kg	No Report	No Report	No Report	No Report
Pakistan	No Report	No Report	No Report	1824.000 kg	6839.260 kg	27777.550 kg
				7850 u.		
Saudi Arabia	No Report	149.491 kg ICPO	No Report	No Report	No Report	No Report
United Arab Emirates	0.018 kg	0.030 kg	No Report	No Report	0.015 kg	No Report
Sub-Total	22291.120 kg	22949.370 kg	20774.610 kg	10492.040 kg	16360.270 kg	40925.620 kg
			18 u.	7850 u.	50 u.	137 u.
South Asia						
Bangladesh	No Report	No Report	No Report	108 u. ICPO	No Report	No Report
India	19.000 kg	30.000 kg	39.000 kg	26.000 kg	66.000 kg	109.000 kg
Sub-Total	19.000 kg	30.000 kg	39.000 kg	26.000 kg	66.000 kg	109.000 kg
				108 u.		
Total region	22555.770 kg	23011.720 kg	20837.070 kg	10525.900 kg	16758.380 kg	41205.480 kg
	0.002 lt.	202 u.	218 u.	9668 u.	0.001 lt.	1271 u.
	146 u.				227 u.	
EUROPE						
East Europe						
Belarus	0.154 kg	0.005 kg	0.078 kg	No Report	0.032 kg	0.005 kg
Russian Federation	15.000 kg F.O	2.427 kg	2.000 kg F.O	11.024 kg	1.896 kg ICPO	7.196 kg
Sub-Total	15.154 kg	2.432 kg	2.078 kg	11.024 kg	1.928 kg	7.201 kg
Southeast Europe						
Albania	No Report	No Report	10 u. ICPO	No Report	10 u.	10 u.
Bulgaria	No Report	16 u.	No Report	No Report	No Report	0.014 kg
Croatia	79 u.	652 u.	27 u.	No Report	No Report	No Report
Romania	86 u.	132 u.	0.112 kg	248 u.	414 u.	101 u.
Turkey	754.494 kg	440.750 kg Govt	2500.219 kg Govt	797.493 kg	7889.741 kg	1009.695 kg
Sub-Total	754.494 kg	440.750 kg	2500.331 kg	797.493 kg	7889.741 kg	1009.709 kg
	165 u.	800 u.	37 u.	248 u.	424 u.	111 u.
West & Central Europe						
Austria	1.522 kg	0.328 kg	0.220 kg	0.200 kg	0.280 kg	0.080 kg
Belgium	0.098 kg		17.400 kg ICPO	17.400 kg UNODC (2		0.104 kg
Cyprus	No Report	No Report	No Report	15 u.	0.013 kg	No Report

Source: Annual Report Questionnaire if not otherwise indicated

269

SEIZURES, 1998 - 2003

Morphine

Region/country or territory	1998	1999	2000	2001	2002	2003
EUROPE						
West & Central Europe						
Czech Republic	No Report	No Report	No Report	0.049 kg	1.739 lt.	No Report
Denmark	3.000 kg	No Report	1.405 kg [ICPO]	No Report	20000 u. [ICPO]	No Report
Estonia	0.003 kg 5 u.	No Report	0.011 kg 40 u.	1.066 kg	0.039 kg	0.134 kg
Finland	No Report	0.910 kg 60 u.	0.054 kg 60 u.	No Report	No Report	No Report
France	0.088 kg	1.566 kg	0.222 kg	0.218 kg	5.459 kg	0.039 kg
Hungary	No Report	0.200 kg	No Report	10 u.	1.802 kg	0.006 kg
Ireland	0.004 kg	90 u. [ICPO]	No Report	No Report	No Report	No Report
Italy	2.270 kg 12 u.	1.314 kg [ICPO]	0.752 kg 5 u.	0.015 kg 452 u.	3.332 kg 5 u.	0.009 kg 57 u.
Norway	0.008 kg 33 u.	0.001 kg 1219 u.	2005 u.	1963 u.	0.003 kg 1859 u.	0.002 kg 3438 u.
Poland	No Report	No Report	0.588 kg [ICPO] 174 u.	No Report	No Report	No Report
Portugal	0.005 kg	85 u.	241 u.	0.043 kg 97 u.	35 u.	No Report
Slovakia	3 u.		0.288 kg		0.600 kg	No Report
Spain	3 u.	13 u.	33 u.	16 u.	15 u.	No Report
Sweden	0.154 lt.	0.011 kg 0.202 lt. 120 u.	0.074 kg 320 u.	0.070 kg	0.300 kg 621 u.	0.289 kg 10 u.
Switzerland	0.054 kg	0.537 kg	0.135 kg	0.492 kg	0.146 kg	0.073 kg
United Kingdom	41.251 kg	1.300 kg [NCIS]	3.278 kg	4.015 kg	2.000 kg	2.000 kg [3]
Sub-Total	48.303 kg 0.154 lt. 56 u.	6.167 kg 0.202 lt. 1587 u.	24.427 kg 2878 u.	23.568 kg 2553 u.	13.974 kg 1.739 lt. 22535 u.	2.736 kg 3505 u.
Total region	817.951 kg 0.154 lt. 221 u.	449.349 kg 0.202 lt. 2387 u.	2526.836 kg 2915 u.	832.085 kg 2801 u.	7905.644 kg 1.739 lt. 22959 u.	1019.646 kg 3616 u.
OCEANIA						
Oceania						
Australia	No Report	No Report	3.205 kg 104 u.	0.036 kg 73 u.	4.097 kg	0.601 kg [4]
New Zealand	1.166 kg	0.312 kg	0.713 lt. 396 u.	0.954 kg 1285 u.	0.887 kg 370 u.	0.458 kg 142 u.
Sub-Total	1.166 kg	0.312 kg	3.205 kg 0.713 lt. 500 u.	0.990 kg 1358 u.	4.984 kg 370 u.	1.059 kg 142 u.
Total region	1.166 kg	0.312 kg	3.205 kg 0.713 lt. 500 u.	0.990 kg 1358 u.	4.984 kg 370 u.	1.059 kg 142 u.

Source: Annual Report Questionnaire if not otherwise indicated

SEIZURES, 1998 - 2003

Morphine

Region/country or territory	1998	1999	2000	2001	2002	2003
TOTAL	23463.050 kg	24270.960 kg	23712.590 kg	11411.860 kg	24697.100 kg	43716.130 kg
	0.601 lt.	1.218 lt.	17.721 lt.	37105 u.	1.740 lt.	25956 u.
	1568 u.	5414 u.	5609 u.		27867 u.	

1) Small quantity. 2) Due to unavailability of 2001 data, year 2000 data were used for analysis purposes. 3) Due to unavailability of 2003 data, year 2002 data were used for analysis purposes. 4) Sum of seizures reported by national, State & Territory law enforcement agencies

Source: Annual Report Questionnaire if not otherwise indicated

SEIZURES, 1998 - 2003
Other opiates

Region/country or territory	1998	1999	2000	2001	2002	2003
AFRICA						
East Africa						
Ethiopia	No Report	No Report	No Report	No Report	0.826 kg	No Report
Mauritius	No Report	No Report	No Report	No Report	204 u. [ICPO]	217 u.
Sub-Total					0.826 kg 204 u.	217 u.
North Africa						
Egypt	No Report	0.030 lt. [(1]	1.140 lt. [ICPO]	No Report	No Report	No Report
Sub-Total		0.030 lt.	1.140 lt.			
Southern Africa						
Zambia	No Report	No Report	No Report	No Report	No Report	0.085 kg
Sub-Total						0.085 kg
West and Central Africa						
Benin	No Report	No Report	1.650 kg [ICPO]	No Report	No Report	No Report
Nigeria	No Report	No Report	No Report	No Report	0.756 kg [ICPO] 68421 u.	No Report
Sub-Total			1.650 kg		0.756 kg 68421 u.	
Total region		0.030 lt.	1.650 kg 1.140 lt.		1.582 kg 68625 u.	0.085 kg 217 u.
AMERICAS						
Caribbean						
Cayman Islands	No Report	0.003 kg [ICPO]	2 u.	No Report	No Report	No Report
Dominican Republic	No Report	8.000 kg [ICPO]	No Report	No Report	No Report	No Report
Puerto Rico	No Report	No Report	No Report	No Report	0.036 lt. [ICPO] 4 u.	No Report
Sub-Total		8.003 kg	2 u.		0.036 lt. 4 u.	
North America						
Canada	1.446 kg 0.093 lt. 8880 u.	0.594 kg 8805 u.	0.682 kg 1.050 lt. 4784 u.	1.124 kg 22045 u.	0.918 kg 28238 u.	1.218 kg 14393 u.
Mexico	No Report	No Report	No Report	No Report	8053.635 kg	207789 u.
United States	No Report	9338 u. [ICPO (1]	No Report	10778580 u.	78081 u.	No Report
Sub-Total	1.446 kg 0.093 lt. 8880 u.	0.594 kg 18143 u.	0.682 kg 1.050 lt. 4784 u.	1.124 kg 10800630 u.	8054.553 kg 106319 u.	1.218 kg 222182 u.
South America						
Argentina	No Report	No Report	No Report	0.200 kg	No Report	No Report
Chile	25 u.	No Report	No Report	No Report	13 u.	64 u. [(1]
Colombia	No Report	3.500 kg [(1]	No Report	1.000 kg [(1]	No Report	No Report
Peru	No Report	38.693 kg [ICPO]	No Report	No Report	No Report	341.863 kg

Source: Annual Report Questionnaire if not otherwise indicated

SEIZURES, 1998 - 2003
Other opiates

Region/country or territory	1998	1999	2000	2001	2002	2003
AMERICAS						
South America						
Sub-Total	25 u.	42.193 kg		1.200 kg	13 u.	341.863 kg
						64 u.
Total region	1.446 kg	50.790 kg	0.682 kg	2.324 kg	8054.553 kg	343.081 kg
	0.093 lt.	18143 u.	1.050 lt.	10800630 u.	0.036 lt.	222246 u.
	8905 u.		4786 u.		106336 u.	
ASIA						
Central Asia and Transcaucasian countries						
Armenia	No Report	0.017 kg [ICPO]	1.679 kg	No Report	No Report	No Report
Azerbaijan	No Report	No Report	72.590 kg [ICPO]	No Report	No Report	No Report
Georgia	No Report	25.003 kg [ICPO (2]	12.871 kg [ICPO]	No Report	No Report	No Report
Kazakhstan	3.219 kg	7.944 kg	No Report	No Report	No Report	No Report
Uzbekistan	No Report	No Report	288.000 kg [ICPO]	No Report	No Report	55.500 kg
Sub-Total	3.219 kg	32.964 kg	375.140 kg			55.500 kg
East and South-East Asia						
Brunei Darussalam	0.057 kg	12.970 lt.	23.000 lt.	1413 u.	0.003 lt. [(1]	25 u. [(1]
	474 u.	2377 u.			2565 u.	
Hong Kong Special Administrative Region of China	No Report	187 u. [(2]	7.600 lt. [ICPO]	5.200 lt.	4930 u.	9574 u. [(1]
			1873 u.	3306 u.		
Indonesia	7179 u.	564 u. [ICPO (1]	0.000 kg [Govt]	0.000 kg [Govt]	0.000 kg [Govt]	4000 u.
Japan	0.006 kg	0.005 kg	No Report	No Report	579 u. [ICPO]	No Report
	0.030 lt.					
	5557 u.					
Macao Special Administrative Region of China	8.000 lt. [ICPO]	No Report	2.000 lt. [ICPO]	No Report	52 u. [ICPO]	No Report
	45 u.		1 u.			
Malaysia	No Report	18453 u.	17982.480 lt. [(1]	No Report	No Report	No Report
Myanmar	No Report	555.000 kg	222.089 lt. [(3]	No Report	338.454 lt. [(3]	98.827 kg
		121.000 lt.				101.510 lt.
Singapore	301 u.	0.438 kg [(2]	1127 u. [(4]	6382.000 kg	No Report	No Report
Thailand	No Report	381.600 lt. [ICPO (1]	569.505 kg [ICPO]	No Report	1057.000 kg [ICPO]	[Govt.]
Sub-Total	0.063 kg	555.443 kg	569.505 kg	6382.000 kg	1057.000 kg	98.827 kg
	8.030 lt.	515.570 lt.	18237.170 lt.	5.200 lt.	338.457 lt.	101.510 lt.
	13556 u.	21581 u.	3001 u.	4719 u.	8126 u.	13599 u.
Near and Middle East /South-West Asia						
Afghanistan	No Report	No Report	No Report	No Report	No Report	498.000 lt.
Bahrain	No Report	No Report	No Report	No Report	58 u.	No Report
Iran (Islamic Republic of)	No Report	1088.000 kg	1459.000 kg [ICPO]	No Report	No Report	1777.000 kg
Iraq	No Report	No Report	No Report	1.000 kg [(1]	No Report	No Report
Israel	No Report	2.121 lt. [ICPO (1]	3.843 kg [ICPO]	No Report	2.600 kg [ICPO]	No Report
		7 u.	15 u.			

Source: Annual Report Questionnaire if not otherwise indicated

273

SEIZURES, 1998 - 2003
Other opiates

Region/country or territory	1998	1999	2000	2001	2002	2003
ASIA						
Near and Middle East /South-West Asia						
Lebanon	No Report	No Report	0.300 kg [ICPO]	No Report	No Report	No Report
Pakistan	No Report	No Report	No Report	No Report	21757.000 kg [ICPO]	No Report
United Arab Emirates	No Report	No Report	No Report	No Report	0.030 kg [1]	0.017 kg
Sub-Total		1088.000 kg 2.121 lt. 7 u.	1463.143 kg 15 u.	1.000 kg	21759.630 kg 58 u.	1777.017 kg 498.000 lt.
South Asia						
Bangladesh	30499 u. [Govt]	5821 u. [Govt]	6518 u. [Govt]	2763 u. [Govt]	290.475 kg 108356 u.	376.800 kg [5] 70879 u.
Nepal	3676 u.	No Report	No Report	No Report	35.000 lt. [ICPO]	No Report
Sub-Total	34175 u.	5821 u.	6518 u.	2763 u.	290.475 kg 35.000 lt. 108356 u.	376.800 kg 70879 u.
Total region	3.282 kg 8.030 lt. 47731 u.	1676.407 kg 517.691 lt. 27409 u.	2407.788 kg 18237.170 lt. 9534 u.	6383.000 kg 5.200 lt. 7482 u.	23107.100 kg 373.457 lt. 116540 u.	2308.144 kg 599.510 lt. 84478 u.
EUROPE						
East Europe						
Belarus	No Report	No Report	No Report	0.088 kg [Govt]	0.361 kg [ICPO]	0.194 kg [Govt]
Republic of Moldova	2100 u.	682 u. [ICPO]	0.858 kg [ICPO]	No Report	171.720 kg [Govt (6]	No Report
Russian Federation	167.700 kg [F.O]	54.575 kg	18.000 kg [F.O]	21469.675 kg	93.446 kg [ICPO]	1003.626 kg
Ukraine	No Report	11600 u. [ICPO (1]	No Report	No Report	20.000 kg	No Report
Sub-Total	167.700 kg 2100 u.	54.575 kg 12282 u.	18.858 kg	21469.760 kg	285.527 kg	1003.820 kg
Southeast Europe						
Albania	No Report	No Report	0.480 lt. [ICPO] 7 u.	No Report	21 u. [7]	No Report
Bosnia and Herzegovina	1 u. [ICPO]	No Report	No Report	No Report	No Report	No Report
Bulgaria	No Report	No Report	3650 u. [ICPO]	No Report	No Report	No Report
Croatia	No Report	No Report	29 u.	No Report	4047 u. [ICPO]	No Report
Romania	19494 u.	26 u. [2]	0.840 lt. [2] 387 u.	No Report	0.046 kg [ICPO]	No Report
The former Yugoslav Republic of Macedonia	No Report	3.988 kg [ICPO] 2.250 lt. 135 u.	No Report	No Report	No Report	No Report
Turkey	No Report	34090 u. [ICPO (2]	0.234 kg [Govt. (2]	No Report	No Report	No Report
Sub-Total	19495 u.	3.988 kg 2.250 lt. 34251 u.	0.234 kg 1.320 lt. 4073 u.		0.046 kg 4068 u.	

Source: Annual Report Questionnaire if not otherwise indicated

SEIZURES, 1998 - 2003
Other opiates

Region/country or territory	1998	1999	2000	2001	2002	2003
EUROPE						
West & Central Europe						
Belgium	0.109 kg	9.100 kg [ICPO] 0.200 lt. 307500 u.	15.070 kg [ICPO]	15.070 kg [UNODC (8]	No Report	0.080 kg
Cyprus	No Report	55 u. [ICPO]	No Report	No Report	0.200 kg [ICPO] 70 u.	39 u. [(1]
Denmark	6.000 kg	No Report	No Report	No Report	No Report	No Report
Estonia	No Report	2 u.	0.003 kg 20 u.	No Report	0.076 kg	0.151 kg
Finland	No Report	46 u. [ICPO]	13808 u.	31967 u.	18700 u.	37300 u.
France	No Report	521 u. [ICPO (2]	4134 u. [ICPO]	No Report	No Report	No Report
Greece	1.529 kg 6774 u.	0.132 kg 7795 u.	0.472 kg 5162 u.	0.070 kg 1466 u.	1576 u.	No Report
Hungary	438 u.	120 u. [ICPO (2]	No Report	262 u.	222 u.	No Report
Ireland	No Report	0.320 kg [ICPO (2] 579 u.	No Report	No Report	6.895 lt. [ICPO] 252 u.	No Report
Italy	0.554 kg 7538 u.	2.426 kg [ICPO (2]	2.967 kg [(9] 7220 u.	No Report	5.447 kg [ICPO] 22442 u.	No Report
Latvia	No Report	No Report	No Report	No Report	No Report	0.001 kg
Lithuania	13 u.	0.210 kg 92 u.	0.888 lt. [(2]	No Report	0.001 kg [ICPO]	No Report
Luxembourg	No Report	0.180 lt. [ICPO (2]	0.098 lt. [ICPO]	No Report	No Report	No Report
Malta	77 u.	No Report	98 u.	No Report	0.230 lt. [ICPO]	No Report
Monaco	No Report	No Report	No Report	No Report	0.003 lt. [ICPO]	No Report
Netherlands	4093 u. [Govt (2]	50.000 kg [Govt (2] 186437 u.	16.000 kg [Govt (2] 5543 u.	No Report	No Report	No Report
Norway	No Report	0.017 kg 9657 u.	0.001 kg 8007 u.	0.255 kg 18879 u.	0.756 kg 68421 u.	0.779 kg 14190 u.
Poland	395.000 lt.	389.000 lt. [(10]	3.500 lt. [ICPO] 174 u.	No Report	193.000 kg [(10]	1551.000 kg
Portugal	35 u.	21 u.	15 u. [(11]	20.910 kg 22 u.	0.009 kg 2 u.	0.017 kg 36 u.
Slovakia	922 u.	278 u.	38 u. [ICPO]	No Report	21 u.	No Report
Slovenia	No Report	0.552 lt.	1.545 lt. [ICPO] 245 u.	No Report	No Report	No Report
Spain	No Report	966 u. [ICPO]	No Report	7708 u.	742 u. [ICPO]	No Report
Sweden	0.003 kg 1.312 lt.	0.053 kg 783 u.	0.052 kg 631 u.	No Report	4629 u.	No Report
Switzerland	No Report	5006 u.	5472 u. [(2]	No Report	4079 u. [ICPO]	No Report
United Kingdom	0.064 kg	60.600 kg [NCIS (2]	0.548 kg	1146.641 kg	No Report	No Report
Sub-Total	8.259 kg 396.312 lt. 19890 u.	122.858 kg 389.932 lt. 519858 u.	35.113 kg 6.031 lt. 50567 u.	1182.946 kg 60304 u.	199.489 kg 7.128 lt. 121156 u.	1552.028 kg 51565 u.

Source: Annual Report Questionnaire if not otherwise indicated

SEIZURES, 1998 - 2003

Other opiates

Region/country or territory	1998	1999	2000	2001	2002	2003
EUROPE						
Total region	175.959 kg	181.421 kg	54.205 kg	22652.710 kg	485.062 kg	2555.848 kg
	396.312 lt.	392.182 lt.	7.351 lt.	60304 u.	7.128 lt.	51565 u.
	41485 u.	566391 u.	54640 u.		125224 u.	
OCEANIA						
Oceania						
Australia	22.243 kg [Govt. (12]	6.792 kg [Govt. (12]	0.384 kg	6.786 kg [Govt. (13]	No Report	5.776 kg [(14]
New Zealand	No Report	0.100 kg	No Report	No Report	0.461 kg	1.580 lt.
					1301 u.	339 u.
Sub-Total	22.243 kg	6.892 kg	0.384 kg	6.786 kg	0.461 kg	5.776 kg
					1301 u.	1.580 lt.
						339 u.
Total region	22.243 kg	6.892 kg	0.384 kg	6.786 kg	0.461 kg	5.776 kg
					1301 u.	1.580 lt.
						339 u.
TOTAL	202.930 kg	1915.510 kg	2464.709 kg	29044.820 kg	31648.760 kg	5212.934 kg
	404.435 lt.	909.903 lt.	18246.710 lt.	5.200 lt.	380.621 lt.	601.090 lt.
	98121 u.	611943 u.	68960 u.	10868410 u.	418026 u.	358845 u.

1) Codeine 2) Methadone 3) Phensedyl 4) Methadone and dihydrocodeine 5) Including codeine preparartion 6) Poppy solution 7) pethidine 8) Due to unavailability of 2001 data, year 2000 data were used for analysis purposes. 9) 2.933 kg,7208 u. methadone 10) Polish heroin (also called "compot") 11) 15 u. liquid heroin, 92 u. methadone 12) Provisional figures. 13) Fiscal year 14) Sum of seizures reported by national, State & Territory law enforcement agencies

Source: Annual Report Questionnaire if not otherwise indicated

6.2. Cocaine: Seizures 1998-2003

Region/country or territory	1998	1999	2000	2001	2002	2003
SEIZURES, 1998 - 2003						
Cocaine (base and salts)						
AFRICA						
East Africa						
Kenya	1.240 kg	0.110 kg	4.017 kg	0.207 kg [Govt]	18.584 kg [Govt]	3.930 kg
Rwanda	No Report	No Report	No Report	No Report	4.000 kg	No Report
Uganda	No Report	0.412 kg	1.910 kg	No Report	No Report	No Report
United Republic of Tanzania	No Report	1.161 kg	2.103 kg [ICPO]	7.389 kg [Govt]	2.461 kg [ICPO]	1.727 kg
Sub-Total	1.240 kg	1.683 kg	8.030 kg	7.596 kg	25.045 kg	5.657 kg
North Africa						
Algeria	No Report	No Report	No Report	0.288 kg [ICPO]	0.268 kg	9.508 kg
Egypt	1.860 kg	0.792 kg	14.288 kg	No Report	4.001 kg	0.550 kg
Libyan Arab Jamahiriya	0.136 kg	0.070 kg [F.O]	0.531 kg [F.O]	0.173 kg [F.O]	No Report	No Report
Morocco	30.111 kg	1.742 kg	0.898 kg	4.298 kg 103 u.	15.801 kg 15 u.	2.590 kg
Sudan	No Report	No Report	0.001 kg 2 u.	0.587 kg [Govt]	No Report	1.922 kg [Govt]
Tunisia	0.127 kg	0.017 kg [ICPO]	No Report	No Report	1.055 kg	0.540 kg
Sub-Total	32.234 kg	2.621 kg	15.718 kg 2 u.	5.346 kg 103 u.	21.125 kg 15 u.	15.110 kg
Southern Africa						
Angola	38.007 kg [ICPO]	15.901 kg	173.724 kg [ICPO]	20.745 kg [ICPO]	No Report	No Report
Botswana	0.700 kg [ICPO]	1.696 kg [ICPO]	No Report	No Report	No Report	No Report
Lesotho	No Report	0.632 kg [ICPO]	No Report	No Report	No Report	No Report
Malawi	1.500 kg	1.200 kg	No Report	0.250 kg	No Report	20.283 kg
Mozambique	2.134 kg [ICPO]	0.385 kg [ICPO]	0.100 kg [ICPO]	0.012 kg [ICPO]	No Report	15.000 kg [HNLF]
Namibia	2.110 kg	No Report	0.093 kg	3.036 kg 100 u.	0.189 kg 89 u.	0.056 kg 79 u.
South Africa	635.908 kg 3825 u.	345.549 kg [ICPO] 12940 u.	91.202 kg	155.305 kg 3470 u.	436.499 kg	776.726 kg 20173 u.
Swaziland	No Report	3.609 kg	6.832 kg	1.006 kg	1.058 kg	4.568 kg
Zambia	0.000 kg [Govt]	1.116 kg	0.005 kg 27 u.	[Govt (1]	17.300 kg	0.055 kg
Zimbabwe	0.501 kg	0.166 kg	0.593 kg	No Report	No Report	No Report
Sub-Total	680.860 kg 3825 u.	370.254 kg 12940 u.	272.549 kg 27 u.	180.354 kg 3570 u.	455.046 kg 89 u.	816.688 kg 20252 u.
West and Central Africa						
Benin	0.628 kg	No Report	21.494 kg [F.O]	31.741 kg [ICPO]	0.050 kg [ICPO]	No Report
Burkina Faso	No Report	No Report	No Report	No Report	No Report	0.028 kg
Cameroon	3.780 kg	No Report	No Report	No Report	No Report	No Report
Chad	No Report	0.015 kg [ICPO]	0.028 kg	No Report	No Report	No Report
Congo	No Report	No Report	40.010 kg	0.020 kg	0.611 kg	0.800 kg
Côte d'Ivoire	19.015 kg	9.287 kg 16 u.	3.442 kg [ICPO]	1.048 kg	3.150 kg	No Report
Gabon	No Report	0.216 kg [ICPO]	No Report	No Report	No Report	No Report

Source: Annual Report Questionnaire if not otherwise indicated

277

SEIZURES, 1998 - 2003
Cocaine (base and salts)

Region/country or territory	1998	1999	2000	2001	2002	2003
AFRICA						
West and Central Africa						
Gambia	0.074 kg [ICPO]	0.060 kg	4.865 kg [Govt]	7.000 kg	No Report	0.107 kg [Govt]
Ghana	5.035 kg	7.062 kg	No Report	No Report	10.400 kg	15.370 kg
Guinea	No Report	No Report	No Report	No Report	No Report	0.771 kg
Niger	0.233 kg [ICPO]	No Report	No Report	No Report	No Report	No Report
Nigeria	9.260 kg [Govt.]	15.064 kg	53.950 kg	195.823 kg	35.347 kg	134.983 kg
Sao Tome and Principe	No Report	0.100 kg	No Report	No Report	No Report	No Report
Senegal	5.321 kg [ICPO]	31.564 kg [ICPO] 110 u.	0.207 kg [ICPO]	No Report	0.837 kg [ICPO]	No Report
Togo	No Report	2.330 kg [HNLF]	6.213 kg	29.927 kg	3.051 kg	1.775 kg [HNLF]
Sub-Total	43.346 kg	65.698 kg 126 u.	130.209 kg	265.559 kg	53.446 kg	153.833 kg
Total region	757.680 kg 3825 u.	440.256 kg 13066 u.	426.506 kg 29 u.	458.855 kg 3673 u.	554.662 kg 104 u.	991.289 kg 20252 u.
AMERICAS						
Caribbean						
Anguilla	0.108 kg	0.020 kg [F.O]	No Report	926.000 kg [F.O]	No Report	No Report
Antigua and Barbuda	1.000 kg [F.O]	26.000 kg [F.O]	24.000 kg [F.O]	767.000 kg [F.O]	No Report	62.000 kg [INCSR]
Aruba	794.000 kg [NAPOL]	465.000 kg [F.O]	346.000 kg [F.O]	266.000 kg [F.O]	490.681 kg [ICPO]	1.000 kg [PROJ.S]
Bahamas	3343.054 kg	1857.000 kg [F.O]	2759.510 kg	1469.000 kg 3238 u.	2477.273 kg	4361.124 kg
Barbados	35.000 kg [NAPOL]	132.760 kg [HONLC]	81.000 kg [F.O]	83.000 kg [F.O]	No Report	97.000 kg [INCSR]
Bermuda	4.330 kg	8.076 kg	11.574 kg	667.000 kg [F.O]	8.860 kg	0.700 kg [PROJ.S]
British Virgin Islands	20.000 kg [NAPOL]	432.000 kg [F.O]	534.000 kg [F.O]	2159.040 kg 34 u.	No Report	No Report
Cayman Islands	1195.142 kg 1824 u.	1926.129 kg	1813.000 kg [F.O]	1006.817 kg 40874 u.	404.825 kg 28199 u.	6.007 kg
Cuba	669.000 kg [NAPOL]	2444.000 kg [F.O]	3145.000 kg [F.O]	1278.000 kg [F.O]	406.001 kg [ICPO]	506.500 kg [HONL]
Dominica	29.000 kg [F.O]	82.769 kg [ICPO]	10.000 kg [F.O]	6.000 kg [F.O]	4.526 kg [ICPO]	8.700 kg [PROJ.S]
Dominican Republic	2341.916 kg	1075.953 kg	1310.000 kg [CICAD]	1913.944 kg	2295.200 kg [HONLC]	735.703 kg
French Guiana	3.000 kg [F.O]	446.000 kg [F.O]	25.000 kg [F.O]	No Report	No Report	74.000 kg [PROJ.S]
Grenada	26.500 kg	43.000 kg [F.O]	103.000 kg [F.O]	53.389 kg	77.320 kg [ICPO]	8.500 kg [PROJ.S]
Guadeloupe	3222.000 kg [F.O]	593.000 kg [F.O]	292.000 kg [F.O]	593.000 kg [F.O]	No Report	608.500 kg [PROJ.S]
Haiti	1272.000 kg [NAPOL]	436.000 kg	594.000 kg [F.O]	414.000 kg	272.760 kg	45.000 kg [CICAD]
Jamaica	1143.000 kg [F.O]	2455.000 kg [ICPO] 3543 u.	1656.000 kg [F.O]	2950.910 kg 3099 u.	3725.000 kg [ICPO] 2750 u.	1586.000 kg [INCSR]
Martinique	46.000 kg [F.O]	36.000 kg [F.O]	15.000 kg [F.O]	No Report	No Report	1138.000 kg [PROJ.S]
Netherlands Antilles	639.000 kg [NAPOL]	18.000 kg [F.O]	965.353 kg [ICPO]	1043.000 kg [F.O]	2455.168 kg [ICPO]	7728.000 kg [PROJ.S]
Puerto Rico	10344.000 kg [F.O]	9977.000 kg [F.O]	5516.000 kg [F.O]	2831.000 kg [F.O]	208.280 kg [ICPO] 76637 u.	No Report
Saint Kitts and Nevis	1.000 kg [F.O]	10.000 kg [F.O]	53.000 kg [INCSR]	20.000 kg [F.O]	No Report	36.000 kg [INCSR]

Source: Annual Report Questionnaire if not otherwise indicated

SEIZURES, 1998 - 2003
Cocaine (base and salts)

Region/country or territory	1998	1999	2000	2001	2002	2003
AMERICAS						
Caribbean						
Saint Lucia	78.137 kg	133.000 kg [CICAD]	110.473 kg	63.000 kg [F.O]	No Report	433.000 kg [INCSR]
Saint Vincent and the Grenadines	13.000 kg [F.O]	15.000 kg [F.O]	51.000 kg [INCSR]	207.000 kg [F.O]	No Report	1.500 kg [INCSR]
Trinidad and Tobago	77.680 kg	137.000 kg [CICAD]	203.000 kg [INCSR]	821.880 kg	172.769 kg	172.771 kg
Turks and Caicos Islands	2075.000 kg	3.000 kg	0.136 kg [ICPO]	4.000 kg [F.O]	1.689 kg	48.209 kg
United States Virgin Islands	No Report	432.028 kg [ICPO]	No Report	No Report	No Report	No Report
Sub-Total	27372.870 kg 1824 u.	23183.730 kg 3543 u.	19618.050 kg	19542.980 kg 47245 u.	13000.350 kg 107586 u.	17658.210 kg
Central America						
Belize	1221.000 kg [NAPOL]	39.515 kg [ICPO]	13.000 kg [F.O]	3854.857 kg	7.549 kg [ICPO]	56.700 kg [INCSR]
Costa Rica	7387.140 kg 104494 u.	1998.720 kg 56514 u.	5871.000 kg 64998 u.	1748.600 kg [Govt] 58948 u.	2955.000 kg [Govt] 100381 u.	4291.850 kg 80579 u.
El Salvador	45.256 kg [ICPO]	38.649 kg	434.700 kg [ICPO]	31.545 kg	2075.154 kg	2044.300 kg
Guatemala	9217.070 kg	9964.788 kg	1537.360 kg	4107.913 kg	2934.265 kg	9200.504 kg
Honduras	1804.000 kg [CICAD] 603 u.	709.000 kg [CICAD] 662 u.	1215.000 kg [CICAD] 1031 u.	717.100 kg [HONL]	79.023 kg 708 u.	5649.133 kg 2357 u.
Nicaragua	4750.265 kg 21235 u.	833.000 kg [CICAD]	963.000 kg [CICAD]	2717.971 kg [ICPO]	2208.437 kg 12739 u.	1110.700 kg [HONL]
Panama	11828.085 kg	3139.889 kg	7413.455 kg	2660.000 kg	2587.700 kg [HONLC]	9487.000 kg [INCSR]
Sub-Total	36252.820 kg 126332 u.	16723.560 kg 57176 u.	17447.520 kg 66029 u.	15837.980 kg 58948 u.	12847.130 kg 113828 u.	31840.190 kg 82936 u.
North America						
Canada	562.983 kg 0.007 lt.	1650.518 kg 0.407 lt. 19 u.	280.866 kg 5.156 lt. 26 u.	1678.488 kg 167 u.	181.391 kg 75 u.	475.574 kg 33 u.
Mexico	22597.072 kg	34622.602 kg	23195.942 kg [(2]	29988.684 kg	12639.347 kg	21107.238 kg
United States	117000.000 [Govt.] kg	132318.000 kg	99700.000 kg 1514.386 lt. 5326 u.	106212.500 kg	101904.500 [(2] kg	117024.800 kg
Sub-Total	140160.100 kg 0.007 lt.	168591.100 kg 0.407 lt. 19 u.	123176.800 kg 1519.542 lt. 5352 u.	137879.700 kg 167 u.	114725.200 kg 75 u.	138607.600 kg 33 u.
South America						
Argentina	1766.900 kg	1660.776 kg	2351.359 kg	2286.858 kg	1638.281 kg	1992.708 kg
Bolivia	11346.000 kg [F.O]	7712.000 kg [F.O]	5599.000 kg [F.O]	4615.000 kg [F.O]	5103.030 kg	12881.000 kg [F.O]
Brazil	6560.414 kg	7646.103 kg	5555.925 kg	9137.265 kg [Govt]	9415.200 kg [F.O]	9766.702 kg
Chile	2952.471 kg	2930.000 kg [CICAD]	2076.100 kg	2428.090 kg	2262.311 kg	2410.508 kg
Colombia	107891.000 [Govt] kg	60512.000 kg [Govt]	105006.000 [Govt] kg	75087.000 kg [Govt]	120579.000 [Govt] kg	145601.000 [Govt] kg
Ecuador	3854.200 kg [Govt]	10163.900 kg [Govt]	3308.000 kg [Govt]	12242.000 kg [Govt]	11212.300 kg [Govt]	6847.590 kg [Govt]
Guyana	3222.000 kg [NAPOL]	40.163 kg [ICPO]	167.000 kg [CICAD]	73.000 kg [ICPO]	No Report	278.783 kg

Source: Annual Report Questionnaire if not otherwise indicated

279

SEIZURES, 1998 - 2003
Cocaine (base and salts)

Region/country or territory	1998	1999	2000	2001	2002	2003
AMERICAS						
South America						
Paraguay	222.352 kg	95.058 kg	96.000 kg [CICAD]	90.000 kg [HONL]	230.152 kg	278.991 kg
Peru	9936.968 kg	11307.116 kg	11847.611 kg	9189.362 kg	14568.175 kg	7940.540 kg
Suriname	283.444 kg	185.000 kg [CICAD]	207.000 kg [INCSR]	2253.000 kg	340.000 kg	814.000 kg [INCSR]
Uruguay	23.604 kg	18.698 kg	20.642 kg	24.758 kg [ICPO]	43.013 kg	49.919 kg
Venezuela	8159.000 kg [CICAD]	12418.839 kg	15063.194 kg	13950.940 kg	17828.940 kg	32339.560 kg
Sub-Total	156218.400 kg	114689.600 kg	151297.800 kg	131377.300 kg	183220.400 kg	221201.300 kg
Total region	360004.100 kg 0.007 lt. 128156 u.	323188.100 kg 0.407 lt. 60738 u.	311540.200 kg 1519.542 lt. 71381 u.	304637.900 kg 106360 u.	323793.100 kg 221489 u.	409307.300 kg 82969 u.
ASIA						
Central Asia and Transcaucasian countries						
Azerbaijan	No Report	0.005 kg	No Report	No Report	No Report	No Report
Georgia	No Report	0.002 kg [ICPO]	No Report	No Report	No Report	No Report
Kazakhstan	20.000 kg	0.035 kg	No Report	0.054 kg [F.O]	0.119 kg [F.O]	No Report
Turkmenistan	1.000 kg [Govt.]	No Report	No Report	No Report	No Report	No Report
Sub-Total	21.000 kg	0.042 kg		0.054 kg	0.119 kg	
East and South-East Asia						
China	No Report	No Report	No Report	No Report	No Report	45.000 kg
Hong Kong Special Administrative Region of China	167.700 kg [Govt.]	11.990 kg	9.004 kg	29.700 kg	8.300 kg	6.630 kg
Indonesia	4.748 kg	0.500 kg	17.415 kg	30.793 kg	2.314 kg	58.116 kg
Japan	20.846 kg	10.349 kg	15.580 kg	23.716 kg	16.900 kg	2.500 kg
Macao Special Administrative Region of China	No Report	No Report	0.008 kg	No Report	0.027 kg	0.001 kg
Malaysia	No Report	No Report	No Report	0.017 kg [ICPO]	No Report	2.500 kg
Mongolia	No Report	2.800 kg [ICPO]	No Report	0.400 kg	No Report	No Report
Philippines	1.080 kg [ICPO]	0.227 kg	0.588 kg	No Report	8.026 kg	No Report
Republic of Korea	2.080 kg	2.251 kg	No Report	0.111 kg	1.170 kg [ICPO]	0.905 kg
Singapore	1.050 kg	No Report	No Report	No Report	No Report	No Report
Thailand	3.555 kg	0.619 kg [ICPO]	4.003 kg [HNLP]	4.625 kg [HNLP]	14.730 kg [ICPO]	11.000 kg [Govt.]
Sub-Total	201.059 kg	28.736 kg	46.598 kg	89.362 kg	51.467 kg	126.652 kg
Near and Middle East /South-West Asia						
Bahrain	No Report	No Report	0.010 kg [ICPO]	No Report	0.002 kg	No Report
Israel	99.800 kg	28.229 kg [ICPO]	11.659 kg	23.617 kg	96.012 kg	80.009 kg
Jordan	0.940 kg	1.912 kg	0.803 kg	0.505 kg	0.188 kg	No Report
Kuwait	0.003 kg	No Report	36.000 kg [ICPO]	No Report	0.002 kg [ICPO]	4.700 kg [ICPO]
Lebanon	11.898 kg	32.013 kg	0.466 kg	7.207 kg	7.839 kg	40.728 kg
Pakistan	0.100 kg	1.100 kg	No Report	No Report	No Report	No Report
Saudi Arabia	2.202 kg	4.908 kg [ICPO]	0.708 kg 3 u.	0.046 kg	1.528 kg [ICPO]	0.900 kg [ICPO]

Source: Annual Report Questionnaire if not otherwise indicated

SEIZURES, 1998 - 2003
Cocaine (base and salts)

Region/country or territory	1998	1999	2000	2001	2002	2003
ASIA						
Near and Middle East /South-West Asia						
Syrian Arab Republic	0.235 kg [Govt]	32.102 kg [Govt]	7.177 kg [Govt]	1.031 kg [Govt]	57.237 kg	36.738 kg
United Arab Emirates	0.146 kg	0.840 kg	0.537 kg	0.007 kg	0.013 kg	0.408 kg
Sub-Total	115.324 kg	101.104 kg	57.360 kg 3 u.	32.413 kg	162.821 kg	163.483 kg
South Asia						
Bangladesh	No Report	No Report	0.550 kg	No Report	No Report	No Report
India	1.000 kg	1.000 kg [ICPO]	0.350 kg [F.O]	2.000 kg	2.000 kg	2.000 kg
Maldives	No Report	No Report	No Report	No Report	15.801 kg [ICPO] 15 u.	No Report
Sri Lanka	No Report	No Report	No Report	0.640 kg	No Report	No Report
Sub-Total	1.000 kg	1.000 kg	0.900 kg	2.640 kg	17.801 kg 15 u.	2.000 kg
Total region	338.383 kg	130.882 kg	104.858 kg 3 u.	124.469 kg	232.209 kg 15 u.	292.135 kg
EUROPE						
East Europe						
Belarus	No Report	No Report	No Report	No Report	0.003 kg	0.003 kg [Govt]
Republic of Moldova	No Report	No Report	No Report	0.001 kg	No Report	No Report
Russian Federation	100.340 kg	12.749 kg	65.000 kg [F.O]	82.502 kg	58.155 kg [ICPO]	53.350 kg
Ukraine	250.586 kg	26.263 kg [ICPO]	0.520 kg [ICPO]	0.018 kg	0.012 kg	0.094 kg
Sub-Total	350.926 kg	39.012 kg	65.520 kg	82.521 kg	58.170 kg	53.447 kg
Southeast Europe						
Albania	No Report	2.159 kg [ICPO]	4.000 kg [Govt]	0.266 kg [Govt]	0.006 kg	1.286 kg
Bosnia and Herzegovina	0.005 kg [NAPOL]	No Report	164.392 kg [NAPOL]	No Report	0.240 kg [ICPO]	No Report
Bulgaria	685.585 kg	17.010 kg	4.333 kg	12.752 kg	36.282 kg	8.884 kg
Croatia	6.426 kg	1.807 kg	913.127 kg	1.487 kg	3.365 kg	350.769 kg
Romania	1.203 kg	9.670 kg	13.140 kg	2.524 kg	2.720 kg	12.680 kg
Serbia and Montenegro	No Report	No Report	No Report	3.623 kg	1.926 kg [ICPO]	6.021 kg
The former Yugoslav Republic of Macedonia	0.040 kg	2.955 kg [NAPOL]	4.689 kg [NAPOL]	5.860 kg [Govt]	0.342 kg	No Report
Turkey	604.880 kg	13.153 kg	8.444 kg [Govt.]	2.010 kg [Govt]	7.734 kg	2.833 kg
Sub-Total	1298.139 kg	46.754 kg	1112.125 kg	28.522 kg	52.615 kg	382.472 kg
West & Central Europe						
Andorra	0.064 kg [ICPO]	0.060 kg	0.023 kg [ICPO]	0.086 kg	0.270 kg [ICPO]	No Report
Austria	99.140 kg	63.377 kg	20.375 kg	108.278 kg	36.896 kg	58.306 kg
Belgium	2088.312 kg	1761.709 kg	2813.991 kg	2813.991 kg [UNODC (3]	3589.000 kg	645.600 kg
Cyprus	0.018 kg	5.361 kg	57.599 kg	0.123 kg	1.944 kg	9.571 kg

Source: Annual Report Questionnaire if not otherwise indicated

SEIZURES, 1998 - 2003
Cocaine (base and salts)

Region/country or territory	1998	1999	2000	2001	2002	2003
EUROPE						
West & Central Europe						
Czech Republic	42.000 kg	140.800 kg	14.712 kg	5.170 kg 9 u.	6.042 kg	2.624 kg
Denmark	44.133 kg	24.200 kg	35.910 kg	25.624 kg	14.152 kg	104.004 kg
Estonia	2.565 kg 71 u.	0.128 kg 139 u.	0.108 kg 37 u.	0.137 kg	2.286 kg	30.486 kg
Finland	1.987 kg	1.703 kg	38.575 kg	6.500 kg	0.442 kg	1.100 kg
France	1076.000 kg	3697.372 kg	1333.119 kg	2102.257 kg	3660.183 kg	4185.011 kg
Germany, Federal Republic of	1133.243 kg	1979.100 kg	915.600 kg	1290.087 kg	2142.894 kg	1014.103 kg
Greece	283.971 kg	45.485 kg 8 u.	156.245 kg 2 u.	227.287 kg	18.035 kg	200.645 kg
Hungary	26.385 kg	121.147 kg	9.200 kg	6.015 kg	58.928 kg	23.467 kg
Iceland	No Report	0.955 kg	0.942 kg	0.257 kg	1.870 kg	1.192 kg
Ireland	334.230 kg	85.553 kg	18.041 kg	5.325 kg	30.467 kg	106.909 kg
Italy	2143.804 kg 1341 u.	2997.611 kg [ICPO] 14 u.	2359.715 kg 2329 u.	1808.910 kg 612 u.	4039.991 kg 646 u.	3521.329 kg 603 u.
Latvia	0.063 kg	1.915 kg	0.027 kg	1.024 kg	No Report	0.616 kg
Liechtenstein	0.151 kg	0.003 kg	0.010 kg	0.750 kg	0.014 kg	0.014 kg
Lithuania	10.133 kg	0.275 kg	1.841 kg	0.129 kg	0.732 kg	0.183 kg
Luxembourg	5.995 kg	0.327 kg	10.757 kg [ICPO]	No Report	2.486 kg [ICPO]	11.153 kg
Malta	0.058 kg	1.366 kg	0.028 kg	2.542 kg	4.535 kg [ICPO]	3.716 kg
Monaco	0.012 kg	0.056 kg [ICPO]	0.001 kg [ICPO]	No Report	0.010 kg	0.000 kg
Netherlands	8998.000 kg [Govt]	10361.000 kg [Govt]	6472.000 kg [Govt]	8382.000 kg	7968.000 kg	17560.000 kg
Norway	93.020 kg	60.477 kg	12.215 kg	20.753 kg	35.828 kg	31.369 kg
Poland	21.157 kg	20.082 kg	5.664 kg	No Report	422.179 kg	401.225 kg
Portugal	624.949 kg	822.560 kg	3075.374 kg	5574.658 kg	3140.103 kg	3021.257 kg
Slovakia	1.642 kg	2.508 kg	0.166 kg	No Report	0.069 kg	0.697 kg
Slovenia	3.522 kg	1.580 kg	0.098 kg	1.080 kg	55.380 kg	1.610 kg
Spain	11687.623 kg	18110.883 kg	6164.770 kg	33681.091 kg	17617.749 kg	49279.342 kg
Sweden	18.505 kg	413.945 kg 1.944 lt. 430 u.	52.257 kg	47.388 kg	41.000 kg	42.071 kg
Switzerland	251.616 kg	288.013 kg	207.476 kg	168.637 kg	185.940 kg	188.617 kg
United Kingdom	2985.323 kg [(4]	2972.700 kg [NCIS]	3970.220 kg	2897.441 kg	3635.000 kg	3635.000 kg [(5]
Sub-Total	31977.620 kg 1412 u.	43982.250 kg 1.944 lt. 591 u.	27747.060 kg 2368 u.	59177.540 kg 621 u.	46712.430 kg 646 u.	84081.220 kg 603 u.
Total region	33626.690 kg 1412 u.	44068.020 kg 1.944 lt. 591 u.	28924.700 kg 2368 u.	59288.580 kg 621 u.	46823.210 kg 646 u.	84517.140 kg 603 u.

Source: Annual Report Questionnaire if not otherwise indicated

SEIZURES, 1998 - 2003
Cocaine (base and salts)

Region/country or territory	1998	1999	2000	2001	2002	2003
OCEANIA						
Oceania						
Australia	103.162 kg Govt. (6	70.725 kg	1437.869 kg	1151.255 kg	105.874 kg	288.164 kg [7]
Fiji	No Report	No Report	0.347 kg ICPO	2.000 kg ICPO	No Report	No Report
New Zealand	0.015 kg	0.454 kg	0.249 kg	0.008 kg	0.267 kg	7.061 kg
Sub-Total	103.177 kg	71.179 kg	1438.465 kg	1153.263 kg	106.141 kg	295.225 kg
Total region	103.177 kg	71.179 kg	1438.465 kg	1153.263 kg	106.141 kg	295.225 kg
TOTAL	394830.100 kg	367898.400 kg	342434.700 kg	365663.100 kg	371509.400 kg	495403.100 kg
	0.007 lt.	2.351 lt.	1519.542 lt.	110654 u.	222254 u.	103824 u.
	133393 u.	74395 u.	73781 u.			

1) Small quantity. 2) Includes crack. 3) Due to unavailability of 2001 data, year 2000 data were used for analysis purposes. 4) Included in cannabis seeds. 5) Due to unavailability of 2003 data, year 2002 data were used for analysis purposes. 6) Provisional figures. 7) Sum of seizures reported by national, State & Territory law enforcement agencies

Source: Annual Report Questionnaire if not otherwise indicated

SEIZURES, 1998 - 2003
Coca leaf

Region/country or territory	1998	1999	2000	2001	2002	2003
AMERICAS						
North America						
Canada	No Report	0.316 kg	0.056 kg	0.050 kg	3.405 kg	6.015 kg
United States	No Report	58.436 kg	45.608 kg [1] 2.181 lt.	0.600 kg	No Report	No Report
Sub-Total		58.752 kg	45.664 kg 2.181 lt.	0.650 kg	3.405 kg	6.015 kg
South America						
Argentina	47847.961 kg	68492.192 kg	95901.272 kg	91352.081 kg	45570.390 kg	46243.113 kg
Bolivia	108568.550 Govt kg	63145.190 kg Govt	58996.100 kg Govt	79620.810 kg Govt	101769.420 Govt kg	152315.340 Govt kg
Brazil	No Report	No Report	0.018 kg ICPO	No Report	No Report	No Report
Chile	No Report	No Report	No Report	No Report	0.249 kg ICPO	No Report
Colombia	340564.000 kg	306782.000 Govt kg	897911.000 kg	583.165 kg	638000.000 Govt kg	688691.000 kg
Ecuador	0.050 kg	5000 u.	No Report	No Report	No Report	No Report
Peru	132209.875 kg	34792.500 kg	48609.597 kg	29324.293 kg	39921.738 kg	51114.752 kg
Uruguay	No Report	No Report	No Report	No Report	0.646 kg	0.215 kg
Venezuela	No Report	No Report	No Report	180.000 kg	No Report	No Report
Sub-Total	629190.400 kg	473211.900 kg 5000 u.	1101418.000 kg	201060.400 kg	825262.400 kg	938364.400 kg
Total region	629190.400 kg	473270.600 kg 5000 u.	1101464.000 kg 2.181 lt.	201061.000 kg	825265.800 kg	938370.400 kg
ASIA						
Central Asia and Transcaucasian countries						
Armenia	0.163 kg	No Report	No Report	No Report	No Report	No Report
Sub-Total	0.163 kg					
Total region	0.163 kg					
EUROPE						
Southeast Europe						
Serbia and Montenegro	No Report	No Report	No Report	No Report	1.226 kg	No Report
Sub-Total					1.226 kg	
West & Central Europe						
Belgium	No Report	No Report	No Report	No Report	No Report	1.256 kg
Denmark	No Report	No Report	0.043 kg	0.000 kg	No Report	No Report
France	No Report	11.133 kg	No Report	No Report	0.203 kg	No Report
Hungary	No Report	No Report	No Report	1.049 kg	0.632 kg	No Report
Italy	0.049 kg	0.109 kg ICPO	0.445 kg	0.055 kg	2.255 kg	0.280 kg 9 u.
Norway	0.001 kg	3.420 kg	No Report	No Report	0.030 kg	0.082 kg
Poland	No Report	No Report	No Report	45.298 kg	No Report	No Report

Source: Annual Report Questionnaire if not otherwise indicated

SEIZURES, 1998 - 2003
Coca leaf

Region/country or territory	1998	1999	2000	2001	2002	2003
EUROPE						
West & Central Europe						
Portugal	0.020 kg	No Report	No Report	No Report	1 u.	No Report
Sweden	No Report	No Report	0.268 kg	No Report	No Report	No Report
Sub-Total	0.070 kg	14.662 kg	0.756 kg	46.402 kg	3.120 kg 1 u.	1.618 kg 9 u.
Total region	0.070 kg	14.662 kg	0.756 kg	46.402 kg	4.346 kg 1 u.	1.618 kg 9 u.
OCEANIA						
Oceania						
Australia	No Report	No Report	No Report	0.019 kg	10.443 kg	0.055 kg[2]
New Zealand	0.019 kg	0.011 kg	No Report	4.253 kg	0.013 kg	0.031 lt.
Sub-Total	0.019 kg	0.011 kg		4.272 kg	10.456 kg	0.055 kg 0.031 lt.
Total region	0.019 kg	0.011 kg		4.272 kg	10.456 kg	0.055 kg 0.031 lt.
TOTAL	629190.700 kg	473285.300 kg 5000 u.	1101464.000 kg 2.181 lt.	201111.700 kg	825280.600 kg 1 u.	938372.100 kg 0.031 lt. 9 u.

1) Includes cocaine other 2) Sum of seizures reported by national, State & Territory law enforcement agencies

Source: Annual Report Questionnaire if not otherwise indicated

6.3. Cannabis: Seizures 1998-2003

	SEIZURES, 1998 - 2003					
	Cannabis herb					
Region/country or territory	**1998**	**1999**	**2000**	**2001**	**2002**	**2003**
AFRICA						
East Africa						
Burundi	No Report	45.847 kg [ICPO]	No Report	No Report	No Report	No Report
Eritrea	No Report	No Report	No Report	No Report	No Report	20.500 kg
Ethiopia	331.561 kg	807.364 kg	181.821 kg	152.064 kg	155.568 kg	No Report
Kenya	2375.240 kg	8762.033 kg	5649.000 kg	383253.486 [Govt (1] kg	77737.711 kg	8371.270 kg
Madagascar	No Report	1265.332 kg [ICPO]	No Report	No Report	No Report	No Report
Mauritius	3.090 kg	5.592 kg	21.931 kg	66.985 kg	43.492 kg	45.261 kg
Rwanda	No Report	No Report	No Report	No Report	6215.000 kg	No Report
Seychelles	2.056 kg [ICPO]	1.005 kg	22.014 kg	0.067 kg [ICPO]	1.042 kg	No Report
Somalia	No Report	No Report	No Report	No Report	1000.000 kg	No Report
Uganda	5530.000 kg	5530.000 kg [ICPO]	6100.000 kg	50000.000 kg	100.000 kg	25000.500 kg
United Republic of Tanzania	4617.862 kg	6021.273 kg	24293.304 kg [ICPO]	249639.026 [Govt] kg	90410.857 kg [ICPO]	733222.063 kg
Sub-Total	12859.810 kg	22438.450 kg	36268.070 kg	683111.600 kg	175663.700 kg	766659.600 kg
North Africa						
Algeria	58.300 kg [ICPO]	No Report	No Report	No Report	No Report	1.797 kg
Egypt	31078.387 kg	22588.505 kg	30397.591 kg	50037.000 kg	No Report	No Report
Morocco	37160.879 kg	46136.058 kg [Govt]	83719.676 kg [Govt]	68168.624 kg [Govt]	88529.162 kg [Govt]	69058.207 kg
Sudan	No Report	No Report	1887.805 kg	No Report	No Report	No Report
Tunisia	2.000 kg	No Report	No Report	No Report	No Report	No Report
Sub-Total	68299.560 kg	68724.560 kg	116005.100 kg	118205.600 kg	88529.160 kg	69060.010 kg
Southern Africa						
Angola	1.975 kg [ICPO]	2829.167 kg	4733.667 kg [ICPO]	621.278 kg [ICPO]	No Report	No Report
Botswana	1186.000 kg [ICPO]	1229.000 kg [ICPO]	No Report	No Report	1000.000 kg [ICPO]	No Report
Lesotho	21583.824 kg [ICPO]	7243.697 kg [ICPO]	No Report	No Report	6513.350 kg [ICPO]	No Report
Malawi	5201.971 kg	27141.583 kg	312471.845 kg	8663.694 kg	7131.989 kg	8165.463 kg
Mozambique	462.000 kg [ICPO]	894.406 kg [ICPO]	1700.562 kg [ICPO]	6721.550 kg [ICPO]	5798.000 kg [ICPO]	5089.474 kg [HNLF]
Namibia	361.395 kg	282.363 kg	302.981 kg	5386.189 kg	949.448 kg [ICPO]	619.749 kg
South Africa	197116.297 kg	289943.561 kg [ICPO]	717701.918 kg	123964.058 kg	104977.750 kg	32928.219 kg
Swaziland	5943.293 kg	33283.707 kg	14946.718 kg	15064.342 kg	10196.081 kg	8463.019 kg
Zambia	3256.366 kg [Govt]	7000.653 kg	7318.199 kg	14.600 kg [Govt]	1605.194 kg	94440.000 kg
Zimbabwe	6117.086 kg	1816.001 kg	3045.908 kg	1530.254 kg	3722.538 kg	1353.049 kg
Sub-Total	241230.200 kg	371664.200 kg	1062222.000 kg	161966.000 kg	141894.300 kg	151059.000 kg
West and Central Africa						
Benin	611.077 kg [Govt]	25.138 kg [Govt]	971.781 kg [F.O]	809.408 kg [ICPO]	2126.210 kg [ICPO]	No Report
Burkina Faso	No Report	No Report	No Report	2404.713 kg	No Report	1419.592 kg
Cameroon	112.875 kg	1154.560 kg	No Report	No Report	443.245 kg 180 u.	No Report
Central African Republic	57.551 kg [ICPO]	No Report	No Report	No Report	6.650 kg [Govt]	No Report

Source: Annual Report Questionnaire if not otherwise indicated

SEIZURES, 1998 - 2003
Cannabis herb

Region/country or territory	1998	1999	2000	2001	2002	2003
AFRICA						
West and Central Africa						
Chad	No Report	686.000 kg [ICPO]	378.000 kg	No Report	No Report	No Report
Congo	No Report	1.000 kg	259.000 kg	222.000 kg	1147.830 kg	282.500 kg
Côte d'Ivoire	898.960 kg	1650.189 kg	1236.644 kg [ICPO]	1876.658 kg	4397.968 kg	No Report
Equatorial Guinea	24.000 kg 6 u.	26.000 kg 46 u.	No Report	No Report	No Report	No Report
Gabon	114.336 kg [ICPO]	45.648 kg [ICPO]	No Report	No Report	No Report	No Report
Gambia	376.145 kg [ICPO]	No Report	229.444 kg [Govt]	700.000 kg	638.959 kg [ICPO]	428.094 kg [Govt]
Ghana	4375.098 kg	4080.049 kg	No Report	No Report	5418.140 kg	9178.980 kg
Guinea	No Report	No Report	640.345 kg [ICPO]	No Report	No Report	2910.000 kg
Guinea-Bissau	No Report	No Report	No Report	367.000 kg	No Report	No Report
Mauritania	17.200 kg [Govt]	No Report	No Report	No Report	No Report	42.237 kg [F.O]
Niger	682.173 kg [ICPO]	1356.162 kg [ICPO]	No Report	No Report	No Report	No Report
Nigeria	16170.500 kg [Govt.]	17691.014 kg	272260.020 kg	317950.204 kg	506846.009 kg	535241.050 kg
Saint Helena	0.183 kg	No Report	0.075 kg		No Report	1.375 kg
Sao Tome and Principe	No Report	No Report	No Report	15.000 kg	No Report	No Report
Senegal	69652.000 kg [F.O.]	7165.830 kg [ICPO]	No Report	No Report	4888.080 kg [ICPO]	No Report
Togo	No Report	569.477 kg [HNLF]	429.056 kg	655.247 kg	234.641 kg	794.429 kg
Sub-Total	93092.090 kg 6 u.	34451.070 kg 46 u.	276404.400 kg	325000.200 kg	526147.700 kg 180 u.	550298.300 kg
Total region	415481.700 kg 6 u.	497278.200 kg 46 u.	1490899.000 kg	1288283.000 kg	932234.900 kg 180 u.	1537077.000 kg
AMERICAS						
Caribbean						
Anguilla	5.037 kg	8.000 kg [F.O]	No Report	1.000 kg [F.O]	No Report	No Report
Antigua and Barbuda	105.000 kg [F.O]	94.000 kg [F.O]	67.000 kg [F.O]	662.000 kg [F.O]	No Report	339.000 kg [INCSR]
Aruba	No Report	142.000 kg [F.O]	12.000 kg [F.O]	1159.000 kg [F.O]	434.247 kg [ICPO]	No Report
Bahamas	2591.065 kg	3610.000 kg [F.O]	4093.000 kg	4174.000 kg 9203 u.	11515.000 kg	6063.624 kg
Barbados	1650.000 kg [CICAD]	333.580 kg [HONLC]	2948.000 kg [F.O]	5748.925 kg [ICPO]	No Report	3000.000 kg [INCSR]
Bermuda	91.800 kg	87.067 kg	136.579 kg	32.000 kg [F.O]	360.000 kg	38.900 kg [PROJ.S]
British Virgin Islands	84.000 kg [F.O]	354.000 kg [F.O]	26.000 kg [F.O]	151.950 kg 80 u.	No Report	26.200 kg [PROJ.S]
Cayman Islands	4063.009 kg 650 u.	5100.371 kg	6621.000 kg	11818.000 kg	6681.000 kg	9027.090 kg
Cuba	4610.000 kg [F.O]	5559.000 kg [F.O]	8581.400 kg [HONL]	6121.000 kg [F.O]	6023.428 kg [ICPO]	5159.900 kg [HONL]
Dominica	361.000 kg [F.O]	192.000 kg [F.O]	468.000 kg [CICAD]	521.000 kg [F.O]	No Report	44.000 kg [INCSR]
Dominican Republic	110.298 kg	184.333 kg	1526.000 kg [CICAD]	3815.900 kg	1749.000 kg [HONLC]	534.945 kg
French Guiana	127.000 kg [F.O]	134.000 kg [F.O]	58.000 kg [F.O]	No Report	No Report	89.000 kg [PROJ.S]

Source: Annual Report Questionnaire if not otherwise indicated

287

SEIZURES, 1998 - 2003

Cannabis herb

Region/country or territory	1998	1999	2000	2001	2002	2003
AMERICAS						
Caribbean						
Grenada	84.000 kg	219.000 kg [F.O]	103.000 kg [INCSR]	133.690 kg	379.280 kg [ICPO] 547 u.	115.000 kg [CICAD]
Guadeloupe	8860.000 kg [F.O]	515.000 kg [F.O]	1017.000 kg [F.O]	516.000 kg [F.O]	No Report	No Report
Haiti	9255.000 kg [F.O]	71.030 kg	401.000 kg [F.O]	1705.000 kg [F.O]	149.050 kg	31.000 kg [CICAD] 70 u.
Jamaica	35911.000 kg [F.O]	56226.940 kg [ICPO]	55870.000 kg [F.O]	74044.000 kg	27137.000 kg [ICPO]	36600.000 kg [INCSR]
Martinique	136.000 kg [F.O]	199.000 kg [F.O]	749.000 kg [F.O]	No Report	No Report	No Report
Montserrat	No Report	2677.000 kg [F.O]	0.497 kg	No Report	0.373 kg	No Report
Netherlands Antilles	No Report	541.000 kg [F.O]	39.782 kg [ICPO]	3772.000 kg [F.O]	5691.000 kg [ICPO]	883.000 kg [PROJ.S]
Puerto Rico	1285.000 kg [F.O]	12605.000 kg [F.O]	1982.000 kg [F.O]	24.000 kg [F.O]	49536.000 kg [ICPO] 1177 u.	No Report
Saint Kitts and Nevis	31.000 kg [F.O]	14124.000 kg [F.O]	119.000 kg [INCSR]	330.000 kg [F.O]	No Report	17000.000 kg [INCSR]
Saint Lucia	363.663 kg	267.000 kg [CICAD]	1803.610 kg	753.000 kg [F.O]	No Report	583.000 kg [INCSR]
Saint Vincent and the Grenadines	1321.000 kg [F.O]	7180.000 kg [F.O]	1709.000 kg [INCSR]	1962.000 kg [F.O]	No Report	1700.000 kg [INCSR]
Trinidad and Tobago	3483.545 kg	8287.000 kg [CICAD]	1546.000 kg [F.O]	2393.950 kg	1135.404 kg	2180.003 kg
Turks and Caicos Islands	8.000 kg	68.500 kg	27.000 kg [F.O]	24.000 kg [F.O]	12.802 kg	57.767 kg
United States Virgin Islands	No Report	48.123 kg [ICPO]	No Report	No Report	No Report	No Report
Sub-Total	74536.420 kg 650 u.	118826.900 kg	89903.870 kg	119862.400 kg 9283 u.	110803.600 kg 1724 u.	83472.420 kg 70 u.
Central America						
Belize	1557.000 kg [F.O]	392.000 kg [F.O]	249.000 kg [F.O]	269.909 kg	392.468 kg [ICPO]	55.000 kg [INCSR]
Costa Rica	469.340 kg	1693.550 kg	1140.650 kg	2887.000 kg [Govt]	728.760 kg [Govt]	1779.270 kg
El Salvador	291.202 kg [ICPO]	604.581 kg	455.700 kg [ICPO]	463.917 kg	666.059 kg	637.400 kg
Guatemala	193.970 kg	814.212 kg	158.450 kg	584.550 kg	1098.310 kg	1853.173 kg
Honduras	1293.000 kg [CICAD]	1583.000 kg [CICAD]	1112.000 kg [CICAD]	1231.000 kg [HONL]	416.142 kg 1127 u.	1472.710 kg
Nicaragua	613.027 kg	754.000 kg [CICAD]	737.000 kg [CICAD]	586.560 kg [ICPO]	631.028 kg	381.100 kg [HONL]
Panama	16536.006 kg	3477.268 kg	3657.498 kg	1639.000 kg	1842.000 kg [HONLC]	1478.000 kg [INCSR]
Sub-Total	20953.540 kg	9318.610 kg	7510.298 kg	7661.936 kg	5774.767 kg 1127 u.	7656.653 kg
North America						
Canada	27299.990 kg 8 u.	44541.000 kg 52 u.	70221.600 kg 738 u.	6833.524 kg 18 u.	13278.116 kg	9888.928 kg
Mexico	1062143.980 kg	1471959.958 kg	2050402.078 kg	1839357.121 kg [Govt]	1633326.209 kg	2160309.136 kg
United States	799000.875 kg [Govt.]	1175373.000 kg	218256.453 kg	682574.100 kg	1110525.400 kg	1224429.600 kg
Sub-Total	1888445.000 kg 8 u.	2691874.000 kg 52 u.	2338880.000 kg 738 u.	2528765.000 kg 18 u.	2757130.000 kg	3394628.000 kg

Source: Annual Report Questionnaire if not otherwise indicated

SEIZURES, 1998 - 2003
Cannabis herb

Region/country or territory	1998	1999	2000	2001	2002	2003
AMERICAS						
South America						
Argentina	10920.230 kg	18301.339 kg	25538.966 kg	33052.239 kg	44823.951 kg	58340.491 kg
Bolivia	320.000 kg Govt	2160.000 kg Govt	3745.000 kg Govt	7055.000 kg Govt	8754.000 kg Govt	8509.000 kg Govt
Brazil	28982.492 kg	69171.506 kg	159073.232 kg	146279.636 kg Govt	194080.000 F.O kg	166254.292 kg
Chile	2238.325 kg	2105.000 kg CICAD	3277.341 kg (2	2418.496 kg	8832.672 kg	4620.464 kg
Colombia	70025.000 kg	69087.000 kg Govt	75173.000 kg Govt	86610.000 kg	76998.000 kg	134939.000 kg
Ecuador	17734.700 kg Govt	2977.000 kg Govt	18263.000 kg Govt	3079.000 kg Govt	1746.000 kg Govt	2673.400 kg Govt
Guyana	51.000 kg F.O	3528.000 kg F.O	4387.000 kg F.O	243.000 kg ICPO	No Report	380.336 kg
Paraguay	80077.914 kg	199282.319 kg	51081.000 kg CICAD	94000.000 kg HONL	48140.946 kg	76975.463 kg
Peru	19880.324 kg	4055.732 kg	1635.419 kg	2601.446 kg	2888.717 kg	19275.553 kg
Suriname	104.754 kg	177.000 kg CICAD	107.000 kg INCSR	46.000 kg	205.000 kg	119.000 kg INCSR
Uruguay	424.778 kg	493.783 kg	805.843 kg	1115.222 kg ICPO	899.704 kg	620.544 kg
Venezuela	4500.000 kg CICAD	13055.778 kg	14999.634 kg	14431.800 kg	20919.610 kg	9588.900 kg
Sub-Total	235259.500 kg	384394.400 kg	358086.400 kg	390931.800 kg	408288.600 kg	482296.500 kg
Total region	2219195.000 kg 658 u.	3204414.000 kg 52 u.	2794381.000 kg 738 u.	3047221.000 kg 9301 u.	3281997.000 kg 2851 u.	3968053.000 kg 70 u.
ASIA						
Central Asia and Transcaucasian countries						
Armenia	0.888 kg	46.675 kg Govt.	53.798 kg	14.081 kg	76.084 kg	6.594 kg
Azerbaijan	40.287 kg	55.395 kg	2773.104 kg ICPO	61.500 kg	2212.550 kg	No Report
Georgia	No Report	31972.800 kg ICPO	No Report	32397.000 kg ICPO	No Report	42.400 kg
Kazakhstan	716.236 kg	10481.505 kg	No Report	11789.000 kg F.O	17072.230 kg F.O	18829.000 kg F.O
Kyrgyzstan	1569.243 kg F.O	1716.475 kg (3	3748.220 kg (4	2250.663 kg (4	2525.915 kg	3398.620 kg
Tajikistan	323.331 kg F.O	No Report	No Report	750.486 kg	998.956 kg	1424.920 kg
Uzbekistan	358.558 kg	288.689 kg	No Report	No Report	417.900 kg	516.800 kg
Sub-Total	3008.543 kg	44561.540 kg	6575.122 kg	47262.730 kg	23303.630 kg	24218.330 kg
East and South-East Asia						
Brunei Darussalam	3.288 kg	0.364 kg	0.054 kg	0.007 kg	1.132 kg	0.451 kg
China	5079.000 kg	No Report	4493.000 kg Govt	751.000 kg Govt	1300.000 kg Govt	703.900 kg
Hong Kong Special Administrative Region of China	585.000 kg Govt	24.727 kg	226.007 kg	No Report	665.910 kg	233.030 kg
Indonesia	1071.862 kg	3741.068 kg	6332.908 kg	27390.075 kg	61291.436 kg	24204.621 kg
Japan	120.884 kg	565.904 kg	310.246 kg	1070.248 kg	256.500 kg 24 u.	558.200 kg 29 u.
Lao People's Democratic Republic	410.000 kg INCSR	2187.000 kg HNLP	1860.000 kg INCSR	1702.000 kg Govt	1932.200 kg	4577.900 kg
Macao Special Administrative Region of China	1.661 kg ICPO	3.000 kg INCB	16.381 kg	0.519 kg	0.124 kg	0.943 kg

Source: Annual Report Questionnaire if not otherwise indicated

289

SEIZURES, 1998 - 2003
Cannabis herb

Region/country or territory	1998	1999	2000	2001	2002	2003
ASIA						
East and South-East Asia						
Malaysia	1781.010 kg	2064.498 kg	1885.450 kg	1570.526 kg [ICPO]	1734.133 kg [ICPO]	2408.380 kg
Mongolia	No Report	5.000 kg [ICPO]	5.800 kg [ICPO]	No Report	No Report	0.600 kg
Myanmar	380.970 kg	274.282 kg	601.508 kg	284.387 kg	281.988 kg	85.201 kg
Philippines	2057.974 kg [Govt (5]	1187.870 kg	1429.474 kg [Govt (5]	706.418 kg [Govt (5]	1361.507 kg	236.091 kg
Republic of Korea	32.751 kg	39.442 kg	39.371 kg [ICPO]	283.869 kg	194.795 kg [ICPO]	37.274 kg
Singapore	21.831 kg [(3]	7.432 kg [(3]	23.903 kg	8.843 kg	2.637 kg [ICPO]	2.065 kg
Thailand	5581.840 kg	14706.198 kg	10320.000 kg [HNLP]	10921.000 kg [F.O]	12095.000 kg [F.O]	13650.000 kg [Govt.]
Viet Nam	379.000 kg [F.O]	400.000 kg [F.O]	2200.000 kg [F.O]	1289.005 kg	243.000 kg [F.O]	750.000 kg
Sub-Total	17507.070 kg	25206.790 kg	29744.100 kg	45977.890 kg	81360.370 kg 24 u.	47448.660 kg 29 u.
Near and Middle East /South-West Asia						
Bahrain	0.041 kg [ICPO]	0.042 kg [ICPO]	7.417 kg [ICPO]	No Report	0.008 kg	No Report
Iran (Islamic Republic of)	No Report	No Report	1495.000 kg [ICPO]	No Report	No Report	No Report
Iraq	No Report	270.000 kg [INCB]	No Report	No Report	No Report	No Report
Israel	3581.000 kg	3400.000 kg [ICPO]	9855.000 kg	11685.000 kg	12382.000 kg	18425.000 kg
Jordan	No Report	No Report	No Report	55.034 kg	1.440 kg	No Report
Kuwait	0.246 kg	[ICPO]	3.099 kg [ICPO]	No Report	715.060 kg [ICPO]	No Report
Lebanon	No Report	1.379 kg	0.017 kg	0.011 kg	0.091 kg	0.464 kg
Oman	No Report	0.269 kg	6823.000 kg [ICPO]	0.001 kg	0.306 kg	No Report
Pakistan	No Report	No Report	1223.205 kg [ICPO]	No Report	68346.000 kg [F.O]	No Report
Qatar	146.250 kg [ICPO]	3.297 kg [ICPO]	0.300 kg [ICPO]	No Report	0.003 kg	No Report
Saudi Arabia	No Report	No Report	No Report	No Report	5591.000 kg [ICPO]	663.000 kg [ICPO]
United Arab Emirates	0.095 kg	0.341 kg	No Report	2.566 kg	0.425 kg	1.350 kg
Yemen	11.350 kg [ICPO]	No Report	24.990 kg [ICPO]	No Report	No Report	No Report
Sub-Total	3738.982 kg	3675.328 kg	19432.030 kg	11742.610 kg	87036.330 kg	19089.810 kg
South Asia						
Bangladesh	3404.466 kg [Govt]	3475.326 kg [Govt]	2593.688 kg [Govt]	2392.130 kg [Govt]	1555.081 kg [Govt]	2392.130 kg [Govt]
India	68221.000 kg	38610.000 kg	100056.000 kg	75943.000 kg [Govt (6]	93477.000 kg [Govt]	79483.000 kg
Maldives	0.001 kg	0.022 kg	No Report	0.004 kg	0.072 kg [ICPO]	No Report
Nepal	6409.669 kg	4064.650 kg	8025.308 kg [ICPO]	No Report	850.031 kg	No Report
Sri Lanka	3450.686 kg	4062.421 kg	5026.336 kg	113238.733 kg	555.135 kg [ICPO]	No Report
Sub-Total	81485.830 kg	50212.420 kg	115701.300 kg	191573.900 kg	96437.310 kg	81875.130 kg
Total region	105740.400 kg	123656.100 kg	171452.600 kg	296557.100 kg	288137.600 kg 24 u.	172631.900 kg 29 u.
EUROPE						
East Europe						
Belarus	117.000 kg [Govt]	425.000 kg	124.000 kg	103.000 kg [ICPO]	89.000 kg	231.000 kg [Govt]

Source: Annual Report Questionnaire if not otherwise indicated

SEIZURES, 1998 - 2003
Cannabis herb

Region/country or territory	1998	1999	2000	2001	2002	2003
EUROPE						
East Europe						
Republic of Moldova	No Report	416.000 kg [ICPO]	No Report	No Report	No Report	No Report
Russian Federation	23510.650 kg	33801.919 kg	23313.000 kg [F.O]	43877.267 kg	29847.879 kg [ICPO]	41844.638 kg
Ukraine	No Report	4045.000 kg [ICPO. (6]	11609.932 kg [ICPO]	8195.320 kg	80.000 kg	0.107 kg
Sub-Total	23627.650 kg	38687.920 kg	35046.930 kg	52175.590 kg	30016.880 kg	42075.740 kg
Southeast Europe						
Albania	No Report	4395.156 kg [ICPO]	6604.000 kg [Govt]	6915.000 kg [Govt]	13717.899 kg	7760.170 kg
Bosnia and Herzegovina	53.815 kg [NAPOL]	59.144 kg [ICPO]	127.982 kg [NAPOL]	467.585 kg [ICPO]	919.545 kg [ICPO]	No Report
Bulgaria	1527.562 kg	29365.000 kg	295.947 kg	183.061 kg	1308.970 kg	689.051 kg
Croatia	20342.877 kg	200.898 kg	797.501 kg	737.911 kg	608.070 kg	435.037 kg
Romania	7.478 kg	4.530 kg [ICPO]	321.000 kg [ICPO]	155.000 kg	14880.000 kg [Govt]	70.030 kg
Serbia and Montenegro	No Report	No Report	No Report	1230.224 kg	1729.501 kg	1464.955 kg
The former Yugoslav Republic of Macedonia	1136.752 kg	698.098 kg [NAPOL]	1333.399 kg [NAPOL]	99.115 kg [Govt]	29.234 kg	180.681 kg
Turkey	9295.822 kg [Govt (3]	9009.040 kg [Govt]	28637.130 kg [Govt (5]	10096.848 kg [Govt (5]	5462.376 kg [Govt]	6959.763 kg
Sub-Total	32364.310 kg	43731.870 kg	38116.960 kg	19884.740 kg	38655.590 kg	17559.690 kg
West & Central Europe						
Andorra	0.116 kg [ICPO]	0.046 kg	0.237 kg [ICPO]	0.200 kg	0.111 kg	No Report
Austria	1211.031 kg	341.402 kg	1562.828 kg	282.255 kg	450.289 kg	553.263 kg
Belgium	2463.270 kg	2914.749 kg	8206.746 kg	8206.746 kg [UNODC (7]	23920.000 kg	13194.778 kg
Cyprus	128.905 kg	30.108 kg	28.875 kg	37.537 kg	9.169 kg	55.545 kg
Czech Republic	5.500 kg	111.200 kg	16.648 kg	190.450 kg	100.728 kg	77.817 kg
Denmark	No Report	52.830 kg	739.819 kg 14032 u.	762.262 kg	50.671 kg	No Report
Estonia	4.789 kg 358 u.	1.468 kg 491 u.	4.190 kg 673 u.	0.903 kg	1.747 kg	1.968 kg
Finland	8.014 kg	18.167 kg	13.825 kg	16.100 kg	32.000 kg	45.000 kg
France	3521.790 kg	3382.205 kg	4865.558 kg	3922.370 kg	6146.700 kg	3994.627 kg
Germany, Federal Republic of	14897.189 kg	15021.800 kg	5870.900 kg	2078.703 kg	6130.199 kg	2582.342 kg
Greece	17510.434 kg	12038.938 kg 10 u.	14908.448 kg	11653.193 kg	6021.447 kg	7153.183 kg
Hungary	42.930 kg	65.725 kg	51.000 kg	131.030 kg	114.755 kg	179.023 kg
Iceland	No Report	0.503 kg	5.092 kg	0.030 kg	1.439 kg	3.362 kg
Ireland	38.909 kg	68.290 kg	207.954 kg	11590.057 kg	6105.710 kg	199.706 kg
Italy	38785.988 kg 1192 u.	21248.982 kg [ICPO]	26071.488 kg 2068 u.	36622.637 kg 967 u.	16397.838 kg 823 u.	15302.848 kg 453 u.
Latvia	2.480 kg	231.200 kg	6.780 kg	193.580 kg	No Report	6.020 kg
Liechtenstein	No Report	No Report	0.972 kg [(3]	422.470 kg	1.442 kg	422.000 kg
Lithuania	30.357 kg	25.667 kg	14.428 kg	15.540 kg	5.300 kg	29.009 kg
Luxembourg	4.956 kg	3.932 kg	8.383 kg [ICPO]	No Report	18.196 kg [ICPO]	15.561 kg

Source: Annual Report Questionnaire if not otherwise indicated

SEIZURES, 1998 - 2003
Cannabis herb

Region/country or territory	1998	1999	2000	2001	2002	2003
EUROPE						
West & Central Europe						
Malta	0.069 kg	0.161 kg	No Report	0.022 kg	0.846 kg [ICPO]	24.533 kg
Monaco	0.032 kg	0.013 kg [ICPO]	0.024 kg [ICPO]	No Report	0.093 kg	0.035 kg
Netherlands	55463.000 kg [Govt]	49115.000 kg [Govt]	10330.000 kg [Govt]	21139.000 kg	42675.000 kg	8246.000 kg
Norway	88.172 kg	16.471 kg	20.905 kg	35.384 kg	105.654 kg	48.247 kg
Poland	62.146 kg	847.901 kg	139.000 kg	74.306 kg	495.700 kg	198.152 kg
Portugal	7.115 kg	65.766 kg	223.212 kg	234.533 kg	361.026 kg	264.821 kg
Slovakia	12539.934 kg	156.000 kg	168.196 kg	No Report	151.500 kg	31.971 kg
Slovenia	2772.604 kg	249.156 kg	3413.025 kg	177.880 kg	1099.940 kg	219.570 kg [HONEU]
Spain	412.866 kg	761.342 kg	353.292 kg	532.420 kg	380.733 kg	397.713 kg
Sweden	98.431 kg	28.228 kg 4 u.	45.597 kg	13.981 kg	76.000 kg	37.991 kg
Switzerland	13163.982 kg	7800.229 kg	18313.602 kg	11106.537 kg	21893.240 kg	13032.240 kg
United Kingdom	21660.666 kg	15410.048 kg [ICPO] 20 u.	25473.979 kg	26740.984 kg	34994.000 kg	34994.000 kg [(8]
Sub-Total	184925.700 kg 1550 u.	130007.500 kg 525 u.	121065.000 kg 16773 u.	136181.100 kg 967 u.	167741.500 kg 823 u.	101311.300 kg 453 u.
Total region	240917.600 kg 1550 u.	212427.300 kg 525 u.	194228.900 kg 16773 u.	208241.400 kg 967 u.	236414.000 kg 823 u.	160946.800 kg 453 u.
OCEANIA						
Oceania						
Australia	15996.628 kg [Govt. (6]	3340.917 kg [Govt. (6]	4365.089 kg [Govt. (9]	6918.357 kg	5310.996 kg [(10]	6020.483 kg [(11]
Fiji	No Report	45.618 kg [ICPO]	106.200 kg [ICPO]	316.750 kg [ICPO]	14.414 kg [ICPO]	No Report
New Caledonia	No Report	132.000 kg [INCB]	No Report	No Report	No Report	No Report
New Zealand	389.182 kg [(12]	323.649 kg	332.396 kg	1847.000 kg	593.078 kg	611.212 kg
Sub-Total	16385.810 kg	3842.184 kg	4803.685 kg	9082.107 kg	5918.488 kg	6631.695 kg
Total region	16385.810 kg	3842.184 kg	4803.685 kg	9082.107 kg	5918.488 kg	6631.695 kg
TOTAL	2997720.000 kg 2214 u.	4041618.000 kg 623 u.	4655765.000 kg 17511 u.	4849385.000 kg 10268 u.	4744702.000 kg 3878 u.	5845341.000 kg 552 u.

1) Includes plants,resin & seeds 2) No. of seizures include seizures of cannabis plant 3) Including cannabis resin. 4) Including cannabis resin and plants 5) Including cannabis resin 6) Provisional figures. 7) Due to unavailability of 2001 data, year 2000 data were used for analysis purposes. 8) Due to unavailability of 2003 data, year 2002 data were used for analysis purposes. 9) Fiscal year 10) Includes 1855.237kg of Cannabis unspecified 11) Sum of seizures reported by national, State & Territory law enforcement agencies 12) Including cannabis resin, liquid cannabis.

Source: Annual Report Questionnaire if not otherwise indicated

SEIZURES, 1998 - 2003
Cannabis resin

Region/country or territory	1998	1999	2000	2001	2002	2003
AFRICA						
East Africa						
Djibouti	No Report	No Report	No Report	No Report	No Report	250.000 kg
Ethiopia	No Report	No Report	No Report	No Report	No Report	642.429 kg
Kenya	No Report	3.200 kg [ICPO]	6356.000 kg	21.000 kg [ICPO]	17.172 kg	No Report
Madagascar	No Report	No Report	No Report	No Report	No Report	6.000 kg
Mauritius	0.130 kg	(1	0.007 kg	0.040 kg	0.027 kg	0.007 kg
Seychelles	1.073 kg [Govt.]	72.883 kg	32.962 kg	17.934 kg [ICPO]	2.986 kg	No Report
Uganda	25.000 kg	8.797 kg	No Report	No Report	No Report	No Report
United Republic of Tanzania	42.162 kg	No Report	15.000 kg [ICPO]	12.500 kg [Govt]	1865.614 kg [ICPO]	No Report
Sub-Total	68.365 kg	84.880 kg	6403.969 kg	51.474 kg	1885.799 kg	898.436 kg
North Africa						
Algeria	1217.179 kg [ICPO]	4080.662 kg	1694.127 kg [ICPO]	1728.258 kg [ICPO]	2148.379 kg	8068.302 kg
Egypt	628.434 kg	626.000 kg	525.000 kg	486.000 kg	1080.000 kg	1199.000 kg
Libyan Arab Jamahiriya	471.955 kg	1.476 kg [F.O]	3.418 kg [F.O]	7.044 kg [F.O]	No Report	No Report
Morocco	55519.734 kg	54755.235 kg	143946.033 kg	61355.736 kg	66394.000 kg	96305.867 kg
Sudan	No Report	No Report	No Report	No Report	No Report	8723.792 kg [HNLF]
Tunisia	806.324 kg	1893.381 kg	536.684 kg [ICPO]	1288.877 kg	977.730 kg	539.886 kg
Sub-Total	58643.630 kg	61356.760 kg	146705.300 kg	64865.920 kg	70600.100 kg	114836.800 kg
Southern Africa						
Malawi	3.000 kg	3.000 kg	No Report	No Report	No Report	No Report
Mozambique	14.160 kg [ICPO]	11.000 kg [ICPO]	15542.000 kg [ICPO]	0.200 kg [ICPO]	No Report	105.415 kg [HNLF]
South Africa	20.568 kg	22.612 kg [ICPO]	11500.000 kg	534.146 kg	696.170 kg	114.173 kg
Swaziland	No Report	No Report	No Report	5.056 kg	No Report	No Report
Zambia	3.111 kg [Govt]	4.201 kg	14.604 kg	0.016 kg [Govt]	1037.000 kg	No Report
Zimbabwe	3.191 kg	No Report	No Report	0.081 kg	11.000 kg	No Report
Sub-Total	44.030 kg	40.813 kg	27056.600 kg	539.499 kg	1744.170 kg	219.588 kg
West and Central Africa						
Benin	No Report	No Report	350.000 kg [ICPO]	13.000 kg [ICPO]	No Report	No Report
Burkina Faso	No Report	No Report	No Report	No Report	No Report	13.000 kg
Gambia	0.420 kg [ICPO]	0.007 kg	No Report	No Report	1.966 kg [ICPO]	0.142 kg [Govt]
Saint Helena	No Report	No Report	No Report	No Report	1 u.	No Report
Senegal	No Report	No Report	5390.000 kg [ICPO]	No Report	No Report	No Report
Sub-Total	0.420 kg	0.007 kg	5740.000 kg	13.000 kg	1.966 kg 1 u.	13.142 kg
Total region	58756.440 kg	61482.460 kg	185905.800 kg	65469.890 kg	74232.040 kg 1 u.	115968.000 kg

Source: Annual Report Questionnaire if not otherwise indicated

293

SEIZURES, 1998 - 2003
Cannabis resin

Region/country or territory	1998	1999	2000	2001	2002	2003
AMERICAS						
Caribbean						
Bahamas	16.082 kg	2.095 kg [ICPO]	27.900 kg	14.220 kg 31 u.	61.690 kg [ICPO]	2.270 kg
Barbados	No Report	1.270 kg [HONLC]	No Report	No Report	No Report	22.200 kg [PROJ.S]
Bermuda	0.609 kg	171.002 kg	1.136 kg	No Report	1.550 kg	No Report
Cayman Islands	No Report	No Report	No Report	No Report	No Report	50.930 kg
Cuba	No Report	66.200 kg [F.O]	21.400 kg [HONL]	No Report	0.192 kg [ICPO]	0.400 kg [HONL]
Dominica	No Report	0.015 kg [ICPO]	No Report	51.580 kg [ICPO]	No Report	No Report
Dominican Republic	No Report	184.000 kg [ICPO]	No Report	0.008 kg	0.007 kg [ICPO]	0.324 kg
Grenada	No Report	No Report	No Report	No Report	No Report	90.000 kg [PROJ.S]
Jamaica	No Report	61.450 kg [ICPO]	20.000 kg [CICAD]	8.100 kg	497.000 kg [ICPO]	No Report
Netherlands Antilles	No Report	No Report	0.061 kg [ICPO]	0.104 kg [ICPO]	0.060 kg [ICPO]	No Report
Saint Lucia	No Report	No Report	0.071 kg	No Report	No Report	No Report
Trinidad and Tobago	2725.305 kg	No Report	No Report	No Report	No Report	No Report
Turks and Caicos Islands	No Report	No Report	0.202 kg [ICPO]	No Report	No Report	No Report
Sub-Total	2741.996 kg	486.032 kg	70.770 kg	74.012 kg 31 u.	560.499 kg	166.124 kg
Central America						
Honduras	No Report	1027 u. [CICAD]	No Report	No Report	No Report	No Report
Panama	No Report	No Report	0.002 kg [ICPO]	No Report	No Report	No Report
Sub-Total		1027 u.	0.002 kg			
North America						
Canada	15925.320 kg 0.002 lt. 97 u.	6477.000 kg 1.000 lt. 5 u.	16317.600 kg 31 u.	1755.997 kg	158.893 kg	1803.932 kg
Mexico	1.743 kg	0.329 kg	0.005 kg	29.507 kg	0.035 kg	1.076 kg
United States	No Report	761.000 kg	945.137 kg	56.500 kg	620.900 kg	155.000 kg
Sub-Total	15927.060 kg 0.002 lt. 97 u.	7238.330 kg 1.000 lt. 5 u.	17262.740 kg 31 u.	1842.004 kg	779.828 kg	1960.008 kg
South America						
Argentina	1.880 kg	5006 u.	9.114 kg	1.219 kg	1.891 kg	12.643 kg
Brazil	No Report	37.550 kg	41.009 kg	43.519 kg [Govt]	36.100 kg [F.O]	55.724 kg
Chile	No Report	No Report	0.001 kg	No Report	No Report	No Report
Colombia	No Report	338.000 kg	38.000 lt. [CICAD]	0.200 kg	No Report	No Report
Falkland Islands (Malvinas)	No Report	0.063 kg	0.120 kg	No Report	No Report	No Report
Paraguay	3.702 kg	2.337 kg	2.097 kg [Govt]	27.693 kg [Govt]	1301.000 kg	2477.000 kg
Suriname	0.529 kg	No Report	No Report	No Report	No Report	No Report
Uruguay	No Report	1.136 kg	0.045 kg	No Report	2.387 kg	No Report
Sub-Total	6.111 kg	379.086 kg 5006 u.	52.386 kg 38.000 lt.	72.631 kg	1341.378 kg	2545.367 kg

Source: Annual Report Questionnaire if not otherwise indicated

SEIZURES, 1998 - 2003
Cannabis resin

Region/country or territory	1998	1999	2000	2001	2002	2003
AMERICAS						
Total region	18675.170 kg 0.002 lt. 97 u.	8103.447 kg 1.000 lt. 6038 u.	17385.900 kg 38.000 lt. 31 u.	1988.647 kg 31 u.	2681.705 kg	4671.499 kg
ASIA						
Central Asia and Transcaucasian countries						
Armenia	No Report	0.178 kg ^{ICPO}	0.169 kg	0.112 kg	0.914 kg	0.106 kg
Azerbaijan	23.256 kg	0.832 kg	No Report	15.500 kg	0.169 kg	No Report
Georgia	No Report	0.003 kg ^{ICPO}	0.009 kg ^{ICPO}	No Report	No Report	0.004 kg
Kazakhstan	298.635 kg	145.462 kg	No Report	276.160 kg $^{F.O}$	192.650 kg $^{F.O}$	199.000 kg $^{F.O}$
Tajikistan	726.449 kg $^{F.O}$	560.000 kg $^{F.O}$	429.981 kg $^{F.O}$	No Report	No Report	No Report
Turkmenistan	22249.000 kg $^{Govt.}$	10413.000 kg $^{F.O}$	No Report	No Report	No Report	108.000 kg ^{Govt}
Uzbekistan	No Report	694.000 kg $^{F.O}$	65.100 kg	86.000 kg $^{F.O}$	44.700 kg	19.400 kg
Sub-Total	23297.340 kg	11813.470 kg	495.259 kg	377.772 kg	238.433 kg	326.511 kg
East and South-East Asia						
Hong Kong Special Administrative Region of China	No Report	14.376 kg	6.004 kg	0.700 kg	0.370 kg	15.310 kg
Indonesia	0.690 kg 230 u.	300.005 kg ^{HNLP}	3.885 kg	5.632 kg	0.687 kg	0.643 kg
Japan	214.560 kg	200.297 kg	185.416 kg	73.499 kg	275.300 kg	323.900 kg
Macao Special Administrative Region of China	0.995 kg ^{ICPO}	No Report	0.043 kg	0.499 kg	No Report	0.027 kg
Mongolia	No Report	No Report	No Report	2 u.	No Report	No Report
Philippines	No Report	No Report	1.770 kg 2 u.	8.015 kg	265.000 kg	No Report
Republic of Korea	0.884 kg	1.963 kg	No Report	4.254 kg	158.968 kg ^{ICPO}	3.279 kg
Thailand	20.592 kg	121.220 kg	91.903 kg ^{ICPO}	No Report	52.170 kg ^{ICPO}	56.600 kg ^{ICPO}
Sub-Total	237.721 kg 230 u.	637.861 kg	289.021 kg 2 u.	92.599 kg 2 u.	752.495 kg	399.759 kg
Near and Middle East /South-West Asia						
Afghanistan	No Report	No Report	No Report	No Report	50314.044 kg	81176.000 kg
Bahrain	1.036 kg ^{ICPO}	1263.049 kg ^{ICPO}	No Report	No Report	3.700 kg	No Report
Iran (Islamic Republic of)	14376.364 kg	18907.000 kg	31581.000 kg ^{NAPOL}	46084.000 kg	64166.000 kg ^{Govt}	76991.000 kg
Iraq	No Report	No Report	569.970 kg	2343.796 kg	No Report	No Report
Israel	60.900 kg	70.000 kg ^{ICPO}	30.218 kg	143.000 kg	2893.000 kg	1053.000 kg
Jordan	166.737 kg	112.410 kg	298.456 kg	785.542 kg	864.966 kg	4133.775 kg
Kuwait	214.103 kg	972.878 kg ^{ICPO}	3488.000 kg $^{F.O}$	No Report	No Report	0.600 kg ^{ICPO}
Lebanon	2492.609 kg	76.698 kg	358.000 kg ^{ICPO}	307.820 kg	28670.335 kg	11488.194 kg
Oman	No Report	14335.695 kg	No Report	2382.645 kg	49.934 kg	1461.000 kg ^{ICPO}
Pakistan	65909.234 kg	81458.142 kg	129181.626 kg	75161.024 kg	85126.407 kg	99123.245 kg
Qatar	374.526 kg ^{ICPO}	680.869 kg ^{ICPO}	134.586 kg ^{ICPO}	144.820 kg	65.969 kg	296.785 kg

Source: Annual Report Questionnaire if not otherwise indicated

SEIZURES, 1998 - 2003
Cannabis resin

Region/country or territory	1998	1999	2000	2001	2002	2003
ASIA						
Near and Middle East /South-West Asia						
Saudi Arabia	2357.874 kg	2003.000 kg [ICPO]	2719.091 kg 18 u.	1767.430 kg	No Report	5866.000 kg [ICPO]
Syrian Arab Republic	231.759 kg [Govt]	819.058 kg [Govt]	No Report	379.957 kg [Govt]	907.427 kg	1863.527 kg
United Arab Emirates	7087.219 kg	2530.511 kg	943.405 kg	6113.923 kg	3127.065 kg	2070.526 kg
Yemen	No Report	No Report	No Report	No Report	26.125 kg	No Report
Sub-Total	93272.360 kg	123229.300 kg	169304.400 kg 18 u.	135614.000 kg	236215.000 kg	285523.700 kg
South Asia						
Bangladesh	0.990 kg [Govt]	6.660 kg [Govt]	0.001 kg [Govt]	0.000 kg [Govt]	28.470 kg [Govt]	1.160 kg [Govt]
India	10106.000 kg	3290.000 kg	5041.000 kg	5664.000 kg	4487.000 kg [Govt]	3012.000 kg
Maldives	No Report	0.004 kg	No Report	No Report	0.007 kg [ICPO]	No Report
Nepal	2585.886 kg [Govt]	1671.413 kg [Govt] [(1]	2539.936 kg [Govt]	No Report	850.031 kg [ICPO]	921.824 kg
Sri Lanka	No Report		0.011 kg	0.015 kg	19979.000 kg [ICPO]	0.010 kg
Sub-Total	12692.880 kg	4968.077 kg	7580.948 kg	5664.015 kg	25344.510 kg	3934.994 kg
Total region	129500.300 kg 230 u.	140648.700 kg	177669.600 kg 20 u.	141748.300 kg 2 u.	262550.400 kg	290184.900 kg
EUROPE						
East Europe						
Belarus	0.509 kg	1.949 kg	0.639 kg	0.663 kg [Govt]	2.174 kg	2.639 kg [Govt]
Republic of Moldova	228.000 kg	No Report	523.000 kg [ICPO]	358.130 kg	No Report	No Report
Russian Federation	1588.700 kg	710.895 kg	845.000 kg [F.O]	1335.671 kg	1424.257 kg [ICPO]	1734.924 kg
Ukraine	6150.100 kg	14.000 kg [ICPO. (2]	49.316 kg [ICPO]	11.130 kg	6.950 kg [Govt]	12.224 kg
Sub-Total	7967.309 kg	726.844 kg	1417.955 kg	1705.594 kg	1433.381 kg	1749.787 kg
Southeast Europe						
Bosnia and Herzegovina	No Report	0.002 kg [NAPOL]	No Report	0.060 kg [ICPO]	No Report	No Report
Bulgaria	0.680 kg	0.010 kg	514.017 kg	422.584 kg	88.476 kg	384.509 kg
Croatia	2.878 kg	6.555 kg	1.041 kg	4.559 kg	2.107 kg	2.281 kg
Romania	1.673 kg	43.530 kg	340.810 kg [(3]	13871.000 kg	38.580 kg	2.060 kg
Serbia and Montenegro	No Report	No Report	No Report	4.534 kg	6.814 kg	1.113 kg
The former Yugoslav Republic of Macedonia	1.164 kg [NAPOL]	0.089 kg [NAPOL]	427.519 kg [NAPOL]	309.846 kg [Govt]	258.406 kg	423.504 kg
Turkey	9434.290 kg [(3]	2060.258 kg [Govt]	71.000 kg [Govt]	268.477 kg	1220.725 kg	863.551 kg
Sub-Total	9440.685 kg	2110.444 kg	1354.387 kg	14881.060 kg	1615.108 kg	1677.018 kg
West & Central Europe						
Andorra	1.372 kg [ICPO]	1.422 kg	3.061 kg [ICPO]	3.790 kg	3.076 kg	No Report
Austria	124.718 kg	109.996 kg	243.673 kg	137.987 kg	133.209 kg	239.144 kg
Belgium	817.622 kg	3130.812 kg [ICPO]	532.163 kg	27993.336 kg [UNODC (4]	5298.000 kg	5655.300 kg

Source: Annual Report Questionnaire if not otherwise indicated

SEIZURES, 1998 - 2003
Cannabis resin

Region/country or territory	1998	1999	2000	2001	2002	2003
EUROPE						
West & Central Europe						
Cyprus	1.201 kg	7.291 kg	9.525 kg	1.443 kg	1.456 kg	0.896 kg
Czech Republic	No Report	1.200 kg	23.099 kg	6.850 kg	11.391 kg	64.805 kg
Denmark	1572.455 kg	14021.300 kg	2914.419 kg	1762.742 kg	2635.235 kg	3829.009 kg
Estonia	0.133 kg 52 u.	1.191 kg 191 u.	9.913 kg 58 u.	0.199 kg	1.067 kg	58.608 kg
Finland	160.972 kg	492.316 kg	196.540 kg	590.000 kg	482.300 kg	423.000 kg
France	52176.426 kg	64096.665 kg	48710.697 kg	58195.515 kg	50836.113 kg	78347.920 kg
Germany, Federal Republic of	6109.549 kg	4885.200 kg	8525.200 kg	6863.057 kg	5003.001 kg	8303.338 kg
Greece	30.817 kg	55.819 kg	56.120 kg	270.780 kg	67.711 kg	89.894 kg
Hungary	6.803 kg	5.242 kg	22.538 kg	0.880 kg	4.181 kg	1.532 kg
Iceland	No Report	41.622 kg	26.626 kg	44.140 kg	57.564 kg	No Report
Ireland	3179.178 kg	2514.975 kg	379.800 kg	567.026 kg	3314.938 kg	5349.000 kg
Italy	15412.128 kg 711 u.	46780.319 kg [ICPO]	20725.364 kg 818 u.	16455.477 kg 811 u.	28600.257 kg 947 u.	25165.812 kg 787 u.
Latvia	3.150 kg	0.685 kg	0.495 kg	0.191 kg	No Report	50.052 kg
Liechtenstein	2.770 kg	No Report	No Report	0.012 kg	0.013 kg	0.032 kg
Lithuania	3.780 kg	1.054 kg	0.169 kg	0.260 kg	0.569 kg	262.600 kg
Luxembourg	1.974 kg	1.270 kg	1.174 kg [ICPO]	No Report	0.697 kg [ICPO]	5.374 kg
Malta	25.116 kg	1.606 kg	3.913 kg	3.562 kg	8.801 kg [ICPO]	34.429 kg
Monaco	0.396 kg	0.111 kg [ICPO]	0.512 kg [ICPO]	No Report	0.095 kg	1383.000 kg
Netherlands	70696.000 kg [Govt]	61226.000 kg [Govt]	29590.000 kg [Govt]	10972.000 kg	32717.000 kg [Govt]	10719.000 kg
Norway	1874.136 kg	1254.762 kg	632.647 kg	808.541 kg	1097.980 kg	2223.410 kg
Poland	8.176 kg	49.203 kg	No Report	9.426 kg	217.346 kg	33.640 kg
Portugal	5747.793 kg	10636.075 kg	30467.121 kg	6472.688 kg	7022.029 kg	31555.686 kg
Slovakia	0.015 kg	No Report	2.085 kg	0.635 kg	No Report	0.067 kg
Slovenia	1.958 kg	64.622 kg	1.022 kg	2.360 kg	0.120 kg	0.590 kg [HONEU]
Spain	428236.375 kg	431165.280 kg	474504.785 kg	514181.600 kg	564808.966 kg	727312.801 kg
Sweden	390.930 kg	1065.387 kg 26 u.	1206.709 kg	772.462 kg	729.000 kg	1010.826 kg
Switzerland	1837.480 kg	651.548 kg	1258.307 kg [ICPO]	317.550 kg	1317.640 kg	323.210 kg
United Kingdom	82837.533 kg	33727.243 kg [ICPO] 194 u.	48346.903 kg	58996.761 kg	44192.000 kg	44192.000 kg [(5]
Sub-Total	671261.000 kg 763 u.	675990.300 kg 411 u.	668394.600 kg 876 u.	705431.300 kg 811 u.	748561.800 kg 947 u.	946634.900 kg 787 u.
Total region	688669.000 kg 763 u.	678827.600 kg 411 u.	671166.900 kg 876 u.	722017.900 kg 811 u.	751610.300 kg 947 u.	950061.800 kg 787 u.
OCEANIA						
Oceania						
Australia	No Report	4.129 kg	17.972 kg	3266.944 kg	55.795 kg	513.495 kg [(6]
New Zealand	3.632 kg	0.676 kg	No Report	0.435 kg	0.482 kg	0.263 kg

Source: Annual Report Questionnaire if not otherwise indicated

SEIZURES, 1998 - 2003
Cannabis resin

Region/country or territory	1998	1999	2000	2001	2002	2003
OCEANIA						
Oceania						
Sub-Total	3.632 kg	4.805 kg	17.972 kg	3267.379 kg	56.277 kg	513.758 kg
Total region	3.632 kg	4.805 kg	17.972 kg	3267.379 kg	56.277 kg	513.758 kg
TOTAL	895604.500 kg 0.002 lt. 1090 u.	889067.000 kg 1.000 lt. 6449 u.	1052146.000 kg 38.000 lt. 927 u.	934492.100 kg 844 u.	1091131.000 kg 948 u.	1361400.000 kg 787 u.

1) Small quantity. 2) Provisional figures. 3) Including cannabis herb. 4) WCO 5) Due to unavailability of 2003 data, year 2002 data were used for analysis purposes. 6) Sum of seizures reported by national, State & Territory law enforcement agencies

Source: Annual Report Questionnaire if not otherwise indicated

SEIZURES, 1998 - 2003
Cannabis oil

Region/country or territory	1998	1999	2000	2001	2002	2003
AFRICA						
East Africa						
Kenya	No Report	4.057 kg	No Report	No Report	No Report	No Report
Madagascar	No Report	No Report	No Report	No Report	No Report	15.500 lt.
Sub-Total		4.057 kg				15.500 lt.
North Africa						
Morocco	14.473 kg	19.000 lt.	0.693 kg	0.008 kg	No Report	6.080 kg
Sub-Total	14.473 kg	19.000 lt.	0.693 kg	0.008 kg		6.080 kg
Southern Africa						
Zambia	0.000 kg [Govt]	0.000 kg [Govt]	0.000 kg [Govt]	8.500 kg [Govt]	No Report	No Report
Sub-Total				8.500 kg		
West and Central Africa						
Benin	26.863 kg	No Report	No Report	No Report	No Report	No Report
Sub-Total	26.863 kg					
Total region	41.336 kg	4.057 kg 19.000 lt.	0.693 kg	8.508 kg		6.080 kg 15.500 lt.
AMERICAS						
Caribbean						
Aruba	No Report	0.002 kg [ICPO]	No Report	No Report	No Report	No Report
Bahamas	No Report	104.089 kg [ICPO]	0.450 kg	No Report	No Report	No Report
Haiti	11.000 kg [CICAD]	No Report	No Report	No Report	No Report	No Report
Jamaica	No Report	371.490 kg [ICPO]	579.091 kg [ICPO]	210.980 kg	No Report	No Report
Saint Vincent and the Grenadines	No Report	No Report	28375 u. [INCSR]	No Report	No Report	No Report
Sub-Total	11.000 kg	475.581 kg	579.541 kg 28375 u.	210.980 kg		
Central America						
Panama	No Report	11.360 lt.	No Report	No Report	No Report	No Report
Sub-Total		11.360 lt.				
North America						
Canada	524.937 kg 20.166 lt. 2 u.	434.000 kg 55.302 lt. 6 u.	28.000 kg 187.392 lt. 13 u.	120.191 kg 16 u.	168.830 kg 66.000 lt.	92.212 kg 62 u.
United States	No Report	490.685 kg	66.152 kg	59.700 kg		No Report
Sub-Total	524.937 kg 20.166 lt. 2 u.	924.685 kg 55.302 lt. 6 u.	94.152 kg 187.392 lt. 13 u.	179.891 kg 16 u.	168.830 kg 66.000 lt.	92.212 kg 62 u.
South America						
Chile	No Report	0.025 kg [ICPO]	No Report	No Report	0.320 kg [ICPO]	No Report
Suriname	No Report	No Report	No Report	0.217 kg	No Report	No Report
Uruguay	No Report	No Report	No Report	No Report	2.386 kg [ICPO]	No Report
Sub-Total		0.025 kg		0.217 kg	2.706 kg	

Source: Annual Report Questionnaire if not otherwise indicated

SEIZURES, 1998 - 2003
Cannabis oil

Region/country or territory	1998	1999	2000	2001	2002	2003
AMERICAS						
Total region	535.937 kg	1400.291 kg	673.693 kg	391.088 kg	171.536 kg	92.212 kg
	20.166 lt.	66.662 lt.	187.392 lt.	16 u.	66.000 lt.	62 u.
	2 u.	6 u.	28388 u.			
ASIA						
Central Asia and Transcaucasian countries						
Armenia	22.353 kg	0.002 kg [ICPO]	0.000 kg [(1]	0.007 kg	No Report	0.001 kg
Georgia	No Report	No Report	No Report	No Report	No Report	0.002 kg
Sub-Total	22.353 kg	0.002 kg	0.000 kg	0.007 kg		0.003 kg
East and South-East Asia						
Brunei Darussalam	No Report	No Report	No Report	0.260 lt.	No Report	No Report
Indonesia	No Report	300.005 kg	3.885 kg [Govt]	5.632 kg [Govt]	0.687 kg [Govt]	0.643 kg [Govt]
Japan	3.750 kg	0.002 kg		0.000 lt.	0.003 lt.	No Report
		0.002 lt.				
Republic of Korea	No Report	No Report	No Report	No Report	0.765 kg [ICPO]	No Report
Thailand	No Report	No Report	0.516 kg [ICPO]	No Report	No Report	No Report
Sub-Total	3.750 kg	300.007 kg	4.401 kg	5.632 kg	1.452 kg	0.643 kg
		0.002 lt.		0.260 lt.	0.003 lt.	
Near and Middle East /South-West Asia						
Iran (Islamic Republic of)	No Report	68.000 kg [ICPO]	No Report	No Report	No Report	No Report
Lebanon	No Report	No Report	10.000 kg	No Report	119.600 kg	12.500 kg
Sub-Total		68.000 kg	10.000 kg		119.600 kg	12.500 kg
South Asia						
Maldives	No Report	0.001 kg	No Report	0.003 kg	No Report	No Report
Nepal	No Report	2.100 kg	No Report	No Report	No Report	No Report
Sub-Total		2.101 kg		0.003 kg		
Total region	26.103 kg	370.110 kg	14.401 kg	5.642 kg	121.052 kg	13.146 kg
		0.002 lt.		0.260 lt.	0.003 lt.	
EUROPE						
East Europe						
Belarus	No Report	0.002 kg	No Report	0.001 kg [Govt]	2.401 kg	0.240 kg
Russian Federation	102.900 kg [F.O]	141.344 kg	291.000 kg [F.O]	366.590 kg	208.747 kg [Govt]	122.914 kg
Sub-Total	102.900 kg	141.346 kg	291.000 kg	366.591 kg	211.148 kg	123.154 kg
Southeast Europe						
Albania	No Report	13.000 lt. [ICPO]	2.100 lt. [ICPO]	No Report	0.600 lt.	48.500 lt.
Bulgaria	No Report	0.100 kg	0.080 kg	6 u.	No Report	No Report
Croatia	0.008 kg	No Report	No Report	No Report	No Report	No Report
Romania	No Report	No Report	No Report	No Report	1.000 lt.	No Report
Turkey	63.411 kg	No Report	2.480 kg	0.001 kg	No Report	0.026 kg
Sub-Total	63.419 kg	0.100 kg	2.560 kg	0.001 kg	1.600 lt.	0.026 kg
		13.000 lt.	2.100 lt.	6 u.		48.500 lt.

Source: Annual Report Questionnaire if not otherwise indicated

SEIZURES, 1998 - 2003
Cannabis oil

Region/country or territory	1998	1999	2000	2001	2002	2003
EUROPE						
West & Central Europe						
Austria	No Report	No Report	0.750 kg [ICPO]	0.188 kg	1.919 kg	6.450 kg
Belgium	No Report	5.000 kg	No Report	No Report	No Report	
Cyprus	No Report	30.294 kg	No Report	No Report	No Report	No Report
Denmark	0.008 kg	3.910 kg	0.962 kg	0.019 kg	[1]	No Report
Estonia	No Report	No Report	0.300 kg 2 u.	No Report	No Report	No Report
France	0.592 kg	1.690 kg	2.830 kg	3.513 kg	5.086 kg	49.329 kg
Germany, Federal Republic of	0.538 kg	2.300 kg	4.500 kg	0.044 kg	2.062 kg	4.296 kg
Greece	No Report	0.200 kg [ICPO]	1.205 kg	1.910 kg	757.000 kg	2.821 kg
Italy	0.635 kg 3 u.	6.772 kg [ICPO]	13.349 kg 5 u.	25.263 kg 171 u.	52.646 kg 753 u.	2.240 kg 1001 u.
Netherlands	150.000 lt. [Govt]	1.000 lt. [Govt]	No Report	No Report	No Report	No Report
Norway	0.034 kg	0.026 kg	0.028 kg	0.009 kg	1.683 kg	0.005 kg
Portugal	No Report	0.001 kg	0.004 kg	0.134 kg	0.011 kg 11 u.	No Report
Slovakia	No Report	No Report	64.000 kg	No Report	No Report	No Report
Spain	74.970 lt.	2346 u.	0.310 lt.	1915.500 kg	0.001 lt.	No Report
Sweden	No Report	0.006 kg	No Report	0.203 kg	No Report	0.004 kg
Switzerland	1.541 kg	0.609 kg	95.082 kg	17.577 kg	191.654 kg	0.722 kg
United Kingdom	7.366 kg	No Report	4.491 kg	6.862 kg	2.000 kg	2.000 kg [2]
Sub-Total	10.714 kg 224.970 lt. 3 u.	50.808 kg 1.000 lt. 2346 u.	187.501 kg 0.310 lt. 7 u.	1971.222 kg 171 u.	1014.061 kg 0.001 lt. 764 u.	67.867 kg 1001 u.
Total region	177.033 kg 224.970 lt. 3 u.	192.254 kg 14.000 lt. 2346 u.	481.061 kg 2.410 lt. 7 u.	2337.814 kg 177 u.	1225.209 kg 1.601 lt. 764 u.	191.047 kg 48.500 lt. 1001 u.
OCEANIA						
Oceania						
Australia	No Report	2.650 kg	0.755 lt.	No Report	0.251 kg 4 u.	0.210 kg [3]
New Zealand	4.159 kg	0.026 kg	8.305 kg	3.147 kg	1.342 kg	1.680 kg
Sub-Total	4.159 kg	2.676 kg	8.305 kg 0.755 lt.	3.147 kg	1.593 kg 4 u.	1.890 kg
Total region	4.159 kg	2.676 kg	8.305 kg 0.755 lt.	3.147 kg	1.593 kg 4 u.	1.890 kg
TOTAL	784.568 kg 245.136 lt. 5 u.	1969.388 kg 99.664 lt. 2352 u.	1178.153 kg 190.557 lt. 28395 u.	2746.199 kg 0.260 lt. 193 u.	1519.390 kg 67.604 lt. 768 u.	304.375 kg 64.000 lt. 1063 u.

1) Small quantity. 2) Due to unavailability of 2003 data, year 2002 data were used for analysis purposes. 3) Sum of seizures reported by national, State & Territory law enforcement agencies

Source: Annual Report Questionnaire if not otherwise indicated

SEIZURES, 1998 - 2003
Cannabis plant

Region/country or territory	1998	1999	2000	2001	2002	2003
AFRICA						
East Africa						
Eritrea	No Report	No Report	No Report	20.000 kg	No Report	120 u.
Kenya	No Report	No Report	No Report	No Report	23625 u.	1845 u.
Madagascar	No Report	No Report	No Report	No Report	1050980.000 kg	6698625.838 kg
Mauritius	43294 u.	45444 u.	55038 u.	30788 u.	22464 u.	17988 u.
Seychelles	No Report	30.700 kg	7.233 kg	No Report	1.073 kg	No Report
Uganda	9411 u.	35000 u.	54700 u.	780000 u.	1431.100 kg	48000.225 kg
Sub-Total	52705 u.	30.700 kg 80444 u.	7.233 kg 109738 u.	20.000 kg 810788 u.	1052412.000 kg 46089 u.	6746626.000 kg 19953 u.
North Africa						
Algeria	No Report	No Report	No Report	No Report	No Report	3361 u.
Egypt	35150384 u.	No Report	No Report	470 u.	No Report	
Morocco	No Report	No Report	No Report	73810.724 kg	93206.000 kg	20284.030 kg
Sub-Total	35150380 u.			73810.730 kg 470 u.	93206.000 kg	20284.030 kg 3361 u.
Southern Africa						
Angola	No Report	5733 u.	No Report	No Report	No Report	No Report
Malawi	6371.045 kg	9428.350 kg	61182.146 kg	51611.136 kg	4127.826 kg	1576.894 kg
Namibia	No Report	25 u.	No Report	67 u.	949.448 kg	No Report
South Africa	784201.063 kg	No Report	864234.300 kg	608330.095 kg	754913.307 kg	94564 u.
Swaziland	7517.000 kg	2528136 u.	36665 u.	No Report	No Report	No Report
Zambia	No Report	No Report	No Report	No Report	No Report	87700.000 kg
Zimbabwe	300.000 kg 2936 u.	165 u.	3555 u.	878 u.	6136 u.	701 u.
Sub-Total	798389.100 kg 2936 u.	9428.350 kg 2534059 u.	925416.400 kg 40220 u.	659941.300 kg 945 u.	759990.600 kg 6136 u.	89276.890 kg 95265 u.
West and Central Africa						
Cameroon	No Report	No Report	No Report	2649.008 kg	No Report	300.000 kg
Congo	No Report	10.000 kg [(1]	No Report	No Report	No Report	No Report
Côte d'Ivoire	200 u.	No Report	No Report	No Report	No Report	No Report
Gambia	No Report	834.982 kg	No Report	700.000 kg	No Report	No Report
Ghana	No Report	No Report	No Report	No Report	5000.000 kg	No Report
Guinea-Bissau	No Report	No Report	No Report	8.000 kg	No Report	No Report
Nigeria	1712580.000 [Govt.] kg	No Report	No Report	270250.000 kg	No Report	No Report
Saint Helena	17 u.	17 u.	6 u.	5 u.	1150 u.	139 u.
Togo	No Report	No Report	50.000 kg	No Report	5.500 kg	No Report
Sub-Total	1712580.000 kg 217 u.	844.982 kg 17 u.	50.000 kg 6 u.	273607.000 kg 5 u.	5005.500 kg 1150 u.	300.000 kg 139 u.
Total region	2510969.000 kg 35206240 u.	10304.030 kg 2614520 u.	925473.700 kg 149964 u.	1007379.000 kg 812208 u.	1910614.000 kg 53375 u.	6856487.000 kg 118718 u.

Source: Annual Report Questionnaire if not otherwise indicated

SEIZURES, 1998 - 2003
Cannabis plant

Region/country or territory	1998	1999	2000	2001	2002	2003
AMERICAS						
Caribbean						
Anguilla	40 u.	No Report	No Report	No Report	No Report	No Report
Antigua and Barbuda	No Report	23384 u. CICAD	9317 u. CICAD	No Report	No Report	No Report
Bahamas	99 u.	No Report	1466 u.	10207 u.	110 u.	14112 u.
Barbados	400 u. CICAD	81 u. HONLC	1078 u. CICAD	No Report	No Report	No Report
Bermuda	No Report	268 u.	230 u.	No Report	34 u.	No Report
British Virgin Islands	No Report	No Report	No Report	4556 u.	No Report	No Report
Dominica	No Report	55120 u. CICAD	123032 u. CICAD	No Report	No Report	No Report
Dominican Republic	346 u.	1991 u.	1114 u. CICAD	6578 u.	4061 u. HONLC	392 u.
Grenada	6212.000 kg	12086 u. CICAD	2091 u. INCSR	6611 u.	No Report	No Report
Haiti	No Report	No Report	No Report	1705.000 kg	No Report	No Report
Jamaica	No Report	No Report	No Report	34 u.	No Report	No Report
Montserrat	No Report	No Report	1008 u.	No Report	No Report	No Report
Saint Kitts and Nevis	36000 u. CICAD	63911 u. CICAD	34057 u. INCSR	No Report	No Report	No Report
Saint Lucia	69200 u.	18047 u. CICAD	83090 u.	No Report	No Report	No Report
Saint Vincent and the Grenadines	1500 u. CICAD	4760 u. CICAD	28375 u. CICAD	No Report	No Report	No Report
Trinidad and Tobago	2869850 u.	4415958 u. CICAD	7200000 u. INCSR	3122894 u.	2671600 u.	396640 u.
Turks and Caicos Islands	No Report	No Report	No Report	No Report	No Report	0.331 kg
Sub-Total	6212.000 kg 2977435 u.	4595606 u.	7484858 u.	1705.000 kg 3150880 u.	2675805 u.	0.331 kg 411144 u.
Central America						
Belize	202803 u. CICAD	270136 u. CICAD	143000 u. CICAD	70607 u.	No Report	No Report
Costa Rica	733089 u.	2153645 u.	2048421 u.	1906454 u.	1235119 u.	981168 u.
El Salvador	No Report	4688 u.	25005 u. HONL	1126 u.	1158 u.	10059 u.
Guatemala	576060 u.	594378 u.	293897 u.	418097 u.	330586 u. HONL	326705.170 kg
Honduras	286414 u. CICAD	133680 u. CICAD	83859 u. CICAD	248951 u. HONL	41402 u.	365881 u.
Nicaragua	833943 u.	13569 u. CICAD	83070 u. CICAD	116003 u. HONL	144967 u.	128749 u. HONL
Panama	No Report	25102 u.	No Report	36950 u.	No Report	No Report
Sub-Total	2632309 u.	3195198 u.	2677252 u.	2798188 u.	1753232 u.	326705.200 kg 1485857 u.
North America						
Canada	1025808 u.	1304477 u.	1199423 u.	86456.827 kg 508039 u.	83444.072 kg 1405304 u.	127326.631 kg 1515786 u.
Mexico	No Report	No Report	No Report	No Report	355578 u.	347277 u.
United States	No Report	497.366 kg	163.344 kg	4561.900 kg		No Report
Sub-Total	1025808 u.	497.366 kg 1304477 u.	163.344 kg 1199423 u.	91018.730 kg 508039 u.	83444.070 kg 1760882 u.	127326.600 kg 1863063 u.

Source: Annual Report Questionnaire if not otherwise indicated

SEIZURES, 1998 - 2003
Cannabis plant

Region/country or territory	1998	1999	2000	2001	2002	2003
AMERICAS						
South America						
Argentina	1296 u.	1222 u.	676 u.	1687 u.	939 u.	14244 u.
Bolivia	No Report	No Report	No Report	705.536 kg	No Report	No Report
Brazil	3371112 u.	3462158 u.	3699601 u.	3823846 u. [Govt]	2594101 u. [F.O]	2345889 u.
Chile	956.942 kg 759 u.	No Report	63621 u.	98892 u.	69891 u.	79228 u.
Colombia	No Report	No Report	No Report	No Report	No Report	11010 u.
Ecuador	126 u. [Govt]	339 u. [Govt]	No Report	No Report	No Report	No Report
Falkland Islands (Malvinas)	1 u.	No Report	No Report	No Report	No Report	No Report
Guyana	No Report	No Report	31698 u. [CICAD]	No Report	No Report	8618.455 kg
Paraguay	1415875.000 kg	3769000 u.	1366500 u. [CICAD]	No Report	4986000.000 kg	1662.000 kg
Peru	No Report	5418.300 kg	29566.400 kg	38106.465 kg 2 u.	103687.000 kg	17296 u.
Suriname	500 u.	No Report	No Report	No Report	No Report	No Report
Uruguay	No Report	No Report	5 u.	No Report	0.410 kg 246 u.	30 u.
Venezuela	No Report	No Report	26 u.	No Report	No Report	No Report
Sub-Total	1416832.000 kg 3373794 u.	5418.300 kg 7232719 u.	29566.400 kg 5162127 u.	38812.000 kg 3924427 u.	5089688.000 kg 2665177 u.	10280.460 kg 2467697 u.
Total region	1423044.000 kg 10009350 u.	5915.666 kg 16328000 u.	29729.740 kg 16523660 u.	131535.700 kg 10381530 u.	5173132.000 kg 8855096 u.	464312.600 kg 6227761 u.
ASIA						
Central Asia and Transcaucasian countries						
Armenia	24.218 kg	No Report	No Report	No Report	No Report	No Report
Azerbaijan	489000.000 kg	405669.000 kg	No Report	317000.000 kg	No Report	No Report
Georgia	No Report	No Report	No Report	No Report	No Report	34600 u.
Kazakhstan	200.077 kg	1869.000 kg	No Report	No Report	No Report	No Report
Uzbekistan	663.316 kg	238.772 kg	No Report	No Report	76.000 kg	No Report
Sub-Total	489887.600 kg	407776.800 kg		317000.000 kg	76.000 kg	34600 u.
East and South-East Asia						
Brunei Darussalam	No Report	No Report	6 u.	No Report	No Report	No Report
Hong Kong Special Administrative Region of China	No Report	No Report	No Report	2103.900 kg	No Report	No Report
Indonesia	47515 u.	78072 u.	No Report	2061 u.	378982 u.	165541 u.
Japan	23.954 kg 1668 u.	26.422 kg	95.617 kg 50 u.	77.020 kg 2022 u.	88.900 kg 4917 u.	49.600 kg 2692 u.
Lao People's Democratic Republic	No Report	No Report	No Report	No Report	2500.000 kg	155154.000 kg
Mongolia	No Report	No Report	No Report	5 u.	No Report	No Report

Source: Annual Report Questionnaire if not otherwise indicated

SEIZURES, 1998 - 2003
Cannabis plant

Region/country or territory	1998	1999	2000	2001	2002	2003
ASIA						
East and South-East Asia						
Philippines	518939.000 [ICPO] kg	5005860 u. [(2]	2599724 u.	754223.844 kg	4399980 u.	5286082 u.
Republic of Korea	3815 u.	10705 u.	No Report	4255 u.	No Report	5724 u.
Singapore	No Report	No Report	No Report	No Report	2.637 kg	No Report
Thailand	13401.892 kg	42996.497 kg	No Report	No Report	No Report	18300.000 kg [Govt]
Sub-Total	532364.900 kg 52998 u.	43022.920 kg 5094637 u.	95.617 kg 2599780 u.	756404.800 kg 8343 u.	2591.537 kg 4783879 u.	173503.600 kg 5460039 u.
Near and Middle East /South-West Asia						
Iraq	55.905 kg	No Report	No Report	No Report	No Report	No Report
Jordan	1.120 kg	62.525 kg	18.032 kg	No Report	No Report	No Report
Lebanon	No Report	4445.880 kg	No Report	80.000 kg	No Report	No Report
Qatar	No Report	No Report	No Report	No Report	0.045 kg	No Report
United Arab Emirates	No Report	No Report	No Report	0.214 kg	No Report	No Report
Sub-Total	57.025 kg	4508.405 kg	18.032 kg	80.214 kg	0.045 kg	
South Asia						
Bangladesh	12383 u. [Govt]	3587 u. [Govt]	2123 u. [Govt]	10293 u. [Govt]	6131 u. [Govt]	5277 u. [Govt]
India	No Report	No Report	No Report	174818.000 kg	No Report	No Report
Nepal	No Report	No Report	No Report	No Report	3320.000 kg	5091.108 kg
Sri Lanka	21375.000 kg	372000.000 kg	32524.344 kg	No Report	25834.000 kg	73774.363 kg
Sub-Total	21375.000 kg 12383 u.	372000.000 kg 3587 u.	32524.340 kg 2123 u.	174818.000 kg 10293 u.	29154.000 kg 6131 u.	78865.470 kg 5277 u.
Total region	1043685.000 kg 65381 u.	827308.100 kg 5098224 u.	32637.990 kg 2601903 u.	1248303.000 kg 18636 u.	31821.580 kg 4790010 u.	252369.100 kg 5499916 u.
EUROPE						
East Europe						
Belarus	117.000 kg	4654.000 kg [Govt]	5058.000 kg [Govt]	2460.000 kg [Govt]	7406 u.	No Report
Ukraine	5103.364 kg	No Report	No Report	No Report	4.155 kg	83.867 kg
Sub-Total	5220.364 kg	4654.000 kg	5058.000 kg	2460.000 kg	4.155 kg 7406 u.	83.867 kg
Southeast Europe						
Albania	No Report	No Report	No Report	No Report	115678 u.	168298 u.
Bosnia and Herzegovina	1445 u. [NAPOL]	16222 u. [NAPOL]	451 u. [NAPOL]	No Report	No Report	No Report
Bulgaria	16000.000 kg 10943 u.	2742 u.	12713.026 kg 3448 u.	21390.000 kg	7457.240 kg	12535.273 kg
Croatia	5131 u.	3050 u.	1739 u.	2843 u.	1828 u.	3496 u.
Romania	215.923 kg	No Report	No Report	No Report	24710.000 kg [Govt]	No Report
Serbia and Montenegro	No Report	No Report	No Report	No Report	1391.066 kg	No Report

Source: Annual Report Questionnaire if not otherwise indicated

305

SEIZURES, 1998 - 2003
Cannabis plant

Region/country or territory	1998	1999	2000	2001	2002	2003
EUROPE						
Southeast Europe						
The former Yugoslav Republic of Macedonia	1457 u.	151262 u.NAPOL	No Report	606 u.Govt	815 u.	858 u.
Turkey	55655864 u.	19736000 u.	327.750 kg 29168530 u.	20243988 u.	25789062 u.	30725276 u.
Sub-Total	16215.920 kg 55674840 u.	19909280 u.	13040.780 kg 29174170 u.	21390.000 kg 20247440 u.	33558.300 kg 25907380 u.	12535.270 kg 30897930 u.
West & Central Europe						
Austria	No Report	No Report	7991 u.	35.721 kg UNODC (3	157.643 kg	127.046 kg
Belgium	6280.000 kg	2911.166 kg			26476 u.	27339 u.
Cyprus	276 u.	190 u.	493 u.	274 u.	248 u.	1329 u.
Czech Republic	No Report	No Report	No Report	343 u.	3173 u.	3125 u.
Denmark	949.969 kg	337.290 kg	No Report	No Report	683.201 kg	No Report
Estonia	23.184 kg 92 u.	41.973 kg 175 u.	67.647 kg 585 u.	192.062 kg	79.271 kg	39.516 kg
Finland	2.334 kg 2900 u.	5.251 kg 2789 u.	14.041 kg 5325 u.	16.000 kg 4900 u.	15.500 kg 6385 u.	20.000 kg 8800 u.
France	34266 u.	23287 u.	24295 u.	No Report	96.671 kg	84.238 kg
Germany, Federal Republic of	81097 u.	168833 u.	25277 u.	68696 u.	29352 u.	35863 u.
Greece	9967 u.	46198 u.	49985 u.	18821 u.	16232 u.	21060 u.
Hungary	1033 u.	620.000 kg	2217 u.	No Report	17.069 kg 2053 u.	27.769 kg
Iceland	No Report	No Report	No Report	No Report	3.692 kg 1207 u.	13.617 kg 1794 u.
Ireland	400 u.	No Report	98 u.	365 u.	467 u.	239 u.
Italy	190240 u.	ICPO	1306469 u.	3219414 u.	297627 u.	191592 u.
Liechtenstein	1300.000 kg	3.686 kg	42.600 kg	No Report	No Report	285.000 kg
Lithuania	No Report	No Report	No Report	No Report	68.140 kg	600.000 kg
Luxembourg	222 u.	No Report	No Report	No Report	No Report	34 u.
Malta	5 u.	35 u.	22 u.	11 u.	No Report	125 u.
Netherlands	353178 u.Govt	582588 u.Govt	661851 u.Govt	884609 u.Govt	900381 u.	11118555 u.
Norway	23.041 kg	28.546 kg	18.854 kg	17.628 kg 123 u.	15.922 kg	21.444 kg
Poland	1904.362 kg	900.000 kg	1.008 kg	15.000 kg	1600.000 kg	86163 u.
Portugal	17316 u.	1184 u.	1.936 kg 2279 u.	3807 u.	1.751 kg 3135 u.	0.550 kg 2663 u.
Slovakia	2830.680 kg	848.797 kg	No Report	817.226 kg	573.900 kg	159.956 kg
Slovenia	14453 u.	8196 u.	6.011 kg 3354 u.	1925 u.	27.750 kg 9425 u.	280.502 kg
Spain	3072.938 kg	2319.031 kg	18156.043 kg	3907.120 kg	5882.218 kg	7242.065 kg
Sweden	6.890 kg	39.820 kg 249 u.	3.213 kg 251 u.	2.789 kg		11.813 kg
Switzerland	26813 u.	79746 u.	227476 u.	189008 u.	557262 u.	570704 u.

Source: Annual Report Questionnaire if not otherwise indicated

SEIZURES, 1998 - 2003
Cannabis plant

Region/country or territory	1998	1999	2000	2001	2002	2003
EUROPE						
West & Central Europe						
United Kingdom	72040 u.	382 u. [ICPO]	47816 u.	71507 u.	57069 u.	57069 u. [4]
Sub-Total	16393.400 kg	8055.560 kg	18311.350 kg	5003.546 kg	9222.728 kg	8913.516 kg
	804298 u.	913852 u.	2365784 u.	4463803 u.	1910492 u.	12126450 u.
Total region	37829.690 kg	12709.560 kg	36410.130 kg	28853.550 kg	42785.190 kg	21532.660 kg
	56479140 u.	20823130 u.	31539950 u.	24711240 u.	27825280 u.	43024380 u.
OCEANIA						
Oceania						
Australia	No Report	176.150 kg	90060 u.	22973 u.	449.703 kg	782.304 kg [5]
					295781 u.	20461 u.
New Zealand	164531 u.	173277 u.	10157 u.	90857 u.	74324 u.	154298 u.
Sub-Total	164531 u.	176.150 kg	100217 u.	113830 u.	449.703 kg	782.304 kg
		173277 u.			370105 u.	174759 u.
Total region	164531 u.	176.150 kg	100217 u.	113830 u.	449.703 kg	782.304 kg
		173277 u.			370105 u.	174759 u.
TOTAL	5015527.000 kg	856413.500 kg	1024252.000 kg	2416071.000 kg	7158802.000 kg	7595484.000 kg
	101924600 u.	45037150 u.	50915700 u.	36037450 u.	41893870 u.	55045540 u.

1) Including cannabis seeds. 2) Includes seedlings 3) Due to unavailability of 2001 data, year 2000 data were used for analysis purposes. 4) Due to unavailability of 2003 data, year 2002 data were used for analysis purposes. 5) Sum of seizures reported by national, State & Territory law enforcement agencies

Source: Annual Report Questionnaire if not otherwise indicated

SEIZURES, 1998 - 2003
Cannabis seed

Region/country or territory	1998	1999	2000	2001	2002	2003
AFRICA						
East Africa						
Mauritius	No Report	No Report	0.076 kg	No Report	No Report	1249 u. [Govt]
Somalia	No Report	No Report	No Report	No Report	15.000 kg	No Report
Uganda	5.000 kg	No Report	102.800 kg	No Report	No Report	No Report
Sub-Total	5.000 kg		102.876 kg		15.000 kg	1249 u.
North Africa						
Algeria	0.930 kg [ICPO]	No Report	No Report	No Report	No Report	No Report
Egypt	11.504 kg	115.819 kg	24.323 kg	No Report	No Report	No Report
Sub-Total	12.434 kg	115.819 kg	24.323 kg			
Southern Africa						
Lesotho	No Report	35.280 kg [ICPO]	No Report	No Report	No Report	No Report
Swaziland	8.096 kg	No Report	263.840 kg	No Report	No Report	No Report
Zambia	38.597 kg [Govt]	126.280 kg	52.261 kg	13.500 kg [Govt]	No Report	163.785 kg
Zimbabwe	0.200 kg	No Report	No Report	No Report	No Report	No Report
Sub-Total	46.893 kg	161.560 kg	316.101 kg	13.500 kg		163.785 kg
West and Central Africa						
Saint Helena	100 u.	80 u.	No Report	No Report	No Report	No Report
Sub-Total	100 u.	80 u.				
Total region	64.327 kg	277.379 kg	443.300 kg	13.500 kg	15.000 kg	163.785 kg
	100 u.	80 u.				1249 u.
AMERICAS						
Caribbean						
Anguilla	8 u.	No Report	No Report	No Report	No Report	No Report
Dominican Republic	1327 u.	3642 u.	679.000 kg [CICAD]	No Report	No Report	No Report
Grenada	0.004 kg	No Report	No Report	No Report	No Report	No Report
Jamaica	No Report	452.630 kg [ICPO]	No Report	No Report	No Report	No Report
Montserrat	No Report	No Report	2500 u.	No Report	No Report	No Report
Saint Lucia	No Report	No Report	0.311 kg	No Report	No Report	No Report
Sub-Total	0.004 kg	452.630 kg	679.311 kg			
	1335 u.	3642 u.	2500 u.			
Central America						
El Salvador	No Report	No Report	No Report	No Report	No Report	4.000 kg [HONL]
Guatemala	5.100 kg	78.473 kg	24.200 kg	No Report	No Report	26.200 kg [HONL]
Honduras	No Report	No Report	2.000 kg [CICAD]	No Report	No Report	9.300 kg [HONL]
Nicaragua	No Report	No Report	1.000 kg [CICAD]	No Report	No Report	No Report
Sub-Total	5.100 kg	78.473 kg	27.200 kg			39.500 kg
North America						
Mexico	4948.744 kg	5847.545 kg	10353.807 kg	7660.910 kg [Govt]	10214.446 kg [Govt]	13775.867 kg [Govt]
United States	No Report	412271.587 kg	417120.258 kg	No Report	No Report	No Report
		451 u.	102 u.			

Source: Annual Report Questionnaire if not otherwise indicated

SEIZURES, 1998 - 2003
Cannabis seed

Region/country or territory	1998	1999	2000	2001	2002	2003
AMERICAS						
North America						
Sub-Total	4948.744 kg	418119.100 kg 451 u.	427474.100 kg 102 u.	7660.910 kg	10214.450 kg	13775.870 kg
South America						
Argentina	42.790 kg 1950 u.	0.091 kg	0.276 kg	1.255 kg	No Report	2.000 kg [HONL]
Brazil	5.179 kg	55.804 kg	99.047 kg	No Report	23.000 kg [F.O]	41.100 kg [HONL]
Chile	0.377 kg	No Report	No Report	No Report	No Report	No Report
Colombia	127.789 kg	53.424 kg	220.000 kg [Govt]	11.000 kg [Govt]	510.000 kg [Govt]	24.000 kg [Govt]
Guyana	No Report	No Report	No Report	No Report	No Report	4.090 kg
Paraguay	503.110 kg	2130.025 kg	668.000 kg [CICAD]	1223.000 kg [Govt]	1478.586 kg [Govt]	No Report
Peru	0.241 kg	19.041 kg	2.841 kg	No Report	No Report	1.600 kg [HONL]
Sub-Total	679.486 kg 1950 u.	2258.385 kg	990.164 kg	1235.255 kg	2011.586 kg	72.790 kg
Total region	5633.333 kg 3285 u.	420908.600 kg 4093 u.	429170.700 kg 2602 u.	8896.165 kg	12226.030 kg	13888.160 kg
ASIA						
Central Asia and Transcaucasian countries						
Uzbekistan	No Report	No Report	222.900 kg	No Report	No Report	No Report
Sub-Total			222.900 kg			
East and South-East Asia						
Indonesia	0.329 kg	1.875 kg	3.300 kg [Govt]	2.641 kg [Govt]	1.647 kg [Govt]	0.114 kg [Govt]
Philippines	85007.000 kg [ICPO] 223459 u.	163.000 kg	28.550 kg	No Report	No Report	No Report
Republic of Korea	No Report	46.067 kg	No Report	No Report	No Report	No Report
Thailand	1.225 kg	No Report	No Report	No Report	No Report	No Report
Sub-Total	85008.550 kg 223459 u.	210.942 kg	31.850 kg	2.641 kg	1.647 kg	0.114 kg
Near and Middle East /South-West Asia						
Bahrain	No Report	0.361 kg [ICPO]	No Report	No Report	No Report	No Report
Jordan	1.412 kg	61.461 kg	3.589 kg	No Report	No Report	No Report
Lebanon	No Report	270.000 kg	424.000 kg	No Report	No Report	No Report
United Arab Emirates	No Report	No Report	0.135 kg	No Report	No Report	No Report
Sub-Total	1.412 kg	331.822 kg	427.724 kg			
South Asia						
Bangladesh	No Report	No Report	No Report	No Report	0.500 kg [Govt]	No Report
Maldives	[1]	No Report	No Report	No Report	No Report	No Report
Sub-Total					0.500 kg	
Total region	85009.970 kg 223459 u.	542.764 kg	682.474 kg	2.641 kg	2.147 kg	0.114 kg

Source: Annual Report Questionnaire if not otherwise indicated

309

SEIZURES, 1998 - 2003
Cannabis seed

Region/country or territory	1998	1999	2000	2001	2002	2003
EUROPE						
Southeast Europe						
Bulgaria	6.556 kg	6.768 kg [ICPO]	1.872 kg	No Report	No Report	No Report
Croatia	0.053 kg 24133 u.	0.868 kg 17054 u.	10437 u.	No Report	No Report	No Report
The former Yugoslav Republic of Macedonia	0.135 kg 508 u.	0.103 kg [NAPOL] 696 u.	No Report	0.120 kg [Govt] 186 u.	298 u.	0.217 kg 1126 u.
Sub-Total	6.744 kg 24641 u.	7.739 kg 17750 u.	1.872 kg 10437 u.	0.120 kg 186 u.	298 u.	0.217 kg 1126 u.
West & Central Europe						
Andorra	0.576 kg [ICPO]	4.900 kg	No Report	No Report	No Report	No Report
Belgium	48.190 kg	16.250 kg	No Report	No Report	No Report	No Report
Finland	0.345 kg 1304 u.	0.100 kg 1150 u.	0.054 kg 1242 u.	No Report	No Report	No Report
Hungary	No Report	No Report	10.000 kg	No Report	No Report	No Report
Iceland	No Report	No Report	No Report	No Report	No Report	54.968 kg 48259 u.
Malta	72 u.	5 u.	4 u.	No Report	No Report	
Poland	No Report	4.016 kg	1200 u.	No Report	No Report	No Report
Portugal	1.563 kg	38.377 kg 45 u.	1.739 kg 201 u.	No Report	4036 u.	No Report
Slovakia	No Report	No Report	No Report	No Report	1.810 kg	No Report
Sub-Total	50.674 kg 1376 u.	63.643 kg 1200 u.	11.793 kg 2647 u.		1.810 kg 4036 u.	54.968 kg 48259 u.
Total region	57.418 kg 26017 u.	71.382 kg 18950 u.	13.665 kg 13084 u.	0.120 kg 186 u.	1.810 kg 4334 u.	55.185 kg 49385 u.
OCEANIA						
Oceania						
Australia	No Report	4.129 kg	5.559 kg	No Report	No Report	No Report
New Zealand	244031 u.	253609 u.	No Report	No Report	No Report	No Report
Sub-Total	244031 u.	4.129 kg 253609 u.	5.559 kg			
Total region	244031 u.	4.129 kg 253609 u.	5.559 kg			
TOTAL	90765.050 kg 496892 u.	421804.200 kg 276732 u.	430315.700 kg 15686 u.	8912.426 kg 186 u.	12244.990 kg 4334 u.	14107.240 kg 50634 u.

1) Small quantity.

Source: Annual Report Questionnaire if not otherwise indicated

6.4. Amphetamine-type stimulants: Seizures 1998-2003

SEIZURES, 1998 - 2003

Amphetamine-type Stimulants (excluding 'Ecstasy')

Region/country or territory	1998	1999	2000	2001	2002	2003
AFRICA						
East Africa						
Djibouti	No Report	No Report	No Report	No Report	No Report	10000 u.
Eritrea	No Report	No Report	6.000 kg [ICPO]	No Report	No Report	No Report
Sub-Total			6.000 kg			10000 u.
North Africa						
Egypt	15.348 lt.	5.222 kg 19.023 lt.	11.650 lt. 57076 u.	No Report	10.925 lt.	3863 u.
Morocco	49561 u.	73917 u.	No Report	No Report	No Report	No Report
Sudan	No Report	No Report	0.250 kg 38 u.	No Report	No Report	No Report
Tunisia	No Report	No Report	No Report	No Report	28038 u.	5882 u.
Sub-Total	15.348 lt. 49561 u.	5.222 kg 19.023 lt. 73917 u.	0.250 kg 11.650 lt. 57114 u.		10.925 lt. 28038 u.	9745 u.
Southern Africa						
Namibia	No Report	No Report	No Report	No Report	No Report	9212 u.
South Africa	527 u.	369 u. [ICPO]	0.013 kg [ICPO] 924 u.	59078 u.	1.259 kg 2294 u.	8189 u.
Zambia	0.000 kg [Govt]	0.018 kg	0.000 kg [Govt]	270 u. [Govt]	No Report	No Report
Zimbabwe	15.729 kg	No Report	No Report	No Report	No Report	No Report
Sub-Total	15.729 kg 527 u.	0.018 kg 369 u.	0.013 kg 924 u.	59348 u.	1.259 kg 2294 u.	17401 u.
West and Central Africa						
Burkina Faso	No Report	No Report	No Report	2.851 kg	No Report	No Report
Cameroon	No Report	No Report	No Report	1000 u.	23 u.	No Report
Chad	No Report	1620 u. [ICPO]	180000 u.	No Report	No Report	No Report
Côte d'Ivoire	6385 u.	56.131 kg	0.200 kg [ICPO]	0.124 kg	66373 u.	No Report
Gambia	No Report	328 u.	No Report	3.000 kg	No Report	No Report
Guinea	No Report	No Report	No Report	No Report	No Report	0.200 kg
Niger	No Report	556537 u. [ICPO]	No Report	No Report	No Report	No Report
Nigeria	No Report	322.071 kg	0.580 kg	No Report	No Report	No Report
Togo	No Report	No Report	No Report	No Report	1.160 kg	No Report
Sub-Total	6385 u.	378.202 kg 558485 u.	0.780 kg 180000 u.	5.975 kg 1000 u.	1.160 kg 66396 u.	0.200 kg
Total region	15.729 kg 15.348 lt. 56473 u.	383.442 kg 19.023 lt. 632771 u.	7.043 kg 11.650 lt. 238038 u.	5.975 kg 60348 u.	2.419 kg 10.925 lt. 96728 u.	0.200 kg 37146 u.
AMERICAS						
Caribbean						
Bahamas	No Report	No Report	60.000 kg [CICAD]	No Report	No Report	2.270 kg
Bermuda	No Report	No Report	No Report	No Report	65 u. [ICPO]	No Report
Cayman Islands	0.040 kg 120 u.	0.001 kg [ICPO]	No Report	No Report	No Report	0.001 kg

Source: Annual Report Questionnaire if not otherwise indicated

311

SEIZURES, 1998 - 2003

Amphetamine-type Stimulants (excluding 'Ecstasy')

Region/country or territory	1998	1999	2000	2001	2002	2003
AMERICAS						
Caribbean						
Netherlands Antilles	541.000 kg [F.O]	No Report	No Report	No Report	No Report	17.000 kg [PRO]
Sub-Total	541.040 kg 120 u.	0.001 kg	60.000 kg		65 u.	19.271 kg
Central America						
Costa Rica	No Report	No Report	195 u.	468 u.	0.005 kg [(1]	No Report
Sub-Total			195 u.	468 u.	0.005 kg	
North America						
Canada	0.590 kg 54.500 lt. 11207 u.	20.218 kg 2.306 lt. 4970 u.	29.482 kg 2.798 lt. 8815 u.	53.231 kg 57798 u.	31.603 kg 4673 u.	23.564 kg 6388 u.
Mexico	98.391 kg	926.011 kg 880 u.	714.920 kg	417.944 kg	459.056 kg	747.868 kg
United States	1824.363 kg 215.776 lt. 411768 u.	2641.000 kg 20217 u.	2451.383 kg 226.682 lt. 43096 u.	2857.600 kg 5494617 u.	1107.205 kg 217437 u.	3853.400 kg 3646276 u.
Sub-Total	1923.344 kg 270.276 lt. 422975 u.	3587.229 kg 2.306 lt. 26067 u.	3195.785 kg 229.480 lt. 51911 u.	3328.775 kg 5552415 u.	1597.864 kg 222110 u.	4624.832 kg 3652664 u.
South America						
Argentina	600 u.	4103 u.	10134 u.	3991 u.	430 u.	89 u.
Brazil	No Report	No Report	No Report	No Report	201 u. [ICPO]	No Report
Chile	0.011 kg 6973 u.	104523 u. [CICAD]	11287 u.	22225 u.	2861 u.	0.110 kg 17735 u.
Peru	No Report	No Report	No Report	0.063 kg 709 u.	No Report	No Report
Sub-Total	0.011 kg 7573 u.	108626 u.	21421 u.	0.063 kg 26925 u.	3492 u.	0.110 kg 17824 u.
Total region	2464.395 kg 270.276 lt. 430668 u.	3587.230 kg 2.306 lt. 134693 u.	3255.785 kg 229.480 lt. 73527 u.	3328.838 kg 5579808 u.	1597.869 kg 225667 u.	4644.212 kg 3670488 u.
ASIA						
Central Asia and Transcaucasian countries						
Georgia	No Report	No Report	0.013 kg [ICPO]	No Report	No Report	No Report
Tajikistan	No Report	No Report	No Report	No Report	No Report	0.750 kg
Uzbekistan	No Report	0.031 kg	No Report	No Report	No Report	No Report
Sub-Total		0.031 kg	0.013 kg			0.750 kg
East and South-East Asia						
Brunei Darussalam	0.237 kg	1.197 kg	1.648 kg	0.661 kg 375 u.	0.248 kg	0.140 kg
Cambodia	25114 u. [F.O]	23032 u. [F.O]	50565 u. [F.O]	75576 u. [F.O]	137660 u. [F.O]	209527 u. [F.O]
China	1608.000 kg [F.O]	16059.000 kg [ICPO]	20900.000 kg [ICPO]	4840.000 kg [F.O]	3190.000 kg	5830.000 kg

Source: Annual Report Questionnaire if not otherwise indicated

SEIZURES, 1998 - 2003
Amphetamine-type Stimulants (excluding 'Ecstasy')

Region/country or territory	1998	1999	2000	2001	2002	2003
ASIA						
East and South-East Asia						
Hong Kong Special Administrative Region of China	232.700 kg [Govt.]	No Report	87.600 kg	63.100 kg	71.565 kg	39.445 kg
			7879 u.	214776 u.	84203 u.	300791 u.
Indonesia	7.761 kg [HNLP]	218.625 kg 29511 u.	88.163 kg	48.793 kg 5355 u.	46.580 kg 421246 u.	22.577 kg 238284 u.
Japan	549.702 kg 0.788 lt. 1 u.	1994.459 kg 0.589 lt. 4589 u.	1030.580 kg [ICPO] 0.471 lt. 954 u.	419.175 kg 142 u.	446.000 kg 0.195 lt. 51830 u.	493.500 kg 0.038 lt.
Lao People's Democratic Republic	No Report	931401 u. [Govt]	1957929 u. [Govt]	851619 u. [Govt]	151750 u.	120.370 kg
Macao Special Administrative Region of China	0.073 kg [ICPO]	No Report	0.272 kg [ICPO]	0.035 kg	1.108 kg	0.005 kg
	187 u.		785 u.	1732 u.	3867 u.	530 u.
Malaysia	No Report	5.411 kg 329265 u.	208.100 kg 195387 u.	No Report	6.046 kg [ICPO] 419216 u.	102.200 kg 1294659 u.
Mongolia	No Report	0.100 kg [ICPO]	No Report	4 u.	No Report	No Report
Myanmar	16026688 u.	22.058 kg 28887514 u.	6.398 kg 26759772 u.	33103548 u.	431.200 kg 9399794 u.	102.000 kg 4002684 u.
Philippines	312.929 kg [Govt] 85.730 lt.	943.700 kg	989.760 kg 30.000 lt.	1777.642 kg	914.335 kg	3122.029 kg
Republic of Korea	28.311 kg	29.233 kg	4.500 kg [ICPO] 9240 u.	169.562 kg 2095 u.	36.817 kg [ICPO]	64.809 kg
Singapore	1.711 kg 4470 u.	1.300 kg 1380 u.	0.759 kg 24723 u.	2.175 kg 19935 u.	52243 u.	0.054 kg 8062 u.
Taiwan, Province of China	No Report	No Report	836.000 kg [PRESS]	1156.000 kg [PRESS]	No Report	No Report
Thailand	3013.000 kg [F.O]	4517.000 kg [F.O]	7557.000 kg [HNLP] 84000000 u.	8338.000 kg [F.O]	8662.223 kg [ICPO]	6505.000 kg [Govt]
Viet Nam	No Report	6025 u. [F.O]	30876 u. [ICPO]	72391 u.	47852 u. [F.O]	27000 u.
Sub-Total	5754.424 kg 86.518 lt. 16056460 u.	23792.080 kg 0.589 lt. 30212720 u.	31710.780 kg 30.471 lt. 113038100 u.	16815.140 kg 34347550 u.	13806.120 kg 0.195 lt. 10769660 u.	16402.130 kg 0.038 lt. 6081537 u.
Near and Middle East /South-West Asia						
Bahrain	28 u. [ICPO]	No Report	0.005 kg [ICPO]	No Report	0.001 kg 645233 u.	No Report
Israel	No Report	190 u. [ICPO]	131 u. [ICPO]	0.014 kg	0.001 kg 424 u.	151 u.
Jordan	262071 u.	518813 u.	5817798 u.	1405872 u.	1421896 u.	3242094 u.
Kuwait	No Report	No Report	110000 u. [ICPO]	No Report	No Report	No Report
Lebanon	No Report	359 u. [ICPO]	41616 u. [ICPO]	No Report	989 u. [ICPO]	No Report
Pakistan	No Report	No Report	20.000 kg	No Report	No Report	No Report
Qatar	220 u. [ICPO]	14 u. [ICPO]	448 u. [ICPO]	No Report	6081 u.	198 u.

Source: Annual Report Questionnaire if not otherwise indicated

313

SEIZURES, 1998 - 2003

Amphetamine-type Stimulants (excluding 'Ecstasy')

Region/country or territory	1998	1999	2000	2001	2002	2003
ASIA						
Near and Middle East /South-West Asia						
Saudi Arabia	3553231 u.	7549665 u. [ICPO]	9698370 u. [(2]	1.000 kg 6715652 u.	10409161 u. [ICPO]	2.400 kg [ICPC]
Syrian Arab Republic	No Report	1470831 u.	1159065 u. [(2]	1911796 u. [Govt (2]	3062393 u.	2255590 u.
United Arab Emirates	No Report	No Report	0.107 kg [ICPO]	0.176 kg	0.037 kg 2 u.	0.007 kg
Yemen	972 u. [ICPO]	3020 u. [ICPO]	0.005 kg [ICPO] 3754 u.	No Report	No Report	No Report
Sub-Total	3816522 u.	9542892 u.	20.117 kg 16831180 u.	1.190 kg 10033320 u.	0.040 kg 15546180 u.	2.407 kg 5498033 u.
South Asia						
India	No Report	No Report	3.000 kg [ICPO]	0.965 kg	No Report	No Report
Maldives	No Report	0.001 kg	No Report	6 u.	No Report	No Report
Nepal	No Report	No Report	No Report	No Report	0.023 kg	No Report
Sub-Total		0.001 kg	3.000 kg	0.965 kg 6 u.	0.023 kg	
Total region	5754.424 kg 86.518 lt. 19872980 u.	23792.120 kg 0.589 lt. 39755610 u.	31733.910 kg 30.471 lt. 129869300 u.	16817.300 kg 44380880 u.	13806.180 kg 0.195 lt. 26315840 u.	16405.290 kg 0.038 lt. 11579570 u.
EUROPE						
East Europe						
Belarus	0.282 kg	1.644 kg	1.267 kg [ICPO]	13.500 kg [Govt]	9.273 kg [Govt]	11.039 kg
Republic of Moldova	No Report	0.105 lt. [ICPO]	No Report	No Report	No Report	No Report
Russian Federation	34.000 kg [F.O]	40.500 kg [F.O]	9.000 kg [F.O (3]	13.513 kg	37.640 kg [ICPO]	44.395 kg
Ukraine	2.482 kg	No Report	4784 u. [Govt (4]	0.716 kg	No Report	No Report
Sub-Total	36.764 kg	42.144 kg 0.105 lt.	10.267 kg 4784 u.	27.729 kg	46.913 kg	55.434 kg
Southeast Europe						
Albania	No Report	0.009 kg [ICPO]	No Report	No Report	10 u.	50 u.
Bosnia and Herzegovina	No Report	No Report	No Report	No Report	117.000 kg [ICPO]	No Report
Bulgaria	150 u.	87.192 kg 22928 u.	209.930 kg 18491 u.	64.676 kg [(2] 760 u.	173.950 kg 135347 u.	587.408 kg [(2] 140688 u.
Croatia	0.765 kg 9106 u.	1.110 kg 15429 u.	2.124 kg	0.931 kg	28.026 kg	3.814 kg
Romania	No Report	10546 u.	15874 u.	11.663 kg [Govt]	0.999 kg	1436 u.
Serbia and Montenegro	No Report	No Report	No Report	0.087 kg	No Report	96816 u.
The former Yugoslav Republic of Macedonia	No Report	No Report	No Report	No Report	7.015 kg	No Report
Turkey	479403 u. [Govt]	1231964 u. [Govt]	295037 u.	1090486 u. [(2]	9063992 u.	5375197 u.

Source: Annual Report Questionnaire if not otherwise indicated

SEIZURES, 1998 - 2003
Amphetamine-type Stimulants (excluding 'Ecstasy')

Region/country or territory	1998	1999	2000	2001	2002	2003
EUROPE						
Southeast Europe						
Sub-Total	0.765 kg	88.311 kg	212.054 kg	77.357 kg	326.990 kg	591.222 kg
	488659 u.	1280867 u.	329402 u.	1091246 u.	9199349 u.	5614187 u.
West & Central Europe						
Andorra	143 u. [ICPO]	43 u.	0.004 kg [ICPO]	No Report	0.004 kg	No Report
					42 u.	
Austria	9763 u.	5165 u.	0.450 kg	2.918 kg	9.491 kg	54.306 kg
			1452 u.			
Belgium	445.000 kg	325.070 kg	75.140 kg [ICPO]	75.140 kg [UNODC (5]	500.000 kg	209.000 kg
	271080 u.	489566 u.	18397 u.	18397 u.		
Cyprus	No Report	0.012 kg	0.005 kg [ICPO]	0.004 kg	0.123 kg	125 u.
					1 u.	
Czech Republic	76.500 kg [ICPO.]	21.400 kg	13.234 kg [ICPO]	23.130 kg	4.715 kg	9.724 kg
		673 u.			132 u.	3134 u.
Denmark	25.236 kg	31.600 kg	57.136 kg	160.640 kg	35.256 kg	65.892 kg
Estonia	1.955 kg	11.507 kg	26.692 kg	25.300 kg	35.119 kg	109.111 kg
	971 u.	2707 u.	955 u.		1023 u.	
Finland	24.784 kg	78.464 kg	79.565 kg	137.730 kg	129.200 kg	114.600 kg
	1003 u.	17665 u.		14967 u.		
France	165.122 kg	232.941 kg	447.234 kg	57.420 kg	168.050 kg	274.965 kg
	1142226 u.		2283620 u.			24697 u.
Germany, Federal Republic of	309.602 kg	360.000 kg	271.200 kg [ICPO]	262.539 kg	361.720 kg	484.055 kg
Greece	0.003 kg	1.380 kg	2.008 kg	0.078 kg	0.500 kg	0.637 kg
	5 u.	257 u.	30109 u.	8 u.	1789 u.	18 u.
Hungary	7.605 kg	9.257 kg	10.000 kg	1.740 kg	3.731 kg	12.118 kg
				19 u.	232 u.	
Iceland	No Report	5.078 kg	10.267 kg	0.132 kg	7.161 kg	2.945 kg
						310 u.
Ireland	43.162 kg	13.300 kg [ICPO]	5.040 kg	17.955 kg	16.473 kg	67.724 kg
	46538 u.	12015 u.	568952 u.		12728 u.	1019 u.
Italy	2.454 kg	5.131 kg [ICPO]	0.197 kg	0.924 kg	2.099 kg	4.304 kg
	2309 u.	16115 u.	77299 u.	327 u.	341 u.	378 u.
Latvia	1.395 kg	0.493 kg [ICPO]	0.853 kg	3.551 kg	No Report	15.877 kg
	1.700 lt.		1114 u.			
	2671 u.					
Liechtenstein	No Report	No Report	No Report	12 u.	0.003 kg	0.004 kg
Lithuania	0.013 kg	0.077 kg	19.492 kg	6.886 kg	4.542 kg	31.560 kg
	0.994 lt.	0.486 lt.	0.482 lt.		229 u.	243 u.
	142 u.	2297 u.	42 u.			
Luxembourg	No Report	0.016 kg [ICPO]	0.157 kg [ICPO]	No Report	0.006 kg [ICPO]	0.152 kg
Malta	No Report	No Report	45 u. [(6]	No Report	No Report	0.000 kg
Netherlands	1450.000 kg [Govt]	853.000 kg [Govt]	293.000 kg [Govt]	579.000 kg	481.000 kg	880.000 kg
	242409 u.	45847 u.			1028 u.	14000 u.
Norway	207.999 kg	52.110 kg	95.506 kg	106.936 kg	232.566 kg	247.275 kg
		6056 u.	1147 u.	2565 u.	11912 u.	1785 u.

Source: Annual Report Questionnaire if not otherwise indicated

315

SEIZURES, 1998 - 2003

Amphetamine-type Stimulants (excluding 'Ecstasy')

Region/country or territory	1998	1999	2000	2001	2002	2003
EUROPE						
West & Central Europe						
Poland	51.503 kg	51.453 kg	141.600 kg	194.960 kg	161.516 kg	192.950 kg
Portugal	1131 u. [7]	0.087 kg	0.029 kg	0.001 kg	0.640 kg	0.033 kg
		31393 u.	22 u.	35 u.	34 u.	125 u.
Slovakia	9.717 kg	0.131 kg	0.281 kg	0.571 kg	0.331 kg	0.033 kg
	35 u.	22 u.				
Slovenia	0.679 kg	0.625 kg ICPO	0.218 kg	0.064 kg	0.030 kg	373 u.
	534 u.	818 u.	28546 u.	98 u.	390 u.	
Spain	176.985 kg	49.538 kg	23.412 kg	18.700 kg	55.642 kg	47.315 kg
		182.000 lt.		29711 u.	31427 u.	2726 u.
Sweden	134.714 kg	120.310 kg	107.039 kg ICPO	253.161 kg	350.300 kg	365.379 kg
		1099 u.				2510 u.
Switzerland	No Report	10.700 kg	39.105 kg	4.608 kg	10.433 kg	23.697 kg
United Kingdom	1807.847 kg	1194.938 kg ICPO	1772.344 kg	1716.626 kg	1407.000 kg	1407.000 kg [8]
		25021 u.	6541808 u.			
Sub-Total	4942.275 kg	3428.618 kg	3491.208 kg	3650.714 kg	3977.650 kg	4620.655 kg
	2.694 lt.	182.486 lt.	0.482 lt.	66139 u.	61308 u.	51443 u.
	1720960 u.	656759 u.	9553508 u.			
Total region	4979.804 kg	3559.073 kg	3713.529 kg	3755.800 kg	4351.553 kg	5267.312 kg
	2.694 lt.	182.591 lt.	0.482 lt.	1157385 u.	9260656 u.	5665630 u.
	2209619 u.	1937626 u.	9887694 u.			
OCEANIA						
Oceania						
Australia	182.220 kg Govt. [9]	276.288 kg [9]	427.312 kg	876.006 kg [4]	561.050 kg	707.551 kg [10]
						136 u.
Fiji	No Report	No Report	0.333 kg ICPO	No Report	No Report	No Report
New Zealand	1.340 kg	1.104 kg	10.175 kg	4.170 kg	7.439 kg	2.193 kg
		1400 u.	103 u.		523 u.	57 u.
Sub-Total	183.560 kg	277.392 kg	437.820 kg	880.176 kg	568.489 kg	709.744 kg
		1400 u.	103 u.		523 u.	193 u.
Total region	183.560 kg	277.392 kg	437.820 kg	880.176 kg	568.489 kg	709.744 kg
		1400 u.	103 u.		523 u.	193 u.
TOTAL	13397.910 kg	31599.250 kg	39148.090 kg	24788.090 kg	20326.510 kg	27026.750 kg
	374.836 lt.	204.509 lt.	272.083 lt.	51178420 u.	11.120 lt.	0.038 lt.
	22569740 u.	42462100 u.	140068700 u.		35899420 u.	20953030 u.

1) Ketamine 2) Captagon 3) Including other hallucinogens. 4) Includes ecstasy 5) Due to unavailability of 2001 data, year 2000 data were used for analysis purposes. 6) Duromine 7) Small quantity. 8) Due to unavailability of 2003 data, year 2002 data were used for analysis purposes. 9) Provisional figures. 10) Sum of seizures reported by national, State & Territory law enforcement agencies

Source: Annual Report Questionnaire if not otherwise indicated

SEIZURES, 1998 - 2003
Ecstasy (MDA, MDEA, MDMA)

Region/country or territory	1998	1999	2000	2001	2002	2003
AFRICA						
North Africa						
Egypt	No Report	No Report	3372 u.	70080 u.	785 u.	3725 u.
Sub-Total			3372 u.	70080 u.	785 u.	3725 u.
Southern Africa						
Lesotho	No Report	No Report	No Report	No Report	1.884 kg [ICPO]	No Report
Namibia	No Report	74 u.	157 u.	546 u.	49 u.	169 u.
South Africa	No Report	30132 u. [ICPO]	1.177 kg 297021 u.	95792 u.	14.540 kg 424258 u.	401267 u.
Zambia	No Report	No Report	No Report	No Report	No Report	0.071 kg
Zimbabwe	No Report	3 u.	No Report	6 u.	58 u.	15 u.
Sub-Total		30209 u.	1.177 kg 297178 u.	96344 u.	16.424 kg 424365 u.	0.071 kg 401451 u.
Total region		30209 u.	1.177 kg 300550 u.	166424 u.	16.424 kg 425150 u.	0.071 kg 405176 u.
AMERICAS						
Caribbean						
Aruba	No Report	873 u. [F.O]	85279 u. [F.O]	59874 u. [F.O]	19445 u. [ICPO]	No Report
Bahamas	No Report	No Report	63.000 kg	0.023 kg 0 u.	0.027 kg	No Report
Bermuda	No Report	No Report	No Report	153 u. [F.O]	65 u.	No Report
British Virgin Islands	No Report	No Report	No Report	No Report	No Report	2.500 kg [PRO]
Cayman Islands	No Report	0.030 kg	80 u. [F.O]	No Report	120 u.	0.002 kg
Cuba	No Report	No Report	1965 u. [HONL]	No Report	0.001 kg [ICPO]	14 u. [HON]
Dominican Republic	No Report	No Report	125073 u. [F.O]	30903 u.	153605 u. [HONLC]	51565 u.
Guadeloupe	No Report	No Report	25540 u. [F.O]	500 u. [F.O]	No Report	No Report
Jamaica	No Report	No Report	No Report	5070 u.	79 u. [ICPO]	No Report
Netherlands Antilles	No Report	No Report	15.464 kg [ICPO]	20465 u. [F.O]	94 u. [ICPO]	No Report
Puerto Rico	No Report	No Report	No Report	1977 u. [F.O]	No Report	No Report
Sub-Total		0.030 kg 873 u.	78.464 kg 237937 u.	0.023 kg 118942 u.	0.028 kg 173408 u.	2.502 kg 51579 u.
Central America						
Costa Rica	No Report	No Report	46 u.	87 u.	83 u.	1341 u.
Nicaragua	No Report	No Report	No Report	No Report	19886 u.	No Report
Panama	No Report	No Report	2256 u.	22166 u.	934 u. [HONLC]	No Report
Sub-Total			2302 u.	22253 u.	20903 u.	1341 u.
North America						
Canada	No Report	No Report	449.814 kg [ICPO] 2069709 u.	421.590 kg 846973 u.	74.992 kg 177450 u.	51.624 kg 39199 u.
Mexico	No Report	No Report	32.302 kg [ICPO]	102.000 kg	31.953 kg	16.300 kg
United States	No Report	No Report	9600000 u. [ICPO]	8539981 u.	7312142 u.	242.700 kg 1320191 u.

Source: Annual Report Questionnaire if not otherwise indicated

SEIZURES, 1998 - 2003
Ecstasy (MDA, MDEA, MDMA)

Region/country or territory	1998	1999	2000	2001	2002	2003
AMERICAS						
North America						
Sub-Total			482.116 kg	523.590 kg	106.945 kg	310.624 kg
			11669710 u.	9386954 u.	7489592 u.	1359390 u.
South America						
Argentina	No Report	No Report	No Report	No Report	430 u. [ICPO]	14456 u.
Brazil	No Report	59612 u. [ICPO]	36796 u.	1909 u. [Govt]	15804 u. [F.O]	70859 u.
Chile	No Report	No Report	140 u. [ICPO]	2626 u.	458 u.	5244 u.
Colombia	0 u. [Govt]	1022 u.	83.000 kg	19142 u. [Govt]	175382 u.	5042 u.
Ecuador	No Report	No Report	No Report	7 u. [Govt]	0.020 kg [Govt]	3.950 kg [Govt]
					172 u.	
Guyana	No Report	626 u. [F.O]	124 u. [F.O]	No Report	No Report	No Report
Peru	No Report	No Report	No Report	35 u.	78 u.	85 u.
Suriname	3000 u. [CICAD]	No Report	61232 u. [INCSR]	No Report	80 u.	No Report
Uruguay	No Report	84 u.	738 u.	No Report	31 u.	18 u.
Venezuela	No Report	No Report	7985 u. [CICAD]	2 u.	16010 u.	62302 u.
Sub-Total	3000 u.	61344 u.	83.000 kg	23721 u.	0.020 kg	3.950 kg
			107015 u.		208445 u.	158006 u.
Total region	3000 u.	0.030 kg	643.580 kg	523.613 kg	106.993 kg	317.076 kg
		62217 u.	12016960 u.	9551870 u.	7892348 u.	1570316 u.
ASIA						
East and South-East Asia						
Brunei Darussalam	No Report	32 u.	No Report	No Report	10 u.	No Report
China	No Report	No Report	200.000 kg [HNLP]	2700000 u.	3000000 u. [ICPO]	409261 u.
			240000 u.			
Hong Kong Special Administrative Region of China	No Report	21202 u. [ICPO]	58.800 kg	0.032 kg	0.053 kg	31.170 kg
			378621 u.	170243 u.	48840 u.	142912 u.
Indonesia	No Report	29510 u. [ICPO]	109567 u. [Govt]	90523 u. [Govt]	84224 u.	253659 u.
Japan	No Report	No Report	77528 u. [ICPO]	0.121 kg	190281 u. [Govt]	0.014 kg
				112542 u.		393757 u.
Macao Special Administrative Region of China	No Report	No Report	2453 u. [ICPO]	1687 u.	672 u.	661 u.
Malaysia	No Report	55975 u.	49901 u. [ICPO]	No Report	164884 u. [ICPO]	231191 u.
Philippines	No Report	No Report	1026 u.	No Report	246 u.	10 u.
Republic of Korea	No Report	No Report	No Report	1672 u.	39011 u. [ICPO]	37784 u.
Singapore	No Report	4.070 kg	10339 u.	0.257 kg	7331 u.	2410 u.
		17232 u.		23846 u.		
Thailand	5878 u. [HNLP]	30615 u. [F.O]	72182 u. [HNLP]	61922 u. [F.O]	145873 u. [F.O]	33.000 kg [Govt]
Sub-Total	5878 u.	4.070 kg	258.800 kg	0.410 kg	0.053 kg	64.184 kg
		154566 u.	941617 u.	3162435 u.	3681372 u.	1471645 u.

Source: Annual Report Questionnaire if not otherwise indicated

SEIZURES, 1998 - 2003
Ecstasy (MDA, MDEA, MDMA)

Region/country or territory	1998	1999	2000	2001	2002	2003
ASIA						
Near and Middle East /South-West Asia						
Israel	No Report	130.687 kg [ICPO] 30335 u.	270000 u.	1.504 kg 121695 u.	4.454 kg 951057 u.	1.041 kg 104324 u.
Jordan	No Report	5000 u. [ICPO]	No Report	No Report	No Report	No Report
Pakistan	No Report	No Report	No Report	No Report	No Report	1980 u.
Sub-Total		130.687 kg 35335 u.	270000 u.	1.504 kg 121695 u.	4.454 kg 951057 u.	1.041 kg 106304 u.
Total region	5878 u.	134.757 kg 189901 u.	258.800 kg 1211617 u.	1.914 kg 3284130 u.	4.507 kg 4632429 u.	65.225 kg 1577949 u.
EUROPE						
East Europe						
Belarus	No Report	No Report	No Report	0.204 kg [Govt]	0.536 kg [ICPO]	2.725 kg [Govt]
Russian Federation	No Report	No Report	No Report	0.850 kg	No Report	6.191 kg
Ukraine	No Report	1.349 kg [ICPO] 18888 u.	0.305 kg [ICPO] 4784 u.	47 u.	No Report	No Report
Sub-Total		1.349 kg 18888 u.	0.305 kg 4784 u.	1.054 kg 47 u.	0.536 kg	8.916 kg
Southeast Europe						
Bosnia and Herzegovina	No Report	No Report	No Report	No Report	1212 u. [ICPO]	No Report
Bulgaria	No Report	No Report	4524 u. [Govt]	7.900 kg 2361 u.	1.500 kg 3135 u.	1097 u.
Croatia	No Report	15421 u. [ICPO]	9979 u.	12906 u.	110632 u.	29840 u.
Romania	No Report	No Report	10945 u. [ICPO]	67210 u.	0.007 kg 19567 u.	70088 u.
Serbia and Montenegro	No Report	No Report	No Report	0.079 kg 10811 u.	10000 u.	0.060 kg 76302 u.
The former Yugoslav Republic of Macedonia	787 u. [NAPOL]	5532 u. [NAPOL]	280 u. [NAPOL]	45 u. [Govt]	0.002 kg 18341 u.	No Report
Turkey	3559 u. [Govt]	No Report	33894 u. [Govt]	121508 u.	98989 u.	473240 u.
Sub-Total	4346 u.	20953 u.	59622 u.	7.979 kg 214841 u.	1.509 kg 261876 u.	0.060 kg 650567 u.
West & Central Europe						
Andorra	No Report	43 u. [ICPO]	283 u. [ICPO]	85 u.	42 u. [ICPO]	No Report
Austria	No Report	31129 u.	162.093 kg	256299 u.	0.099 kg 383451 u.	422103 u.
Belgium	No Report	266.460 kg [ICPO] 467477 u.	37.000 kg [ICPO] 818515 u.	37.000 kg [UNODC (1] 818515 u.	1564.000 kg	58278 u.
Cyprus	No Report	0.001 kg 62 u.	0.005 kg 3317 u.	0.004 kg 2910 u.	0.273 kg 10253 u.	1.093 kg 5751 u.
Czech Republic	No Report	No Report	17502 u.	29.890 kg	1.893 kg 88391 u.	4.851 kg 51692 u.

Source: Annual Report Questionnaire if not otherwise indicated

319

SEIZURES, 1998 - 2003
Ecstasy (MDA, MDEA, MDMA)

Region/country or territory	1998	1999	2000	2001	2002	2003
EUROPE						
West & Central Europe						
Denmark	No Report	26117 u.	21608 u.	150080 u.	25738 u.	62475 u.
Estonia	No Report	1770 u. ICPO	0.431 kg 1351 u.	1.714 kg	3.402 kg	6.763 kg
Finland	No Report	16578 u. ICPO	87393 u.	81228 u.	45065 u.	35216 u.
France	No Report	1860402 u.	2283620 u. HNLP	1503773 u.	2156937 u.	2211727 u.
Germany, Federal Republic of	No Report	1470507 u. Govt	1634683 u.	4576504 u.	3207099 u.	1257676 u.
Greece	No Report	2815 u.	53557 u.	58845 u.	28430 u.	47705 u.
Hungary	No Report	466 u.	13616 u.	0.260 kg 18301 u.	5.575 kg 23730 u.	30.990 kg 135634 u.
Iceland	No Report	7478 u.	22057 u.	93151 u.	0.006 kg 814 u.	0.021 kg 3190 u.
Ireland	No Report	74.609 kg 266462 u.	695133 u. ICPO	469862 u.	0.153 kg 117046 u.	0.616 kg 1288412 u.
Italy	No Report	272288 u. ICPO	501986 u.	0.285 kg 308845 u.	0.006 kg 397566 u.	0.452 kg 234973 u.
Latvia	No Report	0.749 kg ICPO 17 u.	No Report	1620 u.	No Report	9239 u.
Liechtenstein	No Report	No Report	10 u.	No Report	0.001 kg	0.016 kg
Lithuania	No Report	1122 u. ICPO	50724 u. ICPO	0.045 kg 514 u.	0.003 kg 1205 u.	0.440 kg 98458 u.
Luxembourg	No Report	357 u.	318 u. ICPO	No Report	1139 u. ICPO	132 u.
Malta	No Report	459 u.	5191 u.	2242 u.	1012 u. ICPO	8694 u.
Monaco	No Report	3 u. ICPO	5 u. ICPO	No Report	55 u.	0.006 kg
Netherlands	1163514 u. Govt	3663608 u. Govt	632.000 kg Govt 5500000 u.	113.000 kg 8684505 u.	849.000 kg 6787167 u.	435.000 kg 5420033 u.
Norway	No Report	0.025 kg 24644 u.	0.114 kg 49208 u.	0.117 kg 61205 u.	0.077 kg 102409 u.	0.087 kg 99689 u.
Poland	No Report	6319 u.	129513 u.	232735 u.	38179 u.	1.274 kg 95148 u.
Portugal	No Report	0.086 kg Govt 31319 u.	1.089 kg 25499 u.	0.088 kg 126451 u.	1.675 kg 222466 u.	0.201 kg 163525 u.
Slovakia	No Report	9 u.	493 u. ICPO	0.568 kg	435 u.	1663 u.
Slovenia	4496 u. HONEU	1749 u. ICPO	0.053 kg 27974 u.	1852 u.	7877 u.	2847 u.
Spain	No Report	357649 u.	891562 u. ICPO	860164 u.	1396142 u.	771874 u.
Sweden	No Report	No Report	0.262 kg ICPO 184161 u.	0.314 kg 57750 u.	96577 u.	0.107 kg 71086 u.
Switzerland	No Report	No Report	189569 u. (2	86959 u.	88342 u.	19942 u.
United Kingdom	No Report	6323500 u. NCIS	6534813 u.	7662228 u.	5852000 u.	5852000 u. (3
Sub-Total	1168010 u.	341.930 kg 14834350 u.	833.047 kg 19743660 u.	183.285 kg 26116620 u.	2426.163 kg 21079570 u.	481.917 kg 18429160 u.
Total region	1172356 u.	343.279 kg 14874190 u.	833.352 kg 19808070 u.	192.318 kg 26331510 u.	2428.208 kg 21341440 u.	490.893 kg 19079730 u.

Source: Annual Report Questionnaire if not otherwise indicated

SEIZURES, 1998 - 2003
Ecstasy (MDA, MDEA, MDMA)

Region/country or territory	1998	1999	2000	2001	2002	2003
OCEANIA						
Oceania						
Australia	No Report	55.521 kg	No Report	338.400 kg [Govt. (4]	722.000 kg [Govt.]	1083.183 kg [(5]
						4885 u.
New Zealand	No Report	No Report	0.072 kg	3.000 lt.	256350 u.	271799 u.
			8798 u.	83449 u.		
Sub-Total		55.521 kg	0.072 kg	338.400 kg	722.000 kg	1083.183 kg
			8798 u.	3.000 lt.	256350 u.	276684 u.
				83449 u.		
Total region		55.521 kg	0.072 kg	338.400 kg	722.000 kg	1083.183 kg
			8798 u.	3.000 lt.	256350 u.	276684 u.
				83449 u.		
TOTAL	1181234 u.	533.587 kg	1736.981 kg	1056.245 kg	3278.132 kg	1956.448 kg
		15156520 u.	33345990 u.	3.000 lt.	34547720 u.	22909850 u.
				39417380 u.		

1) Due to unavailability of 2001 data, year 2000 data were used for analysis purposes. 2) Includes ecstasy 3) Due to unavailability of 2003 data, year 2002 data were used for analysis purposes. 4) Fiscal year 5) Sum of seizures reported by national, State & Territory law enforcement agencies

Source: Annual Report Questionnaire if not otherwise indicated

SEIZURES, 1998 - 2003

Depressants (excluding Methaqualone)

Region/country or territory	1998	1999	2000	2001	2002	2003
AFRICA						
East Africa						
Kenya	9060 u.	No Report	272 u.	No Report	157 u.	947 u.
Mauritius	11694 u.	952 u.	1758 u.	No Report	2781 u.	296 u.
Sub-Total	20754 u.	952 u.	2030 u.		2938 u.	1243 u.
North Africa						
Algeria	No Report	110786 u.	100555 u. [ICPO]	No Report	244214 u.	571138 u.
Egypt	No Report	No Report	No Report	No Report	85064 u.	856 u.
Morocco	No Report	No Report	71672 u.	No Report	60458 u.	106456 u.
Tunisia	4439 u.	No Report	No Report	No Report	No Report	No Report
Sub-Total	4439 u.	110786 u.	172227 u.		389736 u.	678450 u.
Southern Africa						
Botswana	No Report	0.073 kg [ICPO] 500 u.	No Report	No Report	No Report	No Report
Mozambique	5080 u. [ICPO]	No Report	No Report	No Report	No Report	No Report
South Africa	No Report	No Report	0.025 kg [ICPO] 3026 u.	No Report	0.316 kg 6437 u.	No Report
Zambia	0.908 kg [Govt]	4140 u.	0.000 kg [Govt]	0.064 kg [Govt] 3522 u.	No Report	0.042 kg 8367 u.
Zimbabwe	43.640 kg	No Report	No Report	No Report	No Report	No Report
Sub-Total	44.548 kg 5080 u.	0.073 kg 4640 u.	0.025 kg 3026 u.	0.064 kg 3522 u.	0.316 kg 6437 u.	0.042 kg 8367 u.
West and Central Africa						
Cameroon	No Report	No Report	No Report	No Report	40 u.	No Report
Chad	No Report	5360 u. [ICPO]	961230 u.	No Report	No Report	No Report
Congo	No Report	No Report	0.003 kg	No Report	2 u.	No Report
Côte d'Ivoire	23.600 kg 9367 u.	66.690 kg	48.646 kg [ICPO]	298.041 kg	247356 u.	No Report
Gambia	4500 u. [ICPO]	No Report	1046 u. [Govt]	3.000 kg	99 u. [Govt]	613 u. [Govt]
Guinea	No Report	No Report	No Report	No Report	No Report	1.200 kg
Niger	679484 u. [ICPO]	367823 u. [ICPO]	No Report	No Report	No Report	No Report
Nigeria	No Report	No Report	134.690 kg	282.454 kg	No Report	936.805 kg
Senegal	4063 u. [ICPO]	4737 u. [ICPO]	310 u. [ICPO]	No Report	No Report	No Report
Sub-Total	23.600 kg 697414 u.	66.690 kg 377920 u.	183.339 kg 962586 u.	583.495 kg	247497 u.	938.005 kg 613 u.
Total region	68.148 kg 727687 u.	66.763 kg 494298 u.	183.364 kg 1139869 u.	583.559 kg 3522 u.	0.316 kg 646608 u.	938.047 kg 688673 u.
AMERICAS						
Caribbean						
Cayman Islands	No Report	0.001 kg	1 u.	No Report	No Report	No Report
Dominican Republic	No Report	8 u. [ICPO]	No Report	50 u.	No Report	
Sub-Total		0.001 kg 8 u.	1 u.	50 u.		

Source: Annual Report Questionnaire if not otherwise indicated

322

SEIZURES, 1998 - 2003
Depressants (excluding Methaqualone)

Region/country or territory	1998	1999	2000	2001	2002	2003
AMERICAS						
Central America						
El Salvador	40000 u. [ICPO]	No Report	0.010 kg [ICPO] 22964 u.	No Report	No Report	No Report
Guatemala	52.000 kg	No Report	No Report	No Report	No Report	No Report
Sub-Total	52.000 kg 40000 u.		0.010 kg 22964 u.			
North America						
Canada	0.934 kg 0.686 lt. 12033 u.	0.726 kg 2.439 lt. 8355 u.	173.865 kg 4.511 lt. 10921 u.	5.321 kg 18684 u.	7.497 kg [1] 25017 u.	2.016 kg 74704 u.
Mexico	1484000 u.	182604 u.	734281 u. [ICPO]	823726 u.	5353064 u.	8759938 u.
United States	No Report	2.646 kg 403724 u.	0.508 kg 0.021 lt. 3338 u.	53385 u.	254975 u.	96444 u.
Sub-Total	0.934 kg 0.686 lt. 1496033 u.	3.372 kg 2.439 lt. 594683 u.	174.373 kg 4.532 lt. 748540 u.	5.321 kg 895795 u.	7.497 kg 5633056 u.	2.016 kg 8931086 u.
South America						
Argentina	13125 u.	8055 u.	11779 u.	4795 u.	24028 u.	No Report
Chile	0.002 kg 2545 u.	19813 u. [CICAD]	6993 u.	9341 u.	34882 u.	5345 u.
Ecuador	No Report	No Report	2923 u. [Govt]	48755 u. [Govt]	45 u. [Govt]	21003 u. [Govt]
Uruguay	No Report	No Report	No Report	No Report	4 u.	No Report
Sub-Total	0.002 kg 15670 u.	27868 u.	21695 u.	62891 u.	58959 u.	26348 u.
Total region	52.936 kg 0.686 lt. 1551703 u.	3.373 kg 2.439 lt. 622559 u.	174.383 kg 4.532 lt. 793200 u.	5.321 kg 958736 u.	7.497 kg 5692015 u.	2.016 kg 8957434 u.
ASIA						
Central Asia and Transcaucasian countries						
Armenia	No Report	1209 u. [ICPO]	No Report	No Report	No Report	No Report
Georgia	180 u. [ICPO]	0.018 kg [ICPO] 1060 u.	0.444 kg [ICPO]	No Report	No Report	No Report
Kazakhstan	No Report	56.000 kg	No Report	No Report	No Report	No Report
Uzbekistan	No Report	No Report	No Report	No Report	13774 u.	No Report
Sub-Total	180 u.	56.018 kg 2269 u.	0.444 kg		13774 u.	
East and South-East Asia						
Brunei Darussalam	No Report	53 u.	1 u.	1 u.	232 u.	No Report
Hong Kong Special Administrative Region of China	162850 u. [Govt]	12.208 kg [2] 1134461 u.	0.090 kg [ICPO] 77862 u.	2.000 kg 390550 u.	0.007 kg [1] 0.020 lt. 1155 u.	633.000 kg 0.007 lt. 8521 u.

Source: Annual Report Questionnaire if not otherwise indicated

SEIZURES, 1998 - 2003

Depressants (excluding Methaqualone)

Region/country or territory	1998	1999	2000	2001	2002	2003
ASIA						
East and South-East Asia						
Indonesia	17793 u.	372494 u. [ICPO]	382174 u. [Govt]	37545 u.	421246 u. [Govt]	3547 u.
Japan	0.024 kg	0.003 lt.	0.003 kg	0.002 kg	93733 u.	0.035 kg
	0.010 lt.	97310 u.	32358 u.	20545 u.		68335 u.
	141455 u.					
Macao Special Administrative Region of China	4937 u. [ICPO]	No Report	19421 u.	2583 u.	2374 u.	4305 u.
Mongolia	No Report	No Report	No Report	No Report	No Report	3350 u.
Myanmar	No Report	No Report	No Report	No Report	347662 u.	No Report
Philippines	No Report	No Report	100000 u. [(3]	No Report	No Report	No Report
Republic of Korea	1452896 u.	1030567 u.	2176 u. [ICPO]	No Report	No Report	No Report
Singapore	34911 u.	13069 u.	48061 u.	0.074 kg	800 u.	55327 u.
				1807 u.		
Thailand	No Report	4.630 kg [ICPO]	10.524 kg [ICPO]	No Report	No Report	No Report
Viet Nam	No Report	74274 u. [ICPO]	115000 u. [ICPO]	158007 u.	No Report	No Report
Sub-Total	0.024 kg	16.838 kg	10.617 kg	2.076 kg	0.007 kg	633.035 kg
	0.010 lt.	0.003 lt.	777053 u.	611038 u.	0.020 lt.	0.007 lt.
	1814842 u.	2722228 u.			867202 u.	143385 u.
Near and Middle East /South-West Asia						
Bahrain	No Report	No Report	No Report	No Report	8527 u.	No Report
Israel	No Report	936 u. [ICPO]	No Report	No Report	No Report	No Report
Jordan	No Report	No Report	1014 u.	No Report	No Report	No Report
Kuwait	8943 u.	No Report	No Report	No Report	No Report	No Report
Lebanon	No Report	359 u.	41616 u.	859 u.	989 u.	1117 u.
Oman	No Report	No Report	No Report	1815.000 kg	3554 u.	No Report
Pakistan	No Report	No Report	20000 u. [ICPO]	No Report	No Report	No Report
Qatar	753 u. [ICPO]	2164 u. [ICPO]	15 u. [ICPO]	No Report	99 u.	59 u.
Saudi Arabia	No Report	No Report	854 u. [ICPO]	No Report	No Report	No Report
Syrian Arab Republic	No Report	15117 u. [ICPO]	No Report	No Report	No Report	No Report
United Arab Emirates	No Report	No Report	No Report	0.498 kg	No Report	No Report
Yemen	169 u. [ICPO]	No Report	1486 u. [ICPO]	No Report	No Report	No Report
Sub-Total	9865 u.	18576 u.	64985 u.	1815.498 kg	13169 u.	1176 u.
				859 u.		
South Asia						
Bangladesh	No Report	No Report	No Report	No Report	No Report	32002 u.
Nepal	6811 u.	No Report	1654 u. [ICPO]	No Report	No Report	No Report
Sub-Total	6811 u.		1654 u.			32002 u.
Total region	0.024 kg	72.856 kg	11.061 kg	1817.574 kg	0.007 kg	633.035 kg
	0.010 lt.	0.003 lt.	843692 u.	611897 u.	0.020 lt.	0.007 lt.
	1831698 u.	2743073 u.			894144 u.	176563 u.

Source: Annual Report Questionnaire if not otherwise indicated

SEIZURES, 1998 - 2003
Depressants (excluding Methaqualone)

Region/country or territory	1998	1999	2000	2001	2002	2003
EUROPE						
East Europe						
Belarus	No Report	0.002 kg	0.100 kg	4.770 kg [Govt]	52.144 kg	5.395 kg
Republic of Moldova	1800 u.	No Report	No Report	No Report	No Report	No Report
Russian Federation	No Report	39.500 kg [ICPO]	2.420 kg [ICPO]	61.574 kg	No Report	364.001 kg
Ukraine	No Report	0.001 kg [ICPO] 8427 u.	289318 u. [ICPO]	No Report	606.000 kg	No Report
Sub-Total	1800 u.	39.503 kg 8427 u.	2.520 kg 289318 u.	66.344 kg	658.144 kg	369.396 kg
Southeast Europe						
Bulgaria	93460 u.	1.500 kg	4.682 kg 4142 u.	No Report	1.103 kg	No Report
Croatia	4358 u.	8335 u.	4778 u.	No Report	No Report	No Report
Romania	No Report	No Report	No Report	5961 u.	33686 u.	82623 u.
The former Yugoslav Republic of Macedonia	No Report	No Report	No Report	No Report	10 u.	No Report
Turkey	3559 u.	No Report	No Report	No Report	No Report	No Report
Sub-Total	101377 u.	1.500 kg 8335 u.	4.682 kg 8920 u.	5961 u.	1.103 kg 33696 u.	82623 u.
West & Central Europe						
Andorra	No Report	No Report	11 u. [ICPO]	No Report	No Report	No Report
Austria	No Report	No Report	32207 u. [ICPO]	36132 u.	24000 u.	26476 u.
Belgium	No Report	No Report	No Report	No Report	137009 u. [(4]	No Report
Czech Republic	No Report	50.000 kg	9450 u.	1119 u.	841 u.	No Report
Estonia	No Report	0.103 kg 138 u.	1.525 kg [(1] 846 u.	0.184 kg 14571 u.	27.883 kg [(1]	10.084 kg
Finland	35664 u.	45448 u.	32148 u.	11700 u.	No Report	No Report
France	No Report	No Report	0.039 kg	No Report	No Report	No Report
Germany, Federal Republic of	7071 u.	No Report	No Report	No Report	No Report	No Report
Greece	2.306 kg 18470 u.	80.210 kg 217004 u.	3.700 kg 35354 u.	22.204 kg 43958 u.	39971 u.	0.170 kg 51349 u.
Hungary	No Report	No Report	No Report	0.001 kg	192 u.	0.022 kg 467 u.
Ireland	No Report	13793 u. [ICPO]	1.121 kg	No Report	5040 u.	12336 u.
Italy	0.037 kg 1506 u.	0.232 kg [ICPO] 3316 u.	0.662 kg 1883 u.	No Report	No Report	No Report
Latvia	11244 u.	0.171 kg 13562 u.	No Report	9011 u.	No Report	No Report
Liechtenstein	No Report	No Report	10280 u. [(4]	430 u.	0.304 kg	No Report
Lithuania	1237 u.	580 u.	106 u.	No Report	0.111 kg [(1] 67 u.	26.040 kg 548 u.
Luxembourg	145 u.	No Report	No Report	No Report	No Report	No Report
Malta	353 u.	8 u.	207 u.	No Report	No Report	11 u.

Source: Annual Report Questionnaire if not otherwise indicated

SEIZURES, 1998 - 2003

Depressants (excluding Methaqualone)

Region/country or territory	1998	1999	2000	2001	2002	2003
EUROPE						
West & Central Europe						
Norway	0.071 kg	0.012 kg	0.043 kg	11.361 kg	47.281 kg	911.094 kg
	101295 u.	180500 u.	413548 u.	848206 u.	1251914 u.	561990 u.
Poland	No Report	No Report	No Report	8.000 lt.	5132 u.	3681829 u.
Portugal	2577 u.	2122 u.	0.001 kg	3689 u.	0.007 kg	0.001 kg
			4794 u.		1071 u.	34845 u.
Slovakia	1356 u.	1104 u.		No Report	No Report	No Report
Slovenia	5745 u.	621 u.	735 u.	460 u.	8 u.	105 u.
Spain	99126 u.	343974 u.	6.825 lt.[1]	595619 u.	22016 u.[1]	27253 u.
			132951 u.			
Sweden	0.302 kg	255000 u.	2.320 kg[1]	46.570 lt.	25.400 lt.[1]	0.610 kg
	293508 u.		16.558 lt.	271478 u.	965400 u.	277962 u.
			237312 u.			
Switzerland	1204104 u.	554641 u.	1907207 u.	No Report	No Report	No Report
United Kingdom	No Report	12000 u.[ICPO]	3.360 kg	12.558 kg	13.130 kg	13.130 kg[5]
			37 u.	105513 u.		
Sub-Total	2.716 kg	130.728 kg	12.771 kg	46.308 kg	88.716 kg	961.151 kg
	1783401 u.	1643811 u.	23.383 lt.	54.570 lt.	25.400 lt.	4675170 u.
			2819076 u.	1941886 u.	2452661 u.	
Total region	2.716 kg	171.731 kg	19.973 kg	112.652 kg	747.963 kg	1330.547 kg
	1886578 u.	1660573 u.	23.383 lt.	54.570 lt.	25.400 lt.	4757793 u.
			3117314 u.	1947847 u.	2486357 u.	
OCEANIA						
Oceania						
Australia	No Report	No Report	0.117 kg	0.038 kg	1.049 kg[6]	1.423 kg[Govt]
					100.000 lt.	0.515 lt.
						67509 u.
New Zealand	445 u.	126 u.	317 u.	No Report	5.170 lt.[1]	5138 u.
					339 u.	
Sub-Total	445 u.	126 u.	0.117 kg	0.038 kg	1.049 kg	1.423 kg
			317 u.		105.170 lt.	0.515 lt.
					339 u.	72647 u.
Total region	445 u.	126 u.	0.117 kg	0.038 kg	1.049 kg	1.423 kg
			317 u.		105.170 lt.	0.515 lt.
					339 u.	72647 u.
TOTAL	123.824 kg	314.723 kg	388.898 kg	2519.144 kg	756.832 kg	2905.068 kg
	0.696 lt.	2.442 lt.	27.915 lt.	54.570 lt.	130.590 lt.	0.522 lt.
	5998111 u.	5520629 u.	5894392 u.	3522003 u.	9719463 u.	14653110 u.

1) Including GHB 2) Includes mainly benzodiazapines 3) Diazepam 4) Rohypnol 5) Due to unavailability of 2003 data, year 2002 data were used for analysis purposes. 6) Litre amount for GHB

Source: Annual Report Questionnaire if not otherwise indicated

SEIZURES, 1998 - 2003
Hallucinogens (excluding LSD but incl. "Ecstasy")

Region/country or territory	1998	1999	2000	2001	2002	2003
AFRICA						
North Africa						
Egypt	No Report	No Report	3372 u.	70080 u.	785 u.	3725 u.
Morocco	No Report	No Report	No Report	No Report	No Report	0.019 kg [Govt]
Sub-Total			3372 u.	70080 u.	785 u.	0.019 kg
						3725 u.
Southern Africa						
Lesotho	No Report	No Report	No Report	No Report	1.884 kg [ICPO]	No Report
Namibia	No Report	74 u.	157 u.	546 u.	49 u.	169 u.
South Africa	111733 u.	30132 u. [ICPO]	1.177 kg	95792 u.	14.540 kg	404394 u.
			297021 u.		424258 u.	
Zambia	No Report	No Report	No Report	No Report	No Report	0.071 kg
Zimbabwe	No Report	3 u.	No Report	0.000 kg	58 u.	15 u.
				6 u.		
Sub-Total	111733 u.	30209 u.	1.177 kg	0.000 kg	16.424 kg	0.071 kg
			297178 u.	96344 u.	424365 u.	404578 u.
West and Central Africa						
Central African Republic	No Report	No Report	No Report	No Report	2.000 lt. [Govt]	No Report
Sub-Total					2.000 lt.	
Total region	111733 u.	30209 u.	1.177 kg	0.000 kg	16.424 kg	0.090 kg
			300550 u.	166424 u.	2.000 lt.	408303 u.
					425150 u.	
AMERICAS						
Caribbean						
Aruba	No Report	873 u. [F.O]	85279 u. [F.O]	59874 u. [F.O]	19445 u. [ICPO]	No Report
Bahamas	No Report	No Report	63.000 kg	0.023 kg	0.027 kg	No Report
				0 u.		
Bermuda	No Report	No Report	No Report	153 u. [F.O]	65 u.	No Report
British Virgin Islands	No Report	No Report	No Report	No Report	No Report	2.500 kg [PRO]
Cayman Islands	No Report	0.030 kg	162 u.	No Report	120 u.	0.002 kg
Cuba	No Report	No Report	1965 u. [HONL]	No Report	0.001 kg [ICPO]	14 u. [HON]
Dominican Republic	No Report	29 u.	125073 u. [F.O]	30903 u.	153605 u. [HONLC]	51565 u.
Guadeloupe	No Report	No Report	25540 u. [F.O]	500 u. [F.O]	No Report	No Report
Jamaica	No Report	No Report	No Report	5070 u.	79 u. [ICPO]	No Report
Netherlands Antilles	No Report	No Report	15.464 kg [ICPO]	20465 u. [F.O]	94 u. [ICPO]	No Report
Puerto Rico	No Report	No Report	No Report	1977 u. [F.O]	No Report	No Report
Sub-Total		0.030 kg	78.464 kg	0.023 kg	0.028 kg	2.502 kg
		902 u.	238019 u.	118942 u.	173408 u.	51579 u.
Central America						
Costa Rica	No Report	No Report	46 u.	87 u.	83 u.	1341 u.
Nicaragua	No Report	No Report	No Report	No Report	19886 u.	No Report
Panama	No Report	No Report	2256 u.	22166 u.	934 u. [HONLC]	No Report

Source: Annual Report Questionnaire if not otherwise indicated

327

SEIZURES, 1998 - 2003

Hallucinogens (excluding LSD but incl. "Ecstasy")

Region/country or territory	1998	1999	2000	2001	2002	2003
AMERICAS						
Central America						
Sub-Total			2302 u.	22253 u.	20903 u.	1341 u.
North America						
Canada	64.019 kg	561.837 kg	764.514 kg	459.025 kg	285.733 kg	137.451 kg
	0.022 lt.	0.503 lt.	0.155 lt.	846973 u.	177450 u.	39199 u.
	25451 u.	3427 u.	2136444 u.			
Mexico	93.000 kg	No Report	32.302 kg [ICPO]	102.000 kg	31.953 kg	16.300 kg
United States	No Report	160.515 kg	9600000 u. [ICPO]	9795741 u.	7637544 u.	242.700 kg
		4745097 u.				2019737 u.
Sub-Total	157.019 kg	722.352 kg	796.816 kg	561.026 kg	317.686 kg	396.451 kg
	0.022 lt.	0.503 lt.	0.155 lt.	10642710 u.	7814994 u.	2058936 u.
	25451 u.	4748524 u.	11736440 u.			
South America						
Argentina	No Report	No Report	No Report	No Report	430 u. [ICPO]	14456 u.
Brazil	No Report	59612 u. [ICPO]	36796 u.	1909 u. [Govt]	15804 u. [F.O]	70859 u.
Chile	2.977 kg	No Report	140 u. [ICPO]	2626 u.	583 u.	1.222 kg
						5290 u.
Colombia	0 u. [Govt]	1022 u.	83.000 kg	38284 u. [Govt]	175382 u.	5042 u.
Ecuador	0 u. [Govt]	0 u. [Govt]	0 u. [Govt]	7 u. [Govt]	0.020 kg [Govt]	3.950 kg [Govt]
					172 u.	0 u.
Guyana	No Report	626 u. [F.O]	124 u. [F.O]	No Report	No Report	No Report
Peru	No Report	No Report	No Report	35 u.	78 u.	85 u.
Suriname	6000 u.	No Report	61232 u. [INCSR]	No Report	80 u.	No Report
Uruguay	No Report	84 u.	738 u.	No Report	31 u.	18 u.
Venezuela	No Report	No Report	7985 u. [CICAD]	2 u.	16010 u.	62302 u.
Sub-Total	2.977 kg	61344 u.	83.000 kg	42863 u.	0.020 kg	5.172 kg
	6000 u.		107015 u.		208570 u.	158052 u.
Total region	159.996 kg	722.382 kg	958.280 kg	561.049 kg	317.734 kg	404.125 kg
	0.022 lt.	0.503 lt.	0.155 lt.	10826770 u.	8217875 u.	2269908 u.
	31451 u.	4810770 u.	12083780 u.			
ASIA						
Central Asia and Transcaucasian countries						
Kazakhstan	No Report	1099.000 kg	No Report	No Report	No Report	No Report
Sub-Total		1099.000 kg				
East and South-East Asia						
Brunei Darussalam	No Report	32 u.	No Report	No Report	10 u.	No Report
China	No Report	No Report	200.000 kg [HNLP]	2700000 u.	3000000 u. [ICPO]	409261 u.
			240000 u.			
Hong Kong Special Administrative Region of China	265 u. [Govt.]	21202 u. [ICPO]	58.800 kg	0.032 kg	89.953 kg	31.170 kg
			378621 u.	170243 u.	49374 u.	142912 u.
Indonesia	119655 u.	32361 u.	492741 u.	90523 u. [Govt]	84224 u.	253659 u.

Source: Annual Report Questionnaire if not otherwise indicated

SEIZURES, 1998 - 2003

Hallucinogens (excluding LSD but incl. "Ecstasy")

Region/country or territory	1998	1999	2000	2001	2002	2003
ASIA						
East and South-East Asia						
Japan	16 u. [(1]	5273 u.	0.016 kg 78471 u.	0.121 kg 112542 u.	190281 u. [Govt]	0.014 kg 393757 u.
Macao Special Administrative Region of China	64 u. [ICPO]	No Report	2453 u. [ICPO]	1687 u.	672 u.	661 u.
Malaysia	1733335 u.	55975 u.	49901 u. [ICPO]	No Report	164884 u. [ICPO]	231191 u.
Philippines	No Report	No Report	1026 u.	No Report	246 u.	10 u.
Republic of Korea	No Report	No Report	No Report	1672 u.	39011 u. [ICPO]	37784 u.
Singapore	2175 u.	5.170 kg 17232 u.	2.566 kg 10339 u.	0.257 kg 23846 u.	7331 u.	2410 u.
Thailand	10395 u. [Govt.]	264.130 kg [ICPO (2] 30615 u.	52.601 kg [ICPO] 72182 u.	61922 u. [F.O]	145873 u. [F.O]	33.000 kg [Govt]
Sub-Total	1865905 u.	269.300 kg 162690 u.	313.983 kg 1325734 u.	0.410 kg 3162435 u.	89.953 kg 3681906 u.	64.184 kg 1471645 u.
Near and Middle East /South-West Asia						
Israel	5.000 kg 118501 u.	130.687 kg [ICPO] 30335 u.	270000 u.	1.504 kg 121695 u.	4.454 kg 951057 u.	1.041 kg 104324 u.
Jordan	No Report	5000 u. [ICPO]	No Report	No Report	No Report	No Report
Pakistan	No Report	No Report	No Report	No Report	No Report	1980 u.
Syrian Arab Republic	No Report	No Report	No Report	No Report	19604 u.	No Report
Sub-Total	5.000 kg 118501 u.	130.687 kg 35335 u.	270000 u.	1.504 kg 121695 u.	4.454 kg 970661 u.	1.041 kg 106304 u.
Total region	5.000 kg 1984406 u.	1498.987 kg 198025 u.	313.983 kg 1595734 u.	1.914 kg 3284130 u.	94.407 kg 4652567 u.	65.225 kg 1577949 u.
EUROPE						
East Europe						
Belarus	No Report	No Report	No Report	0.204 kg [Govt]	1.072 kg	2.725 kg [Govt]
Russian Federation	No Report	0.153 kg	No Report	2.526 kg	2.813 kg [Govt]	6.287 kg
Ukraine	No Report	1.349 kg [ICPO] 18888 u.	0.305 kg [ICPO] 4784 u.	47 u.	No Report	No Report
Sub-Total		1.502 kg 18888 u.	0.305 kg 4784 u.	2.730 kg 47 u.	3.885 kg	9.012 kg
Southeast Europe						
Bosnia and Herzegovina	1041 u. [ICPO]	No Report	No Report	No Report	1212 u. [ICPO]	No Report
Bulgaria	No Report	No Report	4524 u. [Govt]	7.900 kg 2361 u.	1.500 kg 3135 u.	1097 u.
Croatia	No Report	0.018 kg [ICPO] 15421 u.	9979 u.	12906 u.	110632 u.	29840 u.
Romania	1093 u.	No Report	10945 u. [ICPO]	67210 u.	0.017 kg 19567 u.	70088 u.

Source: Annual Report Questionnaire if not otherwise indicated

SEIZURES, 1998 - 2003

Hallucinogens (excluding LSD but incl. "Ecstasy")

Region/country or territory	1998	1999	2000	2001	2002	2003
EUROPE						
Southeast Europe						
Serbia and Montenegro	No Report	No Report	No Report	0.079 kg	10000 u.	0.060 kg
				10811 u.		76302 u.
The former Yugoslav Republic of Macedonia	1574 u.	5532 u. NAPOL	280 u. NAPOL	45 u. Govt	0.002 kg	No Report
					18341 u.	
Turkey	480809 u.	No Report	33894 u. Govt.	121508 u.	98989 u.	473240 u.
Sub-Total	484517 u.	0.018 kg	59622 u.	7.979 kg	1.519 kg	0.060 kg
		20953 u.		214841 u.	261876 u.	650567 u.
West & Central Europe						
Andorra	88 u. ICPO	0.002 kg	0.002 kg ICPO	105 u.	42 u. ICPO	No Report
		43 u.	283 u.			
Austria	114677 u.	31129 u.	162.093 kg	256299 u.	0.099 kg	422103 u.
					383451 u.	
Belgium	33.044 kg	279.620 kg	68.000 kg ICPO	68.000 kg UNODC (3	1564.000 kg	0.026 kg
		467506 u.	818515 u.	818515 u.		58278 u.
Cyprus	20 u.	0.001 kg	0.005 kg	0.004 kg	0.273 kg	1.094 kg
		62 u.	3317 u.	2910 u.	10253 u.	5751 u.
Czech Republic	No Report	No Report	17502 u.	29.890 kg	1.893 kg	4.851 kg
					88391 u.	51692 u.
Denmark	27038 u. (1	26117 u.	0.279 kg	150080 u.	25738 u.	62475 u.
			21638 u.			
Estonia	No Report	0.000 lt.	0.431 kg	1.714 kg	3.402 kg	6.765 kg
		1773 u.	1351 u.			
Finland	0.130 kg	16578 u. ICPO	87393 u.	81228 u.	45065 u.	35216 u.
	2396 u.					
France	4.795 kg	14.000 kg	13.314 kg	7.584 kg	2161199 u.	18.239 kg
		1860402 u.	2283620 u.	1503773 u.		2211727 u.
Germany, Federal Republic of	419329 u.	1470507 u. Govt	35.500 kg	21.897 kg	33.603 kg	1257676 u.
			1634683 u.	4576504 u.	3207099 u.	
Greece	85 u.	3095 u.	53557 u.	58845 u.	28430 u.	47705 u.
Hungary	11857 u.	510 u.	13616 u.	0.260 kg	6.132 kg	30.990 kg
				18301 u.	23730 u.	135634 u.
Iceland	No Report	7478 u.	22057 u.	93151 u.	0.006 kg	0.021 kg
					814 u.	3190 u.
Ireland	1.087 kg	74.609 kg	695133 u. ICPO	469862 u.	0.153 kg	0.616 kg
	616439 u.	266462 u.			117046 u.	1288412 u.
Italy	1.580 kg	0.673 kg ICPO	0.492 kg	0.285 kg	0.006 kg	0.452 kg
	15 u.	272397 u.	502070 u.	308845 u.	397566 u.	234973 u.
Latvia	No Report	0.749 kg ICPO	No Report	1620 u.	No Report	9239 u.
		9625 u.				
Liechtenstein	0.500 kg	No Report	10 u.	No Report	0.001 kg	0.016 kg
Lithuania	831 u.	1122 u. ICPO	50724 u. ICPO	0.045 kg	0.845 kg	0.440 kg
				514 u.	1205 u.	98518 u.

Source: Annual Report Questionnaire if not otherwise indicated

SEIZURES, 1998 - 2003
Hallucinogens (excluding LSD but incl. "Ecstasy")

Region/country or territory	1998	1999	2000	2001	2002	2003
EUROPE						
West & Central Europe						
Luxembourg	No Report	0.167 kg 357 u.	0.122 kg [ICPO] 318 u.	No Report	1139 u. [ICPO]	132 u.
Malta	153 u.	459 u.	5191 u.	2242 u.	1012 u. [ICPO]	8694 u.
Monaco	No Report	3 u. [ICPO]	5 u. [ICPO]	No Report	55 u.	0.006 kg
Netherlands	1163514 u. [Govt]	3663608 u. [Govt]	632.000 kg [Govt] 5500000 u.	113.000 kg 8684505 u.	849.000 kg 6787167 u.	713.000 kg 5420033 u.
Norway	1.081 kg 15647 u.	0.025 kg 24644 u.	0.114 kg 49390 u.	0.492 kg 61205 u.	0.916 kg 102439 u.	1.196 kg 99689 u.
Poland	1736 u.	6319 u.	129513 u.	232735 u.	3.727 kg 38179 u.	7.217 kg 124964 u.
Portugal	10 u.	0.089 kg 31319 u.	1.089 kg 25499 u.	0.091 kg 126451 u.	2.240 kg 222479 u.	0.404 kg 163534 u.
Slovakia	No Report	9 u.	493 u. [ICPO]	0.568 kg	435 u.	1663 u.
Slovenia	4496 u. [HONEU]	1749 u. [ICPO]	0.053 kg 27974 u.	1852 u.	7877 u.	0.600 kg 2847 u.
Spain	194527 u.	357649 u.	914974 u. [ICPO]	860164 u.	1396142 u.	772122 u.
Sweden	0.579 kg	0.504 kg	0.591 kg [ICPO] 184161 u.	0.887 kg 57750 u.	96577 u.	0.254 kg 71216 u.
Switzerland	73914 u.	67353 u.	189569 u. [(4]	86959 u.	88342 u.	19942 u.
United Kingdom	2095879 u. [(5]	6323500 u. [NCIS]	6534813 u.	3.399 kg 7662228 u.	5852000 u.	5852000 u. [(6]
Sub-Total	42.796 kg 4742651 u.	370.439 kg 0.000 lt. 14911770 u.	914.085 kg 19767370 u.	248.116 kg 26116640 u.	2466.296 kg 21083870 u.	786.187 kg 18459420 u.
Total region	42.796 kg 5227168 u.	371.959 kg 0.000 lt. 14951620 u.	914.390 kg 19831770 u.	258.825 kg 26331530 u.	2471.700 kg 21345750 u.	795.259 kg 19109990 u.
OCEANIA						
Oceania						
Australia	7.380 kg [Govt. (7]	57.645 kg [(8]	0.773 kg	343.030 kg [(9]	727.171 kg	1088.298 kg [(10] 4885 u.
New Zealand	2665 u.	No Report	0.530 kg [(11] 8858 u.	0.483 kg 3.000 lt. 84744 u.	1.192 kg 256437 u.	0.476 kg 272169 u.
Sub-Total	7.380 kg 2665 u.	57.645 kg	1.303 kg 8858 u.	343.513 kg 3.000 lt. 84744 u.	728.363 kg 256437 u.	1088.774 kg 277054 u.
Total region	7.380 kg 2665 u.	57.645 kg	1.303 kg 8858 u.	343.513 kg 3.000 lt. 84744 u.	728.363 kg 256437 u.	1088.774 kg 277054 u.

Source: Annual Report Questionnaire if not otherwise indicated

SEIZURES, 1998 - 2003

Hallucinogens (excluding LSD but incl. "Ecstasy")

Region/country or territory	1998	1999	2000	2001	2002	2003
TOTAL	215.172 kg	2650.973 kg	2189.133 kg	1165.300 kg	3628.628 kg	2353.473 kg
	0.022 lt.	0.503 lt.	0.155 lt.	3.000 lt.	2.000 lt.	23643210 u.
	7357423 u.	19990620 u.	33820700 u.	40693600 u.	34897770 u.	

1) Small quantity. 2) Ketamine 3) Due to unavailability of 2001 data, year 2000 data were used for analysis purposes. 4) Includes ecstasy 5) Including other opiates. 6) Due to unavailability of 2003 data, year 2002 data were used for analysis purposes. 7) Provisional figures. 8) Mushrooms 9) Fiscal year 10) Sum of seizures reported by national, State & Territory law enforcement agencies 11) Psilocybine

Source: Annual Report Questionnaire if not otherwise indicated

SEIZURES, 1998 - 2003
LSD

Region/country or territory	1998	1999	2000	2001	2002	2003
AFRICA						
North Africa						
Egypt	514 u.	No Report	300 u.	No Report	No Report	10 u.
Sub-Total	514 u.		300 u.			10 u.
Southern Africa						
Namibia	No Report	No Report	127 u. [ICPO]	No Report	3 u.	No Report
South Africa	6426 u.	1549 u. [ICPO]	5506 u.	7841 u.	1782 u.	525 u.
Zambia	0.000 kg [Govt]	0.000 kg [Govt]	0.000 kg [Govt]	0.000 kg [Govt]	No Report	No Report
Zimbabwe	No Report	30 u.	No Report	No Report	No Report	No Report
Sub-Total	6426 u.	1579 u.	5633 u.	7841 u.	1785 u.	525 u.
Total region	6940 u.	1579 u.	5933 u.	7841 u.	1785 u.	535 u.
AMERICAS						
Central America						
Costa Rica	No Report	No Report	1045 u.	277 u.	No Report	No Report
Sub-Total			1045 u.	277 u.		
North America						
Canada	0.295 kg 8955 u.	0.098 kg 9852 u.	0.149 kg 5.000 lt. 1592 u.	0.401 kg 2747 u.	0.027 kg 2135 u.	0.024 kg 1457 u.
Mexico	No Report	No Report	No Report	8 u.	No Report	No Report
United States	No Report	0.330 kg 165504 u.	0.004 kg 1.296 lt. 28459 u.	97057 u.	1624 u.	1646 u.
Sub-Total	0.295 kg 8955 u.	0.428 kg 175356 u.	0.153 kg 6.296 lt. 30051 u.	0.401 kg 99812 u.	0.027 kg 3759 u.	0.024 kg 3103 u.
South America						
Argentina	1435 u.	1085 u.	1093 u.	1239 u.	468 u.	1638 u.
Brazil	No Report	16 u. [Govt.]	2368 u.	No Report	231 u. [F.O]	100864 u. [HON]
Chile	153 u.	11 u. [CICAD]	33 u.	2 u.	30 u.	4 u.
Uruguay	1 u.	4 u.	143 u.	No Report	11 u.	1 u.
Venezuela	No Report	No Report	1675 u.	No Report	No Report	No Report
Sub-Total	1589 u.	1116 u.	5312 u.	1241 u.	740 u.	102507 u.
Total region	0.295 kg 10544 u.	0.428 kg 176472 u.	0.153 kg 6.296 lt. 36408 u.	0.401 kg 101330 u.	0.027 kg 4499 u.	0.024 kg 105610 u.
ASIA						
Central Asia and Transcaucasian countries						
Uzbekistan	40 u.	No Report	No Report	No Report	No Report	No Report
Sub-Total	40 u.					

Source: Annual Report Questionnaire if not otherwise indicated

333

SEIZURES, 1998 - 2003
LSD

Region/country or territory	1998	1999	2000	2001	2002	2003
ASIA						
East and South-East Asia						
Hong Kong Special Administrative Region of China	No Report	21 u.	27877 u.	6858 u.	16 u.	23 u.
Indonesia	103368 u.	53160 u.	0.000 kg Govt	0.000 kg Govt	0.000 kg Govt	0.000 kg Govt
Japan	4802 u.	62618 u.	65043 u.	644 u.	3973 u.	3460 u.
Macao Special Administrative Region of China	No Report	No Report	No Report	8 u.	No Report	1 u.
Republic of Korea	No Report	No Report	No Report	No Report	No Report	0.900 kg
Singapore	No Report	No Report	No Report	807 u.	No Report	No Report
Thailand	No Report	No Report	No Report ICPO	No Report	No Report	No Report
Sub-Total	108170 u.	115799 u.	92920 u.	8317 u.	3989 u.	0.900 kg 3484 u.
Near and Middle East /South-West Asia						
Israel	10337 u.	7346 u. ICPO	7769 u.	0.003 kg 6266 u.	0.001 kg 2491 u.	28643 u.
Sub-Total	10337 u.	7346 u.	7769 u.	0.003 kg 6266 u.	0.001 kg 2491 u.	28643 u.
South Asia						
India	45 u.	20 u.	No Report	No Report	No Report	No Report
Nepal	9 u.	No Report	No Report	No Report	No Report	No Report
Sub-Total	54 u.	20 u.				
Total region	118601 u.	123165 u.	100689 u.	0.003 kg 14583 u.	0.001 kg 6480 u.	0.900 kg 32127 u.
EUROPE						
East Europe						
Russian Federation	No Report	No Report	0.380 kg ICPO	1.676 kg	2.813 kg ICPO	2.707 kg
Ukraine	500 u.	36 u. ICPO	27 u. Govt	47 u. Govt	477 u. Govt	156 u. Govt
Sub-Total	500 u.	36 u.	0.380 kg 27 u.	1.676 kg 47 u.	2.813 kg 477 u.	2.707 kg 156 u.
Southeast Europe						
Croatia	86 u.	247 u.	231 u.	154 u.	192 u.	14 u.
Romania	No Report	1 u.	1 u. ICPO	No Report	22004 u.	No Report
Serbia and Montenegro	No Report	No Report	No Report	5 u.	No Report	No Report
Turkey	No Report	61 u.	No Report	105 u.	No Report	4986 u.
Sub-Total	86 u.	309 u.	232 u.	264 u.	22196 u.	5000 u.
West & Central Europe						
Andorra	28 u. ICPO	No Report	47 u. ICPO	9 u.	2 u.	No Report
Austria	2494 u.	2811 u.	0.865 kg	572 u.	851 u.	298 u.
Belgium	2050 u.	1047 u.	1090 u. ICPO	No Report		4235 u.
Cyprus	No Report	2 u.	11 u.	No Report	No Report	No Report

Source: Annual Report Questionnaire if not otherwise indicated

SEIZURES, 1998 - 2003
LSD

Region/country or territory	1998	1999	2000	2001	2002	2003
EUROPE						
West & Central Europe						
Czech Republic	No Report	19 u.	1001 u.	5 u.	107 u.	65 u.
Denmark	108 u.	83 u.	1109 u.	156 u.	38 u.	No Report
Estonia	No Report	6 u.	0.022 kg 3 u.	0.002 kg	0.020 kg	2 u.
Finland	301 u.	50 u.	2355 u.	1026 u.	4679 u.	1460 u.
France	18680 u.	9991 u.	20691 u.	6718 u.	No Report	10383 u.
Germany, Federal Republic of	32250 u.	22965 u.	43924 u.	11441 u.	30144 u.	34806 u.
Greece	44 u.	212 u. [ICPO]	112 u.	577 u.	884 u.	900 u.
Hungary	3351 u.	1928 u.	1242 u.	973 u.	969 u.	346 u.
Iceland	No Report	339 u.	15 u.	No Report	No Report	1 u.
Ireland	792 u.	648 u.	No Report	325 u.	No Report	33 u.
Italy	0.003 kg 9752 u.	5509 u. [ICPO]	1980 u.	1139 u.	3064 u.	2161 u.
Latvia	38 u.	27 u.	14 u.	16 u.	No Report	20 u.
Liechtenstein	No Report	No Report	No Report	1 u.	No Report	0.002 kg
Lithuania	342 u.	164 u.	26 u.	275 u.	No Report	191 u.
Luxembourg	0.303 kg	1 u.	21 u. [ICPO]	No Report	0.002 kg [ICPO]	No Report
Malta	123 u.	54 u.	462 u.	No Report	No Report	No Report
Monaco	10 u.	No Report	No Report	No Report	No Report	No Report
Netherlands	37790 u. [Govt]	2667 u. [Govt]	9972 u. [Govt]	28731 u.	355 u.	1642 u.
Norway	2833 u.	483 u.	893 u.	417 u.	172 u.	224 u.
Poland	14902 u.	14099 u.	3659 u.	672 u.	797 u.	20602 u.
Portugal	261 u.	1845 u.	6106 u.	3588 u.	9785 u.	515 u.
Slovakia	63 u.	72 u.	110 u.	60 u.	8 u.	42 u.
Slovenia	53 u.	512 u.	59 u.	No Report	No Report	No Report
Spain	9068 u.	3353 u.	7542 u.	26535 u.	893 u.	31769 u.
Sweden	0.002 kg 2704 u.	1508 u.	0.000 kg [(1] 278 u.	635 u.	305 u.	251 u.
Switzerland	2995 u.	3130 u.	15525 u.	8707 u.	1552 u.	657 u.
United Kingdom	40070 u.	67400 u. [NCIS]	25392 u.	9439 u.	20000 u.	20000 u. [(2]
Sub-Total	0.308 kg 181102 u.	140925 u.	0.887 kg 143639 u.	0.002 kg 102017 u.	0.022 kg 74605 u.	0.002 kg 130602 u.
Total region	0.308 kg 181688 u.	141270 u.	1.267 kg 143898 u.	1.678 kg 102328 u.	2.835 kg 97278 u.	2.709 kg 135758 u.
OCEANIA						
Oceania						
Australia	No Report	0.108 kg	0.007 kg	No Report	No Report	0.690 kg [(3] 95 u.
New Zealand	37554 u.	17437 u.	17522 u.	1057 u.	0.013 kg 431 u.	7036 u.

Source: Annual Report Questionnaire if not otherwise indicated

SEIZURES, 1998 - 2003
LSD

Region/country or territory	1998	1999	2000	2001	2002	2003
OCEANIA						
Oceania						
Sub-Total	37554 u.	0.108 kg 17437 u.	0.007 kg 17522 u.	1057 u.	0.013 kg 431 u.	0.690 kg 7131 u.
Total region	37554 u.	0.108 kg 17437 u.	0.007 kg 17522 u.	1057 u.	0.013 kg 431 u.	0.690 kg 7131 u.
TOTAL	0.603 kg 355327 u.	0.536 kg 459923 u.	1.427 kg 6.296 lt. 304450 u.	2.082 kg 227139 u.	2.876 kg 110473 u.	4.323 kg 281161 u.

1) 2 micrograms 2) Due to unavailability of 2003 data, year 2002 data were used for analysis purposes. 3) Sum of seizures reported by national, State & Territory law enforcement agencies

Source: Annual Report Questionnaire if not otherwise indicated

SEIZURES, 1998 - 2003
Methaqualone

Region/country or territory	1998	1999	2000	2001	2002	2003
AFRICA						
East Africa						
Kenya	No Report	No Report	No Report	52693 u. [Govt]	No Report	10000 u.
United Republic of Tanzania	4 u.	7 u.	295.000 kg [ICPO]	2.107 kg [Govt]	1.500 kg [ICPO]	No Report
Sub-Total	4 u.	7 u.	295.000 kg	2.107 kg 52693 u.	1.500 kg	10000 u.
Southern Africa						
Angola	1.050 kg [ICPO]	No Report	No Report	No Report	No Report	No Report
Lesotho	No Report	No Report	No Report	No Report	0.652 kg [ICPO]	No Report
Malawi	1007 u. [Govt.]	1800 u.	No Report	No Report	1 u.	No Report
Mozambique	No Report	No Report	2200 u. [ICPO]	No Report	No Report	No Report
Namibia	6318 u.	2611 u.	10430 u. [ICPO]	16675 u.	9801 u.	No Report
South Africa	160.000 kg 1307109 u.	2498806 u. [ICPO]	114.507 kg 2669813 u.	7297.837 kg 4202835 u.	254.080 kg 2930316 u.	9373952 u.
Swaziland	12015 u.	1621 u.	6 u. [ICPO]	258 u.	4909 u.	473 u.
Zambia	0.125 kg [Govt]	2368 u.	0.125 kg 724 u.	0.020 kg [Govt]	0.039 kg	3.957 kg
Zimbabwe	4.300 kg 4431 u.	1701 u.	1500 u.	No Report	No Report	No Report
Sub-Total	165.475 kg 1330880 u.	2508907 u.	114.632 kg 2684673 u.	7297.857 kg 4219768 u.	254.771 kg 2945027 u.	3.957 kg 9374425 u.
Total region	165.475 kg 1330884 u.	2508914 u.	409.632 kg 2684673 u.	7299.964 kg 4272461 u.	256.271 kg 2945027 u.	3.957 kg 9384425 u.
AMERICAS						
North America						
Canada	0.007 kg	56.000 kg 123 u.	0.139 kg 46 u.	0.002 kg	No Report	No Report
United States	No Report	32030 u.	0.002 kg 76 u.	107 u.	40731 u.	136 u.
Sub-Total	0.007 kg	56.000 kg 32153 u.	0.141 kg 122 u.	0.002 kg 107 u.	40731 u.	136 u.
South America						
Chile	1390 u.	No Report	No Report	No Report	No Report	No Report
Sub-Total	1390 u.					
Total region	0.007 kg 1390 u.	56.000 kg 32153 u.	0.141 kg 122 u.	0.002 kg 107 u.	40731 u.	136 u.
ASIA						
East and South-East Asia						
China	No Report	No Report	No Report	No Report	2955.000 kg	No Report
Hong Kong Special Administrative Region of China	No Report	187 u. [ICPO]	25.000 kg	0.001 kg 1 u.	0.002 kg 4 u.	0.033 kg

Source: Annual Report Questionnaire if not otherwise indicated

SEIZURES, 1998 - 2003
Methaqualone

Region/country or territory	1998	1999	2000	2001	2002	2003
ASIA						
East and South-East Asia						
Indonesia	No Report	2018 u.	No Report	No Report	No Report	No Report
Sub-Total		2205 u.	25.000 kg	0.001 kg 1 u.	2955.002 kg 4 u.	0.033 kg
South Asia						
India	2257.000 kg	474.000 kg	1095.000 kg	2024.000 kg	7458.000 kg^{Govt}	593.000 kg
Sub-Total	2257.000 kg	474.000 kg	1095.000 kg	2024.000 kg	7458.000 kg	593.000 kg
Total region	2257.000 kg	474.000 kg 2205 u.	1120.000 kg	2024.001 kg 1 u.	10413.000 kg 4 u.	593.033 kg
EUROPE						
Southeast Europe						
Romania	1924 u.	8487 u.^{ICPO}	3981 u.^{ICPO}	3 u.	No Report	No Report
The former Yugoslav Republic of Macedonia	No Report	No Report	No Report	No Report	3 u.	No Report
Sub-Total	1924 u.	8487 u.	3981 u.	3 u.	3 u.	
West & Central Europe						
Belgium	11.000 kg 52 u.	No Report	No Report	No Report	No Report	0.676 kg
Switzerland	4620 u.	No Report	No Report	No Report	No Report	No Report
United Kingdom		No Report	No Report	No Report	0.050 kg	0.050 kg⁽¹
Sub-Total	11.000 kg 4672 u.				0.050 kg	0.726 kg
Total region	11.000 kg 6596 u.	8487 u.	3981 u.	3 u.	0.050 kg 3 u.	0.726 kg
TOTAL	2433.482 kg 1338870 u.	530.000 kg 2551759 u.	1529.773 kg 2688776 u.	9323.966 kg 4272572 u.	10669.320 kg 2985765 u.	597.716 kg 9384561 u.

1) Due to unavailability of 2003 data, year 2002 data were used for analysis purposes.

Source: Annual Report Questionnaire if not otherwise indicated

SEIZURES, 1998 - 2003
Psychotropic substances

Region/country or territory	1998	1999	2000	2001	2002	2003
AFRICA						
East Africa						
Kenya	9060 u.[Govt]	No Report	272 u.[Govt]	No Report	No Report	No Report
Mauritius	No Report	No Report	No Report	897 u.	No Report	No Report
Sub-Total	9060 u.		272 u.	897 u.		
North Africa						
Libyan Arab Jamahiriya	No Report	127512 u.[F.O]	245455 u.[F.O]	87047 u.[F.O]	No Report	No Report
Morocco	No Report	No Report	No Report	135769 u.	No Report	No Report
Sudan	154 u.[Govt]	63 u.[Govt]	37935 u.[Govt]	11700 u.[Govt]	8 u.[Govt]	No Report
Sub-Total	154 u.	127575 u.	283390 u.	234516 u.	8 u.	
West and Central Africa						
Mauritania	135 u.[Govt]	No Report	No Report	No Report	No Report	186 u.[F.O]
Nigeria	No Report	No Report	234.282 kg[HNLF]	312.926 kg[HNLF]	791.000 kg[HNLF]	937.405 kg[HNLI]
Sub-Total	135 u.		234.282 kg	312.926 kg	791.000 kg	937.405 kg 186 u.
Total region	9349 u.	127575 u.	234.282 kg 283662 u.	312.926 kg 235413 u.	791.000 kg 8 u.	937.405 kg 186 u.
AMERICAS						
Caribbean						
Cuba	No Report	No Report	No Report	No Report	No Report	942 u.[HON]
Dominican Republic	No Report	No Report	No Report	No Report	99 u.[HONLC]	No Report
Sub-Total					99 u.	942 u.
North America						
Mexico	1484078 u.	1490152 u.	3418369 u.	8313151 u.[Govt]	5343064 u.[HONL]	8857614 u.[HON]
Sub-Total	1484078 u.	1490152 u.	3418369 u.	8313151 u.	5343064 u.	8857614 u.
South America						
Argentina	No Report	8055 u.[HONL]	11779 u.[HONL]	4795.000 kg[HONL]	24028.000 kg[HONL]	12577 u.
Brazil	No Report	No Report	4862 u.[Govt]	No Report	39398 u.[F.O]	5571 u.[HON]
Chile	No Report	410576 u.[HONL]	No Report	481884 u.[HONL]	No Report	178649 u.[HON]
Sub-Total		418631 u.	16641 u.	4795.000 kg 481884 u.	24028.000 kg 39398 u.	196797 u.
Total region	1484078 u.	1908783 u.	3435010 u.	4795.000 kg 8795035 u.	24028.000 kg 5382561 u.	9055353 u.
ASIA						
Central Asia and Transcaucasian countries						
Uzbekistan	No Report	0.639 kg	No Report	No Report	No Report	No Report
Sub-Total		0.639 kg				
East and South-East Asia						
Viet Nam	59000 u.[F.O]	115595 u.[F.O]	No Report	593662 u.[F.O]	110232 u.[F.O]	236830 u.[F.O]
Sub-Total	59000 u.	115595 u.		593662 u.	110232 u.	236830 u.

Source: Annual Report Questionnaire if not otherwise indicated

SEIZURES, 1998 - 2003
Psychotropic substances

Region/country or territory	1998	1999	2000	2001	2002	2003
ASIA						
Near and Middle East /South-West Asia						
United Arab Emirates	No Report	14460 u.	23246 u.	No Report	No Report	No Report
Sub-Total		14460 u.	23246 u.			
Total region	59000 u.	0.639 kg 130055 u.	23246 u.	593662 u.	110232 u.	236830 u.
EUROPE						
East Europe						
Russian Federation	673.400 kg [F.O]	905.500 kg [F.O]	835.000 kg [F.O]	No Report	No Report	No Report
Sub-Total	673.400 kg	905.500 kg	835.000 kg			
West & Central Europe						
Spain	No Report	362174 u. [HONL]	139776 u. [HONL]	No Report	118452 u.	No Report
Sub-Total		362174 u.	139776 u.		118452 u.	
Total region	673.400 kg	905.500 kg 362174 u.	835.000 kg 139776 u.		118452 u.	
TOTAL	673.400 kg 1552427 u.	906.139 kg 2528587 u.	1069.282 kg 3881694 u.	5107.926 kg 9624110 u.	24819.000 kg 5611253 u.	937.405 kg 9292369 u.

Source: Annual Report Questionnaire if not otherwise indicated

7. PRICES

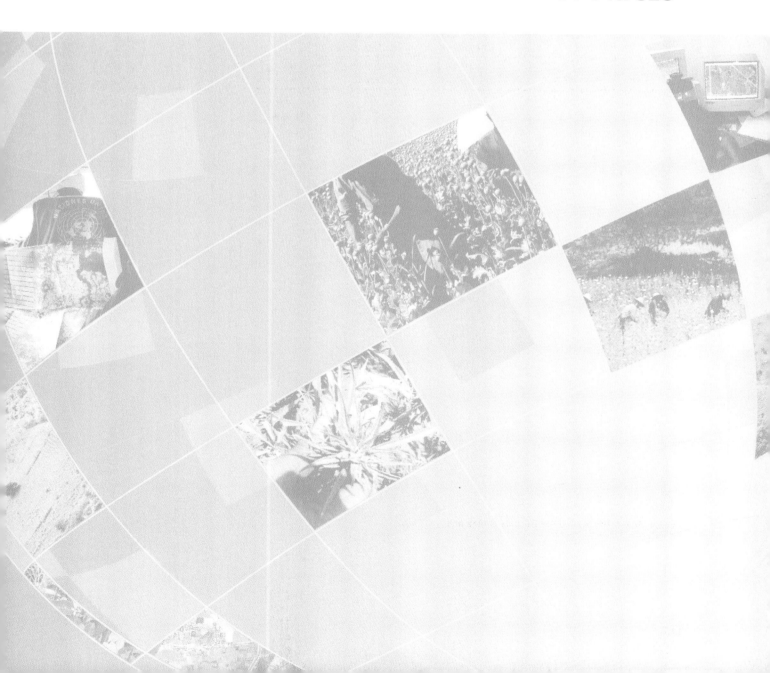

7.1. Opiates: Wholesale, street prices and purity levels

Prices in Europe and in USA, 1990-2004

Retail prices (street price), US$/gram

EUROPE	1990	1991	1992	1993	1994	1995	1996	1997	1998	1999	2000	2001	2002	2003	2004
Austria	270	250	203	132	138	103	87	70	94	57	75	44	92	68	75
Belgium	90	105	105	77	75	75	56	37	41	41	37	27	29	31	32
Denmark	287	265	151	139	228	191	157	188	147	175	116	111	126	122	94
Finland	800	696	770	724	606	455	414	257	254	250	207	121	188	195	195
France	145	153	150	135	144	170	156	113	119	111	32	34	47	57	68
Germany	105	75	96	74	91	90	74	51	43	45	39	38	38	46	49
Greece	120	175	63	44	105	88	77	80	55	55	55	53	45	65	51
Italy	167	148	140	29	55	41	115	98	120	95	71	68	59	63	69
Luxembourg	172	150	150	150	172	202	138	141	133	126	69	67	67	45	76
Netherlands	49	50	55	49	55	61	48	55	34	30	25	43	35	40	40
Norway	1,680	525	510	275	349	300	282	198	186	166	128	157	165	198	148
Iceland	184	376	374	407	380	410	377	372	372	372	372	372	372	372	372
Portugal	83	82	72	63	65	79	68	55	74	37	45	45	41	54	52
Spain	175	185	180	126	132	120	112	88	82	75	59	57	61	75	81
Sweden*	225	210	195	180	165	337	346	135	130	126	113	129	133	128	119
Switzerland	312	221	248	126	164	190	116	81	96	167	53	45	39	48	48
United Kingdom	157	144	144	134	129	125	108	118	120	108	107	86	91	100	110
Ireland	196	180	180	168	161	179	275	228	213	204	176	170	179	179	248
Average unweighted in US-$	290	222	210	168	179	179	167	131	128	124	99	93	100	105	107
inflation adjustment in US-$	**419**	**308**	**283**	**220**	**228**	**222**	**201**	**155**	**149**	**141**	**108**	**99**	**105**	**108**	**107**
Weighted average in US-$	173	149	147	107	118	119	118	93	94	87	64	59	62	70	75
Adjusted for inflation in US-$	**251**	**207**	**198**	**140**	**151**	**148**	**142**	**110**	**109**	**98**	**70**	**63**	**66**	**72**	**75**
Weighted average in Euro	**136**	**120**	**113**	**91**	**100**	**91**	**93**	**82**	**84**	**81**	**69**	**66**	**66**	**62**	**60**
Adjusted for inflation in Euro	**192**	**161**	**146**	**114**	**121**	**107**	**107**	**93**	**94**	**90**	**75**	**70**	**69**	**63**	**60**

Sources: UNODC ARQ and EUROPOL.

	1990	1991	1992	1993	1994	1995	1996	1997	1998	1999	2000	2001	2002	2003
USA	281	279	268	268	204	196	170	151	162	137	126	110	88	116
Adjusted for inflation	**407**	**387**	**361**	**351**	**259**	**243**	**205**	**178**	**188**	**155**	**139**	**117**	**92**	**119**

Sources: ONDCP: 1990-2000 data, UNODC ARQ: 2001-2003 data.

Wholesale, US$/kg

EUROPE	1990	1991	1992	1993	1994	1995	1996	1997	1998	1999	2000	2001	2002	2003	2004
Austria	55,244	46,145	63,000	36,000	37,752	30,491	30,222	28,831	34,565	31,087	25,026	19,553	23,547	33,900	37,260
Belgium	30,000	30,000	28,500	26,600	29,586	32,580	24,307	21,761	20,847	18,557	18,360	20,292	22,229	20,960	23,040
Denmark	110,000	100,000	85,000	95,000	117,625	106,805	86,806	100,465	65,693	61,507	23,585	32,889	20,803	41,770	30,050
Finland	353,774	353,774	353,774	353,774	353,774	353,774	321,586	199,442	197,856	194,357	161,034	44,840	51,804	51,800	51,800
France	180,000	72,250	80,000	63,750	75,000	66,035	46,603	32,230	25,885	25,596	22,158	26,906	23,547	28,250	31,050
Germany	45,244	36,145	41,667	35,206	36,448	35,256	27,890	25,686	25,608	24,770	20,263	17,816	20,325	21,510	25,770
Greece	90,000	70,000	35,000	28,000	29,536	34,362	39,090	28,775	21,020	20,714	17,320	16,592	17,425	18,650	17,540
Italy	67,500	60,000	108,000	42,581	47,690	35,786	48,152	37,795	36,459	36,894	31,163	32,979	33,669	29,830	32,790
Luxembourg	86,000	75,000	75,000	49,500	86,000	57,079	59,852	54,786	52,630	50,368	48,000	50,369	50,369	24,700	31,050
Netherlands	23,850	25,000	26,550	23,850	23,850	24,384	20,572	13,810	14,056	16,985	14,703	15,757	29,199	17,730	17,730
Norway	220,000	200,000	212,500	151,099	101,744	85,000	72,520	62,209	64,918	49,872	44,561	35,874	37,676	17,520	52,520
Portugal	50,000	55,000	46,667	31,500	32,428	43,171	45,902	38,841	30,483	29,339	25,398	31,310	25,839	31,000	34,040
Spain	160,000	125,000	122,500	91,000	74,418	79,880	84,395	63,880	52,755	53,820	43,596	32,000	41,202	48,420	46,840
Sweden*	140,000	130,000	115,000	95,000	117,625	62,655	64,829	65,771	63,190	61,022	41,626	33,702	34,738	41,900	39,028
Switzerland	124,000	153,800	228,875	47,460	52,823	54,850	41,665	37,234	34,294	33,422	29,568	16,082	19,149	22,340	22,340
United Kingdom	53,940	43,940	43,500	43,210	42,500	42,004	34,846	39,491	41,667	29,126	26,718	25,926	30,620	34,340	39,040
Ireland	53,940	53,940	53,500	53,210	52,500	81,479	77,643	36,531	34,396	43,478	37,600	36,441	36,441	30,510	30,510
Average unweighted in US_$	109,029	95,882	101,120	74,514	77,135	72,094	66,287	52,208	48,019	45,936	37,099	28,784	30,505	30,302	33,082
infl.adj. in US-$	**157,752**	**133,138**	**136,227**	**97,480**	**98,341**	**89,396**	**79,852**	**61,466**	**55,636**	**52,103**	**40,701**	**30,710**	**32,049**	**31,120**	**33,082**
Weighted average in US-$	93,652	68,208	77,441	54,923	56,381	52,570	48,000	39,481	36,529	34,283	28,509	25,809	28,196	29,985	32,650
Inflation adj. (kg) in US-$	**135,503**	**94,711**	**104,328**	**71,850**	**71,882**	**65,188**	**57,822**	**46,483**	**42,323**	**38,885**	**31,277**	**27,535**	**29,624**	**30,794**	**32,650**
Inflation adj. (gram) in US-$	**136**	**95**	**104**	**72**	**72**	**65**	**58**	**46**	**42**	**39**	**31**	**28**	**30**	**31**	**33**
Weighted in Euro (g)	74	55	60	47	47	40	38	35	33	32	31	29	30	27	26
Inflation adjusted in Euro (g)	**104**	**74**	**77**	**58**	**57**	**47**	**44**	**39**	**36**	**36**	**33**	**31**	**31**	**27**	**26**

Sources: UNODC ARQ and EUROPOL.
* Calculation for Sweden is based on brown heroin price (80%) and white heroin price (20%)

USA	1990	1991	1992	1993	1994	1995	1996	1997	1998	1999	2000	2001	2002	2003
Average in US-$	162,500	155,000	150,000	146,000	142,500	146,000	141,875	129,375	125,000	107,000	81,200	59,500	50,750	65,500
Inflation adj. (kg) in US-$	**235,118**	**215,227**	**202,078**	**190,999**	**181,675**	**181,041**	**170,909**	**152,318**	**144,829**	**121,365**	**89,085**	**63,480**	**53,319**	**67,269**
Inflation adj. (gram) in US-$	**235**	**215**	**202**	**191**	**182**	**181**	**171**	**152**	**145**	**121**	**89**	**63**	**53**	**67**

Source: UNODC ARQ,

343

OPIUM
Retail and wholesale prices and purity levels:
breakdown by drug, region and country or territory
(prices expressed in US$ or converted equivalent, and purity levels in percentage)

Region / country or territory	RETAIL PRICE (per gram)				WHOLESALE PRICE (per kilogram)				
	Typical	Range	Purity	Year	Typical	Range	Purity	Year
Africa								
North Africa								
Egypt	28.2	21.7 - 34.7		2002	6,730.0	5,860.0 - 7,600.0		2002
Southern Africa								
Zambia	0.7			2003				
Americas								
North America								
Canada	35.3	21.2 - 105.8		2003	17,630.0	15,520.0 - 105,800.0		2003
United States	55.0	30.0 - 80.0		2002	25,000.0	20,000.0 - 30,000.0		2002
South America								
Colombia	0.3			2003	160.0	100.0 - 210.0		2002
Asia								
Central Asia and Transcaucasia								
Armenia	2.5	2.5 - 3.5		2003				
Azerbaijan	2.0	1.8 2.2		2002	1,800.0	1,700.0 - 2,000.0		2002
Georgia	17.5	15.0 - 20.0		2003				
Kazakhstan					1,170.0			2002
Kyrgyzstan	4.0	3.0 - 5.0	14.0 - 22.0	2002	800.0	600.0 - 1,000.0	14.0 - 22.0	2002
Tajikistan	1.0	0.6 - 1.3	40.0 - 90.0	2003	210.0	160.0 - 270.0	40.0 - 90.0	2003
Turkmenistan					3,720.0			2003
Uzbekistan					3,750.0	2,000.0 - 5,500.0		2003
East and South-East Asia								
China					1,250.0	870.0 - 2,500.0		2002
Indonesia	32.4	29.5 - 35.4		2003				
Japan	43.8			2003	3,940.0			
Malaysia	1.5	1.3 - 1.6		2003				
Myanmar	0.2	0.1 - 0.3		2003				
Republic of Korea	29.7	17.0 - 42.4		2003				
Singapore	3.1			2003	4,870.0	4,580.0 - 5,160.0		2003
Near and Middle East /South-West Asia								
Afghanistan	0.5	0.4 - 0.5	90.0 - 95.0	2003	460.0	430.0 - 480.0	90.0 - 95.0	2003
Iran (Islamic Republic of)					1,600.0			2003
Jordan	9.9	8.5 - 11.3		2002				
Lebanon					10,000.0	15,000.0 - 20,000.0		2003
Oman	2.0			2002				
Pakistan	1.3	1.2 - 1.4		2003	110.0	180.0 - 670.0		2003
Qatar	4.0			2003	3,200.0	3,300.0 - 4,110.0		2003
Syrian Arab Republic	6.0	4.5 - 7.5	30.0 - 70.0	2003				
South Asia								
Bangladesh	0.8	0.7 - 1.0	2.0 - 7.0	2002	500.0	400.0 - 700.0	3.0 - 6.0	2002
India					220.0	30.0 - 650.0		2003
Sri Lanka	6.8	5.2 - 8.4		2003				
Europe								
East Europe								
Belarus	11.9			2003	9,900.0			2003
Russian Federation	10.3	3.5 - 27.0		2003	7,800.0	2,660.0 - 16,670.0		2003
Ukraine	1.0	0.8 - 1.2		2002	500.0	400.0 - 600.0		2002
Southeast Europe								
FYR of Macedonia					680.0	570.0 - 790.0		2003
Turkey	2.3				2,260.0	1,700.0 - 2,830.0		2003
West and Central Europe								
Austria	8.5	7.9 - 9.0		2003	2,540.0	2,260.0 - 2,830.0		2003
Czech Rep.	3.3			2003	2,150.0	1,810.0 - 2,490.0		2003
France	16.6			2003				
Norway	33.9			2003	12,430.0	10,170.0 - 14,690.0		2003
Sweden					6,440.0			2003
United Kingdom	14.9	12.0 - 14.9		2002				

HEROIN
Retail and wholesale prices and purity levels:
breakdown by drug, region and country or territory
(prices expressed in US$ or converted equivalent, and purity levels in percentage)

Region / country or territory	RETAIL PRICE (per gram)				WHOLESALE PRICE (per kilogram)				
	Typical	Range	Purity	Year	Typical	Range	Purity	Year
Africa								
East Africa								
Kenya (Heroin no.3)	13.2	13.2 - 19.8		2003	13,210.0	13,210.0 - 19,820.0		2003
(Heroin no.4)	15.9	15.9 - 23.8		2003	23,125.0	19,820.0 - 26,430.0		2003
Mauritius	364.0		20.6	2003				
Rwanda					20,000.0			2002
Uganda	10.4	10.4 - 15.5		2003	30,000.0	25,000.0 - 40,000.0		2003
United Republic of Tanzania	18.0	16.0 - 22.0		2003	18,000.0	15,000.0 - 20,000.0		2003
North Africa								
Egypt	108.5	86.8 - 130.3		2002	23,880.0	17,370.0 - 30,390.0		2002
Morocco	52.4	47.1 - 57.6		2003	26,180.0	20,940.0 - 36,650.0		2003
Southern Africa								
Namibia	56.4	53.1 - 59.7		2003				
South Africa	23.5	19.3 - 26.3		2002	16,930.0	14,110.0 - 20,690.0		2002
Swaziland	39.8	33.2 - 46.4		2003	31,840.0	23,880.0 - 39,800.0		2003
Zambia	31.8			2002				
Zimbabwe	57.1	50.8 - 63.5		2003				
West and Central Africa								
Burkina Faso	43.3	43.3 - 51.9	10.0 - 20.0	2003				
Congo					10,700.0	7,140.0 - 14,270.0		2003
Côte d'Ivoire (Heroin no.4)					9,280.0	20.0 - 18,550.0		2002
Ghana (Heroin no.3 & No.4)	18.5	16.0 - 21.0		2003	18,500.0	16,000.0 - 21,000.0		2003
Guinea	17.5	15.0 - 20.0		2003	17,500.0	15,000.0 - 20,000.0		2003
Nigeria (Heroin no.3)	21.0	16.8 - 21.0		2002	21,040.0	16,830.0 - 21,040.0		2002
Togo (Heroin no.1)	5.2			2003				
Americas								
Caribbean								
Bermuda	20.0			2002				
Trinidad Tobago					6,540.0			2003
Central America								
El Salvador	70.0	65.0 - 69.0		2003	75,000.0	70,000.0 - 80,000.0		2002
Guatemala	63.6	50.9 - 76.3	75.0 - 90.0	2002	50,870.0	47,690.0 - 57,230.0	80.0 - 93.0	2002
Honduras					18,000.0	16,000.0 - 20,000.0	85.0 - 93.0	2003
Nicaragua	75.0		90.0	2002	75,000.0		90.0	2002
North America								
Canada	141.1	127.0 - 282.1	9.0 - 98.0	2003	51,020.0	51,020.0 - 89,290.0	50.0 - 90.0	2002
(Heroin no.3)					56,430.0	56,430.0 - 70,530.0	2.5 - 99.0	2003
(Heroin no.4)					56,430.0	49,370.0 - 10,580.0	2.5 - 99.0	2003
(black tar heroin)	318.9	318.9 - 510.2		2002				
Mexico (Heroin no.4)					32,850.0			2003
United States	115.8		32.0	2003				
(South American)					71,000.0	52,000.0 - 90,000.0	70.0	2003
(Asia)					60,000.0	40,000.0 - 80,000.0	62.0	2003
(Black Tar)					34,000.0	18,000.0 - 50,000.0	37.0	2003
South America								
Argentina					5,330.0	5,150.0 - 5,500.0		2002
Colombia (Heroin no.4)	9.8	8.1 - 11.5	81.0 - 91.0	2003				
Ecuador					10,000.0	8,000.0 - 12,000.0		2003
Venezuela (Heroin no.4)	7.6	6.4 - 7.6	10.0 - 25.0	2003	8,590.0	950.0 - 9,550.0	80.0 - 90.0	2003
Asia								
Central Asia and Transcaucasia								
Armenia	135.0	120.0 - 150.0		2003				
Georgia	275.0	250.0 - 300.0		2003				
Kazakhstan					14,500.0			2002
Kyrgyzstan					6,830.0			2002
(Heroin no.4)	21.0	20.0 - 22.0	40.0 - 60.0	2003	8,000.0	6,000.0 - 10,000.0	50.0 - 90.0	2003
Tajikistan					6,830.0			2002
(Heroin no.3)	1.9	1.3 - 2.6	10.0 - 60.0	2003	1,590.0	480.0 - 2,550.0	10.0 - 60.0	2003
(Heroin no.4)	6.0	4.0 - 8.0	10.0	2002	4,750.0	1,500.0 - 8,000.0	10.0 - 80.0	2002
Uzbekistan	25.0	15.0 - 35.0		2002	16,000.0	7,000.0 - 25,000.0		2003

HEROIN
Retail and wholesale prices and purity levels:
breakdown by drug, region and country or territory
(prices expressed in US$ or converted equivalent, and purity levels in percentage)

Region / country or territory	RETAIL PRICE (per gram)				WHOLESALE PRICE (per kilogram)			
	Typical	Range	Purity	Year	Typical	Range	Purity	Year
East and South-East Asia								
China	50.0	13.0 - 185.0		2002	25,000.0	10,000.0 - 50,000.0		2002
Hong Kong SAR, China (Heroin no.4)	54.7	42.3 - 64.6	50.0 - 66.0	2003	33,070.0	28,350.0 - 35,900.0		2003
Indonesia	41.3	35.4 - 47.2		2003	22,070.0	27,590.0 - 33,100.0		2002
Japan	262.5	175.0 - 350.0		2003				
Laos					10,000.0	10,000.0 - 12,000.0		2003
Macau SAR, China	50.0	37.0 - 62.0		2003				
Malaysia	7.3	6.7 - 8.0		2003				
(Heroin no.3)	4.8	4.3 - 5.3		2003				
(Heroin no.4)	12.6	12.0 - 13.3		2003				
Myanmar					3,480.0	2,880.0 - 4,080.0		2003
(Heroin no.4)	5.6	2.0 - 7.5		2003				
Singapore (Heroin no.3)	128.9	114.6 - 143.3		2003	5,870.0	3,720.0 - 8,020.0		2003
Vietnam	45.1	20.6 - 68.5		2002	20,750.0	16,000.0 - 25,700.0		2002
Near and Middle East/ South- West Asia								
Afghanistan (Heroin no.4)	2.7	2.0 - 3.4	80.0 - 95.0	2003	2,730.0	2,060.0 - 3,400.0	80.0 - 95.0	2003
Iran (Islamic Republic of)	6.4			2003	3,880.0			2003
Israel	33.0	18.0 - 67.0		2003	17,770.0	11,100.0 - 35,500.0		2003
Jordan	49.4	42.4 - 56.5		2002	19,770.0	18,360.0 - 21,190.0		2002
Lebanon (Heroin no.3)	35.0	30.0 - 40.0	40.0 - 60.0	2003	20,000.0	15,000.0 - 25,000.0	30.0 - 50.0	2003
(Heroin no.4)	40.0	35.0 - 45.0		2003	40,000.0	35,000.0 - 45,000.0	80.0 - 90.0	2003
Oman	116.6			2002				
Pakistan					3,690.0	2,280.0 - 5,100.0		2003
(Heroin no.3)	1.2	1.1 - 1.4		2003				
(Heroin no.4)	1.8	1.6 - 2.1		2003				
Qatar	137.0	137.0 - 164.0		2002				
Syrian Arab Republic	20.0	17.0 - 23.0	15.0 - 35.0	2003	17,000.0	15,000.0 - 19,000.0	25.0 - 50.0	2003
South Asia								
Bangladesh (Heroin no.3)	7.0	6.0 - 8.0	2.0 - 4.0	2003	5,500.0	5,000.0 - 7,000.0	4.0 - 6.0	2003
(Heroin no.4)	8.0	7.0 - 10.0	3.0 - 6.0	2003	7,500.0	6,000.0 - 9,000.0	5.0 - 7.0	2003
India					4,330.0	3,250.0 - 10,820.0		2003
Nepal	9.3	5.3 - 13.4		2003	4,000.0	2,670.0 - 5,340.0		2003
Sri Lanka	28.2	23.0 - 33.5	29.0 - 66.0	2003				
Europe								
East Europe								
Belarus	50.7			2003	36,400.0			2003
(Heroin no.2)	35.0	30.0 - 40.0		2002	20,000.0	15,000.0 - 30,000.0		2002
Russian Federation	45.0	20.0 - 100.0		2003	19,150.0	8,300.0 - 30,000.0		2003
Ukraine	60.0	50.0 - 65.0		2002	48,000.0	45,000.0 - 50,000.0		2002
Southeast Europe								
Albania	2.9	2.2 - 3.6		2002	14,500.0	12,000.0 - 17,000.0		2002
Bulgaria (Heroin no.3)	17.0		0.2 - 85.0	2003	9,610.0			2003
Croatia	44.7	29.8 - 59.6	5.0 - 15.0	2003	17,890.0	14,910.0 - 20,870.0	30.0 - 50.0	2003
FYR of Macedonia	19.8	17.0 - 22.6		2003	12,150.0	11,300.0 - 13,000.0		2003
Romania	37.3	35.0 - 39.6	8.0 - 55.0	2003	18,650.0	16,950.0 - 20,340.0		2003
Serbia and Montenegro	36.7	28.3 - 45.2		2003	14,130.0	11,300.0 - 16,950.0		2003
Turkey	9.0			2003	9,610.0	6,780.0 - 12,430.0	25.0 - 70.0	2003
West and Central Europe								
Andorra	33.9			2002				
Austria (Heroin no.3)	67.8	56.5 - 79.1	3.0 - 50.0	2003	33,900.0	28,250.0 - 39,550.0	1.0 - 50.0	2003
(Heroin no.4)	101.7	90.4 - 113.0		2003				
Belgium (Heroin no.3)	30.5	10.2 - 56.5		2003	20,960.0	14,690.0 - 28,250.0		2003
Cyprus	100.0	80.0 - 120.0		2002	22,500.0	20,000.0 - 25,000.0		2002
(Heroin no.3)	141.3			2003	28,820.0			2003
(Heroin no.4)	172.9			2003	38,430.0			2003
Czech Republic	42.4	21.7 - 63.1	4.6 - 41.3	2002	25,100.0	12,530.0 - 37,680.0	20.0 - 41.3	2002
(Heroin no.3)	40.8	28.4 - 53.2	2.0 - 30.0	2003	23,050.0	17,740.0 - 28,360.0	3.3 - 20.3	2003
Denmark (Heroin no.3)	121.5	60.8 - 182.3		2003	41,770.0	22,780.0 - 60,750.0		2003
(Heroin no.4)	144.3	75.9 - 212.6		2003	106,310.0			2003
Estonia (Heroin no.4)	72.5	58.0 - 87.0		2003	29,010.0			2003
Finland	163.9	141.3 - 235.5	7.0	2002	51,800.0	47,090.0 - 56,510.0	7.0	2002
(Heroin no.4)	226.0		2.7 - 31.0	2003	62,150.0		2.5 - 29.0	2003

HEROIN
Retail and wholesale prices and purity levels:
breakdown by drug, region and country or territory
(prices expressed in US$ or converted equivalent, and purity levels in percentage)

Region / country or territory	RETAIL PRICE (per gram)				WHOLESALE PRICE (per kilogram)				
	Typical	Range	Purity	Year	Typical	Range		Purity	Year
France (Heroin no.3)	56.5	50.9 - 79.1	2.0 - 10.0	2003	28,250.0			10.0 - 40.0	2003
(Heroin no.4)	90.4	67.8 - 135.6	2.0 - 10.0	2003	45,200.0			10.0 - 40.0	2003
Germany	46.2	31.8 - 62.6	16.0	2003	21,510.0	17,440.0 -	31,980.0	7.3	2003
Greece (Heroin no.3)	65.0	45.2 - 84.8	2.9 - 43.3	2003	18,650.0	13,560.0 -	23,730.0	1.9 - 32.3	2003
(Heroin no.4)	67.8	50.9 - 84.8	2.9 - 43.3	2003	23,170.0	16,950.0 -	29,380.0	1.9 - 32.3	2003
Hungary	28.3	22.6 - 33.9	3.0 - 30.0	2003	14,690.0	13,560.0 -	15,820.0	3.0 - 60.0	2003
Ireland	226.0	203.4 - 248.6		2003	30,510.0	31,640.0 -	39,550.0	7.0 - 78.0	2003
(Heroin no. 3)	179.0	169.5 - 188.4	25.0 - 35.0	2002					
Italy (Heroin no. 3)	62.7	55.4 - 70.1		2003	29,830.0	26,900.0 -	32,770.0	1.0 - 61.0	2003
(Heroin no. 4)	93.8	85.9 - 101.7		2003	46,270.0	42,300.0 -	50,230.0		2003
Lithuania	32.7	22.8 - 45.9	0.5 - 20.0	2003	25,670.0	13,510.0 -	37,830.0	30.0 - 60.0	2002
(Heroin no.3)					13,043.0			64.0 - 81.0	2003
Luxembourg	40.0		0.9 - 47.8	2003					
Netherlands	40.4	22.6 - 67.8		2003	17,730.0	15,820.0 -	20,340.0		2003
Norway	197.8	113.0 - 282.5	1.0 - 60.0	2003					
(Heroin no.3)					17,520.0			1.0 - 60.0	2003
(Heroin no.4)					17,520.0			40.0 - 90.0	2003
Poland	52.6	47.4 - 73.7	20.0 - 30.0	2003	28,940.0	26,310.0 -	31,580.0	40.0 - 80.0	2003
Portugal (Heroin no.3)	53.7		0.1 - 69.9	2003	31,000.0	28,180.0 -	33,820.0		2003
Slovakia	23.6	18.8 - 28.3		2002	15,070.0	14,130.0 -	16,480.0		2002
Slovenia (Heroin no.3)	44.6	39.6 - 49.7		2003	44,640.0	39,550.0 -	49,720.0		2003
(Heroin no.4)	76.3	73.5 - 79.1		2003	76,280.0	73,450.0 -	79,100.0		2003
Spain	60.8		34.0	2002	41,200.0			51.0	2002
(Heroin no.3)	66.1			2003	48,420.0				2003
Sweden (Heroin no.3)	123.2			2003	30,810.0	24,650.0 -	36,970.0		2003
(Heroin no.4)	147.9			2003	86,260.0	73,940.0 -	98,580.0		2003
Switzerland	48.4	22.3 - 89.4	1.3 - 26.0	2003	22,340.0	14,890.0 -	33,510.0		2003
United Kingdom	100.2	40.9 - 261.6	0.1 - 88.0	2003	34,340.0	19,620.0 -	49,050.0	1.0 - 78.0	2003
Oceania									
Australia	201.9	114.3 - 539.4		2002	75,580.0	53,980.0 -	97,710.0		2002
New Zealand (Heroin no.4)	492.5	405.6 - 579.4		2003					

7.2. Cocaine: Wholesale, street prices and purity levels

Prices in Europe and in USA, 1990-2003

Retail price (street price), US$/gram

EUROPE	1990	1991	1992	1993	1994	1995	1996	1997	1998	1999	2000	2001	2002	2003	2004
Austria	198	180	167	120	126	156	138	118	113	93	94	78	71	90	102
Belgium	80	90	68	95	82	93	90	57	55	60	55	51	50	51	87
Denmark	144	135	111	90	150	176	169	108	119	165	106	120	91	122	83
Finland	159	150	126	105	165	191	184	123	179	157	138	121	111	151	166
France	99	119	140	153	151	174	125	87	84	82	50	87	75	90	87
Germany	120	103	111	95	109	103	90	77	72	68	57	58	57	68	73
Greece	150	120	105	54	116	111	144	91	54	82	69	72	75	96	93
Iceland	167	203	207	200	211	228	226	238	149	134	121	109	150	207	156
Italy	108	120	164	90	104	113	129	109	129	135	100	89	90	101	111
Luxembourg	150	150	150	150	172	194	127	115	110	119	119	119	107	96	84
Netherlands	66	70	74	66	60	79	52	64	38	33	33	33	33	50	50
Norway	176	170	255	156	145	150	153	177	133	128	114	157	165	170	155
Portugal	63	57	60	57	59	66	64	57	51	43	56	48	36	47	49
Spain	110	100	100	63	78	91	72	68	68	63	52	52	56	70	76
Sweden	160	152	183	123	148	118	118	98	88	97	77	79	87	99	93
Switzerland	178	144	188	136	146	148	127	117	110	109	77	69	74	89	89
United Kingdom	131	127	69	123	113	111	102	124	128	104	94	94	84	90	97
Ireland	141	137	120	110	100	119	32	34	32	30	28	28	94	79	87
Average unweighted in US-$	133	129	133	110	124	134	119	103	95	95	80	81	84	98	97
Inflation adjusted in US-$	**193**	**179**	**179**	**144**	**158**	**167**	**143**	**122**	**110**	**107**	**88**	**87**	**88**	**101**	**97**
Weighted average US-$	117	115	118	104	112	118	105	92	92	88	70	74	72	84	88
Inflation adjusted in US-$	**169**	**159**	**159**	**136**	**143**	**147**	**127**	**109**	**106**	**100**	**77**	**79**	**75**	**86**	**88**
Weighted average in Euro	92	93	91	89	94	91	83	81	82	82	76	83	76	74	71
Inflation adjusted in Euro	**130**	**124**	**117**	**110**	**114**	**107**	**96**	**92**	**91**	**91**	**83**	**88**	**79**	**75**	**71**

Sources: UNODC ARQ data and EUROPOL, except 2003 EUROPOL, and in italic UNODC

	1990	1991	1992	1993	1994	1995	1996	1997	1998	1999	2000	2001	2002	2003
USA	184	177	170	147	137	131	126	127	124	118	129	98	86	75
Adjusted for inflation	**267**	**246**	**229**	**193**	**174**	**163**	**152**	**149**	**144**	**134**	**142**	**104**	**90**	**77**

Sources: ONDCP 1990-2000 (prices for 1 gram or less, at street purity), ONDCP, The Price & Purity of Illicit Drugs 1981-2003 (prices for < 2 grams)

Wholesale price, US$/kg

EUROPE	1990	1991	1992	1993	1994	1995	1996	1997	1998	1999	2000	2001	2002	2003	2004
Austria	66,000	60,000	54,000	40,000	41,946	52,084	45,875	56,723	54,440	38,859	47,094	43,995	42,385	59,300	55,890
Belgium	25,000	24,000	38,250	28,000	26,920	30,560	21,927	17,025	19,167	23,859	22,376	26,771	28,111	29,610	32,480
Denmark	80,000	85,000	85,000	82,500	58,516	60,034	46,141	38,640	44,517	78,900	43,462	47,839	37,823	53,160	45,900
Finland	79,500	75,000	62,750	52,500	82,500	95,450	91,750	61,550	89,350	78,460	68,321	59,492	51,804	62,150	68,310
France	117,000	38,250	45,000	38,250	40,000	39,877	48,077	43,554	42,159	27,714	27,000	34,978	37,676	45,200	46,580
Germany	69,000	53,100	60,300	54,142	57,692	54,676	53,925	45,294	41,210	39,639	33,752	33,235	34,476	40,110	44,760
Greece	75,000	60,000	95,000	36,000	46,413	53,098	72,015	43,795	49,180	49,320	41,237	40,359	42,385	53,680	57,450
Italy	54,000	48,000	94,000	41,935	51,097	51,455	55,633	50,629	49,091	47,250	46,000	40,529	41,412	47,440	52,140
Luxembourg	93,919	95,939	113,521	50,847	157,593	141,343	47,625	43,103	41,072	47,718	47,718	47,718	47,718	47,718	31,050
Netherlands	26,500	27,000	29,500	26,500	24,680	33,232	23,894	29,698	22,355	27,500	27,500	27,500	27,500	27,400	27,400
Norway	120,000	120,000	127,500	110,000	39,971	50,000	41,670	60,028	81,699	57,545	51,417	51,569	54,159	56,500	65,210
Portugal	39,500	39,285	33,000	27,000	27,950	34,483	42,591	37,908	33,447	30,000	28,000	29,080	31,046	32,410	36,400
Spain	65,000	60,000	55,000	35,000	36,434	41,322	38,760	36,806	38,924	38,898	30,882	38,898	31,511	38,830	42,540
Sweden	80,000	76,200	91,375	61,450	73,825	55,556	59,255	45,573	50,484	48,508	38,394	34,693	35,763	43,130	43,670
Switzerland	63,900	94,250	116,250	50,847	72,012	75,949	55,949	50,629	41,152	41,000	35,482	23,392	19,274	37,230	37,230
United Kingdom	47,850	46,475	20,625	43,210	45,000	46,774	40,625	47,500	47,500	33,981	38,168	36,008	35,848	40,880	46,480
Ireland	45,000	45,000	40,000	50,000	45,000	42,000	31,646	33,733	31,530	29,891	29,891	29,891	29,891	30,510	30,510
Average unweighted	67,481	61,618	68,298	48,717	54,562	56,347	47,823	43,079	45,722	43,473	38,629	37,997	36,987	43,839	44,941
infl.adj.	**97,636**	**85,560**	**92,011**	**63,731**	**69,562**	**69,870**	**57,610**	**50,718**	**52,975**	**49,309**	**42,380**	**40,539**	**38,859**	**45,022**	**44,941**
Weighted average	67,793	50,687	57,392	43,998	47,040	48,150	47,754	43,975	43,434	38,491	35,580	36,095	35,950	42,322	45,730
Adjusted for inflation (kg)	**98,089**	**70,382**	**77,317**	**57,558**	**59,972**	**59,707**	**57,526**	**51,774**	**50,324**	**43,658**	**39,035**	**38,510**	**37,769**	**43,464**	**45,730**
inflation adjusted (gram)	**98**	**70**	**77**	**57**	**60**	**60**	**58**	**52**	**50**	**44**	**39**	**38**	**38**	**43**	**46**
Weighted in Euro (g)	53	41	44	38	40	37	38	39	39	36	39	40	38	37	37
Inflation adjusted in Euro (g)	**75**	**55**	**57**	**47**	**48**	**43**	**43**	**44**	**43**	**40**	**42**	**43**	**40**	**38**	**37**

Sources: UNODC ARQ or EUROPOL, except 2003 EUROPOL, and in italic UNODC

	1990	1991	1992	1993	1994	1995	1996	1997	1998	1999	2000	2001	2002	2003
USA	45,430	48,300	48,100	44,730	42,180	38,640	35,700	34,320	31,960	30,870	29,580	21,500	23,000	21,500
Adjusted for inflation (kg)	**65,732**	**67,067**	**64,800**	**58,516**	**53,776**	**47,914**	**43,006**	**40,406**	**37,030**	**35,014**	**32,452**	**22,938**	**24,164**	**22,081**
Adjusted for inflation (gram)	**66**	**67**	**65**	**59**	**54**	**48**	**43**	**40**	**37**	**35**	**32**	**23**	**24**	**22**

Sources: ONDCP 1990-2000 (prices for 10-100 gram, at street purity), UNODC ARQ 2001 - 2002 (mid-point of min/max prices)

COCAINE
Retail and wholesale prices and purity levels:
breakdown by drug, region and country or territory
(prices expressed in US$ or converted equivalent, and purity levels in percentage)

Region / country or territory	RETAIL PRICE (per gram)					WHOLESALE PRICE (per kilogram)					
	Typical	Range		Purity	Year	Typical	Range		Purity		Year
Africa											
East Africa											
Kenya	33.0	26.4 -	39.6		2003	46,245.0	39,640.0 -	52,850.0	40.0 -	50.0	2003
Rwanda						26,000.0					2002
United Republic of Tanzania	22.0	20.0 -	24.0		2003	20,000.0	18,000.0 -	22,000.0			2003
North Africa											
Egypt (Coca Base)	184.5	152.0 -	217.1		2002	97,690.0	86,830.0 -	108,540.0			2002
Morocco (Coca Base)	73.3	68.1 -	78.5		2003	52,360.0	41,880.0 -	62,830.0			2003
Southern Africa											
Namibia (Coca Base)	56.4	53.1 -	59.7		2003						
(Crack)	11.9	10.6 -	13.3		2003						
South Africa	21.6	23.5 -	26.3		2002	15,990.0	13,169.0 -	20,694.0			2002
Swaziland (Coca Base)	33.2	26.5 -	53.1		2003						
(Crack)	4.6	6.0 -	6.6		2003	990.0	860.0 -	1,260.0			2003
Zambia						18,300.0	18,300.0 -	19,370.0			2003
(Coca Base)	36.0				2003						
(Crack)	18.3				2003						
Zimbabwe	89.3	114.2 -	128.6		2003						
(Crack)	44.6	35.7 -	53.6		2002						
West and Central Africa											
Burkina Faso (Coca Base)	43.3				2003						
(Crack)	43.3			10.0 - 20.0	2003						
Congo (Coca Base)	26.0	26.0 -	43.3		2003	5,710.0	4,280.0 -	7,140.0			2002
Côte d'Ivoire						12,130.0	20.0 -	24,260.0			2002
Ghana (Coca Base)	21.0	19.0 -	23.0		2003	21,000.0	19,000.0 -	23,000.0			2003
Guinea	20.0	18.0 -	22.0		2003	20,000.0	18,000.0 -	22,000.0			2003
Nigeria	4.7			30.0 - 40.0	2003						
(Coca Base)						15,510.0	15,120.0 -	17,840.0	70.0 -	100.0	2003
Togo	6.1	3.5 -	8.7		2003						
Americas											
Caribbean											
Bahamas	15.0	15.0 -	25.0		2003	16,000.0	20,000.0 -	30,000.0			2003
(Coca Base)	10.0	10.0 -	20.0		2003	16,000.0	20,000.0 -	30,000.0			2003
(Crack)	3.0	2.0 -	5.0		2003						
Bermuda	125.0				2002	65,000.0	60,000.0 -	70,000.0	50.0 -	80.0	2002
(Crack)						65,000.0	60,000.0 -	70,000.0	50.0 -	80.0	2002
Cayman Islands	40.9	32.7 -	49.1		2003	7,362.0	6,544.0 -	8,180.0	78.0 -	92.0	2003
Trinidad Tobago						11,850.0	4,080.0 -	19,610.0	61.0 -	96.0	2003
(crack)	2.9	1.6 -	4.1	21.0 - 76.0	2003						
Turks and Caicos Islands	20.0				2003	8,000.0	7,000.0 -	10,000.0			2003
(Crack)	10.0				2003	6,000.0	5,000.0 -	7,000.0			2003
Central America											
Costa Rica	17.6	15.1 -	20.1		2003	4,400.0	3,770.0 -	5,030.0	53.0 -	90.0	2003
(Crack)	13.2	8.8 -	17.6		2003						
El Salvador	24.0	23.0 -	25.0		2003	24,000.0	23,000.0 -	25,000.0			2003
(Coca Base)	24.0	23.0 -	25.0		2003	24,000.0	23,000.0 -	25,000.0			2003
(Crack)	24.0	23.0 -	25.0		2003	24,000.0	23,000.0 -	25,000.0			2003
Guatemala	6.3	6.3 -	7.6	65.0 - 70.0	2003	12,590.0	10,070.0 -	11,330.0	96.0 -	98.0	2003
(Coca Base)	12.7	10.2 -	12.7	80.0 - 90.0	2002	12,720.0	11,450.0 -	12,720.0	80.0 -	93.0	2002
(Crack)	8.6	7.6 -	9.5	50.0 - 60.0	2002	7,630.0	6,360.0 -	7,630.0	50.0 -	70.0	2002
Honduras	11.8	7.9 -	15.8	75.0 - 85.0	2003						
(Coca Base)	15.3	12.2 -	18.3		2002	4,470.0	3,950.0 -	5,000.0	90.0 -	96.0	2003
(Crack)	5.3	2.6 -	7.9	50.0 - 75.0	2003	3,110.0	2,930.0 -	3,300.0			2002
Nicaragua	5.0				2002						
(Crack)	1.0				2002						

COCAINE
Retail and wholesale prices and purity levels:
breakdown by drug, region and country or territory
(prices expressed in US$ or converted equivalent, and purity levels in percentage)

Region / country or territory	RETAIL PRICE (per gram)				WHOLESALE PRICE (per kilogram)			
	Typical	Range	Purity	Year	Typical	Range	Purity	Year
North America								
Canada					28,210.0	24,690.0 - 42,320.0	73.0	2003
(Coca Base)	51.0	31.9 - 127.6	68.0	2002				
(Crack)	95.7	63.8 - 127.6	72.0	2002				
Mexico					7,880.0			2002
United States	74.6		70.0	2003	21,500.0	13,000.0 - 30,000.0	82.0	2003
(Crack)	140.5		74.0	2003	23,500.0	13,000.0 - 34,000.0		2003
South America								
Argentina	17.0	15.0 - 18.0		2003	5,500.0	2,000.0 - 9,000.0		2003
(Coca Base)					2,060.0	1,720.0 - 2,410.0		2002
(Crack)					1,460.0	1,370.0 - 1,550.0		2002
Bolivia	5.0		80.0	2002	1,500.0			2002
(Coca Base)	3.0			2002	1,200.0			2002
Colombia	1.7	1.5 - 1.9	86.0 - 94.0	2003	1,550.0	1,200.0 - 1,900.0	86.0 - 94.0	2003
(Coca Base)	1.0	0.8 - 1.2	82.0 - 95.0	2003	910.0	420.0 - 1,320.0	85.0 - 95.0	2003
Ecuador					5,000.0	4,000.0 - 6,000.0		2003
(Coca Base)	2.0	1.0 - 3.0		2003	2,500.0	2,000.0 - 3,000.0		
Peru					1,000.0	900.0 - 1,100.0		2003
(Coca Base)					700.0	600.0 - 800.0		2003
Suriname (Coca Base)					4,000.0	3,000.0 - 5,000.0		2002
(crack)	1.7	1.2 - 2.3		2002				
Uruguay	6.0	5.0 - 7.0	15.0 - 40.0	2003	6,250.0	5,000.0 - 7,500.0	25.0 - 100.0	2003
Venezuela	6.4	4.5 - 6.4	10.0 - 20.0	2003	1,270.0	950.0 - 2,230.0	80.0 - 90.0	2003
(Coca Base)	6.4	0.8 - 6.4		2003	70.0	60.0 - 570.0		2003
(Crack)	1.3	1.0 - 1.3		2003	110.0	100.0 - 130.0		2003
Asia								
East and South-East Asia								
Hong Kong SAR, China	148.2	116.0 - 309.3		2003	41,880.0	32,220.0 - 48,970.0		2003
Indonesia	49.7	44.1 - 55.2		2002	11,030.0	9,380.0 - 13,240.0		2002
(Coca Base)	53.1	47.2 - 58.9		2003				
Japan	393.8	350.0 - 437.5		2003				
(Coca Base)	373.3			2002				
Near and Middle East /South-West Asia								
Israel (Coca Base)	88.0	34.0 - 130.0		2003	55,500.0	42,220.0 - 66,670.0		2003
Jordan (Coca Base)					70,620.0	63,560.0 - 77,680.0		2002
Lebanon	70.0	50.0 - 90.0	50.0 - 90.0	2003	65,000.0	50,000.0 - 80,000.0	80.0 - 90.0	2002
Syrian Arab Republic (Coca Base)	100.0	80.0 - 120.0	40.0 - 60.0	2003	60,000.0	50,000.0 - 70,000.0	50.0 - 70.0	2003
South Asia								
India (Coca Base)								
Europe								
East Europe								
Russian Federation	148.0	82.0 - 270.0		2003	82,000.0	60,000.0 - 265,000.0		2003
Ukraine	130.0	110.0 - 150.0		2002	100,000.0	90,000.0 - 110,000.0		2002
Southeast Europe								
Albania	54.2	50.6 - 57.8		2002	45,000.0	40,000.0 - 50,000.0		2002
Bulgaria	79.1		17.0 - 81.0	2003	45,200.0		85.0	2003
Croatia	74.6	59.6 - 89.5	20.0 - 50.0	2003	50,690.0	44,730.0 - 56,660.0	60.0 - 80.0	2003
FYR of Macedonia	37.7	28.3 - 47.1		2002				
(Coca Base)	45.2	33.9 - 56.5		2003	36,730.0	28,250.0 - 45,200.0		2003
Romania	65.0	50.9 - 79.1		2003	28,250.0	22,600.0 - 33,900.0		2003
Serbia and Montenegro	67.8	56.5 - 79.1		2003	45,200.0	33,900.0 - 56,500.0		2003
Turkey	135.6			2003	129,960.0	90,410.0 - 169,510.0		2003

COCAINE
Retail and wholesale prices and purity levels:
breakdown by drug, region and country or territory
(prices expressed in US$ or converted equivalent, and purity levels in percentage)

Region / country or territory	RETAIL PRICE (per gram)				WHOLESALE PRICE (per kilogram)			
	Typical	Range	Purity	Year	Typical	Range	Purity	Year
West and Central Europe								
Andorra (Coca Base)	59.3	56.5 - 62.2		2002				
Austria	90.4	79.1 - 101.7	3.0 - 90.0	2003	42,390.0	37,680.0 - 47,090.0	1.0 - 92.0	2002
(Coca Base)					59,300.0	50,900.0 - 67,800.0	20.0 - 90.0	2003
Belgium	50.9	11.3 - 84.8		2003	29,610.0	22,600.0 - 33,900.0		2003
Cyprus (Coca Base)	166.1			2003	48,040.0			2003
Czech Republic	79.8	53.2 - 106.5	51.0 - 75.0	2003	62,040.0	53,230.0 - 70,970.0	31.7 - 75.0	2003
(Coca Base)					43,940.0	31,080.0 - 56,510.0	75.0 - 86.0	2002
Denmark	121.5	60.8 - 182.3		2003	53,160.0	30,370.0 - 75,940.0		2003
Estonia	72.5	58.0 - 87.0		2003	29,010.0	21,760.0 - 39,170.0		2003
Finland	151.4		59.0 - 74.0	2003	62,150.0		61.0 - 93.0	2003
France	90.4	56.5 - 101.7	10.0 - 40.0	2003	45,200.0	33,900.0 - 56,500.0	60.0 - 90.0	2003
Germany	67.9	49.7 - 88.0	0.3 - 92.0	2003	40,110.0	28,510.0 - 48,940.0	2.4 - 81.4	2003
(Coca Base)	57.1	33.0 - 87.6		2002	34,480.0	25,350.0 - 44,740.0		2002
(Crack)	74.9	58.0 - 73.5		2003				
Greece	96.1	79.1 - 113.0	14.0 - 97.0	2003	53,680.0	39,550.0 - 67,800.0	3.0 - 95.0	2003
Hungary	73.5	67.8 - 79.1	10.0 - 75.0	2003	38,420.0	36,160.0 - 40,680.0	30.0 - 90.0	2003
Iceland	207.0	200.0 - 214.0		2003				
Ireland	79.1	67.8 - 101.7		2003	30,510.0	28,250.0 - 39,550.0	7.0 - 78.0	2003
(Coca Base)	94.2	84.8 - 103.6	60.0 - 70.0	2002				
Italy	100.9	89.8 - 111.9		2003	47,440.0	42,670.0 - 52,200.0	10.0 - 96.0	2003
Lithuania	54.0	39.2 - 68.7	4.0 - 63.0	2003	39,310.0		60.0 - 68.0	2003
Luxembourg	96.1		58.5	2003				
Netherlands	50.0	28.3 - 67.8		2003	27,400.0	20,340.0 - 45,200.0		2003
Norway	169.5	113.0 - 226.0	10.0 - 80.0	2003	56,500.0	28,250.0 - 84,760.0	10.0 - 80.0	2003
(Crack)					56,500.0	28,250.0 - 84,760.0	40.0 - 95.0	2003
Poland	50.0	39.5 - 73.7	14.0 - 21.0	2003	27,670.0	25,160.0 - 30,190.0	40.0 - 84.0	2002
Portugal	46.8		8.4 - 98.9	2003	32,410.0	31,000.0 - 33,820.0		2003
Slovakia	75.3	68.4 - 82.1	65.0 - 82.0	2003	68,440.0	54,750.0 - 82,120.0		2003
(crack)	60.8	55.3 - 66.4		2002				
Slovenia	63.6	61.2 - 65.9		2002	63,580.0	61,220.0 - 65,930.0		2002
Spain	70.0		51.0	2003	38,830.0		73.5	2003
Sweden	98.6	73.9 - 123.2		2003	43,130.0	36,970.0 - 49,290.0		2003
Switzerland	89.4	59.6 - 134.0	38.0 - 58.0	2003	37,230.0	22,340.0 - 59,570.0		2003
United Kingdom	90.4	49.1 - 163.5	51.3 (0.03-95.0)	2003	40,880.0	29,430.0 - 52,320.0	69.1 (3.0-97.0)	2003
(Crack)	155.3	81.8 - 327.0	69.6 (0.4-100.0)	2003	45,780.0	32,700.0 - 58,860.0	77.5 (49.0-90.0)	2003
OCEANIA								
Australia (Coca Base)	146.8	99.0 - 269.9		2002	98,190.0	95,210.0 - 107,110.0		2002
New Zealand	217.3	173.8 - 260.7		2003				

7.3. Cannabis: Wholesale, street prices and purity levels

CANNABIS HERB
Retail and wholesale prices and purity levels:
breakdown by drug, region and country or territory
(prices expressed in US$ or converted equivalent, and purity levels in percentage)

Region / country or territory	RETAIL PRICE (per gram)				WHOLESALE PRICE (per kilogram)				
	Typical	Range		Purity	Year	Typical	Range		Purity	Year
Africa										
East Africa										
Eritrea	4.0	3.0 -	5.0		2003	1,100.0	1,000.0 -	1,200.0	1.0 - 5.0	2003
Kenya	0.2	0.1 -	0.3		2003	99.0	70.0 -	130.0		2003
Madagascar	1.3	1.1 -	1.4	100.0	2002	10.0			100.0	2002
Mauritius	10.1			80.0 - 100.0	2002					
Seychelles						4,140.0	3,680.0 -	4,600.0		
Uganda	0.1	0.03 -	0.1		2003	100.0	50.0 -	100.0		2003
North Africa										
Algeria						520.0				2003
Southern Africa										
Malawi	0.1				2003					
Namibia	0.5	0.4 -	0.7		2003					
South Africa	0.2	0.1 -	0.2		2003	20.0	10.0 -	30.0		2003
Swaziland	2.0	1.3 -	3.3		2003	100.0	70.0 -	130.0		2003
Zambia	0.2				2003	150.0	150.0 -	170.0		2003
Zimbabwe	0.9	0.5 -	1.3	90.0	2003	60.0	50.0 -	80.0	90.0	2003
West and Central Africa										
Burkina Faso	0.2	0.2 -	0.4	100.0	2003	20.0	10.0 -	30.0	100.0	2003
Congo	0.2	0.2 -	0.4		2003	40.0	30.0 -	60.0		2003
Côte d'Ivoire	0.7	0.1 -	1.4		2002	10.0				2002
Ghana	4.0	3.0 -	5.0		2003	290.0	230.0 -	350.0		2003
Guinea						10.0				2003
Nigeria	0.2	0.1 -	0.2		2003	10.0				2002
Saint Helena	8.2				2003	8,175.0				2003
Togo	0.1	0.1 -	0.4		2003	130.0				2003
Americas										
Caribbean										
Bahamas	5.0	5.0 -	10.0		2003	1,500.0	1,500.0 -	2,200.0		2003
Bermuda	50.0				2002	13,000.0	11,000.0 -	11,500.0		2002
Cayman Islands	8.0	6.0 -	10.0		2002	2,000.0	1,500.0 -	2,500.0		2002
Montserrat	5.2	4.7 -	5.7		2002	850.0	750.0 -	940.0		2002
Trinidad Tobago	1.2	0.8 -	1.6		2003	470.0	290.0 -	650.0	100.0	2003
Turks & Caicos Islands	10.0				2003	600.0	400.0 -	800.0		2003
Central America										
Costa Rica	2.0	1.5 -	2.5		2003	190.0	180.0 -	200.0		2003
El Salvador	1.0	1.0 -	1.1		2003	1,070.0	1,000.0 -	1,140.0		2003
Guatemala	2.5	2.5 -	3.2	100.0	2003	110.0			100.0	2003
Honduras	0.3	0.3 -	0.4		2003	90.0	70.0 -	120.0		2003
Nicaragua	0.1				2002	140.0	100.0 -	140.0		2002
North America										
Canada	7.1	7.1 -	17.6	0.5 - 24.0	2003	2,820.0	2,120.0 -	4,230.0	0.1 - 25.0	2003
Mexico						80.0			100.0	2003
United States	11.4				2003	2,035.0	770.0 -	3,300.0	4.8	2003
South America										
Argentina	3.0	2.0 -	4.0		2003	1,750.0	1,000.0 -	2,500.0		2003
Bolivia	0.8				2002	100.0				2002
Colombia	0.1				2003	30.0	10.0 -	70.0		2003
Ecuador	1.0	1.0 -	2.0		2003	1,500.0	1,000.0 -	2,000.0		2003
Paraguay	0.9	0.7 -	1.1		2002	10.0				2002
Suriname	0.9	0.5 -	1.4		2002					
Uruguay	0.3	0.1 -	0.5		2003	200.0	150.0 -	250.0		2003
Venezuela	1.3	1.3 -	1.6		2003	130.0	110.0 -	130.0		2003
Asia										
Central Asia and Transcaucasia										
Armenia	1.8	1.5 -	2.0		2003					
Azerbaijan	0.8	0.8 -	1.0		2002	700.0	650.0 -	800.0		2002
Kyrgyzstan	0.7	0.5 -	1.0	8.0 - 10.0	2003	10.0			8.0 - 10.0	2003
Uzbekistan						700.0	400.0 -	1,000.0		2003

CANNABIS HERB
Retail and wholesale prices and purity levels:
breakdown by drug, region and country or territory
(prices expressed in US$ or converted equivalent, and purity levels in percentage)

Region / country or territory	RETAIL PRICE (per gram)					WHOLESALE PRICE (per kilogram)				
	Typical	Range		Purity	Year	Typical	Range		Purity	Year
East and South-East Asia										
Brunei Darussalam	0.1				2003					
Hong Kong SAR, China	7.5	2.6 -	14.8		2003	2,070.0	1,800.0 -	2,320.0		2003
Indonesia	1.5	1.2 -	1.8		2003	100.0	110.0 -	170.0	100.0	2002
Japan	43.8	8.8 -	87.5		2003	15,750.0	2,890.0 -	39,380.0		2003
Laos						10.0				2003
Macau SAR, China	12.0	10.0 -	15.0		2003	2,350.0	2,200.0 -	2,500.0		2003
Malaysia	0.5	0.4 -	0.5		2003					
Myanmar	0.1				2003					
Republic of Korea	5.9	3.4 -	8.5		2003					
Singapore	4.8	3.8 -	5.7		2003	1,860.0	860.0 -	2,870.0		2003
Near and Middle East /South-West Asia										
Israel	2.2				2003	180.0				2003
Jordan	4.9	2.8 -	7.1		2002	560.0	490.0 -	640.0		2002
South Asia										
Bangladesh	0.3	0.2 -	0.3	3.0 - 6.0	2003	120.0	100.0 -	140.0	6.0 - 8.0	2003
Europe										
East Europe										
Belarus	2.1				2003	1,460.0				2003
Russian Federation	2.7	0.3 -	5.0		2003	1,340.0	180.0 -	2,500.0		2003
Ukraine	1.7	1.5 -	2.0		2002	1,300.0	1,000.0 -	1,500.0		2002
Southeast Europe										
Albania	1.3	1.1 -	1.5		2002	350.0				2002
Bulgaria	0.6	0.5 -	0.7		2003	340.0	20.0 -	450.0		2003
Croatia	3.0	2.2 -	5.2		2003	450.0	370.0 -	520.0		2003
FYR of Macedonia	1.4	1.1 -	1.7		2003	250.0	230.0 -	280.0		2003
Romania	1.0	0.9 -	1.1	0.1 - 5.0	2003	735.0	452.0 -	1,017.0		2003
Serbia and Montenegro	6.8	5.7 -	7.9		2003	100.0	80.0 -	110.0		2003
Turkey	1.1				2003	620.0	340.0 -	900.0	10.0 - 100.0	2003
West & Central Europe										
Austria	4.0	3.4 -	4.5	0.5 - 19.0	2003	960.0	790.0 -	1,130.0	0.5 - 19.0	2003
Belgium	5.7	4.5 -	6.8		2003	2,430.0	2,030.0 -	2,830.0		2003
Cyprus	11.6				2003	2,500.0				2003
Czech Republic	5.8	1.0 -	10.6	0.2 - 20.0	2003	3,160.0	1,020.0 -	5,310.0	0.4 - 18.0	2003
Estonia	3.6	2.2 -	7.3		2003	2,540.0				2003
Finland	6.6	5.7 -	7.5		2002					
France	4.5	2.3 -	5.7		2003	1,130.0	570.0 -	1,700.0		2003
Germany	8.3	5.5 -	11.3	0.1 - 17.5	2003	3,420.0	3,050.0 -	4,500.0	0.03 - 19.5	2003
Greece	3.7	1.7 -	5.7		2003	620.0	340.0 -	900.0		2003
Hungary	7.4	5.7 -	9.0	0.01 - 10.5	2003	1,580.0	1,360.0 -	1,810.0	0.01 - 10.5	2003
Iceland	24.0	14.0 -	36.0		2003					
Ireland	4.5	3.4 -	5.7		2003	850.0	570.0 -	1,020.0		2003
Italy	6.8	6.1 -	7.4		2003	1,290.0	1,010.0 -	1,570.0	2.0 - 15.1	2003
Lithuania	6.4	4.0 -	8.9		2003	2,870.0				2003
Luxembourg	9.4			0.6 - 11.8	2003	4,290.0				2003
Netherlands	6.9	4.5 -	8.5		2003	2,600.0	1,410.0 -	3,960.0		2003
Norway	17.0	11.3 -	22.6		2003					
Poland	6.6	5.3 -	9.2		2003	2,370.0	1,970.0 -	2,760.0		2003
Portugal	4.2			0.3 - 11.5	2003	850.0	560.0 -	1,130.0		2003
Slovakia	4.4	0.2 -	6.6		2002					
Slovenia	9.6	9.0 -	10.2		2003	1,110.0				2003
Spain	3.2				2003	1,200.0				2003
Sweden	5.9				2003					
Switzerland	5.6	2.2 -	14.9	1.5 - 28.0	2003	3,570.0	2,230.0 -	5,960.0		2003
United Kingdom	4.4	1.8 -	11.6	1.0 - 25.0	2003	3,920.0	1,310.0 -	6,540.0		2003
Oceania										
New Zealand	5.8				2003	4,920.0	2,900.0 -	6,950.0	1.0 - 10.0	2003

CANNABIS RESIN
Retail and wholesale prices and purity levels:
breakdown by drug, region and country or territory
(prices expressed in US$ or converted equivalent, and purity levels in percentage)

Region / country or territory	Typical	Range		Purity		Year	Typical	Range		Purity		Year
Africa												
East Africa												
Djibouti							20.0					2003
Kenya	0.9	0.8 -	1.1			2003						
U.R of Tanzania	0.2					2003	150.0	120.0 -	180.0			2003
North Africa												
Algeria	0.5					2003	520.0					2003
Egypt	18.5	10.9 -	26.1			2002	2,280.0	1,740.0 -	2,820.0			2002
Morocco	1.8	1.5 -	2.2			2003	240.0	210.0 -	260.0			2003
Tunisia	1.5					2002						
Southern Africa												
Zambia	0.5					2002						
Zimbabwe	5.7	5.1 -	6.4			2003						
Americas												
Caribbean												
Bahamas	20.0	20.0 -	50.0			2003						
Bermuda	100.0					2002						
Turks & Caicos Islands							900.0	700.0 -	1,000.0			2003
North America												
Canada	7.1	7.1 -	17.6			2003	7,050.0	6,350.0 -	8,460.0			2003
Asia												
Central Asia and Transcaucasia												
Armenia	5.0	4.5 -	5.5			2003						
Azerbaijan	2.0	1.8 -	2.2			2002	1,800.0	1,700.0 -	2,000.0			2002
Georgia	9.0	8.0 -	10.0			2003						
Kyrgyzstan	0.9	0.5 -	1.5	2.0 -	3.0	2003	60.0	50.0 -	70.0	2.0 -	3.0	2003
Tajikistan	0.6	0.3 -	1.0			2003	200.0	100.0 -	300.0			
Uzbekistan							1,350.0	700.0 -	2,000.0			2003
East and South-East Asia												
Hong Kong SAR, China	16.9	2.6 -	35.4			2003						
Indonesia	1.7					2002	1,660.0					2002
Japan	87.5	43.8 -	131.3			2003	2,700.0	1,400.0 -	3,990.0			2002
Macau SAR, China	12.0	10.0 -	15.0			2003	2,350.0	2,200.0 -	2,500.0			2002
Republic of Korea	36.1	29.7 -	42.4			2003						
Near and Middle East /South-West Asia												
Afghanistan	0.2			70.0 -	90.0	2003	160.0	120.0 -	190.0			2003
Iran (Islamic Republic of)							720.0					2003
Israel	5.6	2.2 -	9.0			2003	1,780.0	890.0 -	3,110.0			2003
Jordan	5.7	3.5 -	7.8			2002	710.0	560.0 -	850.0			2002
Lebanon	9.0	8.0 -	10.0	70.0 -	90.0	2003	300.0	200.0 -	400.0	70.0 -	90.0	2003
Oman	2.0					2002						
Pakistan	0.3	0.1 -	0.4			2003	660.0	310.0 -	1,020.0			2003
Qatar	8.8	8.8 -	9.6			2003	5,560.0	6,850.0 -	7,240.0			2003
Syrian Arab Republic	1.0	0.8 -	1.2	70.0 -	90.0	2003	800.0	600.0 -	1,000.0	70.0 -	90.0	2003
Yeman	0.2	0.2 -	0.3			2002	130.0	100.0 -	150.0			2002
South Asia												
Bangladesh	1.2	1.0 -	1.4	2.0 -	5.0	2003						
Nepal	0.2	0.1 -	0.3			2003	90.0	90.0 -	130.0			2003

CANNABIS RESIN
Retail and wholesale prices and purity levels:
breakdown by drug, region and country or territory
(prices expressed in US$ or converted equivalent, and purity levels in percentage)

Region / country or territory	RETAIL PRICE (per gram)				WHOLESALE PRICE (per kilogram)			
	Typical	Range	Purity	Year	Typical	Range	Purity	Year
Europe								
East Europe								
Belarus	11.3			2003	6,900.0			2003
Russian Federation	8.0	2.0 - 24.0		2003	5,200.0	1,000.0 - 19,000.0		2003
Southeast Europe								
Albania					500.0			2002
Croatia	4.5	1.9 - 5.1		2003	890.0	760.0 - 1,020.0		2002
FYR of Macedonia	2.5	1.7 - 3.4		2003	620.0	450.0 - 790.0		2003
Romania	1.8	1.6 - 2.0		2003	904.0	791.0 - 1,017.0		2003
Serbia and Montenegro	6.8	5.7 - 7.9		2003				
Turkey	1.1	0.6 - 1.7		2003				
West and Central Europe								
Andorra	5.2	4.7 - 5.7		2002				
Austria	8.5	7.9 - 9.0		2003	2,540.0	2,260.0 - 2,830.0		2003
Belgium	6.2	4.5 - 7.9		2003	2,150.0	1,750.0 - 2,660.0		2003
Cyprus	16.7			2003	3,840.0			2003
Czech Republic	12.4	7.1 - 17.7	3.0 - 20.0	2003	5,310.0	3,500.0 - 7,120.0	1.7 - 28.0	2003
Denmark	10.6	4.6 - 16.7		2003	3,190.0	1,060.0 - 5,230.0		2003
Estonia	7.3	2.2 - 21.8		2003	2,540.0			2003
Finland	11.3			2003	3,730.0			2003
France	4.5	2.3 - 6.8		2003	2,260.0	1,130.0 - 3,390.0		2003
Germany	6.8	5.0 - 10.2	0.4 - 26.0	2003	2,630.0	1,910.0 - 3,310.0	0.1 - 18.0	2003
Greece	5.7	4.5 - 6.8		2003	1,920.0	1,020.0 - 2,830.0		2003
Hungary	7.9	4.5 - 11.3	0.5 - 8.0	2003	1,580.0	1,360.0 - 1,810.0	0.5 - 8.0	2003
Iceland	34.0	29.0 - 36.0		2003				
Ireland	14.0			2003	3,060.0			2002
Italy	8.8	7.9 - 9.7		2003	2,180.0	1,720.0 - 2,650.0	3.0 - 25.0	2003
Lithuania	11.4	6.6 - 16.4		2003	3,270.0			2003
Luxembourg	9.2			2003	4,520.0			2003
Netherlands	9.2	7.6 - 11.3		2003	1,890.0	450.0 - 6,220.0		2003
Norway	19.8	11.3 - 28.3		2003	3,670.0	2,260.0 - 5,090.0		2003
Poland	7.9	5.3 - 10.5		2003	2,630.0	2,110.0 - 3,160.0		2003
Portugal	2.8		1.0 - 27.0	2003	1,690.0	1,130.0 - 2,250.0		2003
Slovakia	11.0	5.5 - 16.4		2003	2,210.0			2002
Slovenia	3.9	2.8 - 5.0		2003				
Spain	5.0			2003	1,540.0			2003
Sweden	12.3	7.4 - 14.8		2003	4,930.0	4,310.0 - 6,160.0		2003
Switzerland	7.5	3.7 - 11.9	7.0 - 28.0	2003	4,320.0	1,490.0 - 7,450.0		2003
United Kingdom	4.1	1.8 - 6.9	0.3 - 26.0	2003	2,790.0	1,310.0 - 3,270.0		2003
Oceania								
Australia	24.3	16.2 - 27.0		2002				

CANNABIS OIL
Retail and wholesale prices and purity levels:
breakdown by drug, region and country or territory
(prices expressed in US$ or converted equivalent, and purity levels in percentage)

Region / country or territory	RETAIL PRICE (per gram)				WHOLESALE PRICE (per kilogram)			
	Typical	Range	Purity	Year	Typical	Range	Purity	Year
Africa								
Southern Africa								
Zambia	0.8			2002				
Americas								
North America								
Canada	17.6	14.1 - 35.3	12.0 - 88.0	2003	5,640.0	5,640.0 - 8,460.0	9.0 - 88.0	2003
Asia								
Central Asia and Transcaucasia								
Georgia	85.0	80.0 - 90.0		2003				
Europe								
Southeast Europe								
Albania	3.3	2.9 - 3.6		2002	600.0			2003
West and Central Europe								
Austria					4,240.0	3,300.0 - 5,180.0		2002
France	25.9	14.1 - 37.7		2002				
Spain	12.2			2003	2,620.0			2003
United Kingdom	22.4	17.9 - 29.9		2002				
Oceania								
Australia	27.0			2002				
New Zealand	23.2	11.6 - 29.0		2003	18,390.0	12,260.0 - 24,520.0		2003

7.4. Amphetamine-type stimulants: Wholesale, street prices and purity levels

AMPHETAMINE
Retail and wholesale prices and purity levels:
breakdown by drug, region and country or territory
(prices expressed in US$ or converted equivalent, and purity levels in percentage)

Region / country or territory	RETAIL PRICE (per *)						WHOLESALE PRICE (per **)			
	Typical	Range	Purity	Year			Typical	Range	Purity	Year
Africa										
West and Central Africa										
Nigeria	0.7	0.5 - 0.9		2003			430.0	350.0 - 430.0		2003
Asia										
East and South-East Asia										
Indonesia	41.3	35.4 - 47.2		2003						
Malaysia	18.6	16.0 - 21.3		2003						
Vietnam	10.2	4.7 - 11.7		2003						
Near and Middle East /South-West Asia										
Jordan	2.8	2.8 - 4.2		2002	T	TT	2,820.0	2,820.0 - 3,670.0		2002
Qatar	2.7			2003						
Syrian Arab Republic	12.0	10.0 - 14.0		2003	T	TT	8,000.0	6,000.0 - 12,000.0	70.0 - 90.0	2003
Europe										
Eastern Europe										
Belarus	20.7			2003			15,200.0			2003
Ukraine	28.0	25.0 - 30.0		2002						
Southeast Europe										
Bulgaria	4.5	2.3 - 6.8	1.0 - 73.0	2003			3,110.0	2,830.0 - 3,390.0		2003
Croatia	22.4	14.9 - 29.8		2003			8,950.0	5,960.0 - 11,930.0		2003
Serbia and Montenegro	4.5	3.4 - 5.7		2003						
West and Central Europe										
Austria	25.4	22.6 - 28.3	1.0 - 99.0	2003			16,390.0	13,560.0 - 19,120.0	3.0 - 99.0	2003
Belgium	7.9			2003			2,430.0	1,130.0 - 3,390.0		2003
Cyprus	15.4			2003			6,750.0			2003
Czech Republic	33.7	21.3 - 46.1	26.0 - 37.0	2003			26,560.0	17,740.0 - 35,480.0	26.0 - 37.0	2003
Denmark	32.3	11.4 - 53.2		2003			9,110.0	4,560.0 - 13,670.0		2003
Estonia	7.3	3.6 - 18.1		2003			2,540.0	2,030.0 - 3,630.0		2003
Finland	28.3		2.8 - 98.0	2003			6,780.0		17.0 - 96.0	2003
France	15.3	7.9 - 22.6		2003	D	TD	2,270.0	1,130.0 - 3,400.0		2003
Germany	14.2	9.9 - 19.1	0.2 - 72.0	2003			5,760.0	4,080.0 - 8,450.0	1.0 - 52.0	2003
Greece	4.5	3.4 - 5.7		2003			3,050.0	2,710.0 - 3,390.0		2003
Hungary	12.4	11.3 - 13.6	1.0 - 60.0	2003			3,390.0	2,370.0 - 4,520.0	2.0 - 75.0	2003
Iceland	60.0	43.0 - 86.0		2003						
Ireland	17.0	11.3 - 17.0		2003			1,880.0			2002
Italy	22.6	21.5 - 23.7		2003			8,330.0	8,190.0 - 8,480.0		2003
Lithuania	9.7	4.9 - 14.6	4.5 - 50.0	2003			2,620.0		55.0 - 79.0	2003
Netherlands	8.0	5.7 - 11.3		2003			2,180.0	1,580.0 - 2,600.0		2003
Norway	70.6	28.3 - 113.0	10.0 - 80.0	2003			10,450.0	8,480.0 - 12,430.0	10.0 - 80.0	2003
Poland	13.2	6.6 - 23.7	20.0 - 35.0	2003			3,950.0	2,630.0 - 5,260.0	50.0 - 90.0	2003
Slovakia	8.9	4.4 - 13.3		2002						
Slovenia	8.7	7.5 - 9.9		2003			8,700.0	7,460.0 - 9,940.0		2003
Spain	26.6			2003			19,500.0			2003
Sweden	33.9	18.5 - 49.3		2003			6,160.0	4,930.0 - 7,390.0		2003
Switzerland	19.2	12.8 - 25.5		2002			20,520.0	9,570.0 - 31,910.0		2002
United Kingdom	14.7	4.9 - 24.5	10.8 (0.02-74.0)	2003			3,020.0	1,140.0 - 4,910.0	32.9 (6.0.-73.0)	2003
Oceania										
Australia	95.8	21.0 - 215.9		2002			49,480.0	10,800.0 - 86,370.0		2002

(*) in Gram or otherwise as indicated
(**) in Kilogram or otherwise as indicated
D : Doses unit
T : Tablets unit
TD: Thousand of doses
TT: Thousand of tablets

METHAMPHETAMINE
Retail and wholesale prices and purity levels:
breakdown by drug, region and country or territory
(prices expressed in US$ or converted equivalent, and purity levels in percentage)

Region / country or territory	RETAIL PRICE (per gram)					WHOLESALE PRICE (per kilogram)				
	Typical	Range		Purity	Year	Typical	Range		Purity	Year
Africa										
Southern Africa										
Zambia	1.5				2003					
Americas										
North America										
Canada	70.5	70.5 -	141.1		2003	8,460.0	7,050.0 -	12,700.0	0.6 - 100.0	2003
United States	96.5			62.0	2003	18,346.0	3,500.0 -	99,000.0	38.0	2003
Asia										
East and South-East Asia										
Brunei Darussalam	0.1				2003					
China						4,235.0	2,420.0 -	6,050.0	25.0 - 82.0	2003
China (Hong Kong SAR)	48.3	41.6 -	52.1	83.0 - 99.0	2003	3,220.0	5,150.0 -	9,020.0		2003
Indonesia	38.6	33.1 -	44.1		2002	16,550.0	11,030.0 -	22,070.0		2002
Japan	787.5	525.0 -	1,312.5		2003	118,130.0	87,500.0 -	140,000.0		
Laos	10.0	9.0 -	11.0		2003	4,000.0	4,000.0 -	5,000.0	27.0 - 30.0	2003
Macau SAR, China	18.0	12.0 -	25.0		2003					
Malaysia	3.6	3.2 -	4.0		2003					
Myanmar	1.1	0.9 -	2.6		2003					
Philippines	18.5	22.2 -	36.9		2003	16,620.0	14,780.0 -	18,470.0	75.0 - 80.0	2003
Republic of Korea	602.6	297.0 -	848.8	28.8 - 98.5	2003	93,360.0	42,440.0 -	169,750.0	36.1 - 98.5	2003
Singapore	71.6	57.3 -	86.0		2003	51,580.0	45,850.0 -	57,310.0		2003
Europe										
East Europe										
Belarus	16.5				2003	9,900.0				2003
West and Central Europe										
Czech Republic	44.3	17.7 -	71.0	0.2 - 80.0	2003	22,150.0	15,930.0 -	28,360.0	50.0 - 75.0	2003
Estonia						2,990.0				2002
France						2,260.0	1,130.0 -	3,390.0		2003
Lithuania	5.1	3.8 -	6.4	8.5 - 65.0	2003	6,210.0	4,050.0 -	8,110.0	20.0 - 80.0	2002
Norway	70.6	28.3 -	113.0	10.0 - 90.0	2003	10,450.0	8,480.0 -	12,430.0	10.0 - 90.0	2003
Slovakia	8.2	5.5 -	11.0	8.9 - 95.0	2003	16,600.0				2002
Sweden						9,240.0	6,160.0 -	12,320.0		2003
Switzerland	26.1	11.2 -	48.4		2003					
United Kingdom				34.5 (0.57-82.0)	2003					
Oceania										
New Zealand	550.4	405.6 -	695.3		2003	224,810.0	204,370.0 -	245,250.0		2003

L.S.D
Retail and wholesale prices and purity levels:
breakdown by drug, region and country or territory
(prices expressed in US$ or converted equivalent, and purity levels in percentage)

Region / country or territory	RETAIL PRICE (per dose)				WHOLESALE PRICE (per thousand dose)			
	Typical	Range	Purity	Year	Typical	Range	Purity	Year
Africa								
Southern Africa								
Namibia	14.6	13.3 - 15.9		2003				
South Africa	7.5			2002				
Zimbabwe	7.6	6.4 - 8.9		2003				
West and Central Africa								
Ghana	12.0	10.0 - 14.0		2003				
Americas								
Central America								
Costa Rica	15.1			2003				
North America								
Canada	4.6	2.1 - 7.1		2003	2,120.0	1,410.0 - 2,820.0		2003
South America								
Argentina					100.0	20.0 - 150.0		2002
Uruguay	10.0			2003				
Asia								
East and South-East Asia								
Japan	32.0	24.0 - 40.0		2002				
Republic of Korea	10.8	3.4 - 18.2		2003				
Singapore	30.7	27.9 - 33.4		2002	3,900.0			2002
Near and Middle East /South-West Asia								
Israel	15.5	9.0 - 22.2		2003	5,500.0	2,700.0 - 9,000.0		2003
Europe								
East Europe								
Russian Federation	39.0	11.0 - 67.0		2003				
Ukraine	18.0	15.0 - 20.0		2002	12,000.0	10,000.0 - 15,000.0		2002
Southeast Europe								
Croatia	14.9	4.5 - 17.9		2003	7,500.0	6,000.0 - 9,000.0		2003
Romania	26.6	24.9 - 28.3		2003	13,000.0	11,300.0 - 14,690.0		2003
Serbia and Montenegro	4.7	4.7 - 6.6		2003				
West & Central Europe								
Austria	36.7	33.9 - 39.6		2003	12,430.0	7,910.0 - 16,950.0		2003
Belgium	8.2	7.1 - 9.4		2002				
Cyprus	17.3			2003	6,730.0			2003
Czech Republic	6.6	2.5 - 10.6	33.1 - 41.3	2003	4,070.0	1,810.0 - 6,330.0		2003
Denmark	6.3			2002				
Estonia	9.0			2002				
Finland	15.3			2003				
France	11.3	4.7 - 17.0		2003				
Germany	10.7	7.0 - 12.4		2003				
Greece	8.5	6.8 - 10.2		2003	4,520.0	3,390.0 - 5,650.0		2003
Ireland	11.3	9.0 - 13.6		2003				
Italy	29.1	28.3 - 30.0		2003	9,890.0		13.0 - 31.0	2003
Lithuania	14.7	12.9 - 16.4		2003	5,400.0	2,700.0 - 8,110.0		2002
Netherlands	5.7	1.9 - 9.4		2002				
Norway	8.5	5.7 - 11.3		2002				
Poland	9.2	7.9 - 11.8		2003	2,630.0	1,840.0 - 5,260.0		2003
Portugal	7.4			2003				

L.S.D
Retail and wholesale prices and purity levels:
breakdown by drug, region and country or territory
(prices expressed in US$ or converted equivalent, and purity levels in percentage)

Region / country or territory	RETAIL PRICE (per dose)				WHOLESALE PRICE (per thousand dose)			
	Typical	Range	Purity	Year	Typical	Range	Purity	Year
Slovakia	8.2			2003				
Slovenia					1,930.0			2003
Spain	11.5			2003	11,450.0			2003
Sweden	8.8			2003				
Switzerland	14.9	11.2 - 22.3		2003				
United Kingdom	4.9	1.6 - 8.2		2003				
Oceania								
New Zealand	20.3	17.4 - 23.2		2003	8,690.0	5,790.0 - 11,590.0		2003

ECSTASY
Retail and wholesale prices and purity levels:
breakdown by drug, region and country or territory
(prices expressed in US$ or converted equivalent, and purity levels in percentage)

Region / country or territory	RETAIL PRICE (per tablet)				WHOLESALE PRICE (per thousand tablets)			
	Typical	Range	Purity	Year	Typical	Range	Purity	Year
Africa								
North Africa								
Egypt	26.1	19.5 - 32.6		2002	10,850.0			2002
Southern Africa								
Namibia	7.5	7.5 - 11.3		2002				
South Africa	8.5			2002	6,960.0			2002
Zambia	1.6		10.0	2002	1,450.0			2003
Zimbabwe	14.0	12.7 - 15.2		2003				
West and Central Africa								
Ghana	6.0	5.0 - 7.0		2003				
Americas								
Caribbean								
Bahamas	20.0	20.0 - 30.0		2003	30,000.0	25,000.0 - 40,000.0		2002
Bermuda	40.0	30.0 - 50.0		2002				
Cayman Islands	25.0			2002	30,000.0			2002
Trinidad Tobago	19.6			2003				
Central America								
Costa Rica	10.7	8.8 - 12.6		2003				
Nicaragua	25.0		90.0	2002	25,000.0			2002
North America								
Canada	14.1	14.1 - 21.2		2003	4,230.0	4,230.0 - 4,580.0		2003
United States					39,500.0	4,000.0 - 75,000.0	58.0	2003
South America								
Argentina					22,500.0	10,000.0 - 35,000.0		2003
Ecuador	20.0	20.0 - 30.0		2003	20,000.0	20,000.0 - 30,000.0		2003
Suriname	3.5	2.3 - 4.6		2002				
Uruguay	9.0		100.0	2003	21,500.0	18,000.0 - 25,000.0		2002
Venezuela	11.1	9.6 - 12.7	10.0 - 20.0	2003				
Asia								
East and South-East Asia								
Hong Kong SAR, China	11.0	4.4 - 15.9		2003	4,270.0	3,220.0 - 5,150.0		2003
Indonesia	7.7	7.1 - 8.3		2003	7,720.0	6,620.0 - 8,830.0		2002
Japan	43.8	17.5 - 87.5		2003				
Republic of Korea	42.4	34.0 - 50.9		2003				
Macau SAR, China	22.0	18.0 - 31.0		2003				
Malaysia	16.0	10.6 - 21.3						
Singapore	12.9	11.5 - 14.3	38.7	2003	10,320.0	8,020.0 - 12,610.0		2003
Vietnam	36.7			2002				
Near and Middle East /South-West Asia								
Israel	11.5	5.6 - 22.2		2003	2,330.0	1,550.0 - 5,560.0		2003
Europe								
East Europe								
Belarus	13.1			2003	8,500.0			2003
Russian Federation	20.3	7.0 - 46.0		2003				
Southeast Europe								
Bulgaria	9.9	8.5 - 11.3	13.0 - 62.0	2003	8,760.0	8,480.0 - 9,040.0		2003
Croatia	4.5	3.0 - 7.5		2003	2,240.0	1,490.0 - 2,980.0		2003
FYR of Macedonia	8.5	5.7 - 11.3		2003	7,060.0	4,710.0 - 9,420.0		2002
Romania	10.2	9.0 - 11.3		2003	4,520.0	3,390.0 - 5,650.0		2003
Serbia and Montenegro	6.8	5.7 - 7.9		2003	3,300.0	1,880.0 - 4,710.0		2002
Turkey	14.7			2003	15,260.0	7,910.0 - 22,600.0	15.0 - 20.0	2002

ECSTASY
Retail and wholesale prices and purity levels:
breakdown by drug, region and country or territory
(prices expressed in US$ or converted equivalent, and purity levels in percentage)

Region / country or territory	RETAIL PRICE (per tablet)				WHOLESALE PRICE (per thousand tablets)			
	Typical	Range	Purity	Year	Typical	Range	Purity	Year
West and Central Europe								
Andorra	7.1	5.7 - 8.5		2002				
Austria	14.1	11.3 - 17.0	3.0 - 80.0	2003	4,520.0	3,960.0 - 5,090.0	3.0 - 80.0	2003
Belgium	11.3	7.9 - 14.7		2003	1,320.0	450.0 - 2,490.0		2003
Cyprus	16.7			2003	6,740.0			2003
Czech Republic	11.5	5.3 - 17.7	3.2 - 42.0	2003	4,410.0	1,810.0 - 7,120.0	3.2 - 42.0	2003
Denmark	11.1	6.8 - 15.2		2003	3,420.0	1,520.0 - 5,320.0		2003
Estonia	1.5	1.1 - 7.3		2003	14,510.0	8,700.0 - 29,010.0		2003
Finland	18.1			2003	15,070.0	11,300.0 - 18,840.0		2003
France	11.3	7.9 - 17.0		2003	1,750.0	1,130.0 - 2,500.0		2003
Germany	8.5	5.2 - 12.2	26.5	2003	2,620.0	1,900.0 - 3,410.0	2.4	2003
Greece	28.3	22.6 - 33.9		2003	11,870.0	6,780.0 - 16,950.0		2003
Hungary	9.0		6.0 - 47.0	2003	4,520.0	2,260.0 - 6,780.0	6.0 - 47.0	2003
Iceland	37.0	29.0 - 50.0		2003				
Ireland	11.3	6.8 - 13.6		2003	1,070.0	900.0 - 2,260.0		2003
Italy	24.6	22.1 - 27.1		2003	5,730.0	5,490.0 - 5,960.0	26.8	2003
Lithuania	6.5	3.8 - 13.0	15.0 - 45.0	2003	2,290.0		15.0 - 45.0	2003
Luxembourg	11.3			2003				
Netherlands	4.5	2.3 - 5.7		2003	810.0	370.0 - 1,240.0		2003
Norway	42.4	28.3 - 56.5	20.0 - 50.0	2003	37,680.0	28,260.0 - 47,090.0	20.0 - 50.0	2003
Poland	5.3	2.6 - 7.9		2003	1,840.0	1,580.0 - 2,110.0		2003
Portugal	6.1		7.5 - 86.9	2003	2,110.0	1,410.0 - 2,810.0		2003
Slovakia	7.5	5.5 - 9.6	4.7 - 16.4	2003				
Slovenia	9.0	7.9 - 10.2		2003	9,040.0	7,910.0 - 10,170.0		2003
Spain	11.6			2003	11,620.0			2003
Sweden	12.8	10.2 - 15.3		2002	4,930.0			2003
Switzerland	14.9	7.5 - 29.8	23.0 - 33.0	2003	13,500.0	6,380.0 - 25,530.0		2002
United Kingdom	8.7	1.6 - 19.6		2003	2,610.0	2,240.0 - 2,990.0		2002
Oceania								
New Zealand	40.5	34.8 - 46.4		2003	26,070.0	17,380.0 - 34,760.0		2003

8. CONSUMPTION

8.1. Consumption: Annual prevalence of drug abuse
8.1.1. Opiates

OPIATES
Annual prevalence of abuse as percentage of the population aged
15-64 (unless otherwise indicated)

AFRICA		ASIA	
North and Eastern Africa		**Central Asia and Transcaucasia**	
Mauritius, 2003	2.0	Kyrgyzstan, 2001	2.3
Kenya**	0.2	Kazakhstan, 2001	1.3
Morocco**	0.2	Tajikistan, 2001	1.0
Egypt **	0.06	Uzbekistan, 2001	0.5
Ethiopia**	0.05	Georgia, 2000	0.6
Rwanda**	0.05	Armenia**	0.3
Ethiopia**	0.04	Turkmenistan**, 1998	0.3
Uganda**	0.04	Azerbaijan, 2000	0.2
Tanzania, United Rep.,1998	0.02	**East and South-East Asia**	
Southern Africa		Macao SAR, China,2003	1.1
Zambia*,2003	0.4	Lao People's Dem. Rep.,2004	0.9
South Africa*,2003	0.2	Myanmar, 2003	0.7
Namibia,2000	0.03	Thailand, 2001	0.5
Zimbabwe**	0.01	Taiwan province, China,2002*	0.3
West and Central Africa		Viet Nam,2002	0.3
Ghana, 1998	0.7	Hong Kong SAR,China,2003	0.2
Nigeria*, (10+),1999	0.6	Malaysia*,2000	0.2
Chad, 1995	0.2	Indonesia*,2002	0.2
Senegal**	0.03	China,2003	0.2
Sierra Leone,1997	0.01	Republic of Korea**	0.1
		Singapore, 2002	0.1
AMERICA		Japan,2002	0.1
Central America		Brunei Darussalam,1998	0.01
El Salvador**	0.2	**Middle East and South-West Asia**	
Guatemala*	0.2	Iran, Islamic Republic,1999	2.8
Panama**	0.2	Pakistan*,2000	0.8
Honduras,1995	0.1	Afghanistan*,2001	0.6
Costa Rica*	0.1	Bahrain,1998	0.3
North America		Israel, (18-40), 2001	0.3
USA, 2000	0.6	Jordan*, 2001	0.2
Canada, (Ontario,18+), 2000	0.4	Lebanon*, 2001	0.1
Mexico, 2002	0.1	Oman,1999	0.09
South America		Yemen**,1999	0.09
Brazil, (12-65),2001	0.6	Saudi Arabia,2000	0.01
Chile, 2002	0.3	Syrian Arab Rep.,1998	0.01
Venezuela*, 2002	0.3	Kuwait,1998	0.01
Colombia*, 1998	0.2	Qatar,1996	0.01
Argentina, (16-64), 1999	0.1	**South Asia**	
Ecuador*,1999	0.1	India, 2001	0.4
Bolivia**	0.04	Nepal,1996	0.4
Suriname, 1998	0.02	Sri Lanka*,2000	0.3
Uruguay, 2001	0.01	Bangladesh**	0.3
The Caribbean		Maldives**,2001	0.2
Bahamas*,2003	0.2		
Dominican Rep.*, (12-70),2001	0.09		
Antigua Barbuda,2000	0.05		
Barbados**	0.01		

OPIATES
Annual prevalence of abuse as percentage of the population aged 15-64 (unless otherwise indicated)

EUROPE

East Europe

Russian Federation,2001	2.1
Ukraine*, 2002	0.8
Belarus*, 2003	0.4
Moldova, Rep., 2000	0.07

Southeast Europe

Croatia,1999	0.7
Bulgaria, 2001	0.5
Albania*,2000	0.5
FYR of Macedonia,1998	0.4
Romania*, 2002	0.3
Turkey, 2003	0.05

Western and Central Europe

Latvia,2001	1.7
Estonia, 2001	1.2
United Kingdom, 2001	0.9
Luxembourg,2000	0.9
Italy,2002	0.8
Denmark, 2001	0.7
Portugal, 2000	0.7
Spain,2000	0.6
Switzerland,2000	0.6
Ireland,2001	0.6
Lithuania,2002	0.6
Slovenia,2001	0.5
Czech Rep.,2001	0.5
Austria, 2002	0.5
France,1999	0.4
Norway,1997	0.4
Belgium,1997	0.4
Greece, 2001	0.4
Slovakia, 2002	0.3
Hungary, (18-54), 2003	0.3
Germany, 2000	0.3
Netherlands, 2001	0.3
Iceland*,1998	0.3
Malta, 2001	0.2
Poland,2002	0.2
Cyprus,1999	0.2
Sweden,1998	0.1
Finland,1999	0.1

OCEANIA

Australia,2004	0.5
New Zealand,2001	0.5

*UNODC estimates based on local studies, special population group studies, and /or law enforcement agency assessments.
** Tentative estimates.
Sources: Annual Reports Questionnaires, Government Reports, US Department of State, European Monitoring Center for Drugs and Drug Abuse (EMCDDA).

8.1.2. Cocaine

<table>
<tr><td colspan="2" style="text-align:center">COCAINE
Annual prevalence of abuse as percentage of the population aged
15-64 (unless otherwise indicated)</td></tr>
</table>

AFRICA		The Caribbean	
East Africa		Aruba*,1997	1.3
Kenya**	0.1	St. Lucia*,2002	1.0
Southern Africa		Barbados*,2002	1.0
South Africa*, 2003	0.8	Dominican Rep.,(12-70),2000	0.9
Zambia**, 2000	0.2	Grenada, 2003	0.9
Namibia, 1998	0.2	Jamaica*,2001	0.9
Zimbabwe, 2000	0.1	Bahamas*, 2001	0.8
Angola, 1999	0.1	St.Vincent Grenadines*, 2002	0.7
North Africa		Cayman Is.*,2000	0.6
Morocco*,1999	0.01	Haiti*,2000	0.3
West and Central Africa		Antigua Barbuda,2000	0.1
Ghana, 1998	1.1	Dominica,1996	0.01
Nigeria, 1999	0.5	Montserrat,1997	0.01
Sierra Leone, 1996	0.02		
Chad, 1995	0.01		
Sao Tome Principe,1997	0.01	**EUROPE**	
ASIA		**East Europe**	
		Russian Fed.*,2003	0.1
East & South-East Asia		Ukraine*, 2003	0.1
Japan*, 2003	0.03	Belarus*, 2003	0.02
Indonesia**	0.01	**Southeast Europe**	
Singapore, 2000	0.01	Bulgaria*, 2003	0.3
Thailand,2001	0.01	Croatia,1999	0.2
Hong Kong SAR China, (11+), 2003	0.001	Romania*, 2003	0.1
Near and Middle East / South-West Asia		Turkey*, 2003	0.04
Israel, (18+), 2001	0.3	FYR of Macedonia**, 2000	0.02
Lebanon*, 2001	0.1	**West and Central Europe**	
Jordan**	0.1	Spain, 2003	2.7
AMERICA		United Kingdom, (16-59), 2003	2.1
Central America		Switzerland*, 2003	1.1
Panama,(16-60),1996	1.4	Netherlands, 2001	1.1
Guatemala*, 2001	1.0	Italy, (15-44), 2001	1.1
Nicaragua*, 2001	1.0	Ireland, 2002	1.1
Honduras*, 2002	0.9	Iceland*, 2003	1.1
El Salvador*, 2002	0.8	Belgium*, 2003	1.1
Belize*, 1998	0.6	Germany, (18-59), 2003	1.0
Costa Rica,(12-70), 2000	0.4	Luxembourg*, 2003	0.9
North America		Denmark, (16-64), 2000	0.8
USA, 2003	3.0	Austria*, 2003	0.8
Canada, (15+), 2004	1.9	Norway,1999	0.7
Mexico, (12-65),2002	0.4	Cyprus, (15-65), 2003	0.7
South America		Slovakia, 2002	0.6
Argentina, (16-64),1999	1.9	Greece,1998	0.5
Chile,2002	1.7	Liechtenstein, 1998	0.4
Colombia*,2001	1.6	Greenland*,2003	0.4
		Slovenia*, 2003	0.3
Bolivia, (12-50),2000	1.1	Portugal, 2001	0.3
Venezuela*, 2001	1.1	Malta, (18-65),2001	0.3
Ecuador,1995	0.9	Hungary, (18-54), 2003	0.3
Peru, 2002	0.7	France, 2002	0.3
Paraguay*, 2001	0.6	Finland, (15-69), 2002	0.3
Suriname*, 2002	0.5	Sweden*, 2003	0.2
Brazil, (12+), 2001	0.4	Latvia, 2003	0.2
Uruguay, 2001	0.3	Lithuania*, 2003	0.2
OCEANIA		Estonia*, 2003	0.2
Australia, 2004	1.3	Poland, (16-99), 2002	0.1
New Zealand*, 2001	0.5	Czech Rep.*, 2003	0.1

*   UNODC estimates based on local studies, special population group studies, and /or law enforcement agency assessments.
** Tentative estimates.
Sources: Annual Reports Questionnaires, Government Reports, US Department of State, European Monitoring Center for Drugs and Drug Abuse (EMCDDA).

8.1.3. Cannabis

CANNABIS
Annual prevalence of abuse as percentage of the population aged
15-64 (unless otherwise indicated)

AFRICA

East Africa

Mauritius*,2000	7.2
Kenya*, 1994	4.0
Comoros*, 2002	2.9
Ethiopia*,1999	2.6
Somalia, 2002	2.5
Uganda**	1.4
Tanzania, United Rep.**,1999	0.2

North Africa

Morocco, 2003	11.8
Egypt**, 1997	5.2
Libyan Arab Jamahiriya,1998	0.05

Southern Africa

Zambia*, 2003	17.7
South Africa*, 2002	8.4
Zimbabwe, 2000	6.9
Namibia, 2000	3.9

West and Central Africa

Ghana, 1998	21.5
Sierra Leone, 1996	16.1
Nigeria, 2000	13.8
Mali*, 1995	7.8
Angola,1999	2.1
Chad, 1995	0.9
Cote d'Ivoire, 1997	0.01
Sao Tome Principe, 1997	0.01

AMERICA

Central America

Guatemala, 2003	9.1
Belize*, 2003	6.7
Panama*, 2003	4.0
Nicaragua*, 2002	2.2
El Salvador*, 2003	2.0
Honduras*, 2002	1.6
Costa Rica, 2001	1.3

North America

Canada, (15+), 2004	14.1
USA, 2003	13.0
Mexico,(12-65),2002	0.6

South America

Chile, 2002	5.5
Colombia*, 2001	4.3
Argentina, (16-64), 1999	3.7
Venezuela*, 2002	3.3
Ecuador*, (12-49), 1995	3.0
Guyana*, 2002	2.6
Bolivia, (12-50), 2000	2.2
Suriname*, 2002	2.0
Paraguay*, 2002	1.8
Peru, 2002	1.8
Uruguay, (15-65),2001	1.5
Brazil, (12-65), 2001	1.0

The Caribbean

Haiti*, 2000	16.10
Jamaica*, 1997	10.45
Barbados*, 2002	7.30
Grenada*, 2003	6.70
Bahamas*, 2003	4.70
Montserrat, 1997	0.75
Dominica, 1997	0.05

ASIA

Central Asia and Transcaucasia

Kyrgyzstan*, 2001	6.4
Kazakhstan*, 2000	4.2
Uzbekistan*, 2003	4.2
Armenia*, 2003	3.5
Azerbaijan*, 2004	3.5
Tajikistan*, 1998	3.3

Near and Middle East / South-West Asia

Philippines*, 2003	5.5
Cambodia*, 2003	3.5
Macao SAR, China*, 2003	2.6
Malaysia*, 2003	1.6
Thailand, (12-65), 2001	1.5
Myanmar*, 2001	1.4
Indonesia*, 2003	1.3
Lao People's Dem. Rep.*, 2002	0.7
China (Hong Kong SAR)**	0.6
Taiwan province, China**	0.5
Viet Nam*, 2002	0.3
Japan, 2002	0.1
Republic of Korea**	0.1
Singapore, 1998	0.03
Brunei Darussalam, 1996	0.02

Near and Middle East / South-West Asia

Afghanistan**	7.5
Lebanon*, 2001	6.4
Israel*, 2001	5.7
Iran, Islamic Republic, 1999	4.2
Pakistan*, 2000	3.9
Jordan*, 2001	2.1
Syrian Arab Rep.**, 2002	2.0
Bahrain**	0.4
Oman, 1999	0.1
Qatar, 1996	0.1

South Asia

Bangladesh, 1997	3.3
India, 2000	3.2
Maldives,1994	1.5
Nepal*, 1998	3.2
Sri Lanka, 2000	1.5

CANNABIS
Annual prevalence of abuse as percentage of the population aged 15-64 (unless otherwise indicated)

EUROPE

East Europe

Russian Federation*, 2003	3.9
Ukraine*, 2003	3.6
Belarus*, 2003	2.6

Southeast Europe

Bulgaria*, 2003	4.1
Croatia*, 2003	4.0
Albania*, 2001	2.6
Turkey*, (15-65), 2003	1.9
Romania*, 2003	1.7

Western and Central Europe

Spain, 2003	11.3
Czech Rep., 2002	10.9
United Kingdom, (16-59), 2003	10.9
France, 2002	9.8
Switzerland*, 2003	9.6
Belgium*, 2003	8.0
Luxembourg*, 2003	7.6
Greenland*,2003	7.6
Germany, (18-50), 2003	6.8
Slovenia*, 2003	6.2
Denmark, (16-64), 2000	6.2
Italy, (15-45), 2001	6.2
Austria*, 2003	6.1
Netherlands, 2001	6.1
Liechtenstein*, 1998	6.0
Ireland, 2003	5.1
Iceland, (18-75), 2001	5.0
Norway, 1999	4.5
Greece, 1998	4.4
Latvia, 2003	3.8
Cyprus*, 2003	3.7
Slovakia, 2002	3.6
Portugal, 2001	3.3
Finland, 2002	3.2
Hungary, 2003	3.0
Poland, 2002	2.8
Lithuania*(15-66), 2003	2.4
Estonia, (18-70), 1998	2.0
Sweden*, 2003	1.7
Malta, (18-65), 2001	0.8

OCEANIA

Papua New Guinea, 1995	29.5
Micronesia Fed.State., 1995	29.1
Australia, 2004	13.9
New Zealand, 2001	13.4
New Caledonia**	1.9
Fiji, 1996	0.2
Vanuatu, 1997	0.1

*UNODC estimates based on local studies, special population group studies, and /or law enforcement agency assessments.
** Tentative estimates.
Sources: Annual Reports Questionnaires, Government Reports, US Department of State, European Monitoring Center for Drugs and Drug Abuse (EMCDDA).

8.1.4. Amphetamines-type stimulants

AMPHETAMINES
Annual prevalence of abuse as percentage of the population aged
15-64 (unless otherwise indicated)

AFRICA

East Africa	
Kenya**	0.6
Ethiopia**	0.3
North Africa	
Egypt**	0.5
Morocco, 1999	0.3
West & Central Africa	
Nigeria, 1999	1.1
Ghana**	1.0
Cameroon**	0.9
Chad, 1996	0.01
Southern Africa	
Namibia, 2000	0.1
South Africa*, 2002	0.1
Zambia*, 2003	0.1
Zimbabwe, 2000	0.1

AMERICA

Central America	
Honduras, 1997	2.5
Guatemala, 1998	1.7
Panama, 1991	1.2
Costa Rica, 2000	1.0
El Salvador*, 2001	0.7
North America	
USA, 2003	1.4
Canada, 2002	0.6
Mexico, 2002	0.1
South America	
Argentina, (16-64), 1999	0.7
Colombia*, 2001	0.7
Chile*, (16-65), 2002	0.6
Venezuela*, 2002	0.6
Suriname*, 2002	0.6
Brazil, (12-65), 2001	0.3
Ecuador*, 2003	0.3
Uruguay*, 2002	0.1
Peru*, 1998	0.1
Bolivia*,1998	0.1
Caribbean	
Dominican Republic, 2000	0.4
Bahamas*, 2003	0.3
Barbados*, 2002	0.2

ASIA

Central Asia and Transcaucasia	
Uzbekistan, 1997	0.01
East, South & South-East Asia	
Philippines, 2000	2.8
Thailand, 2001	2.5
Macao SAR, China, 2001	1.6
Malaysia*, 2003	1.3
Taiwan province, China, 2000	1.2
Indonesia*, 2003	1.2
Lao PDR*, 2000	0.5
Cambodia*, 2002	0.4
Japan[a], 2003	0.4
Republic of Korea**	0.2
Myanmar, 2002	0.1
Brunei Darussalam, 2000	0.06
Singapore, 1999	0.04
Hong Kong SAR, China, 2002	0.03
India, 2001	0.02
Near and Middle East / South-West Asia	
Israel, (18-40), 2001	0.5
Jordan*, 2001	0.4
Lebanon*, 2001	0.4
Bahrain**	0.1
Oman, 1998	0.1
Qatar, 1996	0.02
Syria, 1998	0.003
Saudi Arabia, 2000	0.002

[a] Life-time prevalence (15+)

AMPHETAMINES
Annual prevalence of abuse as percentage of the population aged 15-64 (unless otherwise indicated)

EUROPE

East Europe

Russian Federation*, 2003	0.2
Ukraine*, 2003	0.2
Belarus*, 2003	0.1
Moldova, Rep., 1998	0.01

Southeast Europe

Croatia*, 2003	0.5
Bulgaria*, 2003	0.4
Albania*, 2003	0.4
Turkey*, 2003	0.2
Romania*, 2003	0.1
FYR of Macedonia, 1995	0.01

West and Central Europe

United Kingdom, 2003	1.6
Estonia*, 2003	1.4
Denmark, 2000	1.3
Czech Rep., 2002	1.1
Norway,1999	1.0
Lituania*, 2003	1.0
Germany, (18-59), 2003	0.9
Iceland*, 2003	0.9
Spain, 2003	0.8
Belgium*, 2001	0.8
Hungary, 2003	0.8
Poland, 2002	0.7
Austria*, 2003	0.6
Latvia*, 2003	0.6
Netherlands, 2001	0.6
Switzerland*, 2003	0.5
Finland, 2002	0.5
Ireland, 2003	0.4
Luxembourg*, 1999	0.4
Malta, 2001	0.4
Slovakia, 2002	0.2
France, 2002	0.2
Slovenia*, 1999	0.2
Cyprus, 2003	0.2
Sweden, 2000	0.2
Greece, 1998	0.1
Italy, 2003	0.1
Portugal, 2001	0.1

OCEANIA

Australia, 2004	4.0
New Zealand, 2001	3.4

*UNODC estimates based on local studies, special population group studies, and /or law enforcement agency assessments.
** Tentative estimates.
Sources: Annual Reports Questionnaires, Government Reports, US Department of State, European Monitoring Center for Drugs and Drug Abuse (EMCDDA).

8.1.5. Ecstasy

ECSTASY
Annual prevalence of abuse as percentage of the population aged
15-64 (unless otherwise indicated)

AFRICA

South Africa*, 2002	0.3
Zambia*, 2003	0.3
Zimbabwe*, 2003	0.1
Namibia, 2000	0.1
Ghana*, 1995	0.01

AMERICA

Central America

Guatemala*, 2003	0.4
Belize*, 2003	0.2
Panama*, 2002	0.2
Nicaragua*, 2002	0.1
El Salvador*, 2003	0.1

North America

USA, 2003	1.1
Canada, 2002	0.9
Mexico, 2002	0.01

South America

Colombia*,2001	0.3
Ecuador*, 2003	0.3
Brazil*, 2001	0.2
Venezuela*, 2001	0.2
Guyana*, 2002	0.1
Chile, 2002	0.1
Peru, 2002	0.1
Suriname*, 2002	0.1
Uruguay*, 2002	0.1
Paraguay*, 2002	0.1
Argentina*, 2001	0.04

The Caribbean

Barbados*, 2002	0.3
Dominican Rep.*, 2000	0.2
Bahamas*, 2003	0.1

ASIA

East & South-East Asia

Indonesia*, 2002	0.1
Thailand, 2001	0.1
Japan*, 2003	0.1
Malaysia*, 2003	0.1
Hong Kong SAR, China, 2003	0.02
Philippines*, 2002	0.02
Singapore, 2000	0.01

Near and Middle East / South-West Asia

Israel, 2001	0.8
Lebanon*, 2001	0.5

EUROPE

East Europe

Ukraine*, 2003	0.1
Russian Federation*, 1999	0.1

Southeast Europe

Bulgaria*, 2003	0.4
Croatia*, 2003	0.3
Turkey*, 2003	0.3
Romania*, 2003	0.1
FYR of Macedonia*, 1999	0.1

West and Central Europe

Czech Rep., 2002	2.5
United Kingdom, (16-59), 2003	2.0
Netherlands, 2001	1.5
Hungary, (18-54), 2003	1.4
Spain, 2003	1.4
Belgium*, 2003	1.1
Ireland, 2003	1.1
Estonia*, 2003	0.8
Latvia, 2003	0.8
Slovakia, 2002	0.8
Germany, (18-59), 2003	0.8
Slovenia*, 1999	0.7
Austria*, 2003	0.7
Iceland*, (15-65), 2003	0.6
Norway, 1999	0.6
Switzerland*, 2003	0.6
Denmark, 2000	0.5
Finland, 2002	0.5
Lithuania*, 2003	0.4
Luxembourg*, (15-65), 1998	0.4
Portugal, 2001	0.4
Sweden*, 2003	0.4
Cyprus*, 2003	0.4
Italy, (15-45), 2001	0.3
Liechtenstein, 1998	0.2
Poland, 2002	0.2
France, 2002	0.2
Malta, (18-65), 2001	0.2
Greece, 1998	0.1

OCEANIA

Australia, 2004	4.2
New Zealand*, 2001	2.2

*UNODC estimates based on local studies, special population group studies, and /or law enforcement agency assessments.
** Tentative estimates.
Sources: ARQs, Government Reports, US Department of State, European Monitoring Center for Drugs and Drug Abuse (EMCDDA).

8.2. Treatment demand (Primary drugs of abuse)

PRIMARY DRUGS OF ABUSE AMONG PERSONS TREATED FOR DRUG PROBLEMS IN WEST EUROPEAN COUNTRIES, 2003 (or latest year available)

Country*	Source	Year	Distribution of main drug in percentages							
			Opiates	Cocaine	Amphetamines	Ecstasy	Hallucinogens	Cannabis	Other Illegal Drugs
Austria	Govt.	2003	87.0%	-	-	-	-	-	-
Belgium	Focal Point EMCDDA	2002	61.3%	15.0%	5.5%	0.8%	0.4%	14.6%	-
Denmark	EMCDDA	2002	46.0%	3.0%	5.0%	1.0%	0.0%	27.0%	18.0%
Finland	EMCDDA	2002	34.1%	0.2%	34.0%	0.6%	0.2%	25.6%	5.3%
France	UNODC	2001	62.1%	7.3%	0.9%	1.4%	0.9%	23.2%	4.2%
Germany	EMCDDA	2003	66.2%	25.6%	14.9%	13.4%	6.9%	58.0%	-
Greece	UNODC	2003	88.4%	1.6%	0.0%	0.4%	0.1%	7.8%	1.7%
Ireland	UNODC	2002	74.7%	1.8%	0.4%	3.1%	0.2%	17.6%	2.2%
Italy	UNODC	2002	79.8%	6.9%	0.2%	1.0%	0.1%	9.0%	3.0%
Luxembourg	EMCDDA	2002	80.0%	6.0%	0.0%	0.0%	0.0%	11.0%	3.0%
Netherlands	UNODC	2002	56.7%	27.5%	1.9%	0.9%	0.0%	13.1%	-
Norway	Focal Point EMCDDA	2001	58.2%	-	12.5 %	-	-	13.9 %	15.4%
Portugal	Focal Point EMCDDA	2002	67.0%	32.0%	3.0%	2.0%	0.0%	36.0%	-
Spain	UNODC	2002	60.7%	25.5%	0.7%	1.0%	0.2%	10.2%	1.8%
Sweden	UNODC	2002	31.1%	1.2%	38.2%	1.0%	0.0%	17.6%	10.8%
United Kingdom	UNODC	2002	75.0%	6.0%	3.0%	1.0%	0.1%	11.0%	3.6%
Average (unweighted)			64.3%	10.0%	7.5%	1.7%	0.6%	18.5%	5.8%

* Patients may be treated for more than one substance

- Austria: data was drawn from a sample of 849 drug users in Vienna. Overall, 6,413 people were treated for heroin abuse in substitution treatment in 2003 in Austria; the number of people treated for drug related psychic behavioural disturbances and intoxication amounted to 11,753.
- Belgium: data for opiates, cocaine and cannabis refer to treatment centres in the French community in 2000; data for amphetamine and ecstasy refer to outpatient treatment in Belgium in 1999.
- Denmark: data on opiates refer to heroin only.
- Germany: data refer to specialized outpatient treatment centres (695 out of 1017 centres); patients (30,109) are being treated for more than one substance of abuse.
- France: total number of reported patients 28,363; estimate based on 51% of responses of specialized drug treatment centres in 2001.
- Italy: total number of patients treated for drug abuse:156,000; data refer to public and private in- and out-patient treatment centres.
- Netherlands: number of people treated: 28,311; data refer to outpatient treatment centres.
- Portugal: data refer to out-patient treatment institutions, concern 53% of all clients in such out patient institutions. Breakdown according to drugs based on reports of the main substance used in the last 30 days prior to treatment.
- Sweden: number of people receiving treatment: 2997; data refer to hospitals, institutional care, walk-in clinics, prisons; 138 units of approx. 600 in Sweden.
- UK: number of people receiving treatment 74,546; data refer to specialized treatment agencies, general practitioners and residential rehabilitation. Data refer to period 1 April 2001 to 31 March 2002.

Sources: UNODC, Annual Reports Questionnaires data; EMCDDA, 2004 Annual Report on the State of the Drug Problem in the European Union; Govt. reports.

PRIMARY DRUGS OF ABUSE AMONG PERSONS TREATED FOR DRUG PROBLEMS IN EUROPE, 2003 (or latest year available)

Country*	Source	Year	Distribution of main drug in percentages		Amphetamine-type stimulants							People treated*
			Opiates	Cocaine	Amphetamines	Ecstasy	Hallucinogens	Cannabis	Hypnotics and Sedatives	Inhalants/solvents	
Austria	Govt.	2003/2	87.0%	-		-	-	-	-	-	11,753
Albania	UNODC	2003	97.1%	-		-	-	-	-	-	1,185
Belarus	UNODC	2003	70.7%	2.00%	1.7%	1.3%	0.9%	2.9%	2.8 %	13.4%	128
Belgium	Focal Point EMCDDA	2002	61.3%	15.0%	5.5%	0.8%	0.4%	7.4%	1.2 %		10,200
Bulgaria	UNODC	1999	96.9%	0.5%				14.6%	1.1 %		1,065
Croatia	UNODC	2003	70.4%	0.5%	1.2 %	0.6 %	-	1.2 %	2.0 %	0.4 %	5,215
Cyprus	UNODC	2003	69.6%	8.9 %	0.7 %	3.0 %	-	23.7 %	1.0 %		303
Czech Republic	UNODC	2003	25.0%	0.3%	52.8 %	0.6%	-	16.2 %		2.7 %	9,237
Denmark	UNODC	2002	30.1%	2.5%	3.3%	0.6%	0.1%	16.5%	-	27.8 %	4,310
Estonia	Focal Point EMCDDA	2001	53.8%	-	18.6%	0.6%	-	16.7%	-	-	2,034
Finland	EMCDDA	2002	34.1%	0.2%	34.0%	1.4%	0.2%	25.6%	-	-	3,497
France	UNODC	2001	62.1%	7.3%	0.9%	1.4%	0.9%	23.2%	4.0 %	-	28,363
Germany	UNODC	2003	66.2%	25.6%	14.9%	13.4%	6.9%	58.0%	-	-	30,109
Greece	UNODC	2003	88.4%	1.6%	0.0%	0.4%	0.1%	7.8%	-	-	3,195
FYR of Macedonia	UNODC	2003	99.6%	-		-	-	0.4%	-	-	568
Hungary	UNODC	2003	17.0%	0.9%	3.6 %	2.3 %	-	25.3 %	33.4 %	-	15,333
Iceland	UNODC	2000	0.1%	7.1%	65.6 %	0.9 %	-	26.3 %	-	-	2,285
Ireland	UNODC	2002	74.7%	1.8%	0.4%	3.1%	0.2%	17.6%	-	-	8,596
Italy	UNODC	2002/3	79.8%	6.9%	0.2%	1.0%	0.1%	9.0%	0.6 %	-	181,572
Latvia	UNODC	2003	44.9%	0.0%	7.5 %	-	-	1.3 %	8.2 %	-	523
Liechtenstein	UNODC	2002	33.3%	8.3%		-	-	50.0 %	-	-	12
Lithuania	UNODC	2003	80.2%	0.1%	3.1 %	-	-	0.8 %	-	4.4 %	2,913
Luxembourg	EMCDDA	2002	80.0%	6.0%	0.0%	0.0%	0.0%	11.0%	-	-	470
Malta	EMCDDA	2001	86.8%	3.8%		0.7 %	0.1 %	8.5 %	0.1 %	-	1,444
Netherlands	UNODC	2002	56.7%	27.5%	1.9%	0.9%	0.0%	13.1%	-	-	28,311
Norway	Focal Point EMCDDA	2001	58.2%	-	12.5 %	-	-	13.9 %	-	-	11,424
Poland	UNODC	2002	39.3%	0.8%	8.1 %	2.0%	-	3.4 %	-	3.3 %	11,915
Portugal	Focal Point EMCDDA	2002/3	67.0%	32.0%	3.0%	0.1 %	0.0%	36.0 %	0.2 %	-	29,596
Romania	UNODC	2003	74.1%	0.4%	0.3 %	-	-	1.9 %	-	23.2 %	2,734
Russian Fed.	UNODC	2003	88.4%	0.02%	1.6 %	-	-	6.1 %	-	-	343,335
Slovakia	UNODC	2003	52.5%	0.8%	17.5 %	0.5 %	-	14.2 %	-	8.7 %	2,119
Slovenia	UNODC	2002	90.9%	0.7%	0.2 %	0.2 %	0.2%	7.7 %	-	0.1 %	2,860
Spain	UNODC	2002	60.7%	25.5%	0.7%	1.0%	0.2%	10.2%	1.3 %	-	46,744
Sweden	UNODC	2002	31.1%	1.2%	38.2%	1.0%	0.0%	17.6%	7.5 %	-	2,997
Switzerland	Govt.	2003/2	42.0%	28.9%	0.6 %	0.6 %	0.3 %	5.6 %	2.3 %	-	20,316
Turkey	UNODC	2001	58.6%	0.0%			0.1%	13.0%	8.0 %	20.5 %	386
United Kingdom	UNODC	2002	75.0%	6.0%	3.0%	1.0%	0.1%	11.0%	2.0 %	-	74,546
Europe - average (unweighted)			**62.3%**	**6.0%**	**8.2%**	**1.0%**	**0.3%**	**14.0%**	**2.0%**	**3.0%**	**901,593**
East-Europe - average (unweighted)			66.2%	0.4%	7.3%	0.3%	0.1%	7.9%	3.5%	4.8%	401,550
West-Europe - average (unweighted)			59.2%	10.3%	8.8%	1.5%	0.5%	18.7%	1.0%	1.3%	500,043

* Please note that treatment definitions differ from country to country

In some countries people are being treated for more than one substance; sum of the percentages may thus exceed 100%.

Sources: UNODC, Annual Reports Questionnaire data; EMCDDA, Data Library.

PRIMARY DRUGS OF ABUSE AMONG PERSONS TREATED FOR DRUG PROBLEMS IN ASIA, 2003 (or latest year available)

Country	Source	Year	Distribution of main drug in percentages							People treated*
			Opiates	Cocaine	Amphetamine-type stimulants		Cannabis	Inhalants	Sedatives	
					Amphetamines	Ecstasy				
Armenia	Govt./UNODC estimate	2003	28.6%	-	14.3%	-	57.1%	-	-	7
Azerbaijan	ARQ / UNODC est.	2003	75.0%	-	-	-	20.0%	5.0%	-	n.a.
Bahrein	ARQ	1998	100.0%	-	-	-	-	-	-	1,488
Bangladesh	ARQ	2003	90.0%	-	-	-	3.0%	-	7.0%	5,605
Brunei Darussalam	ARQ	1999	-	-	96.4%	-	-	3.6%	-	56
China	UNODC FO	2003	98.5%	-	-	-	-	-	-	105,151
Hongkong, SAR of China	Govt	2000	72.5%	-	3.9%	-	4.2%	-	-	1,283
India	ARQ	2003	28.1%	0.4%	0.1%	-	14.0%	-	3.9%	129,000
Indonesia	ARQ	2003	95.4%	-	1.3%	-	1.4%	-	1.7%	4,097
Iran	Govt.	2001	91.6%	-	-	-	2.5%	-	-	33,990
Japan	Govt	2002	0.6%	0.1%	55.8%	0.2%	1.9%	17.9%	4.9%	1,124
Jordan	ARQ	1999	21.4%	-	45.2%	-	-	6%	-	85
Kazakhstan	UNODC FO	2000	74.6%	-	0.1%	-	20%	-	-	41,356
Kuwait	ARQ	2002	69.0%	-	25.0%	-	71.0%	4.0%	61.0%	197
Kyrgyzstan	ARQ	2002	71.4%	-	-	-	28.6%	-	-	5,611
Macao, SAR of China	ARQ	2003	85.9%	-	0.0%	1.3%	0.5%	-	1.6%	384
Malaysia	ARQ	2003	65.7%	-	7.5%	2.3%	23.3%	-	-	36,996
Maldives	ARQ	1998	50.0%	-	-	-	50.0%	-	-	120
Mongolia	ARQ	2001	71.4%	-	-	-	28.6%	-	-	7
Myanmar	ARQ	2003	90.2%	-	6.6%	-	1.7%	-	-	1,373
Nepal, Kathmandu	AMCEWG	1994	87.2%	-	-	-	5.4%	-	-	n.a.
Oman	ARQ	2002	100.0%	-	-	-	-	-	-	7
Pakistan	ARQ/UNODC Study	2002	97.6%	-	-	-	1.0%	-	-	17,425
Philippines	UNODC FO	2003	0.2%	0.5%	87.1%	0.8%	31.3%	-	0.4%	8,189
Qatar	ARQ	1997	25.4%	-	1.7%	-	5.1%	10.2%	-	59
Republic of Korea	ARQ	2003	1.7%	-	57.4%	5.1%	34.1%	-	0.6%	176
Saudi Arabia	ARQ	2001	15.1%	-	41.3%	-	15.9%	27.8%	-	1,368
Singapore	ARQ	2003	100.0%	-	-	-	-	-	-	258
Sri Lanka	ARQ	2003	100.0%	-	-	-	-	-	-	4,664
Taiwan, Province of China	AMCEWG	1999	37.5%	-	44.8%	-	-	8.2%	7.2%	2,589
Tajikistan	ARQ	2002	98.6%	-	-	-	1.4%	-	-	427
Thailand	Govt.	2003	5.4%	-	57.1%	-	6.8%	1.7%	-	355,491
Uzbekistan	ARQ	2003	78.8%	-	-	-	16.8%	0.9%	0.6%	n.a.
Viet Nam	UNODC FO	2003	98.0%	-	2.0%	-	-	-	-	36,478
Average (unweighted)			**62.5%**	**0.0%**	**16.1%**	**0.3%**	**12.9%**	**2.4%**	**2.6%**	**795,100**

* Please note that treatment definitions differ from country to country

This table does not include "other drugs"; therefore the percentages will not add up to 100%.

Sources: UNODC, Annual Reports Questionnaire Data, Asian Multicity Epidemiology work group (AMCEWG); Govt. reports

375

PRIMARY DRUGS OF ABUSE AMONG PERSONS TREATED FOR DRUG PROBLEMS IN OCEANIA
2003 (or latest year available)

Country and year	Source	Year	Opiates	Cocaine	Cannabis	Amphetamie-type stimulants		Inhalants	Sedatives	People treated*
						Amphetamines	Ecstasy			
Australia**	Govt	2002/03	33.3%	0.4%	36.3%	17.7%	0.6%	-	4.7%	74,592
New Zealand***	Govt	1998/2003	31.7%	0.4%	23.1%	7.8%		3.2%	38.6%	6,489
Average			32.5%	0.4%	29.7%	12.8%	0.6%	1.6%	21.7%	81,081

* Please note that treatment definitions differ from country to country.

** Data for Australia refer to closed drug related treatment episodes over the July 2002-June 2003 period (N = 74,600).

*** Data for New Zealand refer to 1998, the latest year for which a breakdown of drug related treatment data has been published; the proportion shown for amphetamines refers to 2003.

The proportion of methamphetamine related telephone helpline calls is used as a proxy for the importance of methamphetamine in overall treatment.

In 1998 0.4% of treatment cases concerned amphetamines; telephone helplines reported a major increase with regard to methamphetamine from 0.5% in 2001 to 1.4% in 2002 & 7.8% in 2003, in parallel,

to hospital reports of large increases in methamphetamine related cases.

PRIMARY DRUG OF ABUSE AMONG PERSONS TREATED FOR DRUG PROBLEMS IN AFRICA, 2003 (or latest year available)

Country	Source	Year	Distribution of main drugs in percentages							People treated*
			Cannabis	Opiates	Cocaine	Amphetamine - type stimulants	Methaqualone	Inhalants	Khat	
Algeria	ARQ	1999	81.3 %	6.6 %	0.2 %	-	-	2.1 %	-	10
Botswana	SENDU	2003	100.0 %	-	-	-	-	-	-	17
Cameroon**	RAS	1995	48.5 %	12.1 %	13.6 %	-	-	36.4 %	-	
Chad	ARQ	1996	50.6 %	-	0.2 %	18.8 %	-	6.3 %	-	16
Congo	ARQ	1995	100.0 %	-	-	-	-	-	-	41
Cote d'Ivoire	ARQ	1998	91.0 %	4.1 %	3.0 %	-	-	-	-	
Egypt	Field	1999	22.1 %	45.1 %	0.4 %	-	-	-	-	
Ethiopia	ARQ	1999/2003	14.6 %	9.6 %		-	-	-	75.6 %	462
Ghana	ARQ	2003	88.2 %	0.9 %	0.6 %	-	-	-	-	932
Kenya***	RAS	1995	33.8 %	4.8 %	2.9 %	5.2 %	-	20.5 %	14.3 %	142
Lesotho	SENDU	2003	100.0 %	-		-	-	-	-	44
Madagascar	ARQ	2003	56.9 %	-		-	-	-	-	663
Malawi	SENDU	2003	99.7 %	-		-	-	-	-	645
Mauritius	ARQ	2003	22.3 %	58.3 %	-	-	-	0.5 %	-	592
Mozambique	SENDU	2003	46.1 %	47.3 %	4.5 %	-	-	-	-	91
Namibia	SENDU	2002	35.2 %	-	16.5 %	5.0 %	42.8 %	-	-	948
Nigeria	ARQ	2003	85.7 %	3.7 %	0.6 %	-	-	-	-	934
Sao Tome & Principe	ARQ	1997	22.2 %	5.5 %	72.2 %	-	-	-	-	
Seychelles	ARQ	2003	94.6 %	2.7 %		2.7 %	-	-	-	37
Sierra Leone	ARQ	1997	96.8 %	-	0.6 %	-	-	-	-	2,067
South Africa	ARQ	2003	37.3 %	12.7 %	12.1 %	3.1 %	26.8 %	-	-	5,780
Tanzania	SENDU	2003/4	62.7 %	32.7 %		-	-	-	-	340
Togo	ARQ	2002	56.2 %	4.3 %	4.9 %	-	-	34.6 %	-	162
Zambia	ARQ	2002	86.2 %	1.8 %		2.8 %	-	-	-	109
Average			**63.8 %**	**10.5 %**	**9.5 %**	**6.3 %**	**2.9 %**	**4.4 %**	**3.7 %**	**14,032**

*   Please note that treatment definitions differ from country to country

**   Proxy: drugs locally consumed, based on key informants from social services (health affairs,), from traditional healers, and repression.

**   Proxy: drugs consumed, based on health workers.

Source: UNODC, Annual Reports Questionnaires data, Southern African Development Community Epidemiology Network on Drug Use.

PRIMARY DRUGS OF ABUSE AMONG PERSONS TREATED FOR DRUG PROBLEMS IN THE AMERICAS, 2003 (or latest year available)

Country and year	Source	Year	Cocaine-type (cocaine, basuco & crack-cocaine)	Cocaine	Basuco	Crack	Cannabis	Amphetamine - type		Inhalants	Tranquilizers	Opiates	People treated*
								Amphetamines	Ecstasy				
Argentina	ARQ	2004	32.6%	24.8%	7.3%	0.2%	31.9%	1.8%	0.4%	15.3%	15.2%	0.6%	144,120
Bahamas	ARQ	2003	36.7%				46.4%						536
Barbados	SIDUC	1998	72.3%	5.6%		66.7%	27.8%						n.a.
Bolivia	SIDUC/ARQ	1998/2003**	54.8%	23.1%	31.8%		14.7%	1.4%		23.5%			5,491
Canada	CCENDU	2001	25.6%				24.7%	0.4%			21.2%	8.1%	29,214
Brazil	SIDUC	1998	59.2%	14.4%		44.8%	27.2%			2.0%	2.4%	0.4%	n.a.
Chile	SIDUC/ARQ	1998/2003**	89%	21.2%	67.8%		4.1%	4.1%					18,300
Colombia	SIDUC	1998	56.3%	28.1%	28.2%		13.4%	3.6%		4.8%			n.a.
Costa Rica	ARQ	2002/03**	54.3%	23.8%		30.5%	30.1%						12,500
Dominican Rep.,	ARQ	2001/03**	76.4%				20.0%					3.6%	2,728
Ecuador	SIDUC	1998/2003**	66.1%	13.5%	52.5%		10.2%			4.6%			5,250
El Salvador	ARQ	1998/2002**	100.0%				58.3%						6,000
Grenada	ARQ	2001	75.0%				25.0%						12
Guatemala	ARQ	2003	75.0%										2,000
Haiti	ARQ	2002	37.5%				35.4%				6.3%	2.1%	51
Honduras	SIDUC	1998	9.0%	3.1%		5.9%	34.4%			9.0%			n.a.
Jamaica	SIDUC/ARQ	1998/2001**	58%			58%	28.9%						1,362
Mexico	ARQ	2003	62.6%				56.6%	13.7%		28.8%	14.6%	4.9%	9,621
Nicaragua	SIDUC	1998	77.3%	14.5%		62.8%	7.3%			12.7%			n.a.
Panama	SIDUC/ARQ	1998/2001**	49.4%	48.9%	0.5%		5.1%			0.5%			5,838
Peru	SIDUC/ARQ	1998/99**	90.8%	20.4%	70.4%		5.6%						4,000
St.Vincent & Grenadines	ARQ	2001	13.4%				86.6%						134
Trinidad & Tobago,	ARQ	2001	35.9%				17.6%						501
Uruguay	SIDUC	1998	46.4%	46.4%			12.2%	0.6%		9.2%			n.a.
USA	SAMHSA/DAWN	2003	30.9%	8.4%		22.5%	54.1%	19.1%	0.6%	7.5%	5.9%	15.6%	1,802,000
Venezuela	ARQ	2003	76.9%				12.5%	0.1%	0.2%	0.3%	0.7%	2.0%	7,321
Unweighted average			56.2%				27.6%	5.0%	0.4%	9.9%	9.5%	1.4%	2,056,979
Average North America			39.7%				45.1%	11.1%	0.6%	18.2%	13.9%	9.5%	1,840,835
Average South America			58.4%				24.1%	0.5%	0.0%	3.6%	1.1%	0.4%	216,144

Note: These drugs represent the most common drugs of impact across countries, therefore the percentages may not add up to 100% for all countries.

* Please note that treatment definitions differ from country to country

** The second year specified is for the number of people treated (last column).

Sources: SIDUC, Treatment Centres Data 1998, Drug of impact; SIDUC 1997 Report; Treatment episode dataset TEDS, USA 1992-2002;

Secretaria Nacional Antidrogas, Brazil (Data refer to one treatment centre in Minas Gerais (985 cases); Canadian Community Epidemiology Network on Drug Use (CCENDU),

Morbidity Statistics 2000/2001 (separations related to illicit drug use).

Methodology

Considerable efforts have been made over the last few years to improve the estimates presented in this report. Nonetheless, the data must still be interpreted with caution because of the clandestine nature of drug production, trafficking and abuse. Apart from the 'hidden' nature of the phenomenon being measured, the main problems with regard to data relate to the irregularity and incompleteness in reporting. This affects the quantity, quality and comparability of information received. First, the irregular intervals at which some Governments report may result in absence of data in some years but availability in others. The lack of regular data, for which UNODC tries to compensate by reference to other sources, can influence trend patterns. Secondly, submitted questionnaires are not always complete or sufficiently comprehensive. All figures should thus be seen as likely orders of magnitude of the drug problem, but not as precise results. It should be also noted that all figures provided, particularly those of more recent years, are subject to updating.

Sources and limitations of data on the supply side

Cultivation, production and manufacture

Global estimates are, in general, more robust on the production side, notably data for plant based drugs, than on the demand side. In line with decisions of the Member States (1998 UNGASS and subsequent CND resolutions), UNODC launched an Illicit Crop Monitoring Programme (ICMP) in 1999. The objective of the programme is to assist Member States in establishing national systems to monitor the extent and evolution of the illicit cultivation of narcotics crops on their territories. The results are compiled by UNODC to present global estimates on an annual basis. Data on cultivation of opium poppy and coca bush and production of opium and coca leaf, presented in this report for the main producing countries (Afghanistan, Myanmar and the Lao PDR for opium and Colombia, Peru and Bolivia for coca) have been derived from these national monitoring systems operating in the countries of illicit production. UNODC also conducted in 2004, for the second time, a survey on cannabis resin production in Morocco, in close cooperation with the Government of Morocco. Estimates for other countries presented in this report have been drawn from replies to UNODC's Annual Reports Questionnaire, from various other sources including reports from Governments, UNODC field offices and the United States Department of State's Bureau for International Narcotics and Law Enforcement Affairs.

The key indicator for measuring progress made towards the supply reduction goals set out in the UNGASS Political Declaration of June 1998 is the area under cultivation of narcotic crops. Since 1999, UNODC has been supporting the establishment of national monitoring systems in the main narcotics production countries. These monitoring systems are tailored to national specificities. The direct participation of UNODC ensures the transparency of the survey activities. Through its network of monitoring experts at headquarters and in the field, the UNODC ensures the conformity of the national systems so that they meet international methodological standards and the information requirements of the international community. Most of these monitoring systems rely on remote sensing technology (i.e. analysis of satellite imagery) in combination with extensive field visits which is made possible through UNODC's field presence in all of the main narcotics producing countries. Satellite images, in combination with ground information, offer a reliable and objective way of estimating illicit crops. Depending on the local conditions, the surveys are conducted either on a census approach (coca cultivation in Colombia, Peru and Bolivia, cannabis cultivation in Morocco) or a sample approach (opium poppy cultivation in Afghanistan, Myanmar and Laos). The accuracy assessment of the individual estimates differs, but is often close to 90%, i.e. 'ground truthing' shows that about 90% of the areas analysed from satellite photos were correctly identified as poppy fields or coca fields. In the case of sampling, the potential error depends on the number of villages investigated and/or on the number of satellite photos taken which form the basis for subsequent extrapolations to the agricultural land. In the case of Afghanistan, for instance, the estimated area under poppy cultivation in the 2004 opium poppy survey showed a potential margin of error +/- 17% (or, for the areas covered by satellite photos, of +/- 13%, suggesting a 90% probability that the actual results fall within the confidence interval).

In addition, the ground surveys, assist UNODC to obtain information on yields, drug prices and various other socio-economic data that is useful for alternative development interventions. Detailed discussion of the methodological approaches can be found on http://www.unodc.org/unodc/en/crop_monitoring.html.

UNODC has also started to conduct yield surveys in some countries, measuring the yield of test fields, and to develop methodologies to extrapolate the yields from proxy variables, such as the volume of poppy capsules. This approach is already used in South-East Asia and in 2004 UNODC used this approach for the first time in Afghanistan as well, following 4 years of testing. All of this is intended to further improve yield estimates, aiming at information that is independent from farmers' reports. The accuracy of the calculated yields depends on a number of factors, including the number of sites investigated. In the case of Afghanistan the confidence interval for the mean yield results in the 2004 survey was, for instance, +/- 8% of the mean value (based on alpha = 0.05).

In countries in which UNODC has not, as yet, undertaken yield surveys, results from other surveys conducted at the national level are used instead. This is currently still the case in Andean countries, though UNODC has started to become involved in such yield surveys and expects better yield estimates over the next few years. The disadvantage of having to take recourse to yield data from other sources is that year on year variations, due to weather conditions, or due to the introduction of improved seeds, fertilizers and pesticides, are not properly reflected in the end results.

The transformation ratios used to calculate the potential cocaine production from coca leaf or the heroin production from opium are more problematic. In order to be precise, these calculations would require detailed information at the local level on the morphine content in opium or the cocaine content in the coca leaf, as well as detailed information on the clandestine laboratory efficiency, which in turn is a function of know-how, equipment and precursor chemicals. This information is not available. A number of studies conducted by enforcement agencies in the main drug producing countries have provided some orders of magnitude for the transformation from the raw material to the end product. The problem is that this information is usually based on just a few cases studies which are not necessarily typical for the production process in general. Potential margins of error in this rapidly changing environment, with new laboratories coming on stream while others are being dismantled, are thus, substantial. This also applies to the question of the psychoactive content of the narcotic plants. One study conducted in Afghanistan by UNODC over a couple of years, indicated, for instance, that the morphine content of Afghan opium was significantly higher than had been thought earlier. Based on this study in combination with information on the price structure (which suggested that at a 10:1 conversion ratio of opium to morphine/heroin laboratory owners would lose money) the transformation ratio for opium produced in Afghanistan was changed from a 10:1 to a new ratio of 6.5 : 1 in 2004. For other countries the traditional 10:1 ratio continues being applied. An open question remains, however, the effective laboratory efficiency in this country[a]. On the cocaine side, a number of studies have been conducted in the Andean region over the last decade investigating the transformation ratios of coca leaf to cocaine base and cocaine HCL - which also form the basis for UNODC's estimates. However, these conversion ratios are not in line with reported price patterns of these substances, raising some questions as to their appropriateness and indicating a need to revisit them. At the same time, it is obviously impossible for UNODC to set up clandestine laboratories and hire 'cooks' in order to improve its statistical basis. All of this underlines the ongoing difficulties to accurately assess global heroin and cocaine production, even though information on areas under cultivation has greatly improved over the last few years.

'Potential' heroin or cocaine production, the indicator used throughout this report, shows the level of production of heroin or cocaine if all of the opium or coca leaf were transformed into the end products. In reality, however, part of the opium or the coca leaf is directly consumed in the producing countries or in neighbouring countries, prior to the transformation into heroin or cocaine. There are important illicit opium markets in Iran or Pakistan and coca leaf is used by the local population in Bolivia, Peru and northern Chile. In addition, significant quantities of the intermediate products, coca paste or morphine, are also consumed in the producing countries.

As the transformation ratios used are rather conservative, total 'potential' production, however, may well be close to 'actual' production of the end products if one takes the *de-facto* lower amounts available for starting the transformation process into account. There are thus two kinds of potential biases in the estimates which (at least partly) can be expected to offset each other.

---

[a] In 2004, the German Bundeskriminalamt conducted a very interesting case study on heroin production in that country which indicated rather low levels of laboratory efficiency. However, it is difficult to generalize these findings and more such studies would be needed to determine overall laboratory efficiency in that country.

The use of the concept of 'potential production' at the country level also means that actual heroin or cocaine production is under-estimated in some countries, and over-estimated in others while the estimate for the global level should not be affected by this. The calculation of 'potential' cocaine production estimates for Peru, for instance, exceeds actual local cocaine production as some of the coca paste or coca base produced in Peru is exported to neighbouring Colombia for further processing into cocaine. Based on the same reasoning, potential cocaine production estimates for Colombia under-estimate actual cocaine production in the country. Actual cocaine manufacture in Colombia takes place from locally produced coca leaf as well as from coca base imported from Peru.

In the case of cannabis herb, the globally most dispersed illegal drug, all available production estimates were aggregated. In most cases, however, these estimates are not based on scientific studies (often reflecting potential yields of eradicated areas rather than total production) and often refer to different years (as only a limited number of countries provided such estimates in the last Annual Reports Questionnaire for the year 2003). A significant number of countries did not provide estimates at all. Thus, in addition to last year's *World Drug Report*, a systematic review was undertaken of all the countries which over the last decade were identified by other countries as a significant cannabis source countries or which reported the seizures of whole cannabis plants (which is indicative of domestic cultivation). For these countries, production was estimated to cover domestic demand, multiplying the number of estimated cannabis users by the average global cannabis herb consumption rate, derived from previous calculations. For countries that were identified as cannabis producing countries but were not identified as major cannabis exporting countries, a certain percentage of domestic demand was used to estimate local production. The percentages chosen depended on quantitative and qualitative information available for different regions. Clearly, this is not an ideal estimation technique but the best that is currently available. In a number of cases, subsequent indications of likely orders of magnitude, referred in scientific literature, came rather close to these results. This approach increased the estimate from 35,000 tons to 42,000 tons. Cross-checks with existing seizure statistics suggest that the magnitude of the overall cannabis estimate is a feasible order of magnitude. Current estimates suggest that the global cannabis herb interception rate in 2003 was 14%, more than the 'traditional' 10% rule of thumb ratio, though lower than the interception rates calculated for opiates (18% in 2002, 23% in 2003), which should be expected as heroin is far more targeted by enforcement bodies than cannabis. Using the 'traditional' 10% ratio, the production estimate would rise to 58,000 tons; but it is difficult to imagine such amounts actually being consumed. Current UNODC estimates of cannabis herb consumption are around 30,000 tons, which – taking seizures into account – would indicate a gross production of around 36,000 tons. These considerations suggest that the potential error for the cannabis herb estimate remains large although the actual figures should fall well within a +/- 50% error margin.

In the case of cannabis resin, scientific information on the – most likely - largest cannabis resin producing country is available which, in combination with seizure statistics, forms a basis for extrapolations to the global level. Given no dramatic changes of cannabis resin production in Morocco, last year's global cannabis resin estimate was maintained. That estimate was based on calculating backward from cannabis herb estimates (based exclusively on explicitly reported cannabis production estimates) and on the assumption of similar interception rates for both substances. Though the resulting global cannabis resin estimates cannot be considered to be very precise, any significant difference (>50%) in the order of magnitude is not very likely.

The potential margins of error for the ATS estimates are less than those of cannabis, but probably larger than those for the heroin or the cocaine estimates. The approach taken in this case was one of triangulation, estimating production based on reported seizures of the end products in combination with some assumptions of law enforcement effectiveness, seizure data of precursor chemicals and estimates based on the number of consumers and their likely levels of *per capita* consumption. While each individual calculation may well raise some questions, the overall results of the three approaches showed similar orders of magnitude, suggesting that actual production levels of ATS may not be too far-off (+/- 30%) from the resulting mid-point estimates. The estimation procedure remains unchanged from the one used for last year's *World Drug Report*.

Trafficking

The information on trafficking, as presented in this report, is mainly drawn from the Annual Reports Questionnaires (ARQ), submitted by Governments to UNODC in 2004 and early 2005 and refers to the year 2003 (and previous years). Additional sources, such as other governmental reports, the International Criminal Police Organization (Interpol), the World Customs Organization (WCO) and UNODC's field offices, were used to supplement the information. Priority was, however, given to officially transmitted data in the Annual

Reports Questionnaire. The analysis of quantities seized, shown in this report, was based on information provided by 157 countries and territories in 2002 and 156 in 2003. Seizures are thus the most comprehensive indicator of the drug situation and its evolution at the global level. Though they may not always reflect trafficking trends correctly at the national level, they tend to show good representations of trafficking trends at the regional and global levels.

There are some technical problems as – depending on the drugs - some countries report seizures in weight terms (kg), in volume terms (litres) while other countries report seizures in 'unit terms'. In Volume II, seizures are shown as reported. In the analytical sections of Volume I of the report, seizure data have been aggregated and transformed into a unique measurement: seizures in 'kilogram equivalents'. For the purposes of the calculations a 'typical consumption unit' (at street purity) was assumed to be: cannabis herb: 0.5 grams, cannabis resin: 0.135 grams; cocaine and ecstasy: 0.1 grams, heroin and amphetamines: 0.03 grams, LSD: 0.00005 grams (50 micrograms). A litre of seizures was assumed to be equivalent to a kilogram. For opiate seizures (unless specified differently in the text), it was assumed that 10 kg of opium were equivalent to 1 kg of morphine or heroin. Though all of these transformation ratios can be disputed, they at least provide a possibility of combining all the different seizure reports into one comprehensive measure. The transformation ratios have been derived from those used by law enforcement agencies, in the scientific literature, by the INCB, and were established in consultation with UNODC's Laboratory and Scientific Section. No changes in the transformation ratios used in last year's *World Drug Report* were made.

Seizures are used as an indicator for trends and patterns in trafficking. In combination with changes in drug prices or drug purities, changes in seizures can indicate whether trafficking has increased or declined. Increases in seizures in combination with stable or falling drug prices is a strong indication of rising trafficking activities. Increasing seizures and rising drug prices, in contrast, may be a reflection of improved enforcement effectiveness. Changes in trafficking can also serve as an indirect indicator for global production and abuse of drugs. Seizures are, of course, only an indirect indicator for trafficking activities, influenced by a number of additional factors, such as variations in law enforcement practices and changes in reporting modalities. Thus, the extent to which seizure statistics from some countries constitute all reported national cases, regardless of the final destination of the illicit drug, can vary and makes it sometimes difficult to assess actual trafficking activities. The problem is exacerbated by increasing amounts of drugs being seized in countries along the main transit routes, the increasing use of 'controlled deliveries', in which countries forego the possibility of seizing drugs immediately in order to identify whole trafficking networks operating across countries, and 'upstream disruptions', making use of intelligence information to inform partner countries and enable them to seize such deliveries prior to entering the country of final destination. Some of the increase of cocaine seizures in the Andean region in recent years, for instance, may have been linked to such upstream market disruptions.

However, over longer periods of time and over larger geographical entities, seizures have proven to be a good indicator to reveal underlying trafficking trends. While seizures at the national level may be influenced by large quantities of drugs in transit or by shifts in law enforcement priorities, it is not very likely that the same is true at the regional or at the global level. If a large drug shipment, while in transit, is taken out of the market in one country, fewer drugs will be probably seized in the neighbouring countries. Similarly, if enforcement efforts and thus seizures decline in one country, the neighbouring countries are likely to suffer from intensified trafficking activities, resulting in rising levels of seizures. The net results, emerging from changes of enforcement priorities of an individual country, are thus, in general, not significant at the regional or at the global level. Actual changes in trafficking can thus be considered to be among the main reasons for changes in seizures at the regional level or the global level. Indeed, comparisons, on a time-series basis, of different indicators with statistical dependence have shown strong correlations (e.g. global opium production estimates and global seizures of opiates, or global coca leaf production and global cocaine seizures), supporting the statistical worth of seizure statistics at regional and global levels. At the same time, data also show that interception rates have gradually increased over the last decade, reflecting improved law enforcement effectiveness at the global level.

Price and purity data

UNODC also collects and publishes price and purity data. Price and purity data, if properly collected, can be very powerful indicators for the identification of market trends. As supply changes in the short-run are usually stronger than changes on the demand side (which tend to take place over longer time periods), shifts in prices and purities are a good indicator for actual increases or declines of market supply. Research has also shown that short-term changes in the consumer markets are – first of all - reflected in purity changes while prices tend to be rather stable over longer periods as traffickers and drug consumers at the retail level prefer 'round' prices.

UNODC collects its price data from the Annual Reports Questionnaire, and supplements this data set by other sources, such as price data collected by Europol and other organisations. Prices are collected for the farm-gate level, the wholesale level ('kilogram prices') and for the retail level ('gram prices'). Countries are asked to provide minimum, maximum and typical prices and purities. In case no typical prices/purities are provided, UNODC calculates the mid-point of these estimates as a proxy for the 'typical' prices/purities (unless scientific studies are available which provide better estimates). What is not known, in general, is the way such data were collected and their actual statistical representativeness. While some improvements have been made in some countries over the last few years, a number of law enforcement bodies in several countries have not, as yet, discovered the powerful strategic value of such data, once collected in a systematic way, at regular intervals, so that it can be used for statistical analysis, drug market analysis and as an early warning system.

Sources and limitations of data on consumption

Extent of drug abuse

a. Overview

UNODC estimates of the extent of drug abuse in the world have been published periodically since 1997 (see *World Drug Reports 1997, 2000,* 2004 and *Global Illicit Drug Trends 2002 and 2003).* The sixth round of estimates, presented in this report, is based on information received until May 2005.

Assessing the extent of drug abuse (the number of drug users) is a particularly difficult undertaking because it involves measuring the size of a hidden population. Margins of error are considerable, and tend to multiply as the scale of estimation is raised, from local to national, regional and global levels. Despite some improvements in recent years, estimates provided by Member States to UNODC are still very heterogeneous in terms of quality and reliability. These estimates cannot simply be aggregated globally to arrive at the total number of drug users in the world. Yet it is both desirable and possible to establish basic orders of magnitude - which are obviously subject to revision as new and better information is generated.

A global estimate of the level of use of specific drugs involves the following steps:

1. Identification and analysis of appropriate sources.
2. Identification of key benchmark figures for the level of drug use in selected countries (annual prevalence of drug abuse among the general population age 15-64) which then serve as 'anchor points' for subsequent calculations.
3. 'Standardization' of existing data (e.g. from age group 12 and above to a standard age group of 15-64).
4. Extrapolation of existing results based on information from neighbouring countries with similar cultural, social and economic situations (e.g. life-time prevalence or current use to annual prevalence, or school survey results to annual prevalence among the general population).
5. Extrapolation of available results from countries in a region to the region as a whole, using all available quantitative and qualitative information.
6. Aggregation of regional results to arrive at global results.

The approach taken to arrive at the global estimates has remained essentially the same since the first attempt was made in 1997.

Estimates of illicit consumption for a large number of countries have been received by UNODC over the years (in the form of Annual Reports Questionnaires (ARQ) submitted by Governments), and have been identified from additional sources, such as other governmental reports and research results from scientific literature. Officially transmitted information in any specific year, however, would not suffice to establish global estimates. For 2003, for instance, 66 countries provided UNODC with quantitative estimates of their drug situation in their country, including 40 countries providing estimates of the prevalence of drug consumption among the general population and 53 countries providing estimates of prevalence of drug use among their student populations. For countries that did not submit information, other sources, where available, were identified. Alternatively, information provided by Governments in previous years was used. In such cases, the prevalence rates were left unchanged and applied to new population estimates for the year 2003. In addition, a number of estimates needed to be 'adjusted' (see below). Using all of these sources, estimates were established for 137 countries. Results from these countries were extrapolated to the sub-regional level and then aggregated into the global estimate.

Detailed information is available from countries in North America, a large number of countries in Europe, a number of countries in South America, a few countries in Oceania (though including the two largest countries) and a limited number of countries in Asia and in Africa. For other countries, available qualitative information on the drug situation only allows for some 'guess estimates'. In the case of complete data gaps for individual countries, it was assumed that drug use was likely to be close to the respective sub-regional average, unless other available indicators suggested that they were likely to be above or below such an average.

One key problem in currently available prevalence estimates from countries is still the level of accuracy, which varies strongly from country to country. While a number of estimates are based on sound epidemiological surveys, some are obviously the result of guesswork. In other cases, the estimates simply reflect the aggregate number of drug addicts found in drug registries which probably cover only a small fraction of the total drug using population in a country.

Even in cases where detailed information is available, there is often considerable divergence in definitions used - registry data (people in contact with the treatment system or the judicial system) versus survey data (usually extrapolation of results obtained through interviews of a selected sample); general population versus specific surveys of groups in terms of age (e.g. school surveys), special settings (such as hospitals or prisons), life-time, annual, or monthly prevalence, etc.

In order to reduce the error from simply aggregating such diverse estimates, an attempt was made to standardize - as a far as possible - the very heterogeneous data set. Thus, all available estimates were transformed into one single indicator – annual prevalence among the general population age 15 to 64 and above - using transformation ratios derived from analysis of the situation in neighbouring countries, and if such data were not available, on estimates from the USA, the most studied country worldwide with regard to drug abuse.

The basic assumption is that the level of drug use differs between countries, but that there are general patterns (e.g. lifetime time prevalence is higher than annual prevalence; young people consume more drugs than older people) which apply universally. It also assumed that the ratio between lifetime prevalence and annual prevalence among the general population or between lifetime prevalence among young people and annual prevalence among the general population, do not vary too much among countries with similar social, cultural and economic situation. Data from a number of countries seem to confirm these assumptions.

In order to minimize the potential error from the use of different methodological approaches, all available estimates for the same country - after transformation - were taken into consideration and - unless methodological considerations suggested a clear superiority of one method over another - the mean of the various estimates was calculated and used as UNODC's country estimate.

b. Indicators used

The most widely used indicator at the global level is the annual prevalence rate: the number of people who have consumed an illicit drug at least once in the last twelve months prior to the survey. As "annual prevalence" is the most commonly used indicator to measure prevalence, it has been adopted by UNODC as the key indicator to measure the extent of drug abuse. It is also part of the Lisbon Consensus[b] (20-21 January 2000) on core epidemiological demand indicators (CN.7/2000/CRP.3). The use of "annual prevalence" is a compromise between "life-time prevalence" data (drug use at least once in a life-time) and data on current use (drug use at least once over the last month). Lifetime prevalence data are, in general, easier to generate but are not very illustrative. Data on current use are of more value. However, they often require larger samples in order to

---

[b] The basic indicators to monitor drug abuse, agreed by all participating organizations that formed part of the Lisbon Consensus in 2000, are:
- Drug consumption among the general population (estimates of prevalence and incidence);
- Drug consumption among the youth population (estimates of prevalence and incidence);
- High-risk drug abuse (estimates of the number of injecting drug users and the proportion engaged in high-risk behaviour, estimates of the number of daily drug users);
- Utilization of services for drug problems (number of individuals seeking help for drug problems);
- Drug-related morbidity (prevalence of HIV, hepatitis B virus and hepatitis C virus among illicit drug consumers);
- Drug-related mortality (deaths directly attributable to drug consumption).
While in the analysis of the drug abuse situation and drug abuse trends all these indicators were considered, when it came to provide a global comparison a choice was made to rely on the one key indicator that is most available and provides an idea of the magnitude for the drug abuse situation: annual prevalence among the population aged 15 to 64.

obtain meaningful results, and are thus more costly to generate, notably if it comes to other drugs than cannabis which is widespread.

The "annual prevalence" rate is usually shown as a percentage of the youth and adult population. The definitions of the age groups vary, however, from country to country. Given a highly skewed distribution of drug use among the different age cohorts in most countries (youth and young adults tend to have substantially higher prevalence rates than older adults or retired persons), differences in the age groups can lead to substantially diverging results. Typical age groups used by UNODC Member States are: 12+; 16-59; 12-60; 14+: 15+; 18+; 18-60; 15-45; 15-75; and increasingly age 15-64. In the past UNODC used to work on the basis of a 15+ age group. The revised version of the Annual Reports Questionnaire (ARQ), adopted by Member States, which since 2001/02 has replaced the previous ARQ, stipulates the age group 15-64 as the key population group for which drug use to be measured against. Prevalence data in this report, like in last year's *World Drug Report*, are thus reported for the age group 15-64. In case the age groups reported by Member States did not differ significantly from this age group, they were presented as reported and the age group was explicitly added. In cases where studies were based on significantly different age groups, results were adjusted to the age group of 15-64. (See below).

The methods used for collecting data on illicit activities vary from country to country. This reduces comparability. Possibilities to reduce differences – ex post – arising due to different methodological approaches are limited. UNODC thus welcomes efforts at the regional level to arrive at more comparable data (as is currently the case in Europe under the auspices of EMCDDA and in the Americas under the auspices of CICAD).

In a number of cases, diverging results are also obtained for the same country, applying differing methodological approaches. In such cases, the sources were analysed in-depth and priority was given to the methodological approaches that are usually also used in other countries. For example, it is generally accepted that household surveys are reasonably good instruments to estimate cannabis, ATS or cocaine use among the general population. Thus household survey results were usually given priority over other sources of prevalence estimates, such as reported registry data from the police or from treatment providers.

However, when it comes to heroin abuse (or drug injecting), there seems to be a general agreement that annual prevalence data derived from national household surveys tend to grossly under-estimate such abuse because severe heroin addicts often do not live in households[c] They may be homeless, in hospitals or in prisons. Moreover, heroin abuse is highly stigmatized so that the willingness to openly report a heroin abuse problem is limited. However, a number of indirect methods have been developed over the last two decades to provide estimates for this group of problem drug users. They include various multiplier methods (e.g. treatment multipliers, police data multipliers, HIV/AIDS multipliers or mortality multipliers), capture-recapture methods, and multivariate indicators.

---

[c] The problem of under-estimation is more widespread for heroin, but it is not excluded for other drugs, especially drugs related to problem drug use such as cocaine or methamphetamine.

Indirect methods to measure problem drug use

Treatment multiplier: If a survey among heroin addicts reveals, for instance, that one quarter of them was in treatment in the last year, the multiplication of the registered treatment population with a multiplier of four provides an estimate of the likely total number of problem heroin users in a country. Police data multiplier: Similarly, if a survey among heroin addicts reveals that one out of five addicts was arrested in the previous year, a multiplication of the persons arrested for heroin possession by the multiplier (five) provides another estimate for the number of heroin users. Establishing various multipliers and applying them to the registered drug using population, provides a range of likely estimates of the heroin abuse population in a country. Either the mid-point of the range, the median or the mean of these estimates can be subsequently used to arrive at a national estimate.

Capture-recapture models are another method based on probability considerations, which can be undertaken without additional field research[d]. If in one register (e.g. arrest register) 5000 persons are found (for possession of heroin) and in a second register (e.g. treatment register) 2000 persons are found (for treatment of heroin abuse), and there are 400 persons who appear in both registries, it can be assumed that 20% (400/2000) of the drug addicts have been arrested, so that the total heroin addict population could be around 25,000 (5000/20%), five times larger than the total number of arrested heroin users.[e] Results can usually be improved if data from more than two registers are analysed (e.g. data from arrest register, treatment register, ambulance register, mortality register, substitution treatment register, HIV register etc). More sophisticated capture-recapture models exist, and are used by some advanced countries, in order to make calculations based on more than two registries. However in order to arrive at reasonable orders of magnitude of the heroin problem in a particular country it is probably sufficient to calculate the various combinations shown above and subsequently report the mid-point, the median or the mean of the resulting estimates.

Another interesting approach is the use of *multivariate indicators*. For this approach, a number of local/regional studies are conducted, using various multiplier and/or capture-recapture methods. Such local studies are usually far cheaper than comprehensive national studies. They serve as anchor points for the subsequent estimation procedures. The subsequent assumption is that drug abuse at the local level correlates with other data that are readily available. For instance, heroin arrest data, heroin treatment data, IDU related HIV data, etc. are likely to be higher in communities where heroin abuse is high and lower in communities where heroin abuse is low. In addition, heroin abuse may correlate with some readily available social indicators (higher levels in deprived areas than in affluent areas; higher levels in urban than in rural areas etc). Taking all of this additional information into account, results from the local studies are then extrapolated to the national level.

Whenever such indirect estimates for problem drug use were available, they were given priority over household survey results. Most of the estimates for problem drug use were obtained from European countries. Unless there was evidence that a significant proportion of problem drug use was related to the use of other drugs, it was assumed that the problem drug use concerned opiates. In the case of some of the Nordic countries, where amphetamine use is known to account for a significant proportion of overall problem drug use, the data of reported problem drug users were corrected by applying the proportion of opiate consumers in treatment in order to arrive at estimates for opiate abuse.

For other drugs, priority was given to annual prevalence data found by means of household surveys. A number of countries, however, did not report annual prevalence data, but lifetime or current use of drug consumption, or they provided annual prevalence data but for a different age group. In order to arrive at basically comparable

---

[d] Such methods were originally developed to estimate the size of animal population. If, for instance, 200 fish are caught ('capture'), marked, and released back into the lake, and then the next day 100 fish are caught, of which 10 were already marked ('re-captured'), probability considerations suggest that the number of fish captured the first day were a 10% sample of the total population. Thus the total population of the lake can be estimated at around 2000 fish.

[e] The advantage of this method is that no additional field research is necessary. There are, however, problems as the two 'sampling processes' for the registries in practice are not independent from each other so that some of the underlying assumptions of the model may be violated (e.g. the ratio could be higher as some of the people arrested are likely to be transferred to a treatment facility; thus the ratio does not correspond any longer to the true proportion of people arrested among the addicts population, and may lead to an under-estimation of the total heroin addict population).

results, it was thus necessary to extrapolate from reported current use or lifetime prevalence data to annual prevalence rates and/or to adjust results for differences in age groups.

c. Extrapolation methods used

The methods used for these adjustments and extrapolations are best explained by providing a number of concrete examples:

Adjustment for differences in the age groups:

New Zealand, for instance, undertook a household survey in 2001, covering the population age 15-45. According to this survey, annual prevalence of ecstasy use was found to affect 3.4% of the population 15-45, equivalent to about 56,000 people. Given the strong association between ecstasy use and younger age groups it can be assumed that there is little ecstasy use in the 45+ age group. Thus, dividing the ecstasy using population established above by the age group 15-64 gives an estimated prevalence rate of 2.2%.

The situation is slightly more complex when it comes to cocaine. The same approach for New Zealand would lower the annual cocaine prevalence rate from 0.6% of the population age 15-45 to 0.4% of the population age 15-64. In this case, however, it must be assumed that there are still some people above the age of 45 consuming cocaine. A rate of 0.4% is thus a minimum estimate. An alternative estimation approach is indicated. Thus, the relationship between cocaine consumption among the group of those age 15-45 and those age 15-64 in other countries was investigated. The finding was that the prevalence rate of cocaine use among those age 15-64 tends to be around 75% of the prevalence rate of those age 15-45. Instead of 0.4%, the cocaine prevalence rate in New Zealand has thus been estimated to affect 0.45% of the population age 15-64.

Similar considerations were also used for the age-group adjustment of data from other countries. A number of countries reported prevalence rates for the age groups 15+ or 18+. In these cases it was generally assumed that there was no significant drug use above the age of 65. The number of drug users based on the population age 15+ (or age 18+) was thus simply shown as a proportion of the population age 15-64.

Extrapolation of results from lifetime prevalence to annual prevalence

Some countries have conducted surveys in recent years, but did not ask the question whether drug consumption took place over the last year. In such cases, results can be still extrapolated to arrive at annual prevalence estimates and reasonably good estimates can be expected. Taking data for life-time and annual prevalence of cocaine use in countries of Western Europe, for instance, it can be shown that there is a rather strong positive correlation between the two measures (correlation coefficient R = 0.94); i.e. the higher the life-time prevalence, the higher is, in general, annual prevalence and *vice versa*. Based on the resulting regression curve (y = 0.3736 * x - 0.0455 with y = annual prevalence and x = life-time prevalence) it can be estimated that a West European country with a life-time prevalence of 2% is likely to have an annual prevalence of around 0.7% (also see figure).

Annual and life-time prevalence rates of cocaine use in Western Europe

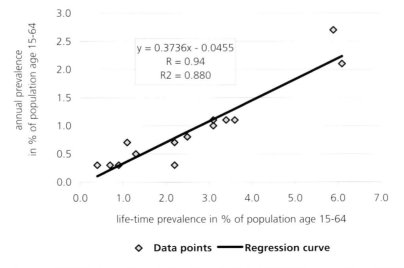

y = 0.3736x - 0.0455
R = 0.94
R2 = 0.880

◇ Data points ▬▬ Regression curve

Sources: UNODC, Annual Reports Questionnaire Data / EMCDDA, Annual Report 2004.

Almost the same result is obtained by calculating the ratio of the unweighted annual prevalence rates of the West European countries and the unweighted life-time prevalence rate (0.93/2.61 = 0.356) and multiplying this ratio with the life-time prevalence of the country concerned (2% * 0.356 = 0.7%).

A similar approach used was to calculate the overall ratio by averaging the annual/life-time ratios, calculated for each country[f]. Multiplying the resulting average ratio (0.387) with the lifetime prevalence of the country concerned provides the estimate for the annual prevalence (0.387 * 2% = 0.8%). This approach also enables the calculation of a confidence interval for the estimate. With a 95% probability the likely annual prevalence estimate for the country concerned falls within a range of 0.6% to 1%[g]. Given this close relationship between life-time and annual prevalence (and an even stronger correlation between annual prevalence and monthly prevalence), extrapolations from life-time or current use data to annual prevalence data was usually given preference to other kinds of possible extrapolations.

However, data also show that good estimation results (showing only a small potential error) can only be expected from extrapolations done for a country located within the same region. If instead of using the West European average (0.387), the ratio found in the USA was used (0.17), the estimate for a country with a lifetime prevalence of cocaine use of 2% would decline to 0.3% (2% * 0.17). Such an estimate is likely to be correct for a country with a drug history similar to the United States, but it is probably not correct for a West European country where the dynamics of the drug markets showed a different pattern. The reason for the difference is that the USA has had a cocaine problem for more than two decades and is thus confronted with very high lifetime prevalence rates while it made considerable progress in reducing cocaine consumption as compared to the mid 1980s. All of this leads to a small proportion of annual prevalence to lifetime prevalence. In Western Europe, by contrast, the cocaine problem is largely a phenomenon of the last decade and still growing. The result, obviously, is a much larger ratio.

Against this background, data from countries in the same region were used, wherever possible, for extrapolation purposes. Thus, data from Central and Eastern Europe were used to extrapolate results for countries located in Central and Eastern Europe which did not collect annual prevalence rates. All of the East European countries had very low drug abuse levels during the cold war, but they grew rapidly in the 1990s. UNODC received annual prevalence estimates from the Czech Republic, Slovakia, Poland and Estonia, and lifetime prevalence estimates from Hungary and Estonia which served as a basis for developing a model for Central and Eastern Europe.

Extrapolation of results from IDU related HIV cases and other indicators

In a number of cases, countries have supplied UNODC with information that is not directly comparable with information from other countries. In such cases reported data as well as all available estimates based on extrapolation from other sources have been used to arrive at an 'UNODC estimate'.

The problem can be demonstrated using the example of the Ukraine, for which UNODC established an estimate for last year's *World Drug Report*. Official data for the year 2002 showed a prevalence rate of opiate abuse of 0.16%. Using such data would have implied that the country – in comparative terms – would have had one of the lowest levels of opiate abuse in Europe. Other available (mainly qualitative) information suggested, however, that this was not likely to be the case. Indeed, the data provided only covered the number of registered opiate users, and thus represented the lowest possible estimate of opiate abuse in the country.

---

[f] For each country the ratio between annual prevalence and lifetime prevalence is calculated. The results are than averaged: In our example:
(0.64 + 0.32 + 0.43 + 0.14 + 0.32 + 0.38 + 0.35 + 0.32 + 0.75 + 0.31 + 0.32 + 0.33 + 0.46+ 0.34) : 14 = 0.387

[g] The calculation of the *confidence interval* can be done as follows:
1). Determination of alpha (usually 0.05);
2). Determination of the number of observations (14 in this case) and 3. Calculation of the standard deviation (0.1502 in this example). This allows to calculate the standard error (standard deviation : (square root of n), i.e. (0.1502 : (square root of 14)) = 0.040)). The z value for alpha equalling 0.05 is 1.96. Multiplying the standard error with the z-value (0.040*1.96) would give the confidence interval (+/- 0.078). But, given the low number of observations (where n< 30), the use of t-statistics is indicated instead. In this case, the standard error must be multiplied with the appropriate t-value (2.145 for n-1 degrees of freedom (14-1) and alpha equalling 0.05 for two-sided t-statistics as can be found in t-value statistics). The result is a confidence interval of +/- 0.0858 (=0.040 * 2.145). Several spreadsheet programs provide such statistics automatically. In Excel, for instance, the 'descriptive statistics' in tool menu under 'data analysis' calculates the confidence interval automatically and uses the t-statistics, wherever appropriate. Applying the +/-0.086 confidence interval to the average ratio calculated above to the mean ratio of 0.387 gives a range of ratios of 0.301 to 0.473. Using the two ratios one arrives at a minimum estimate of the annual prevalence rate of 0.6% (2% * 0.301) and a maximum estimate of the annual prevalence rate of 0.95% (2% * 0.473).

Based on the country's participation in the ESPAD school surveys, a regression analysis[h] with data from other countries in the region suggested that a prevalence rate of around 0.9% could be expected. Based on the number of newly registered HIV cases in this country in 2002, related to injecting drug use (and thus to injecting of opiates), a linear regression analysis with opiate abuse in other countries of the region suggested that a prevalence rate of 1.2% of the population age 15-64 could be possible. However, it must be taken into account that the correlation of opiate use and school survey results is not very strong and that the correlation between opiate abuse and IDU-related HIV is very weak, as shown by available data from Eastern Europe and Western Europe. The actual spread of the HIV virus among IDUs and differences in drug policies seem to account for this. It is thus not possible to rely merely on school survey data or HIV data for extrapolation purposes. It is nonetheless likely that the actual prevalence rate falls within the range of 0.2% to 1.2%. Given the lack of any clear indication of the superiority of one method over another, the average of all three estimates was calculated (0.8%) and used as UNODC's estimate for the country. This estimate is about 4 times the number of registered opiate users in the country. This is not uncommon, as similar ratios between total use and registered use have also been found in a number of other countries.

Estimate for opiate abuse based on IDU-related HIV data and other indicators

	Opiate abuse in % of population age 15-64	Source	ESPAD 1999 in % of 15-16 year olds	IDU related HIV cases per million inhabitants in 2002 based on Euro HIV
Estonia	1.20	EMCDDA (problem drug use)	2	516
Latvia	1.72	EMCDDA (problem drug use)	4	164
Poland	0.24	EMCDDA (problem drug use)	2	5
Russia	2.10	Russian authorities	2	125
	Estimates of opiate abuse (for population age 15-64)	Source / method		
Ukraine	0.16	ARQ, registered users,	1	94
Ukraine	0.9	ESPAD, using a regression analysis		
Ukraine	1.2	HIV, using a regression analysis		
Ukraine	**0.8**	Average ('UNODC estimate')		

Extrapolations based on treatment data

For a number of developing countries, the only drug related data available on the demand side was treatment demand. In such cases, the approach taken was to look for other countries in the region with a similar socio-economic structure, which reported annual prevalence data and treatment data. As a next step, the ratio of people treated per 1000 drug users was calculated for each country. The results from different countries were then averaged and the resulting ratio was used to extrapolate the likely number of drug users from the number of people in treatment.

Extrapolations based on school surveys

Analysis of countries which have conducted both school surveys and national household surveys shows that there is, in general, a positive correlation between the two variables, particularly for cannabis, ATS and cocaine. The correlation, however, is weaker than that of lifetime and annual prevalence or current use and annual prevalence among the general population but stronger than the correlation between opiate use and IDU-related HIV cases and, stronger than the link between treatment and drug use.

---

[h] The linear regression was calculated by using the 'forecast' function in an Excel spreadsheet.
The equation for FORECAST is a+bx, where:

$$a = \overline{Y} - b\overline{X}$$

and:

$$b = \frac{n\sum xy - (\sum x)(\sum y)}{n\sum x^2 - (\sum x)^2}$$

The following examples shows extrapolations of school survey results for cannabis for Western Europe. The basis were the ESPAD School Survey results undertaken in 2003 and the annual prevalence estimates provided by European Member States to UNODC. As can be seen from the figure below, there is a positive correlation between the two variables; the strength of this link, as indicated above, is however, less (R = 0.79) than the strength of the link between life-time and annual prevalence.

Annual prevalence among the general population (age 15-64) and life-time prevalence among 15-16 year old students in Western Europe, 2003

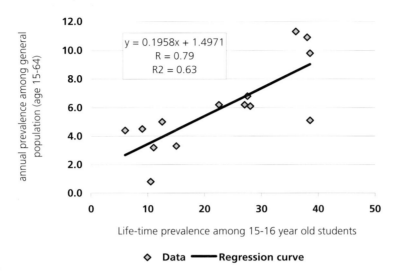

Sources: UNODC, Annual Reports Questionnaire Data, EMCDDA,
Annual Report 2004, Council of Europe, The ESPAD Report 2003.

In order to arrive at UNODC's final estimates for individual countries a number of additional steps were taken. This will be shown for the case of Austria. Participating in the school surveys (ESPAD) that were conducted under the auspices of the Council of Europe, Austria reported a life-time prevalence rate of cannabis use among 15-16 year students of 20.5% (average of 23% for male and 18% for female students) for the year 2003. Applying the regression curve model, cannabis use could be estimated at 5.5% (=20.5 * 0.1958 + 1.4971). Similar models were also established linking annual prevalence among the general population with annual prevalence of cannabis use and with monthly prevalence of cannabis use. The results showed very similar values (5.6% in the other two cases). In addition, the unweighted ratios of student surveys results versus general population use were calculated for all of the West European countries. This resulted in a ratio of 0.3, indicating that annual prevalence of cannabis use among the general population is, on average, equivalent to 30% of life-time use of this drug among the general population. Applying this ratio, cannabis use in Austria could be around 6.15% (=20.5 * 0.3). The confidence interval (at α = 0.05) for this estimate was calculated to range from 4.2% - 8%. Applying the same procedure for annual and 30 days use among students, results amounted to 6.4% and 7.4%, respectively. In the final step, the average of all of these estimates was calculated, resulting in an UNODC estimate of 6.1%.

The reason for using this rather unconventional approach can be demonstrated for the case of Turkey. This country is generally known to have surprisingly low levels of drug consumption by European standards -which was also re-confirmed in the 2003 ESPAD studies. However, applying the results of a simple linear regression curve, would show rather high levels of cannabis consumption. Using the combination of the two approaches (linear regression curve and use of the unweighted ratios) brings the estimates – probably – more in line with reality. As compared to the classical linear regression model, estimates based on this combination of the two methods outlined above, are slightly lower for countries with low levels of prevalence rates among their student population and slightly higher for countries with already high levels of prevalence rates. There would be, of course, a number of non-linear curves with similar properties that statisticians would prefer; given the large number of calculations and the many country specific (qualitative) information, provided to UNODC, that was attempted to be taken into account in making such estimates, it was decided to stay with simple models, as shown above, and to adjust results, wherever needed (e.g. to various combinations of estimates).

It goes without saying that each method of extrapolating results from other countries is not without problems and the results of these estimations for individual countries must be still interpreted with caution as they may well differ from reality. However, this should not influence the overall results as some under-estimates are, most probably, offset by over-estimates, and *vice-versa,* and every attempt has been made to avoid any systematic bias in the estimation process.

Estimates of annual prevalence of cannabis from school survey data in Western Europe							
	General population	Student surveys			Students survey / general population ratios			UNODC estimates of annual prevalence:
	Annual prevalence	Life-time	Annual prevalence	30 days prevalence	lifetime	Annual	30 days	
United Kingdom	10.9	38.0	75.6	19.5	0.29	0.35	0.56	
Spain	11.3	36.0	76.4	22.0	0.31	0.35	0.51	
France	9.8	38.5	75.9	22.0	0.25	0.31	0.45	
Germany	6.8	27.5	82.9	11.5	0.25	0.32	0.59	
Denmark	6.2	22.5	85.7	7.5	0.28	0.36	0.83	
Italy	6.2	27.0	83.4	15.5	0.23	0.28	0.40	
Netherlands	6.1	28.0	83.0	13.0	0.22	0.27	0.47	
Ireland	5.1	38.5	78.2	16.5	0.13	0.16	0.31	
Iceland	5.0	12.5	91.3	4.0	0.40	0.50	1.25	
Norway	4.5	9.0	93.3	2.5	0.50	0.75	1.80	
Greece	4.4	6.0	94.8	2.0	0.73	0.88	2.20	
Portugal	3.3	15.0	90.9	8.0	0.22	0.24	0.41	
Finland	3.2	11.0	92.9	2.5	0.29	0.43	1.28	
Malta	0.8	10.5	94.4	4.0	0.08	0.09	0.20	
Correlations (R) with annual prevalence among general population					0.79	0.80	0.84	
Average ratios					**0.30**	**0.38**	**0.80**	
Austria		20.5	17	9.5				
Turkey		4.0	3.0	2.0				
Estimates for:		Estimates of annual prevalence based on regression curve			Estimates of annual prevalence based on average ratios			Overall averages
		lifetime	12months	30 days	lifetime	12months	30 days	
Austria		5.5	5.6	5.6	6.1	6.4	7.6	**6.1**
Turkey		2.3	2.4	3.0	1.2	1.1	1.6	**1.9**

Sources: UNODC, Annual Reports Questionnaire Data, EMCDDA, Annual Report 2004, Council of Europe, The ESPAD Report 2003.

d. Extrapolation to regional and global level

The next step, after having filled, as far as possible, the data gaps, was to calculate the average prevalence for each sub-region. For this purpose the reported/estimated prevalence rates of countries were applied to the population age 15-64, as provided by the United Nations Population Division for the year 2003. For the remaining countries, for which no estimate could be made, the average prevalence rate of the respective sub-region was applied, unless some additional information suggested that the sub-regional average would be too high or too low for the countries concerned. In general, all of these 'adjustments', based on qualitative information, affected the overall sub-regional estimate only slightly. Following the detailed calculation of all of the sub-regional estimates, the individual sub-regional estimates ('number of drug users') were aggregated to form a regional estimate, and the regional estimates were then aggregated to arrive at the global estimates.

e. Concluding remarks

This process of estimation and the methods used for extrapolating the estimates are not free from risk. All of the extrapolations can potentially lead to substantial over-estimation or under-estimation. While this is definitely true for individual countries, it can be expected that over-estimates and under-estimates partly offset each other at the global level. Moreover, in order to reduce the risk of any systematic bias, estimations were based, as far as possible, on the data from a series of neighbouring countries in the region. It is, however, recognized that the currently provided estimations can change considerably once actual survey data becomes available. UNODC's methodology to arrive at global estimates by extrapolating results from a sample of countries (for which data is available) to a sub-region, also means that methodological changes in some countries can have a significant impact on the final estimates.

The global estimates presented in this report must therefore be treated with a high degree of caution. They provide likely orders of magnitude, as opposed to precise statistics on the prevalence and evolution of global drug abuse. Further changes can be still expected as countries provide more robust estimates based on rigorous scientific methods. Nonetheless, in the absence of global studies on drug abuse, the estimations and the estimation procedures provided in this report guarantee the best picture that is currently obtainable.

Trends in drug use

a. Overview

Ideally, global trends in drug abuse should be monitored by comparing estimates of drug use in one year with those found in a subsequent year. In practice, however, this approach does not always work – at least not for the time being - as a number of changes in the global estimates are due to methodological improvements and not due to underlying changes in drug use. Moreover, general population surveys are very expensive to conduct and only a few countries have an ongoing monitoring system based on these instruments. Some major trends at the global level may be visible, such as the increase in cannabis use. For the identification of other trends, however, the estimates are often not precise enough.

Estimates of annual prevalence of drug use at the global level in the late 1990s and in 2001-2003

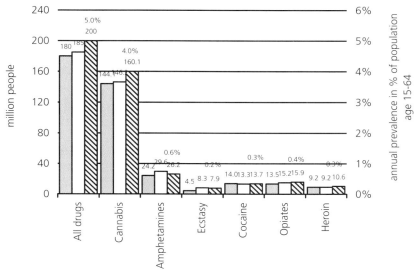

☐ **Drug users in the late 1990s (WDR 2000)** ☐ **Drug users in 2001/02 (WDR 2004)**
☒ **Drug users in 2003/04 (WDR 2005)**

What many countries do collect, however, is routine data such as number of persons arrested for drug abuse, urine testing of arrestees, number of persons undergoing drug treatment, or they monitor drug use based on school surveys. In addition, drug experts dealing on a regular basis with drug issues – even without having precise data at hand – often have a good feeling about whether use of certain drugs is increasing, stabilizing or declining in their constituency.

This knowledge base is regularly tapped by UNODC. Member States usually pass the Annual Reports Questionnaire to drug experts in the country (often in the ministry of health) who provide UNODC with their perception, on a five-point scale, of whether there has been a 'large increase', ' some increase', ' no great change', some decrease' or a 'large decrease' in the use of the various drugs over the past year. The perceptions may be influenced by a number of factors and partial information, including police reports on seizures and arrests, reports from drug treatment centres, reports from social workers, press reports, personal impressions, etc. Any of these influencing factors could contain a reporting bias which has the potential to skew the data towards a misleading increase or decrease. Prioritization of the drug issue is another factor which influences reporting. It can probably be assumed that the countries which reply regularly to the ARQ are those which take the drug problem more seriously. In a number of cases this is a consequence of rising levels of drug use and thus increased public awareness of the problem. All of this suggests that the sample of countries replying to the ARQs may be slightly biased towards countries faced with a deteriorating drug problem. Results must thus be treated with some caution and should not be over-interpreted.

Despite these caveats, trend data provide interesting insights into the growth patterns of individual drugs as well as into regional and global growth patterns. They represent the most comprehensive data set of expert opinion available on the development of drug abuse at the global level, provided in a consistent manner over more than a decade.

Number of countries & territories reporting drug use trends to UNODC

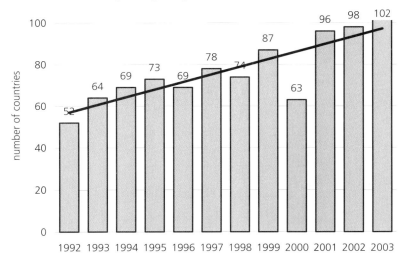

Source: UNODC, Annual Reports Questionnaire Data

Replies to the Annual Report Questionnaire (ARQ) on trends in drug use are more comprehensive than on estimating the number of drug users. The analysis on drug use trends for the year 2003 was based on the replies of 102 countries and territories, about the same number as a year earlier, up from 52 countries and territories in 1992. Overall 163 countries and territories reported drug use trends to UNODC over the last decade. The distribution of countries reporting in 2003 was roughly the same as a year earlier and provides a reasonably good coverage across all regions.

Regional distribution of reports received on drug use trends for the years 2001-2003

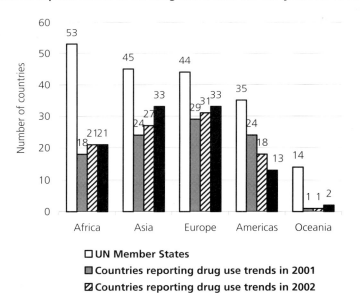

□ UN Member States
▨ Countries reporting drug use trends in 2001
▧ Countries reporting drug use trends in 2002
■ Countries reporting drug use trends in 2003

Source: UNODC, Annual Reports Questionnaire Data.

Aggregating trend data

Various methods have been developed and have been used in this report for the trend aggregation.

The 'traditional' method consisted of simply counting the number of countries reporting increasing, stable and declining levels of drug use. Changes in the 'net results', i.e. number of respondents reporting increases less those reporting declines, have proven to be a good and useful indicator for showing overall changes in the trend. This is in line with business cycle trend analysis where enterprises are asked on a routine basis about their perceptions of whether production is expected to increase, remain stable, or fall over the new few months, and where the net results (Number of increasing trends less number of falling trends) are recorded and presented in order to identify changes in trends. For the purpose of calculating this indicator, the categories 'strong increase' and 'some increase' were combined into a new category 'increase'. Similarly, the categories 'strong decline' and 'some decline' were combined into a new category 'decline'.

The advantage of using this method for describing drug trends at the global level is that a large number of actors, independent of each other, express their views on the trend in their countries. Though some experts may well report wrong trend data, it is unlikely that mistakes all go in the same direction.

Drug use trends 2001, 2002 and 2003

(Number of countries reporting increases less number of countries reporting declines)

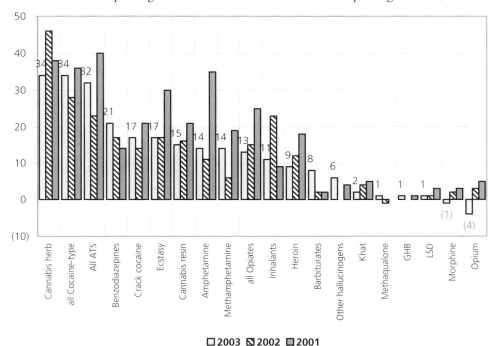

☐ 2003 ▨ 2002 ▨ 2001

Source: Annual Reports Questionnaire Data.

Drug Use Trend Index

A rather new analytical tool, referred to in this report as *Drug Use Trend Index,* has been designed by UNODC to allow for a better presentation of regional and global trends in drug use. The *Drug Use Trend Index* builds on work done by UNODC last year which resulted in the concept of a *Weighted Analysis on Drug Abuse Trends (WADAT),* first published in UNODC's Report to the Commission on Narcotic Drugs on the *World Situation with Regard to Drug Abuse (E/CN.7/2004/2),* and subsequently used in last year's *World Drug Report* as a *Drug Abuse Trend Index.*

The index is constructed as follows: each degree of trend estimation is given a numerical value ranging from –2 to +2 (–2 representing a 'large decrease'; –1, 'some decrease'; 0, 'no great change'; +1, 'some increase'; and +2, 'a large increase'). Estimates for each drug type are then multiplied by the proportion of the drug using population of the country in relation to the drug using population at the global level. The national estimates are subsequently added to represent a global trend estimate for each drug type. The results are finally shown as a cumulative trend curve.

In last year's version of the index, the trends provided by Member States had been weighted by the size of a country in terms of its population. However, it was already pointed out in the methodology section of last year's WDR that – ideally - the weighting should be based on the size of the drug using population instead. The problem was that actual estimates of the size of a country's drug using population were not available for all countries. It was feared that this could mean that trends reported by a number of countries would have to be ignored. Thus the size of the population was chosen to weight the trends reported by member states.

Using the population as the weighting mechanism showed, in general, reasonable results at the regional level where drug use patterns tend to be rather similar. It created, however, a serious problem once an attempt was made to apply the index to the global level, notably for drugs which have a distinct regional distribution pattern. For instance, cocaine use is concentrated in the Americas and in Western Europe and consumption levels in Asia are still minimal. In 2002, India reported a rise in cocaine use, though rising from very low levels. The weight of this country in terms of its population meant, however, that the index showed a sharp rise at the global level, due to this information from India. The results of the index were thus potentially misleading. Against this background UNODC refrained from making use of this index at the global level for the analysis of trends in the use for cocaine or opiates, as these two substances have very distinct distribution patterns.

Thus, an alternative solution was sought to overcome the weighting by population as well as the hurdle of the non-existence of drug use estimates for some countries. The option, finally taken, was that for countries, for which no prevalence estimates exist, the average prevalence rate of the respective sub-region was taken as a proxy for the unknown actual prevalence rate of that country. Using this assumption, prevalence estimates are now available for all countries of the world. Of course, for some countries the 'weight' given to their trend data may slightly be too small or slightly too big, but the potential error resulting from this procedure is far less than the potential error from weighting the index with the general population.

The following graph shows the results for cannabis, starting with 1992 as a baseline. The fact that the index is now at 4.2, and thus above 0, indicates that experts are of the opinion that there was a net increase in cannabis consumption at the global level over the last decade, and the index also indicates that this upward movement gained momentum in recent years. But, how significant has been the increase? If all countries had reported a 'strong increase' every year from 1993 to 2003, the cumulative trend index would have reached a level of 22 (11*2); if all countries had reported 'some increase' every year, the index would be now at 11 (11*1); if countries had considered the trend to have been stable, the index would have remained at 0. If countries had reported every year 'some decline', the index would be at –11, and in case of 'strong decline' at –22.

Drug Use Trend Index – cannabis - based on expert opinion; weighted by estimated number of cannabis users, 1993-2003

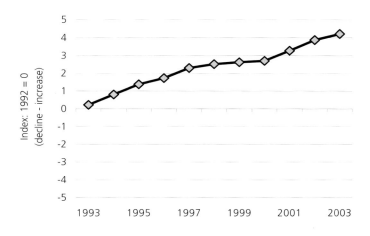

Source: NODC, Annual Reports Questionnaire Data / DELTA.

One advantage of this tool is that it takes the trends reported by Member States and the size of their drug using population into account. In other words, the index gives more weight to the results reported from countries with a large drug using population than to those with small numbers of drug users. This is in line with the observation that the overall impact of a rise in drug consumption in a country with large numbers of drug users has a far greater impact on global drug consumption than the rise in some small countries where drug use just started to become noticed. Another advantage is that the index takes into account the degree of change in drug use levels, thus making better use of all information made available to UNODC by Member States.

There are, of course, also important limitations that need to be taken into account when interpreting the results. The information provided remains – in most cases – an expert opinion and is not necessarily based on hard scientific evidence. While this tool assists in the analysis of trends as reported by Member States to UNODC, the key remains the quality of the input data. A mistake made by one expert in a country with a large drug using population can now seriously distort the global trend estimates. There is also a danger, that some experts may have a political agenda. Thus, this tool cannot be seen as a substitute for serious scientific studies on trends in drug consumption in any given country. Moreover, it cannot be assumed that the difference between various degrees of drug use trends (for example, between "some decrease" and "large decrease") are always interpreted in the same way in different countries or even in the same country in different reporting years, as the ARQs are often filled in by different persons.

Reporting trends in the use of a drug type, such as cannabis, may be also biased by differing trends in the use of substances in the same drug category (for example, the trend in the use of cannabis herb may be increasing while the trend in the use of cannabis resin is decreasing). For the purposes of this report, not just the drug groups but each individual drug category was taken into consideration. The unweighted average of all reported trends (e.g. cannabis herb, cannabis resin) within a drug group (e.g. 'cannabis') was calculated. This was mainly done, in order to have consistency over time. (The drug group headings did not exist in the past). Of course, this is not without problems. In some countries, for instance, cannabis resin does not play a role while cannabis herb is of major importance. The use of a simple average may thus under-estimate the actual increase of cannabis in this country. While for some countries, the detailed profile of substance use is well known, this would not be the case for others. Thus the general rule of averaging all drugs within one category was applied.

It should be also be noted that the Drug Use Trend Index is limited in that it only provides general directions with regard to the main drug types reported by Member States, inevitably leading to very broad generalization. Thus, there is a need for more drug-specific trend analysis to support its conclusions.